PREVENTION OF REOFFENDING
PRÉVENTION DE LA RÉCIDIVE

PREVENTION OF REOFFENDING

The value of rehabilitation and the management of high risk offenders

PRÉVENTION DE LA RÉCIDIVE

Valeur de la réhabilitation et gestion des délinquants à haut risque

Edited by

P.H.P.H.M.C. van Kempen
W. Young

intersentia
Cambridge – Antwerp – Portland

Intersentia Publishing Ltd.
Sheraton House | Castle Park
Cambridge | CB3 0AX | United Kingdom
Tel.: +44 1223 370 170 | Email: mail@intersentia.co.uk

Distribution for the UK:
Hart Publishing Ltd.
16C Worcester Place
Oxford OX1 2JW
UK
Tel.: +44 1865 517 530
Email: mail@hartpub.co.uk

Distribution for the USA and Canada:
International Specialized Book Services
920 NE 58th Ave. Suite 300
Portland, OR 97213
USA
Tel.: +1 800 944 6190 (toll free)
Email: info@isbs.com

Distribution for Austria:
Neuer Wissenschaftlicher Verlag
Argentinierstraße 42/6
1040 Wien
Austria
Tel.: +43 1 535 61 03 24
Email: office@nwv.at

Distribution for other countries:
Intersentia Publishing nv
Groenstraat 31
2640 Mortsel
Belgium
Tel.: +32 3 680 15 50
Email: mail@intersentia.be

Prevention of reoffending. The value of rehabilitation and the management of high risk offenders
Prévention de la récidive. Valeur de la réhabilitation et gestion des délinquants à haut risque
P.H.P.H.M.C. van Kempen and W. Young (eds.)

ISBN 978-1-78068-227-3
D/2014/7849/70
NUR 820

British Library Cataloguing in Publication Data. A catalogue record for this book is available from the British Library.

ACKNOWLEDGMENTS

In editing this forty-fifth publication of the International Penal and Penitentiary Foundation I am delighted to have been joined by Dr. Warren Young. He joins me in offering grateful thanks first of all to all contributors to this book, for the energy they have put into their contributions. It has been a pleasure to work with them all. I must further express my warm gratitude to Judge Phillip Rapoza and Dr. Manon Jendly, my fellow members on the Board of the International Penal and Penitentiary Foundation. They made this book possible as well as the colloquia that are its foundation, which were held in Dublin, Ireland, in June 2011, and Wellington, New Zealand, in February 2013. In this respect I am also indebted to Judge Michael Reilly and Michael Mellett from Ireland, and Judge Bruce Robertson and Dr. Warren Young from New Zealand, respectively, for the outstanding colloquia they organized and for their overwhelming hospitality. Ms. Juliet Van der Voort, LLM, MA, also deserves great appreciation for her assistance in organizing and editing the book, as does Mrs. Fiorina Argante, MA, for supporting me with the enormous amount of correspondence that this project has entailed.

Piet Hein van Kempen
Secretary General International Penal and Penitentiary Foundation
Professor of Criminal Law and Criminal Procedure Law, Radboud University Nijmegen, The Netherlands

REMERCIEMENTS

Dans le cadre de l'édition de cette quarante-cinquième publication de la Fondation Internationale Pénale et Pénitentiaire, je suis ravi d'avoir été secondé par Dr Warren Young. Ce dernier se joint à moi pour remercier vivement, avant toute chose, toutes les personnes ayant contribué à cet ouvrage pour l'énergie qu'elles y ont consacré. Ce fut un plaisir de travailler avec chacune d'entre elles. Je me dois ensuite d'exprimer ma plus profonde gratitude à juge Phillip Rapoza et Dr. Manon Jendly, mes collègues au Conseil de la Fondation Internationale Pénale et Pénitentiaire. Ils ont rendu ce livre possible, ainsi que les colloques qui en furent à l'origine, tenus à Dublin en Irlande en juin 2011, et à Wellington en Nouvelle-Zélande en février 2013. À cet égard, je suis également reconnaissant au juge Michael Reilly et à Michael Mellett d'Irlande, ainsi qu'au juge Bruce Robertson et à Dr Warren Young de Nouvelle-Zélande, respectivement, pour l'organisation exceptionnelle des colloques et pour la chaleureuse hospitalité dont ils ont fait preuve. Je prie également Mademoiselle Juliet Van der Voort, titulaire d'une maîtrise en droit et en lettres, de trouver ici l'expression de toute ma reconnaissance pour son aide précieuse dans l'organisation et l'édition de ce livre, tout comme Madame Fiorina Argante, titulaire d'une maîtrise en lettres, pour le soutien qu'elle m'a apporté dans le cadre des innombrables courriers échangés à l'occasion de la réalisation de ce projet.

Piet Hein van Kempen
Secrétaire Général de la Fondation Internationale Pénale et Pénitentiaire
Professeur de droit criminel et de procédure pénale à l'université Radboud de Nijmegen, Pays-Bas

PREFACE

Incarceration rates are at record levels around the world. This fact can be attributed to a number of causes, including the view that getting "tough" on crime requires a more aggressive use of imprisonment as a criminal sanction. The persistence of such high rates of incarceration, however, challenges us to revisit fundamental concepts and to ask "What is the purpose of incarceration?" or, more broadly, "What is the purpose of punishment?"

This book attempts to suggest answers to those questions by considering how the rehabilitation of offenders in general and the management of high risk offenders in particular can help prevent such persons from reoffending. These issues were addressed at two four-day colloquia conducted by the International Penal and Penitentiary Foundation (IPPF) in Dublin, Ireland and Wellington, New Zealand. The Dublin program focused on the rehabilitation of offenders and the Wellington colloquium centered on the management of high risk offenders. During the course of these two events, scholars, researchers, prison administrators, judges and policy makers from around the world presented papers, participated in panels and engaged in lively debates relating to these issues. Indeed, a number of the chapters that follow started as papers delivered at the two colloquia or were substantially influenced by the discussions that took place there.

As reflected in this book, the role of rehabilitation is unquestionably of great significance in any penal regime. Although the concepts of deterrence, retribution and containment are, to a greater or lesser degree, also reflected in sentencing frameworks, the rehabilitation of offenders should be a paramount consideration. Indeed, rehabilitation is an essential aim of any penitentiary system, with the reformation of prisoners and their social rehabilitation specifically referenced in the 1966 International Covenant on Civil and Political Rights. There is little doubt that the successful rehabilitation of a prisoner is of value not only to the individual prisoner, but also to his or her family, the prison administration, the taxpaying public, and ultimately, society itself. In addition to considering rehabilitation from each of those perspectives, this book discusses the benefit of prisoner rehabilitation to the victims of crime as well, especially where such rehabilitation supports efforts to achieve restorative justice.

Following the discussion of rehabilitation, this book considers how to deal with offenders who pose a substantial risk of re-offending. Criminal sanctions have traditionally sought to reduce such risks by means of deterrent sentences or rehabilitative programs that aim to minimize the likelihood of reoffending. In recent years, however, many jurisdictions have come to regard such measures as insufficient to deal with the most serious offenders, such as sexually violent offenders, pedophiles, members of organized criminal groups and those engaged in terrorist activity. Although many such offenders may be incarcerated for extended periods of time, there remains the issue of how to deal with them both during and after the service of their sentence. As reflected in the chapters devoted to this topic, a variety of special measures have been employed to manage the risks that such offenders pose. Of course underpinning any discussion of such alternatives remains the practical consideration of how to assess both an offender's dangerousness as well as the risk of that person either reoffending or committing new offenses.

In sum, this book significantly contributes to the ongoing public discourse concerning important matters of penal policy. It is an impressive undertaking and it is appropriate to thank the various authors whose timely and thought-provoking contributions make this book the valuable resource that it is. Similarly, gratitude is owed to the publisher Intersentia for its willingness to publish this forty-fifth book in its IPPF series, their second after *Pre-trial detention: Human rights, criminal procedural law and penitentiary law, comparative law (2012).*

Finally, I would like to acknowledge both Professor Dr. Piet Hein van Kempen, the Secretary General of the IPPF, and Dr. Warren Young, first Vice-President of the IPPF, for their exceptional contribution as editors of this book. The publication of this book was achieved largely through their hard work and their willingness to commit considerable time and effort to the project. For their truly unselfish service they are entitled to both our appreciation and our most sincere thanks.[1]

Hon. Phillip Rapoza
President of the International Penal and Penitentiary Foundation

1 Note: the original language of this text is English.

PRÉFACE

Les taux d'incarcération atteignent des niveaux record dans le monde entier. Ce phénomène peut être attribué à plusieurs de causes, notamment le point de vue selon lequel lutter « sévèrement » contre la criminalité nécessite de recourir de manière plus agressive à la sanction pénale qu'est l'emprisonnement. Toutefois, la persistance de ce taux élevé d'incarcération nous incite à revoir les concepts fondamentaux et à nous poser la question suivante : « Quel est l'objectif de l'incarcération ? » ou, plus généralement, « Quel est l'objectif de la sanction ? »

Cet ouvrage tentera de répondre à ces questions en examinant comment la réhabilitation des délinquants en général et la gestion des délinquants à haut risque en particulier peuvent contribuer à prévenir la récidive. Ces questions ont été abordées lors de deux colloques de quatre jours animés par la Fondation Internationale Pénale et Pénitentiaire (FIPP) à Dublin en Irlande et à Wellington en Nouvelle-Zélande. Tandis que le colloque de Dublin s'est penché sur la réhabilitation des délinquants, celui de Wellington s'est intéressé à la gestion des délinquants à haut risque. Au cours de ces deux événements, des universitaires, chercheurs, administrateurs pénitentiaires, juges et décideurs politiques issus du monde entier ont présenté des exposés, participé à des panels et pris part à des débats animés sur le sujet. Plusieurs chapitres de ce livre sont d'ailleurs nés d'exposés présentés lors de ces deux colloques ou ont été fortement influencés par les discussions qui y ont eu lieu.

Comme le démontreront les différents chapitres de ce livre, le rôle capital de la réhabilitation est indiscutable, indépendamment du régime pénal. Bien que les concepts de dissuasion, punition et confinement soient également abordés plus ou moins largement dans le cadre de la fixation des peines, c'est la réhabilitation des délinquants qui doit être la principale considération. Elle est en effet l'un des objectifs principaux de tout système pénitentiaire, avec l'amendement des détenus et leur réinsertion sociale spécifiquement mentionnés dans le Pacte international relatif aux droits civils et politiques de 1966. Il est indéniable que le succès de la réhabilitation d'un détenu sera profitable non seulement à ce dernier, mais également à sa famille, à l'administration pénitentiaire, au contribuable et, en fin de compte, à la société elle-même. Outre ces différents points de vue sur la réhabilitation des détenus, ce livre traitera des bienfaits de cette dernière pour les victimes de la criminalité, tout particulièrement lorsqu'elle soutient les efforts consentis pour appliquer une justice réparatrice.

Au terme de cette discussion sur la réhabilitation, cet ouvrage examinera la meilleure manière de gérer les délinquants qui présentent un risque élevé de récidive. Traditionnellement, les sanctions pénales ont pour objectif de réduire ces risques par des peines dissuasives ou des programmes de réhabilitation visant à minimiser la probabilité de récidive. Ces dernières années, bon nombre de juridictions ont toutefois été amenées à considérer ces mesures comme inadéquates pour traiter le risque généré par les pires délinquants, tels que les délinquants sexuels violents, les pédophiles, les membres de groupes criminels organisés et les personnes engagées dans des activités terroristes. Bien que nombre de ces délinquants puissent être incarcérés durant de longues périodes, il subsiste la question de leur prise en charge pendant l'exécution de leur peine ainsi qu'au terme de celle-ci. Comme le démontreront les chapitres consacrés à ce sujet, diverses mesures spéciales ont été mises en place pour gérer les risques que présentent de tels délinquants. Il va de soi qu'étayer une discussion sur ces solutions reste la préoccupation pratique de l'évaluation tant de la dangerosité d'un délinquant que du risque qu'il récidive ou commette de nouveaux délits.

Somme toute, cet ouvrage contribue de manière significative au débat public actuel concernant les questions importantes en matière de politique pénale. Il s'agit d'un projet imposant, pour lequel il convient de remercier les auteurs dont la contribution opportune et inspirante a permis à ce livre de devenir la ressource précieuse qu'il est aujourd'hui. Je suis également reconnaissant à la maison d'édition Intersentia d'avoir accepté de publier ce quarante-cinquième livre dans sa série FIPP, après *Détention avant jugement : droits de l'homme, droit de la procédure pénale et droit pénitentiaire, droit comparé (2012).*

Enfin, je souhaite remercier le Professeur Dr Piet Hein van Kempen, Secrétaire général de la FIPP, et le Dr Warren Young, premier Vice-président de la FIPP, pour leur contribution exceptionnelle en tant qu'éditeurs de cet ouvrage. Si ce livre a pu voir le jour, c'est en grande partie grâce à leur travail acharné ainsi qu'au temps et aux efforts qu'ils ont bien voulu consacrer à ce projet. Pour leur travail on ne peut plus désintéressé, nous leur adressons à tous deux notre reconnaissance et nos remerciements les plus sincères.[1]

L'Honorable Phillip Rapoza
Président de la Fondation internationale pénale et pénitentiaire

1 La langue originale de ce texte est l'anglais.

CONTENTS

PART TWO
REHABILITATION OF PRISONERS

2ÈME PARTIE
LA RÉHABILITATION DES DÉTENUS

PART ONE

INTRODUCTORY SYNTHESIS AND ANALYSES

1ÈRE PARTIE

SYNTHÈSE ET ANALYSES INTRODUCTIVES

OBLIGATIONS AND MEANS TO PREVENT REOFFENDING: INTRODUCTION, CONTEXT AND CONCLUSIONS

Piet Hein van Kempen*
Warren Young**

1. INTRODUCTION

The necessity to prevent convicted prisoners and other offenders from reoffending constitutes a major challenge to both criminal justice and penitentiary systems. Most countries experience great difficulty in reducing recidivism rates either through these systems or by other means. Reoffending rates are considerable – in many instances they are even high – while the issue is tremendously complicated. This poses a formidable challenge to the state, the central function of which is to provide for the security of its citizens.[1] In that sense, it may be seen as imperative to prevent reoffending. However, even from the perspective of the community and the potential victims of crime, there is a great need to control crime and thus the recidivism of offenders. The criminal justice system is an important mechanism for establishing such control, although it is certainly not the only one. The primary purpose of the criminal

* Dr. P.H.P.H.M.C. van Kempen M.Law (Hons), PhD, is Professor of Criminal Law and Criminal Procedure Law and Chair of the department of Criminal Law and Criminology, Radboud University Nijmegen, The Netherlands. He is also a part-time Justice at the Court of Appeal, 's-Hertogenbosch, The Netherlands, and Secretary General of the International Penal and Penitentiary Foundation.

** Dr. W. Young BA LLB (Hons) PhD is a policy and law reform consultant in Wellington, New Zealand. He has been Deputy President of the New Zealand Law Commission, a Deputy Secretary for Justice and a Professor of law.

Note by authors: the original language of this text is English.

1 On the State's obligation to offer security, see Piet Hein van Kempen, 'Four Concepts of Security – A Human Rights Perspective', 13 *Human Rights Law Review* 1 (2013), p. 1–23 (see particularly p. 20). The United Nations' Secretary General even stressed that "*prevention is the first imperative of justice*"; see Report of the Secretary-General, 'The rule of law and transitional justice in conflict and post-conflict societies', 23 August 2004, *UN Doc.* S/2004/616, par. 4.

justice system is to help define and preserve the legal order, prevent intrusions on that order, and act against the perpetrators of crime. Trying, convicting and punishing offenders is one of several important tools in this endeavour. Even sentencing, however, may be used for a variety of different purposes. Retribution, deterrence (general and special prevention), incapacitation, restoration (repair) and rehabilitation are all widely accepted goals of punishment, or at least justifications for it, although they are often inconsistent with each other in specific cases.[2] Nevertheless, the structural neglect of any of these goals may easily result in a less effective criminal justice system in terms of reducing crime and enhancing public safety. In that case one could argue that the State is remiss in its obligations.

Since the importance of rehabilitation (sometimes described as resocialisation, reintegration or treatment) has clearly become less self-evident in many jurisdictions during recent decades,[3] this volume – in part II – first of all focuses on the value of restoring offenders to a useful life through, *inter alia*, education, vocational guidance, therapy, work programmes and the fostering of personal responsibility, in order to enable them to contribute to their own development and to society. It is asserted and explained that rehabilitation is an important value within the criminal justice and prison system, from the offender's point of view as well as in many other respects. This value should be reflected in both legislative and operational criminal justice policy, as well as being taken into account when the appropriate sentence is being decided in individual cases before the courts. It should also be taken into consideration when punishment is executed. So both the criminal justice and the penitentiary systems can be utilized in a "socially constructive" manner: legislators and courts can decide in favour of punishments that inherently meet the resocialisation interest (such as community service or electronic monitoring); and even when the most punitive sanction is applied (viz., imprisonment[4]) it can be implemented in such a manner that it too contributes to the offender's rehabilitation.[5] Unfortunately, in many instances, however, imprisonment does not serve the goals of rehabilitation and crime reduction.[6] For example, at the

---

2 Cf. in this volume also the chapters by Pradel (par. 1) and Jendly & Delgrande (par. 2).

3 Cf. Francis T. Cullen & Karen E. Gilbert, *Reaffirming Rehabilitation*, Anderson Publishing, 2013, p. xi-xxvi; D.A. Andrews & James Bonta, 'Rehabilitating criminal justice policy and practice', 16 *Psychology, Public Policy, and Law* 1 (2010), p. 39–55.

4 That is, at least in all jurisdictions that do not have capital punishment.

5 See, for example, Francis T. Cullen & Cheryl Lero Jonson, 'Rehabilitation and Treatment Programs', in: James Q. Wilson & Joan Petersilia (eds), *Crime and Public Policy*, Oxford: Oxford University Press, 2011, p. 293–344; James Gilligan & Bandy Lee, 'The Resolve to Stop the Violence Project: reducing violence in the community through a jail-based initiative', 27 *Journal of Public Health* 2 (2005), p. 143–148; and in this volume the chapter by Jendly & Delgrande.

6 See, *e.g.*, Paula Smith *et.al.*, *The Effects of Prison Sentences and Intermediate Sanctions on Recidivism: General Effects and Individual Differences 2002-01*, University of New Brunswick, Saint John/Public Works and Government Services Canada, 2002 (at: www.ccoso.org/library%20articles/200201_Gendreau_e.pdf) (last visited: 1 January 2014).

12th UN Congress on Crime Prevention and Criminal Justice in 2010 it was emphasized that inhumane overcrowding in prisons is a major cause of recidivism, which does nothing to improve public safety.[7]

Although rehabilitation measures are potentially relevant to all categories of offenders,[8] their application alone may not, as indicated above, be sufficient to prevent someone from reoffending. This particularly applies to high risk offenders, *i.e.* those who pose a substantial risk of further serious offending. These include, for example, those with a predisposition to commit sex offences, arson or violent crimes, terrorists, and members of organised criminal groups. Criminal sanctions imposed upon such offenders are often designed to reduce their risk to society – for example, through sentences designed to have an individual deterrent effect or to provide rehabilitative programmes. However, in the last two or three decades many jurisdictions have come to regard these measures as inadequate to deal with the risk posed by the worst offenders. Legislation has been passed, for instance, to impose restrictions on offenders after the expiry of their penal sentence, and to provide for a variety of civil orders as an alternative to criminal sanctions. This volume – in part III – will therefore consider measures to deal with high risk offenders during and after their sentence, and the arguments for and against their use.

The present chapter – which is also part I of this volume – next pays attention to what reoffending may mean, formally speaking, and presents a survey of reoffending rates in various jurisdictions around the world (section 2). We then proceed (in section 3) to look more closely at different values of rehabilitation, introducing the chapters that deal with that topic. In order to offer further context to these chapters we also discuss how rehabilitation treatment may be considered to be a legal obligation. Following on from that, the volume's chapters on measures to deal with high risk offenders during and after their sentence are introduced (section 4). Again, to flesh out the background somewhat, we briefly examine the form that those measures have taken and some of the fundamental issues and dilemmas posed by them. The chapter ends with conclusions.

2. DEFINITION OF REOFFENDING AND RECIDIVISM RATES

Before illustrating the problem of repeat offending with rates on recidivism it is important to emphasise that these rates of course depend greatly on the

---

7 12th UN Congress on Crime Prevention and Criminal Justice, Committee I, 8th & 9th Meetings (AM & PM), Meetings Coverage, 16 April 2010, SOC/CP/352.

8 Cf. United Nations Office on Drugs and Crime, *Introductory Handbook on the Prevention of Recidivism and the Social Reintegration of Offenders* (Criminal Justice Handbook Series), New York: United Nations, 2012, p. 129–145, with attention to reintegration programmes for many different specific groups of offenders.

definition of reoffending on which they are based. The definitions used in various criminological researches vary widely. There is no international agreed standard for measuring and reporting recidivism, so, in the broadest material sense, one could argue that anyone who has ever committed a crime becomes a recidivist when committing another crime. Formally, however, reoffending is usually given a much more limited meaning, which gives rise to such questions as the following: Does reoffending encompass a relapse into crime in general or only the commission of the same offence? Must the new offence have been committed within a certain period after the first crime – for example one, two or five years – or is there no such limitation? Does recidivism take all crimes into account that have been registered by the authorities, or only certain crimes and/or only crimes that have been sentenced, or for which only a prison sentence has been applied? Different studies answer these questions differently, as a result of which statistics on recidivism often have completely different bases. It is useful to bear this in mind when reading the following brief reports on twenty different jurisdictions from six continents, which are presented here – in alphabetical order – as an illustration of the problem of reoffending.[9]

Argentina

Researchers using data of all offenders released from the Buenos Aires penal system from January 1998 until October 2007 found that the recidivism rate (*i.e.* the proportion of individuals released from the penal system that returned to prison after committing another crime) was just above 22% for offenders released from prison, whereas it dropped to just over 13% for those released after electronic monitoring. The average annual recidivism rate for the prison sample – *i.e.* the proportion of those released from prison who returned within a year – was 7.8%, while that for the Electronic Monitoring sample was 4.6%.[10] However, different sources state recidivism rates for Argentina of 60% and 70%.[11]

Bolivia

A recent journal article refers to several studies that report recidivism rates between 20% and 30%. This is considered quite low for Latin America.[12]

9 For the definitions of reoffending that are used in the studies referred to below, see these studies.

10 Rafael Di Tella & Ernesto Schargrodsky, 'Criminal Recidivism after Prison and Electronic Monitoring', 121 *Journal of Political Economy* 1 (2013), p. 54.

11 Gabriel Bouzat, 'Inequality, Crime, and Security in Argentina', SELA (Seminario en Latinoamérica de Teoría Constitucional y Política), Paper 91 (2010), p. 23, footnote 36 (at: http://digitalcommons.law.yale.edu/yls_sela/91) (last visited: 1 January 2014). With further references, see also Cristal Downing, 'Bolivian prison entrepreneurship. An unexpectedly successful rehabilitation method?', 6 *Journal of Enterprising Communities: People and Places in the Global Economy* 4 (2012), p. 346.

12 Cristal Downing, 'Bolivian prison entrepreneurship. An unexpectedly successful rehabilitation method?', 6 *Journal of Enterprising Communities: People and Places in the Global Economy* 4 (2012), p. 346.

Denmark, Finland, Iceland, Norway and Sweden

A survey of almost 60,000 offenders in the Nordic countries – Denmark, Finland, Iceland, Norway and Sweden – shows that Norway has the lowest overall re-offending rate among correctional clients in these countries. Within two years about 20% of all those released from prison and a similar percentage of those who began serving a sentence in the community in Norway incurred a new conviction that had to be served in the correctional services. In the other Nordic countries the overall re-offending rate varies from 24% to 31%.[13]

England & Wales

Between July 2010 and June 2011, around 630,000 offenders were cautioned, convicted (excluding immediate custodial sentences) or released from custody. Around 170,000 of these offenders committed a proven further offence within a year. This gives a one-year proven re-offending rate of 26.9%, which represents a rise of 0.5 percentage points compared to the previous 12 months and a fall of 1.0 percentage points since 2000. These re-offenders committed an average of 2.88 re-offences each. In total, this represents around 490,000 further offences, of which 82% were committed by adults and 18% by juveniles. 56.5% (around 280,000) were committed by those with 11 or more previous offences. 0.7% (around 3,300) were serious violent/sexual offences. 5.1% (around 25,000) were committed by re-offenders on the Prolific and other Priority Offender Programme (PPO); this programme uses a multi-agency approach to focus on a very small, but hard-core group of prolific/persistent offenders who commit a disproportionate amount of crime.[14]

Estonia

According to an Estonian study the recidivism rate for the 2007 procedural decisions and releases from prisons was the lowest in case of terminated proceedings (18%) and the highest in case of people released from prison (40%). Within six months after release from prison about 25% of the offenders had been interrogated as a suspect in the commission of a new crime; within 18 months, suspicion was filed against 50% of former prisoners and against more than 60% within three years. Data indicate that the recidivism rate of people released from prison has decreased somewhat over the years: while 43% of people released in 2004 committed a new criminal offence within a year and 41% in 2005 and 2006,

---

13 Derived from Ragnar Kristoffersen *et al.*, *Retur. En nordisk undersøgelse af recidiv blandt klienter i kriminal-forsorgen*, 2010.

14 All of this is derived from Ministry of Justice, 'Proven Re-offending Statistics Quarterly Bulletin, July 2010 to June 2011, England and Wales', *Statistics Bulletin* 25 April 2013, p. 7 and 20.

in 2007 40% of people released committed new criminal offences. The recidivism rate for people released from prison is highest among those who have fully served their sentence: 50% of these offenders commit a new criminal offence within a year – this indicator has remained at a steady 48%-49% over a four-year period (2004 – 2007), in spite of the fact that the proportion of people released after serving their sentence to all released people has decreased from 82% to 49%.[15]

France

A recent French study shows that over the years from 2000 to 2010 the proportion of convicts who had already been dealt with by the law during the five years preceding their conviction increased between 2000 to 2004 from 35.5% for 2000 to 37.6% for 2004, then declined two points in 2006 (35.7%) and grew again to 40% in 2010, which implies a slight increase in the overall reoffending rate. After ten years the recidivism rate was almost 50%. The rate varies considerably for different offenses. In a period of six years the reoffending rate was high for property crimes: theft and confidence tricks (55%) and property destruction (53.5%), as well as firearms offenses, defamation and drugs (between 53% and 50%). These offenses constituted a little less than a third of the offenses punished in 2004. In contrast, the recidivism rate was lower for traffic offenses (40%), which constituted 30% of the 2004 cohort, as well as sexual abuse. Furthermore, after six years the recidivism rate was higher in cases in which the offender was sentenced to imprisonment (61%) than when the penalty did not include imprisonment (36%).[16]

Germany

For most offenders who were sanctioned in 2004 or released from prison, criminal penalties were a one-time event in the observation period (2004–2007). Approximately 35% of the offenders who were sanctioned or released from prison reoffended within the observation period of three years. If a criminal sanction was imposed for the new offence, it predominantly involved not a deprivation of liberty but a milder sanction. Offenders punished with a custodial sentence had a higher risk of relapse than those who were sentenced to milder sanctions. So convicted prisoners do clearly have a higher reoffending rate than other convicted offenders, but still significantly less than half of them are seen

15 Derived from Andri Ahven, Jako Salla & Siim Vahtrus, *Retsidiivsus Eestis/Recidivism in Estonia*, Tallinn: Justiitsministeerium, 2010, p. 160.

16 Derived from Ministère de la Justice, *Mesurer la récidive. Contribution à la conférence de consensus de prévention de la récidive*, 2013, p. 7–11. See also Benjamin Monnery, 'The determinants of recidivism among ex prisoners: a survival analysis on French data', May 2013 (at: http://halshs.archives-ouvertes.fr/docs/00/82/28/47/PDF/1320.pdf) (last visited: 1 January 2014).

back in the criminal justice system within three years. In addition, the recidivism rate shows a close relationship with the number of previous convictions: the higher this number is, the more the relapse rate increases.[17]

Ireland

A study by the Probation Service showed that almost 63% of offenders under Probation Service supervision had no conviction for a further offence within two years of the imposition of a Probation or Community Service order. The overall recidivism of offenders in the study was 37.2%. In this study 75% of further offences in the two year period occurred in the first year and 25% in the second. Recidivism levels were higher for offenders on Probation Orders (39.3%) than for those on Community Service Orders (33.5%).[18] A study of recidivism among all prisoners released by the Irish Prison Service shows a recidivism rate of 62.3% within three years. Over 80% of those who re-offended did so within 12 months of release.[19]

Japan

According the Ministry of Justice's White Paper on Crime[20] the number of repeat offenders found guilty of non-traffic penal code offenses continued to increase from 1997, but then decreased slightly over four consecutive years from 2007, to reach 137,614 in 2010 (down 2.0% from the previous year). The rate of repeat offenders continued to rise consistently from 1997, reaching 42.7% in 2010 (up 0.5 points (id.)).[21] Examining previously convicted adults cleared for non-traffic penal code offenses in 2010 according to the number of their previous convictions revealed that those with one previous conviction accounted for the highest proportion at 39.1%, but the proportion of those with five or more previous convictions was also high at 21.9%. In addition, those with previous convictions for the same type of offense accounted for 51.6% of the total. The rate of previously convicted persons among adults cleared was 28.2% for total non-traffic penal code offenses, but was remarkably high for robbery (46.0%) and

---

17 Adopted from Jörg-Martin Jehle, Hans-Jörg Albrecht, Sabine Hohmann-Fricke & Carina Tetal, *Legalbewährung nach strafrechtlichen Sanktionen Eine bundesweite Rückfall-untersuchung 2004 bis 2007*, Berlin: Bundesministerium des Justiz, 2010, p. 6–7.

18 Taken from The Probation Service, *Probation Service Recidivism Study 2007–2011. Probation Service Research Report 2*, November 2012, p. 2, 8, 17.

19 Irish Prison Service & Central Statistics Office, *Irish Prison Service Recidivism Study 2013. A study of recidivism among all prisoners released by the Irish Prison Service on completion of a sentence in 2007 – based on reoffending and reconviction data up to the end of 2010*, Longford, Ireland, 2013, p. 3.

20 See also Hiroyuki Kuzuno, 'Neoliberalism, Social Exclusion, and Criminal Justice – A Case in Japan', 40 *Hitotsubashi Journal of Law and Politics* (2012), p. 16.

21 See Ministry of Justice, *White paper on crime 2011*, Part 4, Chapter 6, Section 1/1 (see at: http://hakusyo1.moj.go.jp/en/nendo_nfm.html) (last visited: 1 January 2014).

fraud (39.8%).[22] Of inmates released in 2001 the cumulative percentage of re-imprisonment within ten years was 63.3% for those released on completion of their term of imprisonment and 42.8% for parolees, with 89.2% and 81.9% of these respectively being re-imprisoned within five years. The difference between those imprisoned for the first time and those imprisoned twice is remarkable. About half of those imprisoned twice or more were re-imprisoned within five years, thus indicating the increased difficulty of reforming/rehabilitating them.[23]

The Netherlands

In the Netherlands a first offender is a defendant against whom no previous record of arrest has been made. A repeat perpetrator is a defendant against whom 2 to 5 records (for juveniles) or 2 to 10 records (for adults) are made in the entire criminal career. With more than 5 or 10 records, respectively, one is regarded a multiple offender. Of all the suspects arrested in 2010, 39% were first offenders, 46% repeat offenders, and 14% multiple offenders. For 2005 the corresponding figures were 44%, 43% and 13%. This means that the share of repeat offenders and multiple offenders increased slightly over that period.[24] According to the Recidivism report 2002–2008, citing the 2004 figures, the percentage of repeat adult offenders sanctioned by the court or Public Prosecutor's Service decreased slightly. Of the adults, 27.5% sentenced for committing a crime in 2008 relapsed within two years. In 2002 this was 30.8%. The decline in recidivism started somewhat later for juvenile offenders sanctioned by the court or Public Prosecutor's Service. The national reconviction rate for this population decreased from 2006. In 2002 it was 39.1%. In 2008 35.9% of all minors with a criminal case disposed of by a court or Public Prosecutor's Service were prosecuted again within two years after the index case. The reconviction rate of ex-prisoners has also decreased over the past few years. From 2002, the recidivism percentages in the sector of the adult prison system show a downward trend. Of all the adults leaving a penitentiary institution in 2008, 48.5% came into contact with the judicial system again within two years. In 2002, this was 55.2%. The two-year reconviction rate among former inmates of juvenile detention centres who were released in 2002 was 55.3%. For juveniles released in 2008 this was 52.0%. A decrease can be seen from 2006. This population also includes minors institutionalised under a civil suit.[25]

---

22 See Ministry of Justice, *White paper on crime 2011*, Part 4, Chapter 6, Section 1/2.

23 See Ministry of Justice, *White paper on crime 2011*, Part 4, Chapter 6, Section 3/2.

24 See M.M. van Rosmalen, S.N. Kalidien & N.E. de Heer-de Lange (eds), *Criminaliteit en rechtshandhaving 2011*, Den Haag: CBS/WODC/Raad voor de Rechtspraak, 2012, p. 108.

25 Adopted from B.S.J. Wartna *et.al.*, *Recidivism report 2002–2008. Trends in the reconviction rate of Dutch offenders* (Fact sheet 2011–5a), The Hague: Dutch Ministry of Security and Justice/WODC, p. 2 (at: www.wodc.nl/onderzoeksdatabase/actualisering-recidivemeting-sancties-2011.aspx) (last visited: 1 January 2014).

New Zealand

According to a study over a 48-month period, 18% of the offenders who commenced Supervision, Community Work and Front-end Home Detention in 2002/03, were convicted of a new offence and started a prison sentence at least once during the 48-month follow-up period. During the same period, 36% were convicted and started a community sentence. This means that the overall reconviction rate of offenders who started Supervision, Community Work and Front-end Home Detention was 54% over four years. Interestingly, after one year 59% of these reoffenders had already been reconvicted, while the second year accounted for 20% of these reoffenders, the third year 12% and, of course, the remaining 9% in the fourth year. In other words, by far the most re-offenders re-offend in the first twelve months. The reconviction rates of recidivists for both Supervision and Community Work was 65%, and for Home Detention was 55%, over four years.[26]

Russia

Levels of recidivism are rising considerably. In 2003 about 27% of the crimes were committed by persons who had previously been convicted. This percentage has been rising steadily every year since.[27] According to "The state of crime: January-December 2012", almost every second investigated crime (46.6%) is committed by persons who have previously committed crimes. Members of organised criminal groups committed 17.3 million grave and especially grave crimes (a rise of 2.4%); their share in the total number of investigated crimes within these categories has increased from 5.2% in 2011 to 5.7% in 2012.[28] The statistics reported in "Criminality in January-October 2013" show that the general recidivism rate has risen to 49.1%, while the rate for members of organised criminal groups increased to 6.0%.[29]

Singapore

Recidivism, defined as the percentage of every cohort released who re-offend and subsequently return to prison, is a key performance indicator for the Singapore Prison Service. They use a 2-year rate, and have been tracking it since 1998.

---

26 Derived from A. Nadesu, *Reconviction patterns of offenders managed in the community: A 48-month follow-up analysis*, New Zealand: Department of Corrections, 2008, p. 3, 4, 12–13.

27 See Ilya Kokorin, *Probation services in Europe and Russian experience of social reintegration and rehabilitation of offenders* (LL.M. thesis), Budapest: Central European University, 2013, p. 63 (at: www.etd.ceu.hu/2013/kokorin_ilya.pdf), referring to official reports of the Ministry of Internal Affairs of Russia (at: http://mvd.ru/presscenter/statistics/reports/) (both websites last visited: 1 January 2014).

28 See par. 19, at: http://mvd.ru/presscenter/statistics/reports/item/804701/ (last visited: 1 January 2014).

29 See par. 19, at: http://mvd.ru/presscenter/statistics/reports/item/1317409/ or http://mvd.ru/upload/site1/document_file/tcAeqVoQFq.pdf (last visited: 1 January 2014).

Singapore is witnessing a sustained improvement in the recidivism rate. It has fallen to an all-time low of 23.7% for the cohort released in 2004, down from 44% for the batch released in 1998. 25.1% of inmates released in 2006 returned to prison within 2 years.[30] In 2010 a 2-year recidivism rate of 26.7% was achieved.[31]

South Africa

Official statistics regarding recidivism in South Africa are absent, but according to some the rate is estimated to lie between 55% and 97%.[32] A representative sample study on the basis of all sentenced offenders released from correctional centres in 2006 indicated that during a 36-month follow-up period between 2006 and 2008 about 24% of the offenders were recidivists or re-offenders.[33] Other information, based on an analysis of three samples, showed that in 2010 about 32% of offenders with a first conviction in 1999 had reoffended, 22% with a first conviction in 2005, and 7% with a first conviction in 2009.[34]

Thailand

As of October 2006, the number of convicted prisoners in Thai correctional institutions who were imprisoned for the first time was 95,334 (86.02%) of all 110,827 convicted inmates. The number of offenders with multiple instances of imprisonment was 15,493 or 13.98% of all convicted inmates. From October 2003 – September 2005, the total number of released prisoners was 103,321. The number of these who reoffended from October 2005 – September 2006 was 1,587 or about 1.53% of all released prisoners during two fiscal years. In addition, drug

30 Peter Joo Hee Ng, 'Offender Rehabilitation, Community Engagement, and Preventing Re-Offending in Singapore', UNAFEI, *Resource Material Series* No. 80 (2010), p. 20 (at: www.unafei.or.jp/english/pdf/RS_No80/No80_00All.pdf) (last visited: 1 January 2014).

31 Timothy Hee Sun Leo, 'Using Evidence-Based Knowledge to Create an Offender Throughcare System', UNAFEI, *Resource Material Series* No. 88 (2012), p. 96 (at: www.unafei.or.jp/english/pdf/RS_No88/No88_00All.pdf) (last visited: 1 January 2014).

32 Tharina Guse & Daphne Hudson, 'Psychological Strengths and Posttraumatic Growth in the Successful Reintegration of South African Ex-Offenders', *International Journal of Offender Therapy and Comparative Criminology* XX(X) (2013), p. 1, 2, referring to Merelize Schoeman, 'Recidivism: a conceptual and operational conundrum', *Acta Criminologica* (CRIMSA Conference: Special Edition 1) (2010), p. 80–94. But see *Report on the Open Society Foundation for South Africa (OSF-SA) conference on recidivism and reoffending in South Africa*, 29 and 30 November 2010, p. 1, where it is stated: "A scan of the criminal justice literature shows that discussions of recidivism almost always say the recidivism rate in South Africa is between 80% and 90%. However, this oft-quoted figure has never been scientifically quantified".

33 See Marry Magoro, 'Measuring re-offending in South Africa', in: *Report on the Open Society Foundation for South Africa (OSF-SA) conference on recidivism and reoffending in South Africa*, 29 and 30 November 2010, p. 9 (at: http://osf.org.za/wp/wp-content/uploads/2012/09/Meeting-Report_-Recidivism-conference_20101.pdf) (last visited: 1 January 2014).

34 Albert Mangale, 'Recidivism and the SAPS Criminal Record Centre', in: *Report on the Open Society Foundation for South Africa (OSF-SA) conference on recidivism and reoffending in South Africa*, 29 and 30 November 2010, p. 10–11.

offenders represented the majority of all released prisoners in Thailand who reoffended and were re-imprisoned: they numbered 791 (49.84%).[35] It is also interesting to look at the numbers of juvenile recidivists. More than 12% of the incarcerated juveniles committed repeated infractions; therefore, the recidivism rate indicator of Thai juveniles was higher than the universal standard. Moreover, from 1996 to 2006, juvenile recidivism increased by approximately 1.6 times, and youth recidivism with violence increased by 4.7 times. A violent peer group and the parents' education were crucial determinants of juvenile violent recidivism.[36]

United States of America

During 2007, a total of 1,248,337 persons on parole were at risk of re-incarceration in the whole of the USA. This includes persons under parole supervision on 1 January or those entering parole during the year. Of these parolees, nearly 16% were returned to incarceration in 2007.[37] Another report asserts that among nearly 300,000 prisoners released in 15 states in 1994, 67.5% were rearrested within three years. A study of prisoners released in 1983 gave an estimate of 62.5%. Of the 272,111 persons released from prisons in 15 states in 1994, an estimated 67.5% were rearrested for a felony or serious misdemeanour within three years, 46.9% were reconvicted, and 25.4% were resentenced to prison for a new crime. These offenders had accumulated 4.1 million arrest charges before their most recent imprisonment and another 744,000 charges within three years of release. Released prisoners with the highest re-arrest rates were robbers (70.2%), burglars (74.0%), larcenists (74.6%), motor vehicle thieves (78.8%), those in prison for possessing or selling stolen property (77.4%), and those in prison for possessing, using, or selling illegal weapons (70.2%). Within three years, 2.5% of released rapists were arrested for another rape, and 1.2% of those who had served time for homicide were arrested for homicide.[38]

---

35 Somphop Rujjanavet, 'Improving the Reintegration of Offenders into the Community: the Current Situation of Thai Corrections', 135th International Senior Seminar Participants' Papers, UNAFEI, *Resource Material Series* No. 74 (2008), p. 144 (at: www.unafei.or.jp/english/pdf/RS_No74/No74_15PA_Rujjanavet.pdf) (last visited: 1 January 2014).

36 Adopted from Pimpan Silpasuwan *et.al.*, 'Violence Recidivism among Thai Juvenile Delinquents', 2 *Asia Journal of Public Health* 1 (2011), p. 13, 14. Cf. UNICEF, *Toolkit on Diversion and Alternatives to Detention 2009. Compilation of evidence in relation to recidivism* (at: www.unicef.org/tdad/evidencecostbenefit(2).doc) (last visited: 1 January 2014).

37 Thomas P. Bonczar & Lauren E. Glaze, *Probation And Parole In The United States, 2007. Statistical Tables*, Bureau of Justice Statistics, 11 December 2008, NCJ 224707, p. 7. See also Pew Center on the States, *State of Recidivism: The Revolving Door of America's Prisons*, Washington, DC: The Pew Charitable Trusts, April 2011.

38 Taken from Patrick A. Langan & David J. Levin, *Recidivism of Prisoners Released in 1994*, Bureau of Justice Statistics, Special Report, June 2002, NCJ 193427, p. 1.

Concluding remarks

Although the different definitions on which the statistics presented above are based, covering twenty jurisdictions, make it practically impossible to compare the statistics, they do demonstrate that reoffending constitutes a serious challenge in all the countries represented. The criminological reports and literature on which these statistics are based show that recidivism is higher (and often much higher) in case of offenders released from prison than when criminal proceedings have been terminated or when other sanctions are applied, such as fines, community service or electronic monitoring. These of course are general observations. The degree to which imprisonment influences recidivism positively or negatively also depends on the specific individual and the actual circumstances and regime in prison – for example, whether it is more rehabilitative or punitive in nature and the degree to which it is adapted to the specific personality and social circumstances of the individual offender.[39] That there are differences in results on preventing re-offending between imprisonment and other sanctions might furthermore be because offenders with a higher risk of relapse may also be those offenders who more often receive prison sentences. However, some studies do indicate that the risk of recidivism relative to the same offenders is considerably higher when they receive a prison sentence instead of an alternative sanction.[40]

3. REHABILITATION: OBLIGATION AND VALUES

As mentioned above, the idea of rehabilitation is to restore offenders to a useful life, through, *inter alia*, education, vocational guidance, therapy, work programmes and fostering personal responsibility, in order to enable them to contribute to their own development and to society. In order to achieve this, the State must have legal provisions and operational policies that create the opportunity for rehabilitation. Given that rehabilitation can contribute to the prevention of crime and recidivism, and considering the central function of the state to provide security for its citizens, this function presupposes – at least on an abstract level – that States must use rehabilitation policies and measures at least in so far as they have on balance a positive effect on the reduction of reoffending. The recognition that rehabilitation is a policy that demands to be pursued is furthermore imperative for any State that regards human dignity as a core value of the community it encompasses and that considers itself to be a state under the

39 See Francis T. Cullen, Cheryl Lero Jonson & Daniel S. Nagin, 'Prisons Do Not Reduce Recidivism: The High Cost of Ignoring Science', 91 *The Prison Journal* Supplement to 3 (2011), p. 48S-65S.

40 See, for example, Rafael Di Tella & Ernesto Schargrodsky, 'Criminal Recidivism after Prison and Electronic Monitoring', 121 *Journal of Political Economy* 1 (2013), p. 28–53.

rule of law, *i.e.* the so-called Rechtsstaat.[41] States moreover also have more tangible and legal obligations in this respect. Article 10 (3) of the International Covenant on Civil and Political Rights 1966 (ICCPR)[42] acknowledges the need for the state to be active in this respect. This provision holds: "*The penitentiary system shall comprise treatment of prisoners the essential aim of which shall be their reformation and social rehabilitation. Juvenile offenders shall be segregated from adults and be accorded treatment appropriate to their age and legal status.*"[43] Indeed, although the International Covenant is a human *rights* treaty, this provision is formulated rather as a general obligation on the State than as a particular entitlement of individuals. More such obligations follow from the Human Rights Committee's General Comment 21 on Article 10 ICCPR,[44] which states that no penitentiary system should be retributive only; it should essentially seek the reformation and social rehabilitation of the prisoner.[45] It further refers to legislative and administrative provisions, and to practical measures to ensure the re-education of convicted persons, and to measures to provide teaching, education and re-education, vocational guidance and training and work programmes for prisoners inside the penitentiary establishment as well as outside.[46] These obligations apply to all convicted persons, and thus also to high-risk offenders.

On the basis of international law, European law, the law and practice of the European Convention on Human Rights' Contracting States, and even the case law of several other jurisdictions, the European Court of Human Rights (ECtHR) also recognizes the principle that all prisoners – thus including those serving life sentences or high-risk offenders – be offered the possibility of rehabilitation and the prospect of release if that rehabilitation is achieved.[47] The European Court holds that it is axiomatic that a prisoner cannot be detained unless there are legitimate penological grounds for that detention. Rehabilitation not only entails one of these grounds, the Court also sides with the German Constitutional Court that the prison authorities have "the duty to strive towards

41 Cf. German Constitutional Court, *BVerfGE* 45, 187 (Lebenslange Freiheitsstrafe), nr. 176: "*Das Gericht hat mehrfach betont, daß die Forderung nach Resozialisierung verfassungsrechtlich dem Selbstverständnis einer Gemeinschaft entspreche, die die Menschenwürde in den Mittelpunkt stelle und dem Sozialstaatsprinzip verpflichtet sei.*"

42 999 UNTS 171.

43 Rehabilitation is also set as an important goal in, for example, the United Nations Standard Minimum Rules for the Treatment of Prisoners; see paragraphs 24, 61–67, 76, 80 and 95. See also Rule 6 of the European Prison Rules 2006: "*All detention shall be managed so as to facilitate the reintegration into free society of persons who have been deprived of their liberty.*"; this whole instrument suffuses the importance of rehabilitation; see more expressly also Rules 72(3), 83(b), 102 and 107.

44 *UN Doc.* HRI/GEN/1/Rev.1 at 33 (1994).

45 Para. 10.

46 Para. 11.

47 ECtHR, Grand Chamber Judgement of 9 July 2013, Nrs. 66069/09, 130/10 and 3896/10, par. 110–122 and 73 (*Vinter/the United Kingdom*).

a life sentenced prisoner's rehabilitation".[48] Rather than as a right, the European Court too presents rehabilitation primarily as an obligation that States must fulfil.

Naturally, the legal human rights instruments just mentioned connect the obligation to pursue rehabilitation primarily to its value for the individual offender and prisoner. However, it is useful not to put the emphasis on the state's obligation or the value of rehabilitation for the offender only, but also look at how it serves other goals and may thus also constitute a welcome instrument for the state in that respect. Rehabilitation is valuable in many different respects, as the chapters in part II of this volume set out.

As a further introduction to the topic of rehabilitation and to part II, the chapter by PRADEL (II.1) points out that there were strong doubts regarding the value of rehabilitation (*i.e.* Robert Martinson's "Nothing Works" essay of 1974). He then goes on to deal with two questions: why do we rehabilitate; and how do we rehabilitate? PRADEL concludes that the theory of rehabilitation is diffuse and ill-bounded, but that there are nevertheless hopeful developments and that more research is needed.

In their chapter JENDLY & DELGRANDE (II.2) employ a criminological approach to the value of rehabilitation. After a brief exposé of the history of rehabilitation and the functions of sentencing, they discuss various strategies, such as the "What works" movement, the "Risk-Need-Responsivity" model, "Short, sharp, shock" intervention, "New Public Management" policies, the "Good Lives Model", and "Theories of Distance". On the basis of a number of studies the authors criticise criminal justice policies that put too much emphasis on predictors of recidivism and ignore the social processes that drive the penal institution and the offender's trajectory. They assert that the "Good Lives Model" as well as "Theories of Distance" appear to be fruitful avenues. In this perspective, the important thing is not only to identify the components or motivations involved in the termination of criminal activity, but rather to see how these elements interact over time and could lead to a sustainable abandonment of criminal conduct.

The chapter by DALTON (II.3) explores the value of rehabilitation to prisoners. He pays specific attention to special categories of prisoners and ex-prisoners: members of the travelling community, detainees in mental hospitals, and politically motivated prisoners. An important question in this chapter is how we can expect to convince prisoners – especially prisoners in overcrowded or inhumane prison environments – that it is valuable for them to undergo rehabilitation and of the need to respect the rights of their fellow citizens. His exposé implies that even if rehabilitation did nothing to prevent reoffending, it is

48 See par. 113: "*Similar considerations must apply under the Convention system, the very essence of which, as the Court has often stated, is respect for human dignity*".

still a crucial instrument to improve and humanise prison conditions in many countries and to forestall prison regimes that are contrary to human dignity or to enforce the prohibition of ill-treatment.

Next, Bouzón de Terzano's chapter (II.4) considers the value of rehabilitation from the viewpoint of the prisoner's family. She asserts that the best strategy for rehabilitating prisoners and crime prevention is to protect and strengthen the family. Indeed, it is undeniable that the prisoner's family can help him/her rehabilitate. This is also in the interest of the family itself, not only because criminal behaviour is often also directed against the perpetrator's family members, while imprisonment of the wage earner often causes a mental and economic crisis within the family group, but also because the offender sets the wrong example, which might generate criminality among his/her children or other family members. Bouzón de Terzano sees an obligation on the State to support the family in this respect, by means of legislation, with its direct intervention and through the grant of subsidies.

Not only the family, but also society at large is relevant to the prevention of crime and reoffending. In his chapter Cilliers (II.5) argues that crime and its related problems can only be tackled effectively if society is involved and co-operative. He explains how to get society involved (through a "needs test") and discusses several models of how it can be involved. In order to realize these possibilities, Cilliers concludes that it will be very important for the correctional environment to develop the necessary policy and practical framework in relation to community participation.

Of course, society is also concerned with rehabilitation in other senses, such as the interests of the taxpayer. Therefore, in his chapter Aylward (II.6) discusses the challenges faced generally by policy makers in convincing taxpayers of the relative merits of prisoner rehabilitation. He also examines the value of rehabilitation to the taxpayer and highlights a number of evidence-based studies that have sought to determine the financial benefits of prisoner rehabilitation to the taxpayer. There is some evidence that offender programmes are or can be cost-beneficial.

Rehabilitation might furthermore be valuable to the prison staff and administration, in the sense that rehabilitation might help to secure a penitentiary system that is also safer for them and professionally more rewarding. The value of rehabilitation to the prison administration can also be viewed from another angle, however, as is done in the chapter by de Miranda Pereira (II.7). He holds that a prison system will have fulfilled its role if it provides a safe prison environment, if it achieves a good and well-thought-out selection of inmates in manageable groups, if it offers all offenders real opportunities for personal improvement, if it ensures high-level training, cohesion and motivation among its staff, and if it actively pursues the best possible co-operation and interaction with the free community. Alas, the value of rehabilitation to the prison administration tends to be defined by its capacity to fulfil the former rather than latter purposes.

Finally, Oliveira (II.8) approaches the value of rehabilitation from the perspective of the victim's interests. He explains that rehabilitation of the offender is desirable for the victim in a number of ways. Of major importance in this regard is that rehabilitation can be instrumental to conflict resolution and restorative justice. As a corollary, Oliveira asserts that the victim may play a paramount role in the process of reintegrating prisoners into society.

4. MEASURES TO DEAL WITH HIGH-RISK OFFENDERS DURING AND AFTER THEIR SENTENCE

While rehabilitation that enables offenders to become a law-abiding and productive member of the community is a core responsibility of the State, the statistics set out above on recidivism rates in selected jurisdictions demonstrate that current strategies and programmes frequently fail to protect the community against further offending. As we have already noted, that is more often than not because the penal responses to offenders – and in particular the conditions in which they are confined if they are sent to prison – are not conducive to rehabilitation. But it is also because many offenders are difficult to rehabilitate and often grow out of offending only with the passage of time.

Not surprisingly, the perceived ineffectiveness of the penal system in curbing reoffending rates has led to increasing calls over the last three decades for the adoption of measures not to reintegrate offenders into the community but to keep them apart from, or to restrict the role they can play in, the community. That has been driven by an increasing preoccupation with the prediction of the risk of reoffending for incapacitative purposes. However, as Pradel (III.9) points out, it has also been motivated by the need for rehabilitative measures to be properly targeted.

A large number of preventive measures now exist at all stages of the criminal justice system. As the chapters by Tak (III.4), and Shute (III.6) demonstrate, commentators on such measures tend to focus on the long term detention of high risk offenders for the protection of the public by way of a sentence of the court. The concluding chapter from Feest (III.12) also draws on Viano's contribution to the symposium to note the increasing use of community-based supervision involving electronic surveillance after the end of a prison sentence, particularly for sex offenders. However, the chapters by Young (III.1) and Lambropoulou (III.7) draw attention to the fact that such measures are much more pervasive. Risk prediction underpins some aspects of police decision-making; it is often an underlying purpose of community-based alternatives to traditional punishments; it forms the basis for pre-trial decisions on bail or custodial remand; and it generally determines whether or not a prisoner is released early from a prison sentence.

These types of preventive measures, though, are all pursued within the framework of a criminal justice system that has as its primary objective the prosecution, conviction and punishment of offenders. There is an inevitable tension between the limits imposed by the need for just punishment within that system and the longer term intervention that preventive measures for the mitigation of risk require – or, as VALLOTTON's chapter (III.3) puts it, the apparent impossibility of reconciling the two conflicting goals of imposing retributive punishment for the past and at the same time providing protection for the future. Attention has therefore turned to ways of providing protection by way of interventions outside the context, or at the expiry, of criminal proceeding. TAK (III.4) and SHUTE (III.6) both describe regimes in a number of jurisdictions that provide for indefinite civil detention on the expiry of a prison sentence.

CASORLA (III.8) similarly recognises three crucial phases for assessing the risk of reoffending: the stage of deciding the penalty; the stage of incarceration; and the stage after the sentence has come to an end. For each of these phases he sets out the measures that are applicable in France. Several of these measures are also discussed by PRADEL (III.9).

But, as CASORLA (III.8) notes, all such preventive measures pose a number of challenges and problems. First, VIANO (III.5) in his chapter graphically demonstrates the deleterious effects of a policy that leads to the indiscriminate use of life sentences or other long sentences of imprisonment for the protection of the public. He reminds us that the provision of selective incapacitation through general sentencing practice has diminishing returns and low cost-to-benefit ratios, particularly when it is applied on a widespread basis as in the United States.

Secondly, the severity of a prison sentence is dependant not only on the length of it, but also on the means by which it is executed. DELLA CASA (III.10) discusses various modes of incarceration of high risk offenders in Italy and the possibility for prisoners to appeal against placement in a specific prison regime. He notices important shortcomings in the supervision of the courts in this respect.

Thirdly, a number of chapters – *e.g.* by BUTLER (III.2) and JENDLY & DELGRANDE (II.2) – draw attention to the difficulties in developing robust risk assessment instruments, particularly when the base rate is low (as it is in the case of sex offenders). Indeed, one may go so far as to suggest that risk prediction instruments are not far from guesswork, and TAK (III.4) suggests that it is questionable how much protection is afforded to the community from the use of preventive confinement. The question this raises is whether or to what extent society is justified in imposing coercive measures if the instruments to predict who poses a risk of committing further serious offences are not robust. FEEST

(III.12) concludes that it should be permissible only under narrow conditions. In this regard, Young (III.1) agrees but notes that risk prediction measures have improved greatly in the last 20 years. He also argues that the issue is not about the accuracy of prediction (that is, whether the person would in fact have acted in the way predicted), because that is inherently indeterminable. Rather, the issue is whether the prediction of risk is just and fair – that is, whether the belief that the person presents a high risk of harming others is sufficiently robust and soundly based to enable the presumption that people are harmless to be rebutted.

Fourthly, the ongoing detention of people by way of "preventive security detention" (which exists in a number of European jurisdictions and beyond) has generally been regarded as constitutional when it is imposed as part of the initial sentence. As both Tak (III.4) and Feest (III.11) outline, such detention has historically been regarded as justified only in relation to "mentally ill" offenders or "persons of unsound mind"; detention of offenders of sound mind other than as part of the original sentence of the Court has been held by the European Court of Human Rights to violate the Convention. In 2011 the German Constitutional Court went further and declared all forms of preventive detention unconstitutional.

An increasingly common response is for preventive detention to be entirely separated from the criminal justice process and to be dealt with through a parallel civil process. The difficulty, of course, is that conditions of preventive detention are for all practical purposes often indistinguishable from a long term sentence of imprisonment that is imposed as punishment for the offence. Whether or not a "civil" label is attached to them, they thus look like disproportionate punishment. Butler's chapter (III.2) therefore draws attention to the dangers of using semantics to justify otherwise unjust detention, and to the importance of applying the same moral values to predictive justice as we do to retributive justice.

While these issues and problems are less acute when preventive measures do not involve detention but only limited restrictions or surveillance in the community, they are nevertheless equally applicable. Both Young (III.1) and Butler (III.2) therefore argue that there is a pressing need for a coherent theory of preventive justice that would be based on a set of limiting principles. In their respective chapters, they suggest what some of those principles should be.

5. CONCLUSIONS

Although rehabilitation may not be the ultimate panacea to prevent crime and reoffending, many studies have shown that taking rehabilitation goals into consideration – when sentencing offenders and utilizing rehabilitation programmes and rehabilitative regimes in prison – can contribute to the reduction of recidivism and public safety. Studies also indicate that in some instances there might also be a cost-saving effect from effective recidivism measures. But even if such positive effects were not achieved, rehabilitation would still serve important interests: rehabilitative policies, measures and regimes are material to humanizing and improving the prison system; they can serve the wellbeing of the offender's family; they might benefit prison staff and management goals and their professional satisfaction; and they can be supportive of victims in dealing with their suffering. Given these actual values of rehabilitation, and considering the State's central function to provide security to its citizens, as well as legal obligations under international human rights law, we assert that States are under an obligation to at least apply those rehabilitation policies, measures and programs that are effective, and to search for further means to make rehabilitation work.

But, however well States implement rehabilitation policies, many offenders will continue to commit further serious offences and pose an ongoing risk to the community. Given this reality, we assert that States will sometimes be justified in taking protective measures to mitigate that risk. But that must be done justly, and informed by fundamental human rights and moral values. If States continue to develop them in a piecemeal and incremental fashion as a way of appeasing law and order concerns, some of the core principles upon which rights-based democracies are founded will be seriously eroded.

OBLIGATIONS ET MOYENS DE PRÉVENTION DE LA RÉCIDIVE : INTRODUCTION, CONTEXTE ET CONCLUSIONS

Piet Hein VAN KEMPEN*
Warren YOUNG**

1. INTRODUCTION

La nécessité d'empêcher les détenus condamnés et autres délinquants de repasser à l'acte est le défi de taille que la justice criminelle et les systèmes pénitentiaires se doivent de relever. De nombreux pays sont confrontés à la difficulté de réduire les taux de récidive, par ces systèmes ou par d'autres moyens. Les taux de récidive sont considérables (il n'est pas rare qu'ils soient même élevés) et le problème est extrêmement complexe. Les États, dont la fonction centrale consiste à garantir la sécurité de ses citoyens, sont ainsi confrontés à un défi de taille.[1] C'est en ce sens que la prévention de la récidive peut paraître impérieuse. Toutefois, même suivant la perspective de la communauté et des victimes potentielles de la criminalité, il est indispensable de contrôler cette dernière et donc la récidive des délinquants. Le système de justice criminelle est un mécanisme important de la mise en place de ce contrôle, même s'il est loin d'être le seul. Le principal objectif

---

* Dr P.H.P.H.M.C. van Kempen M. Law (Hons), PhD, est Professeur de droit criminel et de procédure pénale. Il est également le président du département de droit criminel et de criminologie à l'université Radboud de Nijmegen, Pays-Bas. Il est aussi magistrat à temps partiel à la Cour d'appel de 's-Hertogenbosch, Pays-Bas, et Secrétaire Général de la Fondation Internationale Pénale et Pénitentiaire.

** Dr W. Young BA LLB (Hons) PhD est consultant dans le domaine de la réforme politique et législative à Wellington, Nouvelle-Zélande. Il a été Vice-président de la commission législative de Nouvelle-Zélande, Secrétaire adjoint à la Justice et Professeur de droit.

Note : la langue originale de ce texte est l'anglais.

1 À propos de l'obligation de l'État de garantir la sécurité, voir Piet Hein van Kempen, 'Four Concepts of Security – A Human Rights Perspective', 13 *Human Rights Law Review* 1 (2013), p. 1-23 (see particularly p. 20). Le Secrétaire général des Nations Unies a été jusqu'à souligné le fait que « *la prévention est le premier impératif de la justice* » ; voir Rapport du Secrétaire général, « État de droit et justice transitionnelle dans les sociétés en situation de conflit ou d'après-conflit », 23 août 2004, *UN Doc.* S/2004/616, par. 4.

du système de justice criminelle est de contribuer à définir et à préserver l'ordre légal, de prévenir les intrusions dans cet ordre, et d'agir contre les auteurs de délits. Dans le cadre de cet effort, juger, condamner et sanctionner les délinquants est un outil important parmi d'autres. La condamnation elle-même peut toutefois être utilisée à différentes fins. Vengeance, dissuasion (prévention générale et spéciale), neutralisation, rétablissement (réparation) et réhabilitation sont autant d'objectifs de sanction largement acceptés, ou à tout le moins une justification des sanctions, bien qu'ils ne soient généralement pas compatibles entre eux dans certains cas spécifiques.[2] La négligence structurelle de l'un de ces objectifs peut cependant amoindrir l'efficacité du système de justice criminelle en termes de réduction de la criminalité et d'amélioration de la sécurité publique. L'on pourrait alors argumenter que l'État manque à ses obligations.

Dans la mesure où au cours des dernières décennies, l'importance de la réhabilitation (parfois décrite comme resocialisation, réinsertion ou encore traitement) s'est clairement amoindrie dans bon nombre de juridictions[3], le présent ouvrage (partie II) se concentre avant tout sur la valeur de la réintégration des délinquants dans une vie utile (*inter alia*, par l'éducation, l'orientation professionnelle, la thérapie, des programmes de travail et la promotion de la responsabilité personnelle) dans le but de leur donner les capacités de contribuer à leur développement personnel et de prendre part à la société. Nombreux sont ceux qui affirment et expliquent que la réhabilitation est une valeur fondamentale du système de justice pénale et du système carcéral, du point de vue du délinquant mais aussi à bien d'autres égards. Cette valeur doit être inscrite dans la politique législative et pénale opérationnelle et elle doit être prise en compte dans le processus décisionnel qui mène à l'adoption de la peine appropriée dans des cas individuels traités par les tribunaux. Elle doit également être prise en compte lors de l'exécution de la peine. La justice criminelle et les systèmes pénitentiaires peuvent ainsi tous deux être utilisés d'une façon « socialement constructive » : les législateurs et les tribunaux peuvent opter pour des sanctions qui s'inscrivent de façon inhérente dans l'intérêt de la resocialisation (par exemple travaux d'intérêt général ou surveillance électronique). Elle peut même être mise en œuvre lorsque les sanctions les plus punitives sont appliquées (c'est-à-dire l'emprisonnement[4]), de manière à contribuer aussi à la réhabilitation du délinquant.[5] Malheureusement, il est très fréquent que l'emprisonnement ne

---

2 Cf. dans ce volume également les chapitres par Pradel (par. 1) et Jendly & Delgrande (par. 2).

3 Cf. Francis T. Cullen & Karen E. Gilbert, *Reaffirming Rehabilitation*, Anderson Publishing, 2013, p. xi-xxvi; D.A. Andrews & James Bonta, 'Rehabilitating criminal justice policy and practice', 16 *Psychology, Public Policy, and Law* 1 (2010), p. 39-55.

4 Du moins dans toutes les juridictions qui n'appliquent pas la peine capitale.

5 Voir par exemple, Francis T. Cullen & Cheryl Lero Jonson, 'Rehabilitation and Treatment Programs', in: James Q. Wilson & Joan Petersilia (eds), *Crime and Public Policy*, Oxford: Oxford University Press, 2011, p. 293-344; James Gilligan & Bandy Lee, 'The Resolve to Stop

serve pas les objectifs de réhabilitation des délinquants et de réduction de la criminalité.[6] Le 12e Congrès des Nations Unies pour la prévention du crime et la justice pénale de 2010 a mis en exergue le fait que la surpopulation carcérale est une cause majeure de récidive et qu'elle ne contribue en rien à la sécurité publique.[7]

Si l'ensemble des mesures de réhabilitation sont potentiellement pertinentes pour toutes les catégories de délinquants[8], leur seule application peut, comme indiqué précédemment, s'avérer insuffisante pour prévenir la récidive. C'est particulièrement vrai dans le cas des délinquants à haut risque, c'est-à-dire ceux qui présentent un risque important de nouveau délit. Il s'agit par exemple de ceux qui ont une prédisposition à commettre des infractions à caractère sexuel, des incendies volontaires ou des infractions violentes, des terroristes et des membres de groupes criminels organisés. Les sanctions pénales appliquées à ces délinquants ont souvent pour objectif de réduire le risque qu'ils représentent pour la société (par exemple les condamnations conçues pour avoir un effet dissuasif individuel ou pour appliquer des programmes de réhabilitation). Au cours des deux ou trois dernières décennies, bon nombre de juridictions ont toutefois été amenées à considérer ces mesures comme inadéquates pour traiter le risque généré par les pires délinquants. Des lois ont été adoptées, par exemple pour imposer des restrictions aux délinquants au terme de leur condamnation pénale et dans le but d'élargir l'éventail des peines civiles comme solution alternative aux sanctions pénales. La partie III du présent volume abordera dès lors les mesures permettant de traiter les délinquants à haut risque durant l'exécution de leur peine et au terme de celle-ci, ainsi que les arguments favorables et défavorables à leur utilisation.

Ce chapitre – qui est aussi la partie I du présent volume – se penche ensuite sur la signification possible de la notion de récidive, suivant un angle de vue formel, et il présente une étude sur les taux de récidive dans plusieurs juridictions dans le monde (section 2). Nous examinerons ensuite (dans la section 3) plus en détail différentes valeurs de réhabilitation dans une introduction aux chapitres consacrés à ce sujet. Pour élargir le contexte de ces chapitres, nous avons

---

the Violence Project: reducing violence in the community through a jail-based initiative', 27 *Journal of Public Health* 2 (2005), p. 143-148 ; et dans le présent volume le chapitre par Jendly & Delgrande.

6 Voir p. *ex.*, Paula Smith *et.al.*, *Effets de l'incarcération et des sanctions intermédiaires sur la récidive : effets généraux et différences individuelles 2002-01*, Université du Nouveau Brunswick, Saint John/Public Works and Government Services Canada, 2002 (sur le site : www.ccoso.org/library%20articles/200201_Gendreau_e.pdf) (dernière visite : 1 janvier 2014).

7 12e Congrès des Nations Unies pour la prévention du crime et la justice pénale, Commission, 8e & 9e Réunions (AM & PM), Couverture de la réunion, le 16 avril 2010, SOC/CP/352.

8 Cf. Office des Nations Unies contre la drogue et le crime, *Manuel d'introduction pour la Prévention de la Récidive et la Réinsertion Sociale des Délinquants* (Série de manuels sur la justice pénale), New York : Nations Unies, 2012, p. 129-145, avec une attention particulière aux programmes de réinsertion conçus pour de nombreux groupes de délinquants différents.

également abordé en quoi le traitement de la réhabilitation peut être considéré comme une obligation légale. Les chapitres suivants du présent volume consacrés aux mesures visant à traiter les délinquants à haut risque pendant et après leur sanction sont ensuite introduits (section 4). Une fois encore, pour étoffer quelque peu le contexte, nous nous penchons brièvement sur la forme que ces mesures ont adoptée et sur quelques problèmes et dilemmes fondamentaux qu'ils posent. Le chapitre se termine par des conclusions.

2. DÉFINITION DE LA RÉCIDIVE ET DU TAUX DE RÉCIDIVE

Avant d'illustrer le problème de la récidive par des taux, il est important de souligner le fait que ceux-ci dépendent dans une grande mesure de la définition de la récidive sur laquelle ils se basent. Les définitions mises en avant dans les diverses recherches criminologiques sont extrêmement variables. Il n'existe pas de norme internationale pour la mesure et la communication de la récidive, de sorte que l'on pourrait argumenter, au sens matériel le plus large, qu'une personne ayant commis un délit devient un récidiviste lorsqu'elle commet un autre délit. Toutefois, sur le plan de la forme, la définition officielle de la récidive est souvent beaucoup plus restrictive, ce qui suscite des questions du type: La récidive implique-t-elle un nouveau délit en général ou uniquement la perpétuation du même délit? Le nouveau délit doit-il être commis dans une période déterminée après le premier délit (par exemple un, deux ou cinq ans après) ou n'existe-t-il aucune limite? La récidive tient-elle compte de tous les délits consignés par les autorités ou seulement de certains délits et / ou uniquement de délits qui ont été sanctionnés, ou encore qui ont donné lieu à une peine d'emprisonnement? Plusieurs études apportent des réponses différentes à ces questions, de sorte que les statistiques en matière de récidive sont souvent établies sur des bases totalement différentes. Il est utile de se souvenir de cette divergence lors de la lecture des brefs rapports consacrés à vingt juridictions différentes réparties sur les six continents présentés ci-après (par ordre alphabétique) pour illustrer le problème de la récidive.[9]

Argentine

Les chercheurs qui ont utilisé les données de tous les délinquants libérés du système pénitentiaire de Buenos Aires entre janvier 1998 et octobre 2007 ont découvert que le taux de récidive (c'est-à-dire la part des personnes individuelles libérées du système pénal qui sont retournées en prison après avoir commis un

9 Pour obtenir les définitions de la récidive utilisées dans les études, veuillez consulter ces dernières.

nouveau délit) était d'un peu plus de 22 % pour les délinquants libérés de prison, taux qui atteint à peine plus de 13 % pour les délinquants libérés après une peine de surveillance électronique. Le taux de récidive moyen annuel pour l'échantillon des délinquants libérés de prison – c'est-à-dire la part des délinquants libérés de prison qui y sont retournés dans un délai d'un an – était de 7,8 %, pour 4,6 % chez les délinquants ayant bénéficié d'une surveillance électronique.[10] Des sources différentes citent cependant des taux de récidive de 60 % et 70 % pour l'Argentine dans son ensemble.[11]

Bolivie

Un article de journal récemment publié fait référence à plusieurs études faisant état de taux de récidive de 20 % à 30 %, ce qui est considéré comme assez faible en Amérique latine.[12]

Danemark, Finlande, Islande, Norvège et Suède

Une étude menée sur près de 60.000 délinquants dans les pays nordiques – Danemark, Finlande, Islande, Norvège et Suède – montre que la Norvège affiche le taux de récidive global le plus faible parmi les délinquants ayant eu affaire à la justice pénale de ces pays. Près de 20 % des détenus libérés de prison et un pourcentage similaire de ceux qui ont réalisé des travaux d'intérêt général en Norvège ont subi une nouvelle condamnation devant être purgée au sein des établissements pénitentiaires. Dans les autres pays nordiques, le taux de récidive global varie entre 24 % et 31 %.[13]

Angleterre & Pays de Galles

Entre juillet 2010 et juin 2011, près de 630.000 délinquants ont été mis en examen, condamnés (à l'exclusion des peines d'emprisonnement immédiates) ou libérés. Près de 170.000 de ces délinquants se sont rendus coupables d'un nouveau délit dans un délai d'un an, soit un taux de récidive avéré à un an de

---

10 Rafael Di Tella & Ernesto Schargrodsky, 'Criminal Recidivism after Prison and Electronic Monitoring', 121 *Journal of Political Economy* 1 (2013), p. 54.

11 Gabriel Bouzat, 'Inequality, Crime, and Security in Argentina', SELA (Seminario en Latinoamérica de Teoría Constitucional y Política), Paper 91 (2010), p. 23, note de bas de page 36 (sur: http://digitalcommons.law.yale.edu/yls_sela/91) (dernière visite: 1 janvier 2014). Pour d'autres références, voir aussi Cristal Downing, 'Bolivian prison entrepreneurship. An unexpectedly successful rehabilitation method?', 6 *Journal of Enterprising Communities: People and Places in the Global Economy* 4 (2012), p. 346.

12 Cristal Downing, 'Bolivian prison entrepreneurship. An unexpectedly successful rehabilitation method?', 6 *Journal of Enterprising Communities: People and Places in the Global Economy* 4 (2012), p. 346.

13 Tiré de Ragnar Kristoffersen *et al.*, *Retur. En nordisk undersøgelse af recidiv blandt klienter i kriminal-forsorgen*, 2010.

26,9 %, ou encore une augmentation de 0,5 point de pourcentage par rapport aux 12 mois précédents et un recul de 1,0 point de pourcentage depuis 2000. Ces récidivistes ont chacun commis en moyenne 2,88 nouveaux délits. Au total, cela représente près de 490.000 nouveaux délits, dont 82 % commis par des adultes et 18 % par des mineurs. 56,5 % (près de 280.000) ont été commis par les délinquants qui s'étaient déjà rendus coupables de 11 délits antérieurs ou plus. 0,7 % (près de 3.300) sont des infractions graves de violence/à caractère sexuel. 5,1 % (près de 25.000) ont été commis par des récidivistes qui bénéficiaient d'un programme Prolific and other Priority Offender (PPO), un programme pluri-organisations axé sur un groupe très petit mais difficile de délinquants prolifiques / récidivistes ayant commis un nombre disproportionné de délits.[14]

Estonie

D'après une étude estonienne, le taux de récidive 2007 chez les délinquants ayant fait l'objet de décisions de procédure et les détenus libérés fut le plus faible dans le cas des procédures clôturées (18 %) et le plus élevé dans le cas des détenus libérés de prison (40 %). Après six mois, près de 25 % des délinquants ont été interrogés en qualité de suspect dans le cadre d'une nouvelle infraction ; dans les 18 mois, 50 % des ex-détenus ont été suspectés de nouveaux actes délictuels et plus de 60 % dans un délai de trois ans. Les données indiquent que le taux de récidive des détenus libérés a quelque peu diminué au fil des ans : si 43 % des personnes libérées en 2004 ont commis un nouveau délit dans l'année qui a suivi leur libération et 41 % en 2005 et 2006, elles sont 40 % à en avoir fait autant en 2007. Le taux de récidive des détenus libérés de prison est le plus élevé chez ceux qui ont purgé la totalité de leur peine : 50 % de ces délinquants ont commis une nouvelle infraction pénale dans l'année qui a suivi. Bien que la proportion de détenus libérés après avoir purgé leur peine au regard de l'ensemble des détenus libérés ait reculé de 82 % à 49 %, cet indicateur est resté stable sur une période de quatre années (2004 – 2007) à 48 %-49 %.[15]

France

Une étude récemment menée en France montre que pour les années 2000 à 2010, la proportion des condamnés ayant déjà eu maille à partir avec la justice durant les cinq années précédent leur condamnation a augmenté entre 2000 et 2004 pour passer de 35,5 % en 2000 à 37,6 % en 2004, avant de reculer de deux points en 2006 (35,7 %) puis de repartir à la hausse à 40 % en 2010, soit une légère

14 Ces chiffres sont tirés de Ministère de la justice, 'Proven Re-offending Statistics Quarterly Bulletin, July 2010 to June 2011, England and Wales', *Statistics Bulletin* 25 avril 2013, p. 7 et 20.

15 Tiré de Andri Ahven, Jako Salla & Siim Vahtrus, *Retsidiivsus Eestis/Recidivism in Estonia*, Tallinn : Justiitsministeerium, 2010, p. 160.

augmentation du taux global de récidive. Après dix années, le taux de récidive a pratiquement atteint 50 %, avec des variations considérables en fonction des types de délits. Sur une période de six années, le taux de récidive était élevé pour les infractions contre la propriété : vol et abus de confiance (55 %) et destruction de biens (53,5 %), ainsi que les infractions en matière d'arme à feu, la diffamation et les infractions liées à la drogue (entre 53 % et 50 %). Ces infractions représentaient un peu moins d'un tiers des infractions sanctionnées en 2004. À contrario, le taux de récidive a reculé pour les faits de roulage (40 %), soit 30 % des délits de 2004, ainsi que les abus sexuels. De plus, après six années, le taux de récidive s'est avéré plus élevé dans les cas où le délinquant a été condamné à une peine de prison (61 %) que lorsque la sanction ne comprenait pas de peine d'emprisonnement (36 %).[16]

Allemagne

Pour la plupart des délinquants sanctionnés ou libérés de prison en 2004, les sanctions pénales furent un événement unique sur la période d'observation (2004-2007). Près de 35 % des délinquants sanctionnés ou libérés ont récidivé pendant la période d'observation de trois années. Lorsqu'une sanction pénale a été imposée pour le nouveau délit, il s'agit dans la majorité des cas d'une peine moins dure qu'une mesure de privation de liberté. Les délinquants soumis à une peine d'emprisonnement présentaient un risque plus important de récidive que ceux qui ont fait l'objet de sanctions moins sévères. Ainsi, les détenus condamnés présentent de toute évidence un taux de récidive plus important que les autres délinquants condamnés, bien qu'ils soient de loin moins de la moitié à avoir de nouveau eu affaire au système de justice pénale dans un délai de trois années. De plus, le taux de récidive est en relation étroite avec le nombre de condamnations antérieures : plus ce nombre est élevé, plus le taux de rechute augmente.[17]

Irlande

Une étude menée par le service de probation a montré que près de 63 % des délinquants placés sous sa surveillance n'étaient pas condamnés pour un nouveau délit dans les deux années qui suivaient la mesure probatoire ou la peine de travaux d'intérêt général. Le taux de récidive global des délinquants mis en avant par cette étude est de 37,2 %. Elle montre en outre que 75 % des nouveaux

---

16 Tiré de Ministère de la Justice, *Mesurer la récidive. Contribution à la conférence de consensus de prévention de la récidive*, 2013, p. 7-11. Voir également Benjamin Monnery, 'The determinants of recidivism among ex prisoners : a survival analysis on French data', mai 2013 (sur : http://halshs.archives-ouvertes.fr/docs/00/82/28/47/PDF/1320.pdf) (dernière visite : 1 janvier 2014).

17 Tiré de Jörg-Martin Jehle, Hans-Jörg Albrecht, Sabine Hohmann-Fricke & Carina Tetal, *Legalbewährung nach strafrechtlichen Sanktionen Eine bundesweite Rückfalluntersuchung 2004 bis 2007*, Berlin : Bundesministerium des Justiz, 2010, p. 6-7.

délits sont commis durant la première année de la période de deux ans et 25 % pendant la seconde année. Les niveaux de récidive sont plus importants pour les délinquants frappés par une mesure probatoire (39,3 %) que pour ceux qui ont effectué des travaux d'intérêt général (33,5 %).[18] Une étude menée sur la récidive chez l'ensemble des prisonniers, publiée par l'administration pénitentiaire irlandaise, révèle un taux de récidive de 62,3 % dans les trois années. Plus de 80 % des récidivistes sont passés à l'acte dans les 12 mois qui ont suivi leur libération.[19]

Japon

D'après le livre blanc sur la criminalité publié par le Ministère de la justice[20], le nombre de récidivistes qui se sont rendus coupables d'infractions au Code pénal, hors infractions de roulage, n'a pas cessé d'augmenter depuis 1997, pour diminuer ensuite légèrement pendant 4 années consécutives à partir de 2007, pour atteindre 137.614 cas en 2010 (soit 2,0 % de moins que l'année précédente). Le taux de récidive a sans cesse augmenté depuis 1997, pour atteindre 42,7 % en 2010 (soit une augmentation de 0,5 points (id.)).[21] L'examen des adultes déjà condamnés et libérés pour des infractions au Code pénal, hors infractions de roulage, en 2010 en fonction du nombre de condamnations antérieures a révélé que ceux qui avaient subi une condamnation antérieure affichaient le taux de récidive le plus élevé à 39,1 %, et que la proportion de ceux qui avaient déjà été condamnés à cinq reprises au moins était elle aussi élevée, à 21,9 %. De plus, ceux qui ont précédemment été condamnés pour des infractions du même type représentent 51,6 % du total. Le taux de personnes précédemment condamnées parmi les adultes libérés était de 28,2 % du total des infractions au Code pénal hors infractions de roulage. Il est toutefois extrêmement élevé pour les vols (46,0 %) et la fraude (39,8 %).[22] Le pourcentage cumulé de nouvelles condamnations à une peine de prison dans un délai de dix ans parmi les détenus libérés en 2001 s'élève à 63,3 % pour ceux qui ont été libérés au terme de leur peine d'emprisonnement et de 42,8 % pour ceux qui ont bénéficié d'une libération conditionnelle. Ces mêmes pourcentages passent respectivement à 89,2 % et 81,9 % de nouvelle peine d'emprisonnement dans

---

18 Tiré de The Probation Service, *Probation Service Recidivism Study 2007-2011. Probation Service Research Report 2*, novembre 2012, p. 2, 8, 17.

19 Irish Prison Service & Central Statistics Office, *Irish Prison Service Recidivism Study 2013. A study of recidivism among all prisoners released by the Irish Prison Service on completion of a sentence in 2007 – based on reoffending and reconviction data up to the end of 2010*, Longford, Ireland, 2013, p. 3.

20 Voir également Hiroyuki Kuzuno, 'Neoliberalism, Social Exclusion, and Criminal Justice – A Case in Japan', 40 *Hitotsubashi Journal of Law and Politics* (2012), p. 16.

21 Voir Ministère de la justice, *White paper on crime 2011*, Part 4, Chapter 6, Section 1/1 (voir sur: http://hakusyo1.moj.go.jp/en/nendo_nfm.html) (dernière visite: 1 janvier 2014).

22 Voir Ministère de la justice, *White paper on crime 2011*, Partie 4, Chapitre 6, Section 1/2.

un délai de cinq années. La différence entre les personnes emprisonnées pour la première fois et celles qui l'étaient pour la seconde fois est remarquable. Pratiquement la moitié des délinquants emprisonnés deux fois ou plus ont purgé une nouvelle peine de prison dans les cinq ans, ce qui traduit la difficulté de les rééduquer / réinsérer.[23]

Pays-Bas

Les Pays-Bas définissent un délinquant primaire comme un suspect qui n'a encore jamais été interpellé. Un récidiviste est un suspect dont le casier judiciaire contient 2 à 5 faits (pour les mineurs) ou 2 à 10 faits (pour les adultes) sur l'ensemble de leur carrière criminelle. Les délinquants qui comptent respectivement plus de 5 ou 10 faits à leur actif sont considérés comme multirécidivistes. Sur l'ensemble des suspects arrêtés en 2010, il s'agissait d'une première infraction pour 39 %, 46 % étaient des récidivistes et 14 % des multirécidivistes. Pour l'année 2005, ces mêmes chiffres étaient respectivement de 44 %, 43 % et 13 %. Cela signifie que la part des récidivistes et multirécidivistes a quelque peu augmenté au cours de cette période.[24] D'après le rapport sur la récidive 2002-2008, qui fait état des chiffres de 2004, le pourcentage de récidivistes sanctionnés par les tribunaux ou par les services du procureur de la Reine a enregistré un léger recul. 27,5 % des adultes condamnés pour avoir commis un crime en 2008 ont recommencé dans les deux années qui ont suivi. En 2002, ce pourcentage était de 30,8 %. Le recul de la récidive chez les délinquants mineurs sanctionnés par les tribunaux ou les services du procureur de la Reine s'est amorcé avec un léger décalage. Le taux de récidive national chez cette population a commencé à diminuer en 2006 (39,1 % en 2002). En 2008, 35,9 % de tous les mineurs saisis par les tribunaux ou les services du procureur de la Reine pour une affaire pénale ont de nouveau été poursuivis deux années après le cas index. Le taux de nouvelle condamnation des ex-détenus a lui aussi reculé au cours des dernières années. Depuis 2002, les pourcentages de récidive dans le secteur du système pénitentiaire pour adultes montrent une tendance à la baisse. Sur l'ensemble des adultes qui ont quitté une institution pénitentiaire en 2008, 48,5 % ont de nouveau eu maille à partir avec le système judiciaire dans les deux années qui ont suivi, contre 55,2 % en 2002. Le taux de nouvelle condamnation dans les deux ans chez les mineurs ex-détenus de centres de détention pour mineurs libérés en 2002 s'élevait à 55,3 % et à 52,0 % pour les mineurs libérés en 2008. Un recul s'observe à partir de 2006. Cette population inclut également les mineurs placés en institution à la suite d'une action civile.[25]

---

[23] Voir Ministère de la justice, *White paper on crime 2011*, Part 4, Chapter 6, Section 3/2.

[24] Voir M.M. van Rosmalen, S.N. Kalidien & N.E. de Heer-de Lange (eds), *Criminaliteit en rechtshandhaving 2011*, Den Haag : CBS/WODC/Raad voor de Rechtspraak, 2012, p. 108.

[25] Tiré de B.S.J. Wartna *et.al.*, *Recidivism report 2002-2008. Trends in the reconviction rate of Dutch offenders* (Fact sheet 2011-5a), The Hague : Dutch Ministry of Security and Justice/

Nouvelle-Zélande

Selon une étude menée sur une période de 48 mois, 18 % des délinquants qui ont entamé une peine de supervision, des travaux d'intérêt général et de détention à domicile en 2002/03, ont été condamnés pour une nouvelle infraction et ont débuté au moins une peine de prison pendant la période de suivi de 48 mois. Pendant cette même période, 36 % ont été condamnés et ont entamé une peine de travaux communautaires. Cela signifie que le taux global de récidive des délinquants qui ont entamé une peine de supervision, des travaux d'intérêt général et de détention à domicile était de 54 % sur quatre ans. Il est intéressant de noter qu'au terme d'un délai d'un an, 59 % de ces récidivistes avaient déjà encouru une nouvelle condamnation, 20 % au terme de la deuxième année, 12 % au cours de la troisième année, et les 9 % restants, évidemment, durant la quatrième année. En d'autres termes, le taux de récidive de loin le plus important s'observe durant les douze premiers mois. Sur une période de quatre années, les taux de condamnation des récidivistes ayant purgé une peine de supervision et de travaux d'intérêt général étaient de 65 % contre 55 % pour les délinquants ayant purgé une peine de détention à domicile.[26]

Russie

Les taux de récidive augmentent de façon considérable. En 2003, près de 27 % des crimes étaient perpétrés par des personnes déjà condamnées par le passé. Depuis lors, ce pourcentage a augmenté progressivement d'année en année.[27] Selon « The state of crime: January-December 2012 », pratiquement un délit sur deux qui fait l'objet d'une enquête (46,6 %) est commis par des personnes ayant déjà commis d'autres délits. Les membres des groupes criminels organisés se sont rendus coupables de 17,3 millions de délits graves et particulièrement graves (soit une augmentation de 2,4 %) ; leur part dans le nombre total de délits ayant fait l'objet d'une enquête dans ces catégories est passée de 5,2 % en 2011 à 5,7 % en 2012.[28] Les statistiques citées dans « Criminality in January-October 2013 » montrent

---

WODC, p. 2 (sur: www.wodc.nl/onderzoeksdatabase/actualisering-recidivemeting-sancties-2011.aspx) (dernière visite: 1 janvier 2014).

26 Tiré de A. Nadesu, *Reconviction patterns of offenders managed in the community: A 48-month follow-up analysis*, New Zealand: Department of Corrections, 2008, p. 3, 4, 12-13.

27 Voir Ilya Kokorin, *Probation services in Europe and Russian experience of social reintegration and rehabilitation of offenders* (LL.M. thesis), Budapest: Central European University 2013, p. 63 (sur: www.etd.ceu.hu/2013/kokorin_ilya.pdf), qui fait référence à des rapports officiels émanant du Ministère de l'intérieur de Russie (sur: http://mvd.ru/presscenter/statistics/reports/) (dernière visite de ces deux sites Internet: 1 janvier 2014).

28 Voir par. 19, sur: http://mvd.ru/presscenter/statistics/reports/item/804701/ (dernière visite: le 1 janvier 2014).

que le taux de récidive général est passé à 49,1 % et à 6,0 % pour les membres de groupes criminels organisés.[29]

Singapour

La récidive, qui est définie comme le pourcentage de toute cohorte libérée qui a commis un nouveau délit suite auquel elle est retournée en prison, est un indicateur de performance clé pour l'administration pénitentiaire de Singapour. Cette dernière a recours à un taux sur 2 ans qu'elle suit depuis 1998. Singapour assiste à une amélioration durable du taux de récidive qui a atteint un niveau plancher à 23,7 % pour la cohorte libérée en 2004, contre 44 % pour les détenus libérés en 1998. 25,1 % des prisonniers libérés en 2006 sont retournés en prison dans les 2 ans.[30] Un taux de récidive à deux ans de 26,7 % était atteint en 2010.[31]

Afrique du Sud

Il n'existe pas de statistiques officielles de récidive pour l'Afrique du Sud. Toutefois, d'aucuns estiment qu'il se situe entre 55 % et 97 %.[32] Une étude réalisée auprès d'un échantillon représentatif sur la base de tous les délinquants condamnés ayant été libérés des centres correctionnels en 2006 indique que durant une période de suivi de 36 mois comprise entre 2006 et 2008, près de 24 % des délinquants étaient des récidivistes ou avaient commis un nouveau délit.[33] D'autres informations, basées sur une analyse de trois échantillons, a montré qu'en 2010, près de 32 % des délinquants condamnés pour la première

29 Voir par. 19, sur : http://mvd.ru/presscenter/statistics/reports/item/1317409/ ou http://mvd.ru/upload/site1/document_file/tcAeqVoQFq.pdf (dernière visite : 1 janvier 2014).

30 Peter Joo Hee Ng, 'Offender Rehabilitation, Community Engagement, and Preventing Re-Offending in Singapore', UNAFEI, *Resource Material Series* No. 80 (2010), p. 20 (sur : www.unafei.or.jp/english/pdf/RS_No80/No80_00All.pdf) (dernière visite : 1 janvier 2014).

31 Timothy Hee Sun Leo, 'Using Evidence-Based Knowledge to Create an Offender Throughcare System', UNAFEI, *Resource Material Series* No. 88 (2012), p. 96 (sur : www.unafei.or.jp/english/pdf/RS_No88/No88_00All.pdf) (dernière visite : 1 janvier 2014).

32 Tharina Guse & Daphne Hudson, 'Psychological Strengths and Posttraumatic Growth in the Successful Reintegration of South African Ex-Offenders', *International Journal of Offender Therapy and Comparative Criminology* XX(X) (2013), p. 1, 2, avec une référence à Merelize Schoeman, 'Recidivism : a conceptual and operational conundrum', *Acta Criminologica* (CRIMSA Conference : Special Edition 1) (2010), p. 80-94. Voir aussi *Report on the Open Society Foundation for South Africa (OSF-SA) conference on recidivism and reoffending in South Africa*, 29 et 30 novembre 2010, p. 1, qui affirme (traduction libre) : « Un examen de la littérature consacrée à la justice pénale montre que les discussions sur la récidive évoquent pratiquement de manière systématique que le taux de récidive en Afrique du Sud oscille entre 80 % et 90 %. Ce chiffre souvent cité n'a toutefois jamais été prouvé scientifiquement ».

33 Voir Marry Magoro, 'Measuring re-offending in South Africa', in : *Report on the Open Society Foundation for South Africa (OSF-SA) conference on recidivism and reoffending in South Africa*, 29 et 30 novembre 2010, p. 9 (sur : http://osf.org.zas/wp/wp-content/uploads/2012/09/Meeting-Report_-Recidivism-conference_20101.pdf) (dernière visite : 1 janvier 2014).

fois en 1999 avaient récidivé, contre 22 % de ceux qui ont été condamnés pour la première fois en 2005 et 7 % dont la première condamnation date de 2009.[34]

Thaïlande

En octobre 2006, le nombre de détenus emprisonnés pour la première fois dans les établissements pénitentiaires thaïlandais s'élevait à 95.334 (soit 86,02 %) sur l'ensemble des 110,827 détenus. Le nombre de délinquants qui n'en étaient pas à leur première peine d'emprisonnement était quant à lui de 15.493, soit 13,98 % de la totalité des détenus. Le nombre total de prisonniers libérés entre octobre 2003 et septembre 2005, s'élevait à 103.321. Ils sont 1.587, ou environ 1,53 % de l'ensemble des prisonniers libérés sur deux exercices fiscaux, a avoir récidivé entre octobre 2005 et septembre 2006. De plus, la majorité des prisonniers libérés dans ce pays et remis en prison après une récidive sont des délinquants condamnés pour faits de drogue : ils sont au nombre de 791 (soit 49,84 %).[35] Il est également intéressant de se pencher sur le nombre de mineurs récidivistes. Plus de 12 % des mineurs incarcérés ont commis plusieurs infractions ; de sorte que l'indicateur du taux de récidive chez les mineurs thaïlandais était supérieur à la norme universelle. De plus, entre 1996 et 2006, la récidive juvénile a été multipliée par environ 1,6, tandis que la récidive violente des mineurs augmentait de 4,7 fois. L'appartenance à un groupe violent et l'éducation dispensée par les parents sont deux éléments déterminants de la récidive violente chez les mineurs.[36]

États-Unis d'Amérique

Pendant l'année 2007, au total, 1.248.337 personnes en libération conditionnelle présentaient un risque de retourner en prison dans l'ensemble des États-Unis. Ces chiffres incluent les libérés sur parole sous surveillance au 1 janvier ou ceux qui ont bénéficié d'une mesure de libération conditionnelle dans le courant de l'année. Parmi ces détenus en libération conditionnelle, près de 16 % sont retournés en prison en 2007.[37] Un autre rapport avance que, sur les 300.000

---

34 Albert Mangale, 'Recidivism and the SAPS Criminal Record Centre', in : *Report on the Open Society Foundation for South Africa (OSF-SA) conference on recidivism and reoffending in South Africa*, 29 et 30 novembre 2010, p. 10-11.

35 Somphop Rujjanavet, 'Improving the Reintegration of Offenders into the Community: the Current Situation of Thai Corrections', 135th International Senior Seminar Participants' Papers, UNAFEI, *Resource Material Series* No. 74 (2008), p. 144 (sur : www.unafei.or.jp/english/pdf/RS_No74/No74_15PA_Rujjanavet.pdf) (dernière visite : 1 janvier 2014).

36 Tiré de Pimpan Silpasuwan *et.al.*, 'Violence Recidivism among Thai Juvenile Delinquents', 2 *Asia Journal of Public Health* 1 (2011), p. 13, 14. Cf. UNICEF, *Toolkit on Diversion and Alternatives to Detention 2009. Compilation of evidence in relation to recidivism* (sur : www.unicef.org/tdad/evidencecostbenefit(2).doc) (dernière visite : 1 janvier 2014).

37 Thomas P. Bonczar & Lauren E. Glaze, *Probation And Parole In The United States, 2007. Statistical Tables*, Bureau of Justice Statistics, 11 décembre 2008, NCJ 224707, p. 7. Voir

prisonniers libérés dans 15 États en 1994, 67,5 % ont fait l'objet d'une nouvelle arrestation dans les trois ans. Une étude réalisée sur les prisonniers libérés en 1983 avance quant à elle l'estimation de 62,5 %. D'aucuns estiment que sur les 272.111 personnes libérées des prisons de 15 États en 1994, 67,5 % ont de nouveau été arrêtés pour un acte délictueux ou un délit dans les trois années. 46,9 % d'entre eux ont récidivé et 25,4 % ont été condamnés à une nouvelle peine de prison pour un autre délit. Avant leur précédente incarcération, ces délinquants avant cumulé 4,1 millions de motifs d'arrestation et 744.000 motifs dans les trois années qui ont suivi leur libération. Les prisonniers libérés ayant le taux de plus élevé de nouvelle arrestation sont les voleurs de banques (70,2 %), les cambrioleurs (74,0 %), les voleurs à la tire (74,6 %), les voleurs de véhicules motorisés (78,8 %), les receleurs (77,4 %), et ceux qui se trouvaient en prison pour possession, utilisation ou vente d'armes illégales (70,2 %). Dans les trois ans qui ont suivi leur libération 2,5 % des violeurs ont été arrêtés pour un nouveau fait de viol et 1,2 % des détenus pour homicide ont été arrêtés pour un nouvel homicide.[38]

Remarques en guise de conclusion

Si les différentes définitions sur lesquelles se fondent les statistiques présentées ci-dessus (qui couvrent vingt juridictions) rendent toute comparaison pratiquement impossible, elles n'en démontrent pas moins que la récidive constitue un défi de taille dans tous les pays passés en revue. Les rapports criminologiques et la littérature sur laquelle ces statistiques s'appuient montrent que le taux de récidive est plus élevé (et souvent beaucoup plus élevé) chez les délinquants libérés de prison que lorsque les poursuites pénales ont été abandonnées ou lorsque d'autres sanctions ont été appliquées, par exemple des amendes, des travaux d'intérêt général ou la surveillance électronique. Bien entendu, ces observations sont générales. La mesure dans laquelle l'emprisonnement influence positivement ou négativement le taux de récidive dépend aussi de la personne ainsi que des circonstances réelles de l'emprisonnement et du régime carcéral, par exemple s'il est plutôt axé sur la punition ou la réhabilitation et la mesure dans laquelle il est adapté à la personnalité et aux circonstances sociales individuelles du délinquant.[39] Les différences qui existent dans les résultats de la lutte contre la récidive par l'emprisonnement et par d'autres sanctions pourraient en outre être dues au fait

également Pew Center on the States, *State of Recidivism: The Revolving Door of America's Prisons*, Washington, DC: The Pew Charitable Trusts, avril 2011.

38 Tiré de Patrick A. Langan & David J. Levin, *Recidivism of Prisoners Released in 1994*, Bureau of Justice Statistics, Special Report, juin 2002, NCJ 193427, p. 1.

39 Voir Francis T. Cullen, Cheryl Lero Jonson & Daniel S. Nagin, 'Prisons Do Not Reduce Recidivism: The High Cost of Ignoring Science', 91 *The Prison Journal* Supplement to 3 (2011), p. 48S-65S.

que les délinquants qui présentent le risque de récidive le plus élevé peuvent aussi être ceux qui sont le plus souvent condamnés à une peine de prison. Toutefois, certaines études indiquent que le risque de récidive des mêmes délinquants est considérablement plus élevé lorsqu'ils se voient infliger une peine d'emprisonnement plutôt qu'une sanction alternative.[40]

3. RÉHABILITATION : OBLIGATION ET VALEURS

Comme indiqué précédemment, le principe de la réhabilitation consiste à réintégrer les délinquants dans une vie utile (*inter alia*, par l'éducation, l'orientation professionnelle, la thérapie, des programmes de travail et la promotion de la responsabilité personnelle) dans le but de leur donner les capacités de contribuer à leur développement personnel et de prendre part à la société. Pour atteindre cet objectif, l'État doit adopter des dispositions légales et des politiques opérationnelles qui créent des opportunités de réhabilitation. Dans la mesure où la réhabilitation peut contribuer à la lutte contre le crime et la récidive et dans la mesure où la fonction centrale de l'État consiste à garantir la sécurité de ses citoyens, cette fonction présuppose – à tout le moins à un niveau abstrait – que les États doivent avoir recours à des politiques et mesures de réhabilitation au moins pour autant qu'au final, elles aient une incidence positive sur la réduction de la récidive. Il est par ailleurs impératif que tout État qui considère la dignité humaine comme une valeur fondamentale de la communauté qu'il représente et qui se considère comme un État de droit, c'est-à-dire un « Rechtsstaat », reconnaisse la nécessité de mener une politique de réhabilitation.[41] Les États sont en outre soumis en la matière à des obligations légales et plus tangibles. L'article 10 (3) du Pacte international relatif aux droits civils et politiques 1966 (PIDCP)[42] entérine la nécessité pour l'État de se montrer actif en la matière. Cette disposition stipule que : « *Le régime pénitentiaire comporte un traitement des condamnés dont le but essentiel est leur amendement et leur reclassement social. Les jeunes délinquants sont séparés des adultes et soumis à un régime approprié à leur âge et à leur statut légal.* »[43] En effet, si le Pacte international est une convention des *droits* de l'homme, la disposition citée

40 Voir par exemple, Rafael Di Tella & Ernesto Schargrodsky, 'Criminal Recidivism after Prison and Electronic Monitoring', 121 *Journal of Political Economy* 1 (2013), p. 28-53.

41 Cf. German Constitutional Court, *BVerfGE* 45, 187 (Lebenslange Freiheitsstrafe), nr. 176: « *Das Gericht hat mehrfach betont, daß die Forderung nach Resozialisierung verfassungsrechtlich dem Selbstverständnis einer Gemeinschaft entspreche, die die Menschenwürde in den Mittelpunkt stelle und dem Sozialstaatsprinzip verpflichtet sei.* »

42 999 UNTS 171.

43 La réinsertion est également présentée comme un objectif important, par exemple, dans l'ensemble des règles minima des Nations Unies pour le traitement des détenus ; voir paragraphes 24, 61-67, 76, 80 et 95. Voir également la Règle 6 des Règles pénitentiaires européennes 2006 : « *Chaque détention est gérée de manière à faciliter la réintégration dans la*

ici constitue plus une obligation générale qui incombe aux États qu'un droit accordé aux individus. D'autres obligations similaires découlent de l'Observation générale 21 du Conseil des droits de l'homme sur l'article 10 PIDCP[44], qui stipule qu'aucun système pénitentiaire ne doit être exclusivement réparateur ; il doit essentiellement viser la réforme et la réhabilitation sociale du prisonnier.[45] Il fait en outre référence à des dispositions législatives et administratives, ainsi qu'à des mesures pratiques visant à assurer la rééducation des condamnés, à des mesures visant à fournir un enseignement, une éducation et une rééducation, une orientation professionnelle et une formation, ainsi que des programmes de travail pour les prisonniers au sein de l'établissement pénitentiaire et en dehors de celui-ci.[46] Ces obligations sont applicables à tous les condamnés et par conséquent également aux délinquants à haut risque.

Partant du droit international, du droit européen, du droit et de la pratique des États contractants de la Convention européenne des droits de l'homme et même de la jurisprudence de plusieurs autres juridictions, la Cour européenne des droits de l'homme (CEDH) reconnaît, elle aussi, le principe selon lequel tous les prisonniers – donc également ceux qui purgent une peine d'emprisonnement à perpétuité ou les délinquants à haut risque – doivent avoir la possibilité de se réhabiliter et une perspective de libération au terme de cette réhabilitation.[47] La Cour européenne estime qu'il est évident qu'un prisonnier ne peut être détenu que si cette détention se fonde sur des motifs pénologiques légitimes. La réhabilitation ne crée pas seulement l'un de ces motifs, la Cour suit également la position de la Cour constitutionnelle allemande selon laquelle les autorités carcérales ont « le devoir d'œuvrer à la réhabilitation des condamnés à perpétuité ».[48] La Cour européenne présente, elle aussi, principalement la réhabilitation comme une obligation à laquelle les États doivent se conformer plutôt que comme un droit.

Évidemment, les instruments légaux en matière de droits de l'homme mentionnés ci-avant associent principalement l'obligation de réhabilitation à sa valeur pour le délinquant et le prisonnier individuel. Toutefois, il est utile de ne pas seulement mettre l'accent sur l'obligation de l'État ou la valeur de la réhabilitation pour le délinquant, mais de se pencher aussi sur la manière dont elle sert d'autres objectifs et peut de ce fait constituer pour l'État un instrument apprécié en la matière. Comme le montrent les chapitres qui composent la partie II du présent volume, la réhabilitation est appréciable à divers égards.

---

société libre des personnes privées de liberté. » ; tout cet instrument transpire l'importance de la réinsertion ; voir plus explicitement aussi les Règles 72(3), 83(b), 102 et 107.

44 *UN Doc.* HRI/GEN/1/Rev.1 at 33 (1994).

45 Para. 10.

46 Para. 11.

47 CEDH, jugement de la Grande Chambre du 9 juillet 2013, N° 66069/09, 130/10 et 3896/10, par. 110-122 et 73 (*Vinter/Royaume-Uni*).

48 Voir par. 113 : « *Des considérations similaires doivent s'appliquer dans le cadre du système de la Convention, dont l'essence même, la Cour l'a souvent dit, est le respect de la dignité humaine* ».

En guise d'introduction plus poussée du sujet de la réhabilitation et à la partie II, le chapitre rédigé par Pradel (II.1) souligne le fait que d'aucun émettent de sérieux doutes concernant la valeur de la réhabilitation (*i.e.* Robert Martinson's «Nothing Works», essai datant de 1974). Il traite ensuite de deux questions: pourquoi réhabiliter et comment. Pradel conclut que la théorie de la réhabilitation est à la fois diffuse et mal délimitée, bien qu'il existe des évolutions qui donnent à espérer et qu'il faut poursuivre la recherche sur le sujet.

Dans leur chapitre, Jendly & Delgrande (II.2) abordent la valeur de la réhabilitation suivant une approche criminologique. Après un bref exposé de l'historique de la réhabilitation et des fonctions des condamnations, ils évoquent diverses stratégies telles que le mouvement «Qu'est-ce qui fonctionne», le modèle «Fondé sur le risque, les besoins et la réceptivité», l'intervention dite «Short, sharp, shock» (bref passage en prison), les politiques de la «Nouvelle gestion publique», le «Modèle des bonnes vies», et les «Théories de la distance». Les auteurs se fondent sur plusieurs études pour critiquer les politiques de justice pénale qui mettent par trop l'accent sur les indicateurs de récidive et ignorent les processus sociaux qui motivent les établissements pénitentiaires et la trajectoire de l'auteur. Ils affirment que le «Modèle des bonnes vies», à l'instar des «Théories de la distance» semblent être des voies fructueuses. Dans cette perspective, l'important n'est pas uniquement d'identifier les composants ou les motivations de la cessation de l'activité criminelle, mais plutôt de percevoir la façon dont ces éléments interagissent au fil du temps et en quoi ils sont susceptibles de mener à un comportement d'abandon durable du comportement délictueux.

Le chapitre rédigé par Dalton (II.3) explore la valeur de la réhabilitation dans le chef des prisonniers. Il accorde une attention particulière aux catégories spéciales de prisonniers et d'ex-prisonniers: les membres de la communauté du voyage, les personnes détenues dans des hôpitaux psychiatriques et les prisonniers politiques. Une question importante posée dans ce chapitre est comment convaincre les prisonniers – et plus particulièrement ceux qui sont détenues dans des environnements carcéraux surpeuplés ou inhumains – qu'il est important pour eux de passer par la réhabilitation et de respecter les droits de leurs concitoyens. Son exposé implique que même si la réhabilitation n'a pas permis d'empêcher la récidive, elle n'en est pas moins un instrument crucial de l'amélioration et de l'humanisation des conditions de détention dans de nombreux pays, mais aussi pour prévenir les régimes carcéraux contraires à la dignité humaine ou pour appliquer l'interdiction des mauvais traitements.

Le chapitre rédigé par Bouzón de Terzano (II.4) examine la valeur de la réhabilitation du point de vue de la famille du prisonnier. Elle affirme que la meilleure stratégie de réhabilitation des prisonniers et de prévention de la criminalité consiste à protéger et à renforcer la famille. En effet, il est indéniable que la famille du prisonnier est à même de l'aider dans son trajet de réhabilitation. Cette démarche va également dans l'intérêt de la famille elle-même, non seulement parce que le comportement délinquant vise souvent les membres de la famille de leur auteur, alors que l'emprisonnement de la personne qui génère les revenus de la famille provoque souvent une crise mentale et économique au sein du groupe familial, mais aussi parce que le délinquant montre le mauvais exemple, ce qui pourrait être source de criminalité chez ses enfants ou les autres membres de sa famille. BOUZÓN DE TERZANO estime que l'État est dans l'obligation de soutenir la famille en la matière, par voie législative, par son intervention directe et par l'octroi de subventions.

La famille, mais aussi la société dans son ensemble, ont un rôle à jouer dans la prévention de la criminalité et de la récidive. Dans son chapitre, CILLIERS (II.5) affirme que l'on ne peut s'attaquer efficacement à la criminalité et aux problèmes qui en découlent que si la société est activement impliquée dans le processus et qu'elle y apporte sa coopération. Il explique comment la société peut être impliquée (par un « examen des besoins ») et évoque plusieurs modèles d'implications la société. CILLIERS conclut que pour réaliser ces possibilités, il sera très important que l'environnement correctionnel développe la politique et le cadre pratique nécessaires à la participation de la communauté.

Bien entendu, d'autres motifs font que la société est concernée par la réhabilitation, l'intérêt du contribuable par exemple. C'est pourquoi dans son chapitre, AYLWARD (II.6) évoque les défis auxquels les décideurs politiques sont généralement confrontés lorsqu'ils tentent de convaincre les contribuables des avantages relatifs de la réhabilitation des prisonniers. Il se penche en outre sur la valeur de la réhabilitation pour le contribuable et met en avant plusieurs études scientifiquement fondées ayant cherché à déterminer l'avantage financier de la réhabilitation des prisonniers pour le contribuable. Certaines preuves montrent que les programmes pour délinquants sont ou peuvent être rentables.

La réhabilitation pourrait par ailleurs être bénéfique pour le personnel et l'administration pénitentiaires en ce sens qu'elle pourrait contribuer à développer un système plus sûr pour eux et plus gratifiant sur le plan professionnel. La valeur de la réhabilitation pour l'administration pénitentiaire peut cependant aussi être abordée suivant un angle différent, comme le fait DE MIRANDA PEREIRA dans son chapitre (II.7). Il affirme qu'un système pénitentiaire aura rempli son rôle s'il crée un environnement carcéral sécurisé, s'il procède à une sélection efficace et bien pensée des détenus en groupes gérables, s'il offre une réelle possibilité d'amélioration personnelle à tous les délinquants, s'il assure une formation de haut niveau à son personnel et fait en sorte que celui-ci soit soudé et motivé et s'il vise la meilleure coopération possible avec la communauté. Hélas, l'administration carcérale tend à définir la valeur de la réhabilitation par sa capacité à remplir ces premiers objectifs plutôt que ces derniers.

Enfin, OLIVEIRA (II.8) aborde la valeur de la réhabilitation suivant la perspective de l'intérêt des victimes. Il explique que la réhabilitation des délinquants est souhaitable pour les victimes, pour plusieurs raisons. À cet égard, la capacité de la réhabilitation à contribuer à la résolution des conflits et à la justice réparatrice revêt une importance cruciale. En corollaire de quoi Oliveira affirme que la victime peut jouer un rôle déterminant dans la réinsertion sociale des prisonniers.

4. MESURES VISANT À TRAITER LES DÉLINQUANTS À HAUT RISQUE PENDANT LEUR CONDAMNATION ET AU TERME DE CELLE-CI

Si la réhabilitation qui donne la possibilité aux délinquants de devenir des membres respectueux des lois et productifs pour la communauté relève des responsabilités clés de l'État, les statistiques des taux de récidive présentées ci-dessus dans plusieurs juridictions sélectionnées démontrent que les stratégies et programmes actuels échouent souvent à protéger la communauté contre de nouvelles infractions. Comme indiqué précédemment, cet échec est souvent la conséquence de ce que les réponses pénales aux délinquants (et en particulier les conditions dans lesquelles ils sont confinés lorsqu'ils sont envoyés en prison) ne sont pas de nature à susciter la réhabilitation. Il est toutefois aussi souvent dû au fait que pour bon nombre de délinquants, la réhabilitation est un processus difficile et que bien souvent, ils ne quittent la voie de la délinquance qu'au fil du temps.

C'est sans surprise que l'inefficacité perçue du système pénal à réduire les taux de récidive a donné lieu, ces trois dernières décennies, à des appels sans cesse plus pressants en faveur de l'adoption de mesures visant non pas à réinsérer les délinquants au sein de la communauté mais à les éloigner de celle-ci ou à restreindre le rôle qu'ils peuvent y jouer. Cette tendance est inspirée par la préoccupation croissante de la prédiction du risque de récidive à des fins dissuasives. Toutefois, comme le souligne Pradel (III.9), elle est également motivée par la nécessité que les mesures de réhabilitation soient correctement ciblées.

Il existe actuellement de nombreuses mesures préventives, à tous les stades du système de justice pénale. Comme le démontrent les chapitres rédigés par Tak (III.4) et Shute (III.6), ceux qui commentent ces mesures ont tendance à se limiter, pour la protection du public par voie de condamnation par les tribunaux, à l'examen de la détention à long terme ou aux délinquants à haut risque. Le chapitre de Feest (III.12) qui conclut l'ouvrage évoque la contribution de Viano au symposium pour noter le recours croissant à la supervision communautaire avec surveillance électronique au terme d'une peine d'emprisonnement, plus particulièrement pour les délinquants sexuels. Les chapitres de Young (III.1) et Lambropoulou (III.7) attirent quant à eux l'attention sur le fait que ces mesures sont de loin plus diffuses. La prédiction du risque sous-tend certains aspects des prises de décisions policières ; il n'est pas rare qu'elle mette en avant un objectif sous-jacent des alternatives communautaires aux sanctions traditionnelles ; elle forme la base des décisions pré-sententielles de libération sous caution ou de détention provisoire ; et elle entre généralement en compte dans la décision de libération anticipée d'un prisonnier.

Les mesures préventives de ce type sont toutefois toutes appliquées dans le cadre d'un système de justice pénale dont les objectifs premiers sont la poursuite, la condamnation et la punition des délinquants. La tension est inévitable entre les limites imposées par la nécessité d'appliquer une sanction équitable dans ce système et l'intervention à plus long terme requise par les mesures préventives de limitation du risque ou, comme indiqué dans le chapitre de Vallotton (III.3), l'impossibilité apparente de réconcilier les deux objectifs conflictuels que sont l'application d'une sanction rétributive pour les faits passés et, dans le même temps, la protection de l'avenir. C'est la raison pour laquelle d'aucuns se sont penchés sur les modes de protection par des interventions en dehors du contexte de la procédure pénale ou au terme de celle-ci. Tak (III.4) et Shute (III.6) décrivent tous deux des régimes en vigueur dans plusieurs juridictions qui prévoient une détention civile indéfinie au terme d'une peine de prison.

Casorla (III.8) identifie, de manière assez similaire, trois étapes cruciales de l'évaluation du risque de récidive : l'étape de fixation de la peine ; l'étape de l'incarcération et l'étape ultérieure à la fin de la sanction. Pour chacune de ces étapes, il définit les mesures applicables en France. Plusieurs d'entre elles sont également abordées par Pradel (III.9).

Toutefois, comme le signale Casorla (III.8), ces mesures préventives présentent toutes des défis et des problèmes. Dans un premier temps, Viano (III.5) démontre par des graphiques, les effets délétères d'une politique qui donne lieu au recours sans discernement à des peines d'emprisonnement à perpétuité ou autres peines d'incarcération à long terme dans un but de protection du public. Il nous rappelle que l'application de mesures incapacitantes sélectives par des pratiques punitives générales a un effet limitatif sur leur efficacité et présentent un faible rapport coût-bénéfice, tout particulièrement lorsqu'elle est largement appliquée comme c'est le cas aux États-Unis.

Deuxièmement, la sévérité d'une peine de prison dépend à la fois de sa durée, mais aussi de la manière dont elle est exécutée. Della Casa (III.10) évoque plusieurs modes d'incarcération des délinquants à haut risque en Italie ainsi que la possibilité pour les prisonniers d'intenter un recours contre leur placement dans un régime carcéral spécifique. Il souligne d'importants manquements dans la supervision des tribunaux en la matière.

Troisièmement, plusieurs chapitres (*e.g.* par Butler (III.2) et Jendly & Delgrande (II.2)) attirent l'attention sur les difficultés de développer des instruments d'évaluation des risques solides, notamment lorsque le taux de base est faible (comme c'est le cas pour les délinquants sexuels). En effet, l'on pourrait aller jusqu'à suggérer que les instruments de prédiction des risques tiennent de la divination et Tak (III.4) suggère que l'on peut s'interroger sur le degré de protection de la communauté qu'offre le recours au confinement préventif. La question ainsi soulevée est de savoir si et dans quelle mesure la société peut légitimement imposer des mesures coercitives si les instruments de prédiction des personnes présentant un risque de commettre de nouvelles infractions graves ne sont pas solides. Feest (III.12) conclut que ces mesures ne devraient être autorisées que moyennant le respect de conditions strictes. Young (III.1) partage cet avis, mais il note cependant que les mesures de prédiction des risques ont été améliorées au cours des 20 dernières années. Il affirme en outre que le problème ne réside pas tant dans l'exactitude des prédictions (c'est-à-dire si une personne agirait réellement conformément à ce qui a été prédit), puisque c'est une donnée intrinsèquement impossible à déterminer. La question qui se pose plutôt est de savoir si la prédiction du risque est juste et équitable, autrement dit, est-ce que l'idée que la personne présente un risque élevé de causer un dommage à autrui est suffisamment sérieuse et fondée pour présupposer que la personne n'est pas inoffensive.

Quatrièmement, la détention permanente de personnes par voie d'« internement de sûreté » (qui existe dans plusieurs juridictions européennes et au-delà) est généralement considérée comme constitutionnelle lorsqu'elle est imposée dans le cadre de la sanction initiale. Comme le soulignent Tak (III.4) et Feest (III.11), cette détention a toujours été considérée comme justifiée pour les délinquants « malades mentaux » ou les « faibles d'esprit ». La détention des délinquants sains d'esprit autrement que dans le contexte de la sanction initiale imposée par le tribunal est considérée par la Cour européenne des droits de l'homme comme une violation de la Convention. En 2011, la Cour constitutionnelle allemande a encore été plus loin en déclarant inconstitutionnelle toute forme de détention préventive.

La réponse de plus en plus fréquente à cette tendance de fond consiste à séparer entièrement la détention préventive du processus appliqué par la justice pénale et à la traiter parallèlement au processus civil. La difficulté réside évidemment en ce qu'il est souvent impossible de distinguer, en tous ses aspects pratiques, les conditions de la détention préventive d'une peine d'emprisonnement à long terme au titre de sanction de l'infraction commise. Qu'elle soit ou non qualifiée de « civile » importe peu, la détention préventive apparaît comme une sanction disproportionnée. Le chapitre de Butler (III.2) attire dès lors l'attention sur les dangers du recours à la sémantique pour justifier une détention par ailleurs injuste et sur l'importance que revêt l'application des mêmes valeurs morales à la justice prédictive qu'à la justice rétributive.

Si ces questions et problèmes sont moins aigus lorsque les mesures préventives n'impliquent pas de détention mais se limitent à des restrictions ou à une surveillance au sein de la communauté, ils n'en sont pas moins applicables de la même façon. YOUNG (III.1) comme BUTLER (III.2) avancent de ce fait l'argument qu'il existe un besoin pressant de théorie cohérente de la justice préventive basée sur un groupe de principes limitatifs. Dans leurs chapitres respectifs, ils suggèrent ce que certains de ces principes devraient être.

5. CONCLUSIONS

Si la réhabilitation n'est sans doute pas la panacée en matière de prévention de la criminalité et de la récidive, nombreuses sont les études qui ont montré que la prise en compte des objectifs de réhabilitation (lorsque les délinquants sont sanctionnés et que des programmes et régimes de réhabilitation sont mis en place dans le milieu carcéral) peut contribuer à réduire la récidive et à accroître la sécurité publique. Des études montrent en outre que dans certains cas, l'application de mesures efficaces de lutte contre la récidive pourrait générer des économies. Pourtant, même en l'absence de ces effets positifs, la réhabilitation n'en servirait pas moins des intérêts importants : les politiques, mesures et régimes de réhabilitation sont importants pour humaniser et améliorer le système carcéral ; ils peuvent contribuer au bien-être de la famille des délinquants ; ils peuvent également s'avérer bénéfiques pour le personnel carcéral et leurs objectifs de gestion et contribuer à leur satisfaction professionnelle et enfin, ils peuvent apporter un soutien aux victimes par le traitement de leur souffrance. Dans le cadre de ces valeurs actuelles de la réhabilitation et eu égard à la fonction centrale de l'État qui consiste à garantir la sécurité de ses citoyens, sans oublier les obligations légales en vertu de la législation internationale des droits de l'homme, nous affirmons que les États sont dans l'obligation d'appliquer au moins les politiques, mesures et programme de réhabilitation qui ont prouvé leur efficacité et de rechercher de nouveaux moyens de rendre la réhabilitation efficace.

Toutefois, peu importe l'efficacité avec laquelle les États mettent les politiques de réhabilitation en œuvre, nombreux sont les délinquants qui commettront d'autres infractions graves et représenteront un risque permanent pour la communauté. Dans ce contexte, les États se verront parfois contraints d'adopter des mesures protectrices visant à limiter ce risque. Dans cette démarche, ils devront cependant se montrer justes et s'appuyer sur les valeurs fondamentales des droits de l'homme et de la morale. Leur développement par les États au coup par coup et de façon incrémentielle comme un moyen de calmer les préoccupations en matière législative et d'ordre public, pourrait provoquer une érosion considérable de certains principes fondamentaux sur lesquels les démocraties basées sur les droits sont construites.

PART TWO
REHABILITATION OF PRISONERS

2ÈME PARTIE
LA RÉHABILITATION DES DÉTENUS

LA RÉHABILITATION DES DÉTENUS – INTRODUCTION GÉNÉRALE

Jean PRADEL*

1. INTRODUCTION

Notre sujet «La réhabilitation des détenus a-t-elle encore une quelconque valeur?» suggèrera avant tout une définition, appelle une inquiétude et impose des distinctions.

Une définition d'abord

La sanction pénale assure trois fonctions principales (à côté de l'élimination et de la neutralisation):

- Une *fonction réparatrice*: elle compense le préjudice causé à la société. La personne en commettant une infraction a enfreint le «pacte social», cette règle jadis non écrite qui veut que personne ne puisse nuire à ses voisins. Les juristes parlent de rétribution, qui vise à infliger à l'auteur d'une infraction un mal équivalent à celui qu'il a causé. Un délinquant purge sa peine comme le débiteur paye sa dette à son créancier.
- Une *fonction intimidatrice* ensuite, qui se dédouble elle-même. La peine vise d'abord à l'intimidation collective, la menace d'une peine devant dissuader les individus de passer à l'acte. La peine vise aussi à l'intimidation individuelle en ce qu'elle tente d'éviter la récidive;
- Une *fonction de réadaptation* enfin, ou réhabilitation. Je n'insisterais pas sur les termes: les Anglo-Saxons parlent de réhabilitation alors qu'en Europe continentale, on parle plutôt de réintégration, réinsertion, resocialisation. Il s'agit toujours d'un processus psycho-médico-social destiné à accroître les chances du détenu de respecter à l'avenir la liberté d'autrui. Le but est évidemment la réduction de la récidive.

---

* J. Pradel (1933) est Professeur émérite de l'Université de Poitiers, France. Après ses études à la Faculté de droit de Poitiers, il a été magistrat pendant dix ans. Il est notamment l'auteur d'un Droit pénal comparé (2008) et le co-auteur d'un Droit pénal européen (2009). Il est membre titulaire de l'Académie internationale de droit comparé.

Cette troisième fonction est la plus récente, encore qu'elle ait eu des précurseurs dès le 19ème siècle: ainsi en Irlande, en 1854, Sir Walter Crofton entendait déjà « réintégrer le prisonnier dans la société ».

Une inquiétude

C'est ici que surgit une inquiétude. Après une période euphorique inspirée par l'Ecole de la défense sociale nouvelle, la réhabilitation a suggéré le doute et notre intitulé de colloque avec son point d'interrogation – inconcevable il y a quelques décennies – le montre bien (encore qu'il faille comparer l'intitulé français à l'intitulé anglais).

En effet, à partir des années 1970, certaines personnes se mettent à douter de la réhabilitation. On connaît le cri de Robert Martison en 1974 « *Nothing Works* »: les programmes de réhabilitation en prison ne préviennent pas la récidive à de rares exceptions près. Ce courant va générer, surtout aux Etats-Unis, toute une législation avec par exemple les « *Mandatory Minimum Sentences* », les sentences minimales obligatoires, et le fameux « *Three strikes and you're out* ».

Pourtant, loi du balancier, l'espoir renaît, mais une approche plus scientifique se manifeste à partir des années 1990: la doctrine canadienne adopte une perspective psycho-criminologique; celle des Etats-Unis adopte une vision plus socio-criminologique en s'attachant au contexte social, économique, culturel, communautaire. Bref au « *nothing works* » succède le « *what works* » (ce qui « *marche* »). Mais ici s'opposent le camp des spécialistes et celui de l'homme de la rue, de l'opinion, peu sensible à la réhabilitation.

Distinctions

On perçoit déjà que la question est d'une robuste complexité et que des distinctions doivent être faites. Se pose en effet d'abord une question de principe: la réhabilitation est-elle légitime et si elle l'est, c'est pour quelles raisons. Se pose ensuite – si l'on répond positivement à la première question – une seconde série de difficultés: de quelles façons peut-on concevoir cette réhabilitation? En somme, il convient de répondre à deux questions: la réhabilitation pourquoi? La réhabilitation comment?

2. LA RÉHABILITATION POURQUOI ?

Pourquoi vouloir « transformer » les délinquants? La question est d'autant plus grave que l'on s'adresse à des individus ayant commis un fait grave par hypothèse puisqu'ils ont été condamnés à une peine privative de liberté. Dès lors deux attitudes se conçoivent:

- Se contenter de faire purger leur peine à ces délinquants, en les neutralisant quelques mois ou années dans une prison;
- Aller au-delà et profiter de l'incarcération pour les resocialiser.

Cette deuxième thèse est la seule valable pour diverses raisons: une raison philosophico-juridique et des raisons pratiques.

2.1. UNE RAISON PHILOSOPHICO-JURIDIQUE

Philosophiquement, la société ayant le droit de punir pour assurer sa sauvegarde (sorte de légitime défense) a corrélativement le devoir d'offrir au délinquant les moyens de se réinsérer. Certes, ce raisonnement a pu être critiqué ici et là et l'on peut se demander si l'Etat peut prétendre changer la personnalité de certains individus, en l'espèce les délinquants. Mais il est cohérent si l'on prend soin d'y apporter certaines précisions.

D'abord la société ne peut qu'offrir des programmes sans les imposer à cause de la liberté de choisir.

Ensuite, on ne peut pas parler au sens strict d'un «droit» du condamné à la resocialisation car un droit appelle une action en justice et l'on n'imagine pas que le condamné puisse actionner l'Etat pour le faire condamner au motif qu'aucun programme sérieux ne lui aurait été offert ou qu'il a échoué.

Enfin, la pression sur la personnalité est minimale: à une demande par un condamné de procéder à une métamorphose de ses conceptions, on lui demande plus manifestement d'adopter des standards minimum de vie sociale.

Juridiquement, nombreux sont les textes qui consacrent l'idéal de la réhabilitation. Certains de ces textes sont internes, nationaux. Ainsi la loi finlandaise sur les prisons rappelle que «le but de la peine privative de liberté est de condamner le détenu à mener une vis sans crime». Il existe aussi des proclamations internationales: règles minimales peu le traitement des détenus; pacte international relatif aux droits civils et politiques; règles pénitentiaires européennes de 2006. Ne méconnaissons pas non plus l'existence de raisons pratiques.

2.2. DES RAISONS PRATIQUES

Ces raisons intéressent les finances publiques, la victime et la détention.

Finances publiques

S'agissant des finances publiques, on a prétendu qu'il ne fallait pas organiser des programmes de réhabilitation: car, ils sont onéreux; car, très souvent ils ne servent à rien pour réduire la récidive; car il est injuste que des prisonniers bénéficient de tels programmes onéreux.

C'est oublier que la prison ne doit pas servir simplement de lieu de placement de délinquants dans une fonction rétributive. Il est certes difficile de mesurer le bénéfice économique de la réhabilitation. Beaucoup d'études ont été faites. Il y a tout de même un léger préjudice en faveur de la réhabilitation car certains programmes font baisser la récidive.

La victime

Quant à la victime, on s'est demandé quels liens elle peut avoir avec la réhabilitation. Plus précisément, est-ce que la réhabilitation des prisonniers est une bonne chose pour la victime?

On peut rappeler un rapport d'avril 2010 réalisé au sein de l'Institut latino-américain pour la prévention du crime et le traitement des délinquants (rapport intitulé « Prisons et justice pénale en Amérique latine et Caraïbes). De ce document, il résulte que la victime a avantage à la réhabilitation du délinquant pour plusieurs raisons, notamment car le prisonnier réhabilité pourra plus facilement effectuer une réparation minimale de la victime ou au moins s'engager à la rembourser et aussi car les relations entre le prisonnier et la victime seront meilleures.

D'ailleurs, l'ONU a émis quatre instruments pour permettre la participation de la victime à la réhabilitation du délinquant: les règles minimales des Nations-Unies pour la justice des mineurs (Bejing, 1985); les principes fondamentaux de justice relatifs aux victimes de 1990; les règles minimales des Nations-Unies pour les mesures non privatives de liberté (Tokyo, 1990); les principes fondamentaux des Nations-Unies sur l'utilité des programmes de justice réparatrice en matière pénale, 2002.

La victime doit d'ailleurs être entendue au sens large, en incluant la famille (qui évidemment souffre de l'incarcération de l'un des siens). Or cette famille bénéficie de la réhabilitation de son membre qui se trouve être détenu.

Le détenu

C'est enfin le détenu lui-même qui profite de la réhabilitation. La plupart des détenus acceptent les programmes de réhabilitation car ils sont conscients de la précarité de leur situation.

Parmi toutes les théories proposées ou appliquées, il en est une qui doit ici retenir l'attention, c'est l'idée de bien être (*Good Lives Model*): on peut parler de meilleure vie. La prise en compte des ressources individuelles dans la direction du bien être individuel provoque un certain équilibre du détenu et contribuera à réduire le risque de récidive.

En somme, la réhabilitation se fonde pratiquement sur de bonnes raisons : possiblement une réduction des dépenses publiques, très probablement un gain pour la victime et plus probablement encore un avantage pour le détenu lui-même.

Mais alors si la réhabilitation se justifie certainement, de quelle façon peut-on l'organiser ? C'est la question de la réhabilitation comment ?

3. LA RÉHABILITATION COMMENT ?

C'est bien là que les plus graves difficultés apparaissent. Pourquoi ? Pour diverses raisons tenant à la nature de l'infraction, à la durée de la peine, à la psychologie du délinquant et à sa proximité éventuelle avec la victime, aux institutions, aux programmes proposés et même à la culture du pays, sans oublier les droits fondamentaux. Il apparaît alors que si certains principes se dégagent en faveur de la réhabilitation, celle-ci comporte des limites.

3.1. LES PRINCIPES

Avant tout, il faut dire que la réhabilitation n'est jamais automatique, la preuve en étant donnée par le taux de récidive. Cela rappelé, le traitement obéit à deux tendances, même si l'on retrouve toujours des constantes.

La variable

La variable consiste dans le fait d'une double analyse. On peut envisager le traitement dans une perspective psycho-criminologique, avec la recherche des éléments clés de programmes de réhabilitation pour faire baisser la récidive. Par exemple, l'on ciblera les personnes présentant les risques les plus forts (Canada). On peut aussi (Etats-Unis) avoir une vision socio-criminologique en mettant au premier plan le contexte social, économique, culturel, communautaire.

Les constantes

Malgré tout, les programmes de réhabilitation présentent d'importantes constantes. S'agissant des règles générales, tout programme de réhabilitation obéit aux directives suivantes :

- Tenir compte des particularités de la culpabilité ;
- Capacité du condamné dans sa socialisation ;
- Droit du condamné à un traitement individuel ;

- Droit de refuser le traitement proposé ;
- Combinaison des responsabilités de l'individu, de la communauté et de l'Etat ;
- Droit de la victime à la réparation.

Il en résulte que les détenus sont invités à participer activement à l'exécution de leur peine, pour pouvoir s'autoréguler dans une certaine mesure.

Peut-être veut-on croire qu'avec ces principes, le détenu est un peu comme un linge sale qui ressort blanc après passage dans cette machine à laver qu'est la prison. Certes non, car ces principes doivent être prolongés par des directives plus pratiques. Ces directives pratiques sont au nombre de trois :

- Une nourriture et des soins convenables et corrélativement une absence de mauvais traitements, la torture n'ayant pas totalement disparue (voir le CPI) ;
- Des programmes d'activités portant sur l'éducation, sur l'aptitude à la vie sociale, sur la morale et la religion, sur le travail en détention, sur l'enseignement professionnel, sur le sport ;
- Des régimes ouverts et des programmes impliquant une interaction avec la communauté et avant tout avec la famille qui peut contribuer à la resocialisation. On peut citer à cet égard l'expérience néo-zélandaise où le juge face à un jeune délinquant demande à la famille conseil sur la meilleure mesure à prendre. Encore faut-il qu'il y ait une famille.

Pour maintenir le contact avec la famille ou plus généralement avec la communauté, on peut envisager d'aller plus loin encore en imaginant soit l'appel au bracelet électronique du condamné qui reste chez lui, soit l'appel à une obligation de résidence en un lieu autre que la maison de la famille. Ces procédés ne sont hélas pas la panacée.

Toutes ces dispositions pratiques doivent évidemment se concilier avec l'impératif de sécurité. Ce n'est pourtant pas une raison pour écarter ces directives car tout doit être centré sur l'idée que le condamné est une personne qui un jour quittera la prison.

Toutes ces directives doivent être complétées par des locaux convenables, par l'absence de surencombrement des prisons et par un personnel motivé, sans oublier l'existence de structures d'accueil à la sortie de prison.

Enfin les directives doivent être complétées par l'attitude à avoir à propos de la victime. C'est ici que se pose le problème de la justice restaurative (médiation) qui est une véritable pacification sociale par voie d'accord entre auteur et victime et, à cet égard, on doit citer le « système Multi-Portes » pratiqué par exemple par l'Institut Vera à New-York.

Il faut cependant se demander si ces principes de réhabilitation peuvent s'appliquer tout le temps. Hélas la réponse est négative car il y a des limites.

3.2. LES LIMITES

Elles sont de deux sortes.

D'abord certains détenus ne veulent pas entendre parler de réhabilitation. On pense aux condamnés politiques qui invoquent un mobile noble, qui se battent pour une cause et qui iront même jusqu'à considérer que c'est la société, notamment les agents du service de justice, qui devraient être réhabilités.

On pense aussi à des personnes si marginales qu'une réhabilitation ne se conçoit pas, tel est le cas des « barons de la drogue » ou des personnes appartenant à des cultures très différentes comme les gens du voyage ou encore des personnes très dangereuses, décidées à vivre en marge de la société.

Voisin est le cas des détenus qui refusent tout programme car ils ne veulent pas sortir de leur état et l'on pense aux condamnés qui *consomment de la drogue*. Il est très difficile de leur imposer un traitement. Certaines législations y parviennent cependant de façon indirecte : en les privant du bénéfice des réductions de peine ou de la libération conditionnelle s'ils rejettent les soins. Mais faut-il envoyer les toxicomanes en prison alors qu'ils peuvent s'en procurer en prison ?

Cette situation n'est pas très éloignée de celle des *délinquants sexuels* pour lesquels un traitement définitif comme la castration physique serait la solution. Mais on se heurte alors à un obstacle énorme, celui de l'intangibilité de la personne, même en cas d'acceptation.

A côté des condamnés qui se refusent à un traitement, il y a ceux qui ne peuvent y consentir. Cette catégorie, étrange à première vue, est faite de condamnés qui ne comprennent pas la portée de leur condamnation.

On nous a dit que, en Afrique du Sud, 25 % seulement des condamnés comprenaient le sens de leur condamnation. Certes le tribunal prononçant la condamnation explique le contenu de celle-ci, ce qui prouve que la réhabilitation commence dès le jour du jugement. Mais si malgré les efforts du juge, le condamné ne comprend pas ce qui lui arrive, sa réhabilitation est hypothétique.

Parmi ces individus qui ne peuvent consentir valablement à un traitement, il faut aussi compter les malades mentaux. Ils sont nombreux dans les prisons, peut-être 30 %. Certes, l'administration peut leur administrer des traitements médicaux. Mais est-ce suffisant ? Et encore doit-on s'assurer d'une sorte de consentement aux soins. Et pourtant le traitement est la condition de réhabilitation.

4. CONCLUSION

Toutes ces questions et encore celles que je n'ai pu aborder montrent que la théorie de la réhabilitation est un puits sans fond. Certes sur le plan des principes, l'accord est unanime : il fait tenter de réhabiliter le condamné. La justice doit être porteuse d'espoir et d'ailleurs les résultats sont parfois au rendez-vous. Mais dans l'application, dès que l'on veut bâtir des programmes de réhabilitation, on est saisi par le doute car la récidive – cet échec de la réhabilitation – existe toujours.

Ce qu'il faut faire, c'est de poursuivre les recherches. Les juristes passent leur temps à tâtonner, à imaginer de nouvelles formules, à multiplier les enquêtes de terrain. Or une vraie réhabilitation se réalisera bien plus facilement par des enquêtes de terrain que par les travaux en chambre des faiseurs de système.

LA VALEUR DE LA RÉHABILITATION D'UN POINT DE VUE CRIMINOLOGIQUE

Manon JENDLY*
Natalia DELGRANDE**

1. INTRODUCTION

La présente contribution s'attache à explorer la question de la « valeur » attribuée à la réhabilitation par la criminologie et ses développements depuis la deuxième moitié du siècle dernier. Dès lors que la criminologie est encore en cours de reconnaissance dans nombre de pays d'inspiration romano-germanique, notre contribution repose essentiellement sur des travaux d'origine anglo-saxonne. Après avoir fixé brièvement certaines notions clés en rapport avec le sujet traité, nous reviendrons sur les faits marquants de l'évolution de la place accordée à la réhabilitation à partir de la fin de la Deuxième Guerre mondiale dans le monde pénitentiaire. L'idéal réhabilitatif a en effet connu son apogée à la fin des années 60 avant d'être assez radicalement remis en question au début des années 70. Pour freiner son déclin, des chercheurs se sont attelés à démontrer la pertinence de certaines actions réhabilitatives, marquant ainsi le début du « mouvement « *What works* » en référence asymétrique au désormais célébrissime « *Nothing works* » de Robert Martinson. Nous illustrerons ce mouvement par les contributions majeures de certains chercheurs canadiens, respectivement américains. Ces contributions ont essentiellement porté sur l'élaboration de méthodologies analytiques spécifiquement dédiées à identifier les « meilleures » pratiques réhabilitatives, et à dégager des principes et modèles de prise en charge de détenus dits « *evidence-based* », en français « fondés sur les données probantes ». Leur engagement dans ce courant n'est toutefois pas sans poser un certain nombre d'enjeux que nous préciserons avant d'identifier quelles peuvent être les voies susceptibles d'y pallier, à tout le moins en partie. Nous porterons

* Dr. M. Jendly est Maître d'enseignement et de recherche à l'Université de Lausanne, l'Ecole des sciences criminelles et l'Institut de criminologie et de droit pénal.

** N. Delgrande est responsable de recherche et chargée de cours à l'Université de Lausanne, l'Ecole des sciences criminelles et l'Institut de criminologie et de droit pénal.

ainsi un intérêt particulier aux nouvelles idées dans le domaine notamment du désistement au crime, perçu comme étant en mesure d'apporter quelques orientations originales et susceptibles de connaître un développement prodigieux en la matière. Nous discuterons enfin de la tendance actuelle à l'importation en les murs des préceptes de la « Nouvelle gestion publique » et des questionnements qui en résultent dans un contexte fortement imprégné d'une logique responsabilisante voire méritocratique, façonnant tant les pratiques des intervenants que le parcours carcéral des détenus.

2. LES FONCTIONS DE LA PEINE ET FINALITÉS ASSIGNÉES À SON EXÉCUTION

Avant d'entrer dans le vif du sujet, il convient de revenir brièvement sur les différentes fonctions de la peine, avant de préciser celles qui sont attribuées à son exécution.[1]

La peine, qu'elle soit ou non privative de liberté, peut être qualifiée de « plurifonctionnelle »[2], bien qu'elle ait pour principal effet d'infliger une souffrance.[3] Les fonctions qui lui sont traditionnellement dévolues sont en effet multiples. Elles consistent tour à tour en la rétribution, la prévention (ou dissuasion), la neutralisation voire l'élimination, la resocialisation (ou la réhabilitation) et la réparation. Ces fonctions coexistent sans jamais que l'une ou l'autre ne s'efface totalement au profit des autres. La prépondérance qui leur est accordée varie en fonction de leur inscription spatio-temporelle.

Comme son nom l'indique, la rétribution s'inscrit dans une perspective *rétributiviste*: elle vise à infliger à l'auteur de l'infraction un mal équivalent à celui qu'il a commis, conformément à une idée de châtiment. La prévention, la neutralisation et la réhabilitation s'inscrivent en revanche dans une perspective *utilitariste*. La prévention est dite générale lorsqu'elle tend à prévenir la commission par d'autres personnes d'infractions semblables à celles déjà commises. Elle est qualifiée de spéciale, lorsqu'elle cherche à prévenir la commission d'une nouvelle infraction par la même personne, le condamné, c'est-à-dire à prévenir sa récidive.[4] La neutralisation vise la « mise hors d'état de

---

1 M. Jendly, *La coexistence des secrets en exécution de peine privative de liberté. Vers un modèle de partage des informations confidentielles en milieu carcéral*, Thèse en droit, Université de Neuchâtel, 2005.

2 H. Dumont, *Pénologie: le droit canadien relatif aux peines et aux sentences*, Montréal: Thémis, 1993.

3 A. Pires, 'La formation de la rationalité pénale moderne au XVIIIe siècle', in: C. Debuyst, F. Digneffe & A. Pires, *Histoire des savoirs sur le crime et la peine: Tome 2, La rationalité pénale et la naissance de la criminologie*, Bruxelles: Larcier, 2008, p. 21-247.

4 M. Killias, *Précis de criminologie*, Berne: Stämpfli, 2001.

nuire» du condamné. Dans sa conception la plus rigoureuse, elle peut être synonyme de prison à vie, d'une mesure [thérapeutique] de durée indéterminée, voire de peine capitale. S'agissant de la réhabilitation enfin, les doctrines d'inspiration continentale lui préfèrent les termes de «resocialisation», de «réintégration» ou de «réinsertion (sociale)». Il n'est pas de véritable consensus dans la littérature quant à l'emploi de ces dernières notions, ni quant à leur contenu. Dans l'absolu, la première formule – la resocialisation – tend à concrétiser les deux dernières. On parle alors de processus de resocialisation visant la réintégration et/ou la réinsertion du condamné («*re-entry*» ou «*resettlement*» au Royaume-Uni), à savoir sa remise en liberté. La notion de réhabilitation s'entend donc généralement d'un processus. Nous éviterons ici d'entrer dans les controverses entourant les contours conceptuels de la cette notion[5] et retiendrons une définition large de la réhabilitation («*rehabilitation*»), comme comprenant l'ensemble des discours, processus et pratiques psycho-médico-sociales destinés à amener le contrevenant à acquérir des attitudes conformes aux normes sociales communément admises.[6] Nous utiliserons cette notion le cas échéant de façon interchangeable avec celle de resocialisation.[7] Il est à noter en outre que cette notion a entrainé dans son sillage celle de désistement («*desistance from crime*») qui renvoie à une idée de cessation des activités criminelles, de retour «sur le droit chemin» («*going straight*»), une approche de plus en plus étayée dans la littérature criminologique.[8]

S'agissant des objectifs fixés à l'exécution de la peine privative de liberté, ils découlent bien entendu en grande partie des fonctions reconnues à la peine en tant que telle. A l'heure actuelle, sous nos latitudes occidentales, deux objectifs principaux semblent lui être assignés, à savoir la réhabilitation et la protection de la collectivité, via la prévention de la récidive et la neutralisation. Aussi, quand il est question de la «valeur» de la réhabilitation en criminologie, force est de

---

5 N. Morris & D. Rothman (eds), *The Oxford History of the Prison*, New York: Oxford University Press, 1995; A.M. Rodrigues, 'Consensualisme et prison', in: *Nouvelles orientations du régime pénitentiaire*, Actes des Journées internationales de la Fondation internationale pénale et pénitentiaire, Lisbonne/Portugal, 21-25 mai 1999, p. 147-171; P. Raynor & G. Robinson, *Rehabilitation, Crime and Justice*, Basingstoke: Palgrave Macmillan, 2005; T. Ward & S. Maruna, *Rehabilitation: Beyond the Risk Paradigm*, Abingdon: Routledge, 2007.

6 F.A. Allen, *The Decline of the Rehabilitative Ideal: Penal Policy and Social Purpose*, New Haven: Yale University Press, 1981; M. Lynch, 'Rehabilitation as Rhetoric. The Ideal of Reformation in Contemporary Parole Discourse and Practices', 2 *Punishment & Society* 1 (2000), p. 40-65.

7 E. De Wree, T. Vander Beken & G. Vermeulen, 'The Transfer of Sentenced Persons in Europe. Much ado about Reintegration', 11 *Punishment and Society* 1 (2009), p. 111-128.

8 J.H. Laub & R.J. Sampson, 'Understanding Desistance from Crime', in: M. Tonry (ed), *Crime and Justice: a Review of Research*, vol. 28, Chicago: University of Chicago Press, 2001, p. 1-69; S. Farrall & A. Calverley, *Understanding Desistance from Crime. Theoretical Directions in Resettlement and Rehabilitation*, London: Open University Press, 2006; D. Healy, *The Dynamics of Desistance. Charting Pathways through Change*, Cullompton: Willan Publishing, 2010.

constater que celle-ci est essentiellement lue à la lumière de la prévention de la récidive, ce sur quoi nous reviendrons ultérieurement. Auparavant toutefois, il paraît essentiel de brosser brièvement l'évolution de la place accordée à la réhabilitation dans le champ pénitentiaire ces dernières décennies.

3. L'ÉVOLUTION DE LA PLACE ACCORDÉE À LA RÉHABILITATION

Sur le vieux comme sur le nouveau continent, l'attention portée à la réhabilitation n'a cessé de croitre tout au long du 20ème siècle.[9] C'est à l'issue de la Deuxième Guerre mondiale et en grande partie à la faveur des revendications de ceux qui ont connu la prison sous l'occupation qu'une réflexion est entamée en Europe notamment sur les conditions de détention et les modalités de prise en charge des personnes incarcérées.[10] Un peu partout sur le continent, de vastes projets de réforme sont entrepris. Des droits subjectifs sont reconnus aux détenus et le pouvoir discrétionnaire de l'administration pénitentiaire se voit partiellement codifié, notamment sous l'impulsion d'instruments supranationaux, tels qu'en attestent les nombreux travaux de la Fondation.[11] Progressivement, l'institution carcérale s'ouvre sur l'extérieur et se «décloisonne».[12] De nouveaux professionnels pénètrent l'enceinte de la prison et participent à la consécration de dispositifs de prise en charge favorisant la resocialisation des personnes incarcérées.

L'objectif de réhabilitation assigné à l'exécution de la peine privative de liberté est également reconnu de l'autre côté de l'Atlantique, en particulier au sein du Service correctionnel du Canada, chargé de l'exécution des peines privatives de liberté de deux ans et plus. Durant plus de deux décennies, sur les deux continents, l'idéal de réhabilitation constitue ainsi une composante forte de la prise en charge des personnes condamnées à une peine privative de liberté. Au tournant des années 70 cependant, cet idéal se voit sérieusement remis en question. Dans le champ criminologique, on attribue – mais certainement avec trop d'emphase – à Robert Martinson d'avoir été son fossoyeur.[13] Au tournant des années 70, son article reçoit un écho pour ainsi dire jamais égalé en la

---

9 M. Jendly, *La coexistence des secrets en exécution de peine privative de liberté. Vers un modèle de partage des informations confidentielles en milieu carcéral*, Thèse en droit, Université de Neuchâtel, 2005.

10 J. Favard, *Des prisons*, Paris: Gallimard, 1987.

11 P.-H. Bolle (sous la dir. de), *Droits fondamentaux et détention pénale*, Actes du septième Colloque international de la Fondation internationale pénale et pénitentiaire, Neuchâtel/ Suisse, 3-7 octobre 1992.

12 P. Combessie, 'Ouverture des prisons, jusqu'à quel point?', in: C. Veil & D. Lhuilier (sous la dir. de), *La prison en changement*, Ramonville Saint-Agne: Erès, 2000, p. 69-99.

13 R. Martinson, 'What Works? Questions and Answers about Prison Reform', 35 *The Public Interest* (1974) (Spring), p. 22-54.

matière, alors même que l'étude fait l'objet de vives critiques, notamment quant à ses biais méthodologiques.[14] Martinson lui-même publie en 1979 un article qui nuance ses conclusions précédentes.[15] Las !, les résultats publiés en 1974 sont relayés massivement par l'appareil médiatique qui rapporte hâtivement que « rien ne marche » en matière d'intervention correctionnelle. Ils sont récupérés également par certaines franges politiques leur servant de prétexte à l'adoption de lois et mesures plus sévères, telles que les sentences minimales obligatoires (« *Mandatory Minimum Sentences* ») adoptées dans plusieurs Etats des Etats-Unis dans les années 80 et 90 ou le « *Three strikes and you're out* » envisagé pour la première fois en Californie en 1994. La formule « *Nothing works* » se voit ainsi progressivement couplée outre-Atlantique à d'autres toutes aussi colorées, tels que « *Tough on crime* », « *Getting tough with criminals* », ou encore « *What you get is what you serve* », « *You do the crime, you do the time* », marquant le retour du « *just deserts* ».[16] Conjuguées à d'autres ressorts sociaux, économiques, politiques et culturels de l'époque, les conclusions de Martinson ont contribué au déclin de l'idéal réhabilitatif et alimenté l'essor punitif subséquent des politiques pénales et pénitentiaires sur les deux continents.[17] La résistance cependant ne tarde pas à s'organiser, tant dans les milieux praticiens qu'académiques. S'agissant de ces derniers en particulier, plusieurs s'attacheront dans les années qui suivent à tenter d'inverser la tendance.

4. DE QUELQUES PRINCIPES, OUTILS ET MODÈLES FONDÉS SUR LES DONNÉES PROBANTES

C'est donc en un contexte pessimiste à l'égard de la réhabilitation et de surenchère répressive que des voix s'élèvent progressivement pour en appeler à son retour. Certaines mettent l'emphase sur les conséquences désastreuses des stratégies punitives qui jalonnent la chaine pénale et dont résultent en bout de course des taux d'incarcération vertigineux, au demeurant sans lien aucun avec

14 T. Palmer, 'Martinson revisited', 12 *Journal of Research in Crime and* Delinquency 2 (1975), p. 133-152; F.T. Cullen & K.E. Gilbert, *Reaffirming Rehabilitation*, Cincinnati: Anderson, 1982.

15 R. Martinson, 'New Findings, New Views: A Note of Caution Regarding Sentencing Reform', 7 *Hofstra Law Review* 2 (1979), p. 243-258.

16 P. Lalande, 'Punir ou réhabiliter les contrevenants ? Du « Nothing Works » au « What Works » (Montée, déclin et retour de l'idéal de réhabilitation)', in: P. Lalande & O. Lamalice, *La sévérité pénale à l'heure du populisme*, Québec: Ministère de la sécurité publique du Québec, 2006, p. 30-77; S. Lewis, 'Rehabilitation: Headline or Footnote in the New Penal Policy?', 52 *Probation Journal* 2 (2005), p. 119-135.

17 T. Mathiesen, *Prison on Trial: a Critical Assessment*, London: Sage Publications, 1990; D. Garland, *The Culture of Control. Crime and Social Order in Contemporary Society*, Oxford: Oxford University Press, 2001; N. Christie, *L'industrie de la punition. Prison et politique pénale en Occident*, Paris: Autrement, 2003.

les niveaux de criminalité constatés. D'autres s'attachent à démontrer les effets particulièrement délétères des incarcérations de masse et sans ou peu d'aménagements de peine possibles sur les populations carcérales et leurs proches, leurs difficultés accrues à recouvrer les mécanismes de vie en liberté et leur plus forte propension alors à récidiver à leur sortie de prison.[18] D'autres encore s'attèlent à restaurer la réhabilitation en développant des principes et modèles de prise en charge testés et approuvés scientifiquement. Tel est l'agenda du mouvement communément dénommé « *What works* »: renverser le paradigme que « rien ne marche » à l'aune de données probantes, pour restituer au cœur du système de justice pénale l'idée de réhabilitation.

4.1. LA CONTRIBUTION CANADIENNE

Parmi les premiers à s'y atteler se trouvent plusieurs chercheurs canadiens motivés à réformer le système correctionnel de l'intérieur qui considèrent la réhabilitation comme un moyen d'« humaniser » l'incarcération.[19] C'est ainsi à la fin des années 70 que Gendreau et Ross publient une revue des études évaluatives de programmes correctionnels réalisées depuis 1973 ayant démontré une certaine « efficacité » à prévenir et/ou à réduire la récidive.[20] Ils réitèrent en 1987 avec une revue systématique de plus de 200 études évaluatives menées entre 1981 et 1987.[21] A leur suite, nombre de chercheurs colligeront les résultats d'études en la matière, s'attachant à identifier les éléments clés de programmes réhabilitatifs menant à une diminution de la récidive. Bonta et Andrews en particulier, deux psychologues rattachés au Service correctionnel canadien, dégagent progressivement trois principes prépondérants qu'ils labelliseront ultérieurement «*principles of effective intervention*», en français «principes d'interventions efficaces ».[22]

18 M. Tonry & R. Frase, *Sentencing and Sanctions in Western Countries*, Oxford: Oxford University Press, 2001; J. Petersilia, *When Prisoners come Home. Parole and Prisoner Reentry*, Oxford: Oxford University Press, 2003.

19 P. Lalande, 'Punir ou réhabiliter les contrevenants ? Du « Nothing Works » au « What Works » (Montée, déclin et retour de l'idéal de réhabilitation)', in: P. Lalande & O. Lamalice, *La sévérité pénale à l'heure du populisme*, Québec: Ministère de la sécurité publique du Québec, 2006, p. 30-77.

20 P. Gendreau, R. Ross, 'Effective Correctional Treatment: Bibliotherapy for Cynics', 25 *Crime and Delinquency* 4 (1979), p. 463-489.

21 P. Gendreau & R. Ross, 'Revivification of Rehabilitation: Evidence from the 1980s', 4 *Justice* Quarterly 3 (1987), p. 349-407.

22 F.T. Cullen, 'The Twelve People who saved Rehabilitation: How the Science of Criminology made a Difference. The American Society of Criminology 2004 Presidential Address', 43 *Criminology* 1 (2005), p. 1-42; D.A. Andrews, 'Principes des programmes correctionnels efficaces', in: L.L. Motiuk & R. C. Serin (eds), *Compendium 2000 des programmes correctionnels efficaces*, Ottawa: Ministère des Approvisionnements et Services Canada, 2001, p. 10-19.

Très succinctement, le principe du *risque* s'intéresse aux destinataires des programmes d'intervention («qui»). Il repose sur l'idée que les interventions doivent cibler davantage les personnes qui cumulent les facteurs de risques les plus grands; ces interventions ne pouvant n'avoir aucun effet, voire même avoir des effets contreproductifs sur les personnes dont le niveau de risque a été évalué de faible. L'intensité du traitement doit ainsi correspondre au niveau de risque identifié de telle sorte à maximiser la réussite de l'intervention.[23] Pour évaluer ce niveau de risque, sont convoqués des instruments dont la validité prédictive a été éprouvée à travers des méta-analyses sur des groupes de populations cibles. Il s'agit d'outils actuariels de type probabiliste, qui s'articulent autour de facteurs spécifiquement associés au comportement criminel et qui se révèlent toujours plus perfectionnés; on en dénombre à l'heure actuelle quatre générations.

Le deuxième principe est celui du *besoin*, lequel cible les problèmes à traiter («quoi»). Deux types de besoins sont identifiés: d'une part les besoins non-criminogènes, dont la recherche estime qu'il ne sert à rien d'y travailler car leur impact est moindre sur la récidive. D'autre part, les besoins criminogènes (ou facteurs criminogènes ou facteurs de risque dynamiques), identifiés par la recherche comme étant directement liés au comportement criminel et sur lesquels il convient d'agir pour diminuer la probabilité de nouveaux passages à l'acte. On part ici du postulat que les résultats en termes de diminution de la récidive sont d'autant plus importants si les besoins criminogènes sont ciblés et travaillés de manière appropriée.[24] Parmi ces besoins, on trouve notamment une faible maîtrise de soi, des relations avec des pairs délinquants ou encore l'abus de substances. A l'inverse, le fait de résider dans un quartier déshérité, de souffrir d'un manque de confiance en soi ou de troubles de la santé mentale sont identifiés comme étant de faibles prédicteurs de risque, contrairement à l'appréhension qui en était faite par des approches plus traditionnelles.

Le dernier principe enfin est celui de la *réceptivité* et porte sur les programmes d'intervention dispensés («comment»). Il repose sur l'idée que ces derniers doivent tenir compte du style d'apprentissage et des habiletés (psycho-sociales) de leur destinataire, ainsi que de ses caractéristiques individuelles qui «augmentent ou diminuent la probabilité d'une récidive».[25] Il préconise à cet effet des programmes d'intervention essentiellement d'inspiration cognitivo-comportementale qui impliquent un travail plus ou moins intensif, dépendamment du niveau de risque identifié du sujet, sur des problématiques

23 D.A. Andrews & C. Dowden, 'Risk Principle of Case Classification in Correctional Treatment: A Meta-analytic Investigation', 50 *International Journal of Offender Therapy and Comparative Criminology* 1 (2006), p. 88-100.

24 D.A. Andrews, 'Principes des programmes correctionnels efficaces', in: L.L. Motiuk & R. C. Serin (eds), *Compendium 2000 des programmes correctionnels efficaces*, Ottawa: Ministère des Approvisionnements et Services Canada, 2001, p. 10-19.

25 F. Cortoni & D. Lafortune, 'Le traitement correctionnel fondé sur des données probantes: une recension', 42 *Criminologie* 1 (2009), p. 61, 65.

éprouvées empiriquement comme porteuses de risque (gestion de la colère, des pulsions sexuelles, etc.).[26] Les programmes réputés «efficaces» vont notamment de la restructuration cognitive à la création de choix, en passant par l'acquisition graduelle d'habiletés diverses et le renforcement de comportements anticriminels.[27]

Ces trois principes constituent au final les fondements du modèle de réhabilitation d'Andrews et Bonta, intitulé le *Risk-Need-Responsivity Model*, en français le Modèle *Risque-Besoin-Réceptivité*, tout entier inspiré de la psychologie du comportement criminel et de l'apprentissage social.[28] Pour ses promoteurs, la force du modèle tient non seulement à ses assises théoriques, mais également à sa nature empirique. Ciblés sur des causes et des facteurs identifiés comme des «prédicteurs de la récidive», les programmes d'intervention qui en découlent indiqueraient une réduction de la récidive de 30 % en moyenne. Il n'en fallait pas tant pour emporter rapidement l'adhésion des décideurs pénitentiaires. Implanté au sein du Service correctionnel du Canada, ce modèle de réhabilitation, résolument utilitariste, a été source d'inspiration pour l'Australie, et l'Angleterre et les Pays de Galles notamment.[29]

4.2. LA CONTRIBUTION AMÉRICAINE

Le «mouvement «*What works*»» est également bien présent aux Etats-Unis, mais sous un prisme différent. Alors que la perspective canadienne est d'inspiration plutôt «psycho-criminologique», diligentée par les caractéristiques du contrevenant, des intervenants et des programmes, la contribution américaine, peu encline à développer une approche psychologisante, est plutôt d'inspiration «socio-criminologique» et s'intéresse plus au contexte social, économique, culturel et communautaire notamment, qui entoure le contrevenant.[30] Les chercheurs américains s'attèlent ainsi à développer des méthodologies rigoureuses d'évaluation des impacts des programmes correctionnels en termes de réduction de la récidive, dont ils rendent compte

---

26 D.A. Andrews, 'Principes des programmes correctionnels efficaces', in: L.L. Motiuk & R.C. Serin (eds), *Compendium 2000 des programmes correctionnels efficaces*, Ottawa: Ministère des Approvisionnements et Services Canada, 2001, p. 10-19.

27 F. Cortoni & D. Lafortune, 'Le traitement correctionnel fondé sur des données probantes: une recension', 42 *Criminologie* 1 (2009), p. 61-89.

28 D.A. Andrews & J. Bonta, *The Psychology of Criminal Conduct*, New Jersey: Anderson Publishing, 2010.

29 G. Robinson, 'Implementing OASys: Lessons from Research into LSI-R and ACE', 50 *Probation Journal* 1 (2003), p. 30-40.
G. Robinson, 'Late-modern Rehabilitation: The Evolution of a Penal Strategy', 10 *Punishment and Society* 4 (2008), p. 429-445.

30 J. Petersilia, *When Prisoners come Home. Parole and Prisoner Reentry*, Oxford: Oxford University Press, 2003.

sous la forme de revues systématiques, d'analyses coûts-bénéfices ou encore de méta-analyses. Ces dernières en particulier consistent à réunir les résultats de nombreuses recherches distinctes portant sur des programmes appliqués à des populations judiciarisées relativement similaires et à les analyser statistiquement pour identifier en bout de course leur impact sur ces dernières selon la typologie des délits commis. La grille d'évaluation de Sherman et son équipe de l'Université de Maryland (*The Maryland Scale of Scientific Methods*) constitue une parmi les nombreuses méthodologies élaborées en ce sens.[31] Les travaux méta-analytiques menés sur divers programmes d'intervention auprès de personnes judiciarisées emportent un écho assez retentissant dès la fin des années 80[32] et depuis lors n'ont cessé de se développer, également en Europe et notamment sous la forme de consortiums (McGuire, 2001; Campbell Collaboration).[33] Ce faisant, nombre de chercheurs ont contribué à démontrer non seulement quels sont les programmes susceptibles de « fonctionner », mais aussi ceux dont les résultats sont nuls ou mitigés en termes de prévention de la récidive, brisant un certain nombre de mythes entourant notamment des interventions à connotation punitive. Il est ainsi désormais un fait établi que les interventions de type « *Short, sharp, shock* », tels que les *Boot camps*, fondés sur une discipline sévère et un entraînement physique intensif, ne portent aucun fruit en termes de réduction de la récidive. Les résultats de méta-analyses démontrent également que les *Intensive Supervision Program* (ISPs), fondés sur un contrôle intensif des probationnaires couplé à la menace d'une punition accrue en cas de bris de conditions notamment, n'ont guère plus de succès, voire même peuvent produire des effets contraires à celui escompté.[34] Inversement, les communautés thérapeutiques, les thérapies cognitivo-comportementales, les approches centrées sur la famille, de type multi-systémique en particulier, ou encore les programmes d'emploi communautaires sont tour à tour identifiés comme de « bonnes » ou « prometteuses » pratiques selon la terminologie consacrée.

---

31 L.W. Sherman, D. Gottfredson, D. MacKenzie, J. Eck, P. Reuter & S. Bushway, *Preventing Crime: What Works, What Doesn't, What's Promising. A Report to the United States Congress*, MD: University of Maryland, Department of Criminology and Criminal Justice, 1997.

32 V. par exemple les travaux de Lipsey, Wilson: M.W. Lipsey & D.B. Wilson, 'The Efficacy of Psychological, Educational, and Behavioral Treatment: Confirmation from Meta-analysis', 48 *American Psychologist* 12 (1993), p. 1181-1209.

33 J. McGuire, 'What Works in Correctional Intervention? Evidence and Practical Implications', in: G.A. Bernfeld, D.P. Farrington, A.W. Leschied (dir.), *Offender Rehabilitation in Practice. Implementing and Evaluating Effective Programs*, Chichester: John Wiley & Sons, LTD, 2001, p. 25-44.

34 D. MacKenzie, R.B. Layton, D. McDowall & C. Souryal, 'Boot Camp Prisons and Recidivism in Eight States', 33 Criminology 3 (1995), p. 327-357; J. Petersilia & S. Turner, *Evaluating Intensive Supervision Probation/Parole: Results of a Nationwide Experiment*, Washington, DC: National Institute of Justice, 1993.

Au terme de ce bref tour d'horizon, nous pourrions être tentées, à l'instar de certains[35], de conclure de façon dithyrambique sur une apologie du dit « mouvement « *What works* » » et de ses figures de proue, parfois dénommés les « nouveaux réhabilitionnistes ».[36] Si leurs travaux ont très certainement participé au retour progressif de la réhabilitation dans le champ pénal et pénitentiaire, ils ne sont cependant pas sans présenter un certain nombre d'enjeux importants.

5. UN COURANT NON EXEMPT D'ENJEUX

Force est de constater que s'agissant du sujet à l'étude, le courant de pratiques fondées sur les données probantes consacre une importance prépondérante à la prévention de la récidive. Les réussites de la réhabilitation sont en effet essentiellement lues à la lumière de la seule prévention de la réitération, dans un but ultime de protection de la collectivité. Il en résulte un surinvestissement de la notion de « risque » et de préceptes managériaux qui laissent entrevoir l'émergence de nouveaux modes de régulation des conduites dans le monde pénitentiaire et post-pénal.

5.1. LE « RISQUE » AU CARREFOUR DE TOUTES LES DÉCISIONS ET INTERVENTIONS

Pour maximiser les chances de réussite des interventions correctionnelles en termes de prévention de la récidive, les condamnés à une peine privative de liberté tendent à être classés, placés en établissement, pris en charge et le cas échéant bénéficier d'aménagements selon le niveau de risque qu'ils représentent. Il peut être reproché à ces stratégies de se focaliser uniquement sur les éléments identifiés comme prédicteurs de récidive. Typiquement, le Modèle *Risque-Besoin-Réceptivité* s'articule essentiellement autour de facteurs de risques dynamiques et peut parfois négliger d'autres problèmes éprouvés par la personne incarcérée. Il n'est ainsi pas rare que le principal intéressé souhaite travailler sur certains besoins, mais que ces derniers soient relégués car non identifiés par la recherche comme étant « criminogènes ». Par ailleurs, ce type de prise en charge insiste essentiellement sur les déficits du sujet à combler, et subsidiairement seulement sur ses potentiels et facteurs de protection, renforçant une vision

---

35 F.T. Cullen, 'The Twelve People who saved Rehabilitation: How the Science of Criminology made a Difference. The American Society of Criminology 2004 Presidential Address', 43 *Criminology* 1 (2005), p. 1-42.

36 E. Rotman, *Beyond Punishment: A New View on the Rehabilitation of Criminal Offenders*, New York: Greenwood Press, 1990; G. Robinson, 'Risk Management and Rehabilitation in the Probation Service: Collision and Collusion', 38 *The Howard Journal of Criminal Justice* 4 (1999), p. 421-433.

plutôt pessimiste de sa dynamique.[37] Enfin, cette approche ne tend pas à saisir toutes les facettes de l'évolution du détenu et les facteurs qui alimentent sa vulnérabilité sociale, bref son inscription contextuelle générale.[38]

Le risque s'immisce également au cœur des pratiques professionnelles, situation qui n'est pas sans poser parfois quelques problèmes aux intervenants de première ligne. Typiquement, les compétences qu'ils sont appelés à mobiliser en évaluation et en gestion du risque peuvent s'avérer relativement éloignées de leurs missions originelles. Les psychologues en milieu correctionnel canadien par exemple ont progressivement été investis de tâches toujours plus nombreuses en la matière. Ils sont amenés à se focaliser essentiellement sur des problématiques identifiées comme porteuses de risque, les démobilisant d'autant dans l'instauration d'un lien thérapeutique avec le détenu, fragmentant leur approche de ce dernier et à terme rendant pratiquement impossible son appréhension de façon holistique.[39] Au-delà, cette situation semble avoir considérablement appauvri la diversité des obédiences cliniques en ce milieu.[40] Les pratiques psychanalytiques ou d'inspiration phénoménologique par exemple, lorsqu'elles existent encore, tendent à plier sous le poids d'interventions cognitivo-comportementales.

Enfin, de façon générale et toujours d'un point de vue criminologique, les assises théoriques sur lesquelles s'appuient les principes et modèles dits «probants» s'inspirent principalement de la criminologie dite «de l'acte» et éludent certains constats relevant notamment des théories de la réaction sociale qui pourraient pourtant être féconds à exploiter. A trop focaliser sur les prédicteurs de récidive, ces modèles font fi non seulement des processus sociétaux qui alimentent l'institution carcérale, mais également de la trajectoire du sujet. On ne s'interroge guère ici sur le recours à l'incarcération pour gérer la

---

37 J. McGuire, 'What Works in Correctional Intervention? Evidence and Practical Implications', in: G.A. Bernfeld, D.P. Farrington, A.W. Leschied (dir.), *Offender Rehabilitation in Practice. Implementing and Evaluating Effective Programs*, Chichester: John Wiley & Sons, LTD, 2001, p. 25-44; T. Ward & S. Maruna, *Rehabilitation: Beyond the Risk Paradigm*, Abingdon: Routledge, 2007; F. Cortoni & D. Lafortune, 'Le traitement correctionnel fondé sur des données probantes: une recension', 42 *Criminologie* 1 (2009), p. 61-89.

38 B. Quirion, 'Traiter les délinquants ou contrôler les conduites: le dispositif thérapeutique à l'ère de la nouvelle pénologie', 39 *Criminologie* 2 (2006), p. 137-164; M. Barry, 'The Mentor/ Monitor Debate in Criminal Justice: «What Works» for Offenders', 30 *British Journal of Social Work* 2 (2000), p. 575-595.

39 K. Hannah-Moffat, 'Criminogenic Needs and the Transformative Risk Subject: Hybridations of Risk/Need in Penality', 7 *Punishment and Society* 1 (2005), p. 29-51; B. Quirion, 'Traiter les délinquants ou contrôler les conduites: le dispositif thérapeutique à l'ère de la nouvelle pénologie', 39 *Criminologie* 2 (2006), p. 137-164.

40 C. Balier, *Psychanalyse des comportements sexuels violents*, Paris: PUF, 1996; F. Digneffe & C. Adam, 'Le développement de la criminologie clinique à l'Ecole de Louvain', 37 *Criminologie* 1 (2004), p. 43-70; C. Adam, 'Innovation «thérapeutique» en milieu carcéral: du «ver dans le fruit» au «levain dans la pâte»', *Champ pénal/Penal field* [En ligne: http://champpenal.revues.org/2522], 2007.

« dangerosité » supposée d'individus « en marge » ou jugés « indésirables »[41], une dynamique d'exclusion qui se voit au demeurant renforcée par des stratégies correctionnelles diligentées par le risque.[42] De même, ce type de modèle saisit le condamné tel un être rationnel, capable notamment de s'autonomiser et se prendre en charge, alors même que la littérature abonde pour souligner combien les populations incarcérées éprouvent des difficultés de ce type, déjà préexistantes à leur incarcération.[43]

Face à ces critiques, une attention plus particulière est désormais portée par les criminologues à l'implantation des interventions et aux interactions des destinataires avec les professionnels chargés de leur mise en œuvre. Les concepteurs du Modèle *Risque-Besoin-Réceptivité* notamment attachent une importance accrue au principe d' « intégrité » des programmes, à la formation de leurs « gestionnaires » et à la motivation des sujets incarcérés.[44] Il n'empêche, son caractère demeure relativement totalisant, d'autant plus qu'il s'épanouit particulièrement bien en un milieu qui depuis quelques décennies se voit contaminé par la pensée managériale.

5.2. L'HÉGÉMONIE MANAGÉRIALE

Dans une recherche menée auprès d'intervenants du Service correctionnel du Canada, nous nous sommes posée la question de savoir quel est l'impact d'une lecture prédictive des risques sur l'exercice de leurs pratiques professionnelles en les murs à partir du sens qu'ils attribuent aux missions qui leur sont confiées (Jendly, à paraître). L'ensemble du matériel tend à confirmer les hypothèses élaborées par d'autres avant nous, à savoir que les exigences liées à l'évaluation et à la gestion des risques répondent aussi, voire surtout, à des préoccupations managériales des autorités du continuum pénal.[45]

---

41 G. Chantraine, 'La prison post-disciplinaire', 30 *Déviance et Société* 3 (2006), p. 273-288.

42 P. Mary, 'Pénalité et gestion des risques. Vers une justice « actuarielle » en Europe ?', 25 *Déviance et société* 1 (2001), p. 33-51; K. Hannah-Moffat & M. Shaw, 'Situation risquée : le risque et les services correctionnels au Canada', 34 *Criminologie* 1 (2001), p. 47-72; K. Hannah-Moffat, 'Criminogenic Needs and the Transformative Risk Subject : Hybridations of Risk/Need in Penality', 7 *Punishment and Society* 1 (2005), p. 29-51.

43 M. Lynch, 'Rehabilitation as Rhetoric. The Ideal of Reformation in Contemporary Parole Discourse and Practices', 2 Punishment & Society 1 (2000), p. 40-65; S. Maruna, 'Reentry as a Rite of Passage', 13 *Punishment and Society* 1 (2011), p. 3-28.

44 F. Cortoni & D. Lafortune, 'Le traitement correctionnel fondé sur des données probantes : une recension', 42 *Criminologie* 1 (2009), p. 61-89.

45 M. Lynch, 'Rehabilitation as Rhetoric. The Ideal of Reformation in Contemporary Parole Discourse and Practices', 2 *Punishment & Society* 1 (2000), p. 40-65; M. Vacheret & G. Lemire, *Anatomie de la prison contemporaine*, Montréal : Presses de l'Université de Montréal, 2007; C. Vigour, 'Ethos et légitimité professionnels à l'épreuve d'une approche managériale : le cas de la justice belge', 50 *Sociologie du* travail 1 (2008) p. 71-90; F. McNeill, N. Burns, S. Halliday, N. Hutton *et al.*, 'Risk, Responsibility and Reconfiguration : Penal Adaptation and Misadaptation', 11 *Punishment and Society* 4 (2009), p. 419-442.

Toute investie à démontrer « ce qui marche » et à emporter l'adhésion des décideurs, la tendance à des pratiques fondées sur les données probantes coïncide en partie avec l'importation en les murs de principes et instruments propres à la « Nouvelle gestion publique ». Appréciées à l'aune de la prévention de la récidive, les interventions ont progressivement été façonnées par des indicateurs de performance, d'efficacité et d'efficience. Cette tendance a pour effet en pratique de soumettre les intervenants et les détenus à des obligations de rendre compte, d'optimiser leurs ressources, de rationaliser leurs investissements et de maximiser leur auto-régulation.

Du côté des détenus, l'injonction qui leur est faite de « participer activement » à l'exécution de leur peine procède aussi de cette rhétorique. Il est attendu qu'ils se « responsabilisent », qu'ils « s'auto-régulent », « s'auto-gèrent » et le cas échéant qu'ils assument la responsabilité de leurs échecs.[46] S'agissant des intervenants, ils sont enjoints à acquérir des compétences techniques toujours plus perfectionnées et rendre compte de leur rendement à l'aune de leur application.[47] Décrié comme arbitraire, le jugement professionnel a progressivement été remplacé par des échelles fondées sur des facteurs de risque statiques (Echelle de Burgess notamment), puis sur des facteurs statiques et dynamiques, auxquels se sont récemment ajoutés des facteurs de protection et de réceptivité. Leur multiplication et l'importance qu'il leur est accordée – les intervenants qui s'en départissent devant sérieusement en argumenter les motifs – induit chez ces derniers un sentiment de perte de la confiance en leur intuition et leur jugement clinique. Ces instruments impliquent en outre des professionnels qu'ils acquièrent des connaissances toujours plus fines dans l'usage de ces instruments très complexes, paradoxalement parfois au détriment de celles relatives au sujet incarcéré.

Pour certains auteurs, ces glissements vers un auto-contrôle accru des détenus et une standardisation des interventions soutenus par le virage actuariel permettraient non seulement de mieux gérer les populations pénitentiaires, mais également de mieux diligenter les activités des professionnels. Dans une perspective gouvernementaliste, cette évolution laisserait présager l'émergence d'une gouvernance pilotée « à distance » des pratiques et des acteurs, aseptisée et défiant à nouveau le modèle réhabilitatif ou à tout le moins le reconfigurant.[48]

---

46 K. Hannah-Moffat, 'Prisons that Empower. Neo-liberal Governance in Canadian Women's Prisons', 40 *British Journal of Criminology* 2 (2000), p. 510-531; A. Liebling, 'Prisons in Transition', 29 *International Journal of Law and* Psychiatry 5 (2006), p. 422-430; B. Quirion, 'Traiter les délinquants ou contrôler les conduites: le dispositif thérapeutique à l'ère de la nouvelle pénologie', 39 *Criminologie* 2 (2006), p. 137-164; B. Quirion, 'Le détenu responsable et autonome: la nouvelle cible de l'intervention correctionnelle au Canada', 7-8 *Revue de droit pénal et de criminologie* (2009) (juillet), p. 818-835.

47 M. Jendly, 'Performance, transparence et accountability: une équation (dé)responsabilisante des professionnels exerçant en prison?', 36 *Déviance et société* 3 (2012), p. 243-262.

48 N. Rose, 'Governing Risky Individuals: The Role of Psychiatry in New Regimes of Control', 5 *Psychiatry, Psychology and Law* 2 (1998), p. 177-195; N. Rose, 'Government and Control', 40

La question se pose alors de savoir, au-delà du seul horizon de la prévention de la récidive et/ou de la gouvernance objectivée, si d'autres avenues sont envisageables.

6. QUELLES AUTRES AVENUES POSSIBLES ?

Deux avenues en particulier nous semblent ici pertinentes d'être relevées. La première porte sur un modèle de réhabilitation fondé sur une idée de bien-être, de « meilleure vie », et la deuxième renvoie à des approches s'intéressant au désistement.

6.1. LE *GOOD LIVES MODEL*

Le *Good Lives Model*, en français Modèle *des bonnes vies*, est inspiré des recherches dans le domaine de la psychologie sociale et, plus particulièrement, de la psychologie positive.[49] Il convient donc de noter d'emblée que le Modèle *Risque-Besoin-Réceptivité* et celui fondé sur les bonnes vies ne poursuivent pas les mêmes objectifs vectoriels. Alors que le premier découle de recherches dans le domaine de la psychologie clinique, de la psychiatrie correctionnelle et de la médecine pénitentiaire, le second par opposition est d'inspiration comportementaliste et extra-pathologique.[50] Par ailleurs, les approches fondées sur le risque, les besoins et la réceptivité répondent en premier lieu au besoin de protection sociale contre la récidive. L'orientation vectorielle est clairement pro-sociale. En soi, il n'existe pas de contradiction évidente avec le modèle fondé sur les bonnes vies, car ce dernier comporte également la dimension pro-sociale ; toutefois, la construction modulaire de ce dernier ne fixe pas comme objectif prioritaire la réduction de tout risque.[51] Le Modèle *des bonnes vies* oriente en effet les ressources individuelles et sociales dans la direction du bien-être individuel et, par extension, dans la diminution des prédispositions de réitération. En théorie, les bénéfices cumulés d'un mode de vie non-déviant devraient trouver leur primauté sur les risques assumés et les plaisirs d'une

---

British Journal of Criminology 2 (2000), p. 321-339; M. Lynch, 'Rehabilitation as Rhetoric. The Ideal of Reformation in Contemporary Parole Discourse and Practices', 2 Punishment & Society 1 (2000), p. 40-65.

49 T. Ward & M. Brown, 'The Good Lives Model and Conceptual Issues in Offender Rehabilitation', 10 *Psychology, Crime & Law* 3 (2004), p. 243-257.

50 M.E.P. Seligman, 'Positive Health', 57 *Applied Psychology: An International Review* 1 (2008), p. 3-18; M. McMurran, E. Theodosi, A. Sweeney & J. Sellen, 'What Do Prisoners Want? Current Concerns of Adult Male Prisoners', 14 *Psychology, Crime & Law* 3 (2008), p. 267-274.

51 W.R. Lindsay, T. Ward, T. Morgan & I. Wilson, 'Self-regulation of Sex Offending, Future Pathways and the Good Lives Model: Applications and Problems', 13 *Journal of Sexual Aggression* 1 (2007), p. 37-50.

carrière criminelle. Ce modèle apparaît ainsi comme une alternative multiphasique au traitement correctionnel[52], soutenant des objectifs primaires d'intégration des besoins réputés non-criminogènes dans des «*Good Lives Plans*». Le travail basé sur l'approche *Risque-Besoin-Réceptivité* tend on l'a dit à se concentrer exclusivement sur les besoins criminogènes et à ignorer les origines de la dynamique personnelle du sujet. Inversement, les recherches dont découlent le Modèle *des bonnes vies* tendent à démontrer l'importance de l'adaptation comme processus déterminant dans la transformation des besoins criminogènes.[53] Par conséquent, besoins criminogènes et non-criminogènes sont réputés ne pas pouvoir être totalement dissociés.

Les exemples d'application du Modèle *des bonnes vies* sur les délinquants sexuels étayent ce constat.[54] Ils soutiennent que tout individu est porteur d'un certain cadre d'accumulation de «biens». Ces biens sont sous-divisés en «biens individuels primaires» («*primary human goods*»), respectivement en «biens secondaires» ou instrumentaux. Si les biens primaires sont ceux qui déterminent la mise en relation des fonctions biologiques avec les fonctions psychologiques (par exemple, la sensation de douleur physique), alors les biens secondaires apportent l'outillage nécessaire pour retrouver l'équilibre dans les besoins primaires. De ce fait, mettre en évidence un déséquilibre dans les besoins primaires et tendre à réduire ce déséquilibre à un facteur de risque est insuffisant. La personne développe un outillage de biens secondaires tout au long de son existence. Elle passera par des phases aigues ou latentes dans le déséquilibre pour parvenir *in fine* à toucher un équilibre (relatif ou absolu) conditionné par des facteurs internes mais aussi externes. Dans ce sens, les recherches menées auprès de sortants de prison montrent la relativité de l'adaptation à un cadre.[55] Les «sur-adaptés carcéraux» ajustent l'équilibre institutionnel à un cadre de vie

---

52 A. Birgden, 'Therapeutic jurisprudence and «Good Lives»: A Rehabilitation Framework for Corrections', 37 *Australian Psychologist*, 3 (2002), p. 180-186; W.R. Lindsay, T. Ward, T. Morgan & I. Wilson, 'Self-regulation of Sex Offending, Future Pathways and the Good Lives Model: Applications and Problems', 13 *Journal of Sexual Aggression* 1 (2007), p. 37-50.

53 T. Ward, R.M. Collie & P. Bourke, 'Models of Offender Rehabilitation: The Good Lives Model and The Risk-Need-Responsivity Model', in: A. R. Beech, L. Craig & K. D. Browne (eds), *Assessment and Treatment of Sex Offenders: A Handbook*, Chichester: Wiley-Blackwell, 2009, p. 293-310; K. Hannah-Moffat, 'Criminogenic Needs and the Transformative Risk Subject: Hybridations of Risk/Need in Penality', 7 *Punishment and Society* 1 (2005), p. 29-51.

54 T. Ward & R. Mann, 'Good Lives and the Rehabilitation of Offenders: A Positive Approach to Sex Offender Treatment', in: P.A. Linley & S. Joseph (eds), *Positive Psychology in Practice*, New Jersey: Wiley, 2004, p. 598-616; T. Ward & C.A. Stewart, 'The Treatment of Sex Offenders: Risk Management and Good Lives', 34 *Professional Psychology: Research and Practice* 4 (2003), p. 353-360; W.L. Marshall, T. Ward, R.E. Mann, H. Moulden *et al.*, 'Working Positively With Sexual Offenders: Maximizing the Effectiveness of Treatment', 20 *Journal of Interpersonal Violence* 9 (2005), p. 1096-1114; T. Ward & T. Gannon, 'Rehabilitation, Etiology, and Self-regulation: The Comprehensive Good Lives Model of Treatment for Sexual Offenders', 11 *Aggression and Violent Behavior* 1 (2006), p. 77- 94.

55 M. Vacheret & G. Lemire, *Anatomie de la prison contemporaine*, Montréal: Presses de l'Université de Montréal, 2007.

extramuros. La personne s'adapte à un cadre selon ses besoins spatio-temporels et son outillage secondaire. Ainsi pour certains, les besoins criminogènes dépistés à l'intérieur de la prison peuvent devenir des biens instrumentaux menant vers un équilibre primaire. Dans cette perspective, il s'avère donc inutile de se concentrer exclusivement sur les besoins identifiés et régis en le cadre existant, le plus souvent le milieu de contrainte, mais plutôt de projeter la recherche de l'équilibre et du bien-être dans un cadre que la personne pourra elle-même s'approprier à moyen ou même à long terme.[56]

Nous arrivons donc à la pierre angulaire de l'approche fondée sur les bonnes vies : il s'agit d'une voie constructive qui ne se concentre pas exclusivement sur le délinquant lui-même, mais tente de reconstruire le puzzle relationnel entre les contextes individuel, interpersonnel et social dans lequel tout individu est susceptible de vouloir chercher un équilibre de ses biens primaires.[57] Contrairement au modèle de réhabilitation fondé sur le risque et les besoins, celui fondé sur les bonnes vies ne prétend pas à un résultat définitif, par exemple suite à un traitement qui aurait été administré. Il est ainsi vrai que le Modèle *Risque-Besoin-Réceptivité* est plus précis, quantifiable et par conséquent plus rassurant pour les décideurs, mais il est totalement imprévisible à long terme. Le Modèle *des bonnes vies* en revanche a l'avantage de la construction modulaire, par étapes et par objectifs intermédiaires, et constitue un processus de type expérientiel : il s'agit d'assimiler en partie, d'ajuster l'accompagnement aux objectifs personnels, enfin d'ignorer le cas échéant ce qui semble inapproprié.[58] L'évaluation finale des résultats du Modèle *des bonnes vies* est certes plus problématique, mais les résultats intermédiaires atteints s'avèrent particulièrement prometteurs, dans le respect des caractéristiques propres au sujet et au contexte en lequel il s'inscrit. Tel est le cas notamment des personnes qui parviennent à-travers ce modèle à une réduction significative de leurs usages de stupéfiants (notamment à une consommation contrôlée et/ou à une réduction de la fréquence de la revente des substances).

6.2. LES APPROCHES FONDÉES SUR LE DÉSISTEMENT

Depuis près de deux décennies, une nouvelle approche alimente en criminologie le débat sur la réhabilitation. Fondée sur le désistement au crime (« *Theories of*

---

56 R.C. Serin & C.D. Lloyd, 'Examining the Process of Offender Change : the Transition to Crime Desistance', 15 *Psychology, Crime & Law* 4 (2009), p. 347-364 ; J. Vess, 'Fear and Loathing in Public Policy : Ethical Issues in Laws for Sex Offenders', 14 *Aggression and Violent* Behavior 4 (2009), p. 264-272.

57 T. McCulloch & L. Kelly, 'Working with Sex Offenders in Context : Which Way forward ?', 54 *Probation Journal* 1 (2007), p. 7-21.

58 P.R. Whitehead, T. Ward & R.M. Collie, 'Time for a Change : Applying the Good Lives Model of Rehabilitation to a High-Risk Violent Offender', 51 *International Journal of Offender Therapy and Comparative Criminology* 5 (2007), p. 578-598.

Desistance») cette perspective a cela de particulier qu'elle renverse la question de la récidive en ces termes: qui et comment pourrait *ne pas* récidiver? Si les approches classiques tentent de répondre à la question des facteurs qui prédéterminent le passage à l'acte, le désistement s'intéresse aux conditions dans lesquelles ces facteurs peuvent évoluer et réduire, voire empêcher la récidive. Cette approche a déjà fait preuve de fiabilité dans le domaine de la probation[59], mais n'est encore que très peu connue et/ou utilisée dans le domaine carcéral.

Le désistement est généralement défini comme un processus – et non comme une valeur statique inchangeable – de distanciation, voire de cessation de l'activité criminelle.[60] Pour les chercheurs qui s'y attardent, les analyses des phénomènes de récidive et du désistement devraient être dissociées.[61] Le désistement est un processus complexe et ses étapes peuvent être interchangeables. Brièvement, il débute par une phase de désistement primaire, durant laquelle la prise de conscience et la motivation de s'engager dans un processus de changement restent relativement limitées. L'image de soi perçue par le délinquant est la même qu'au moment de l'engagement dans la commission des délits. Cette étape cependant est considérée comme partie intégrante du processus de désistement. Alors que les approches qui ont inspiré notamment le Modèle *Risque-Besoin-Réceptivité* s'arrêtent au moment de cette phase initiale, le désistement ne fait ici que commencer. La deuxième phase, celle du désistement secondaire, se caractérise par une stabilité plus importante, le sujet étant capable de développer une nouvelle perception de lui-même en tant que non-délinquant. Pour y parvenir, il est présumé nécessaire qu'il se situe en-dehors de toutes contraintes judiciaires.[62] Certains chercheurs tendent même à soutenir que l'entrée dans le processus du désistement est pratiquement impossible durant la période d'incarcération.[63] Si toutefois l'incarcération fait partie du parcours du sujet, alors ses aptitudes d'adaptation au milieu carcéral et les conséquences de

---

59 T. McCulloch, 'Probation, Social Context and Desistance: Retracing the Relationship', 52 *Probation Journal* 1 (2005), p. 8-22; F. McNeill, 'Desistance-focused Probation Practice', in: W. H. Chui & M. Nellis (eds), *Moving Probation Forward: Evidence, Arguments and Practice*, Edinburgh: Pearson Longman, 2003, p. 146-162; S. Rex, 'Desistance from Offending: Experiences of Probation', 38 *The Howard Journal of Criminal Justice* 4 (1999), p. 366-383.

60 S. Bushway, A. Piquero, L. Broidy, E. Cauffman *et al.*, 'An empirical framework for studying desistance as a process', 39 *Criminology* 2 (2001), p. 491-516.

61 D. Healy, *The Dynamics of Desistance. Charting Pathways through Change*, Cullompton: Willan Publishing, 2010.

62 S. Farrall, A. Bottoms & J. Shapland, 'Social Structures and Desistance from Crime', 7 *European Journal of Criminology* 6 (2010), p. 546-570.

63 S. Farrall, 'Why Do People Stop Offending?', 1 *Scottish Journal of Criminal Justice Studies* 1 (1995), p. 51-59; A. Liebling & S. Maruna, 'Introduction: the Effects of Imprisonment Revisited', in: A. Liebling & S. Maruna (eds), *The Effects of Imprisonment*, Cullompton: Willan Publishing, 2005, p. 1-29.

son parcours en les murs doivent être prises en considération dans son processus d'implication dans le désistement et, *in extenso*, de réhabilitation.[64]

De l'avis des chercheurs versés dans cette approche, les modèles correctionnels existants ne sont pas en mesure de garantir la mise en place des conditions d'entrée dans le processus du désistement, dès lors que leur préoccupation de base et les objectifs qui leur sont assignés sont exogènes, extra-personnels. La notion même d' « individualisation de la peine » est réputée réductrice, dans la mesure où le délinquant doit correspondre à un type préétabli afin de pouvoir bénéficier d'une prise en charge correspondant à son niveau de risque et sa catégorie de délinquance.[65] Le désistement en tant que partie intégrante des approches de réhabilitation est alors d'autant plus important qu'il écarte la catégorisation implicite des délinquants selon le type du délit ou encore de degrés de « dangerosité » à un moment donné. Le processus du désistement met l'accent sur les perspectives individuelles dans un cadre social donné. Très dynamique, cette approche conviendrait particulièrement aux populations qui vivent des déséquilibres personnels importants et/ou dont l'appréhension du monde qui les entoure ne correspond pas aux codes sociétaux. Parmi les jeunes délinquants ou encore les personnes toxicodépendantes par exemple, les notions telles que la « société » et la « norme sociale » ne sont en effet pas toujours univoques.[66] Dans de tels cas, il s'agit essentiellement de faire découvrir à la personne les moyens d'intégrer les principes de fonctionnement de base d'une société normée et de l'accompagner dans sa quête d'équilibre entre son bien-être personnel et le respect des normes sociales communément admises.

Au cœur de ces questionnements, se niche la question de savoir si les facteurs identifiés comme pouvant influencer le désistement sont uniques ou s'ils constituent le simple revers des facteurs de risque de récidive.[67] Si cette dernière lecture prévalait au commencement des travaux portant sur le désistement[68], il est désormais admis qu'il n'est pas de parfaite symétrie et que les facteurs de désistement doivent être différenciés des prédicteurs de la récidive.[69] Un exemple de cette asymétrie porte sur le fait d'avoir des enfants, événement qui

---

64 T. Ward & S. Maruna, *Rehabilitation: Beyond the Risk Paradigm*, Abingdon: Routledge, 2007.

65 D.A. Andrews & J. Bonta, *The Psychology of Criminal Conduct*, New Jersey: Anderson Publishing, 2010.

66 L.R. Huesmann, L.D. Eron & E.F. Dubow, 'Childhood Predictors of Adult Criminality: Are all Risk Factors reflected in Childhood Aggressiveness?', 12 *Criminal Behaviour and Mental Health* 3 (2002), p. 185-208; L. Nadeau & C. Biron, *Pour une meilleure compréhension de la toxicomanie*, Laval: Presses universitaires de Laval, 2002; G.M. Vincent, M.J. Vitacco, T. Grisso & R.R. Corrado, 'Subtypes of Adolescent Offenders: Affective Traits and Antisocial Behavior Patterns', 21 *Behavioral Sciences and the Law* 6 (2003), p. 695-712.

67 R. Sampson & J. Laub, 'Desistance from Crime over the Life Course', in: J. Mortimer & M. Shanahan (eds), *Handbook of the Life Course*, London: Springer, 2003.

68 M.R. Gottfredson & T. Hirschi, *A General Theory of Crime*, Stanford: Stanford University Press, 1990.

69 R. Sampson & J. Laub, 'Desistance from Crime over the Life Course', in: J. Mortimer & M. Shanahan (eds), *Handbook of the Life Course*, London: Springer, 2003.

peut soit inciter au désistement soit être un facteur de risque de récidive s'il est vécu comme stressant.[70] De plus, les facteurs de désistement sont réputés variés d'une personne à l'autre. Ainsi, les résultats des études entreprises en Finlande montrent que le fait de trouver un travail favorise le désistement chez les hommes de plus de 34 ans, bien que le même événement n'ait pas ou peu d'effet pour un mineur.[71] Dans le même ordre d'idées, la détention peut être conçue comme un prolongement d'une trajectoire criminelle ou comme une rupture (partielle ou complète) dans le parcours d'un délinquant.[72] Dans cette perspective, les changements et conditions d'adaptation de la personne induits par la détention sont considérés d'importance. Les modalités, le moment et la durée de l'incarcération, ses répercussions post-libératoires et, par extension, ses conséquences sur le désistement secondaire peuvent en particulier s'avérer des facteurs spécifiques de l'implication dans le processus du désistement dont il convient de tenir compte de façon prospective. Une expérience réalisée en Angleterre et au Pays de Galles sous le nom du projet *OASys* (« *Offender Assessment System* ») en atteste.[73] Conçu initialement comme base de stockage de données résultant des évaluations actuarielles, le OASys a progressivement été envisagé comme un système de transmission des informations entre les services pénitentiaires et de probation. Il s'est avéré que les résultats de type actuariel présents dans le OASys mis au service des projets de désistement personnels facilitent considérablement les tâches d'orientation des programmes de soutien aux personnes en voie de libération. Si nombre de critiques peuvent certes être opposés à ce système[74], il demeure une tentative de créer des passerelles entre les autorités intra et extra-muros et par là même soutient l'importance d'accorder plus d'attention à la transition du sortant de prison.[75] Outre le fait qu'elle restitue le sujet au cœur de son processus de changement, l'approche fondée sur le désistement offre donc des perspectives d'implications pratiques importantes pour une meilleure planification des programmes destinés à aider les détenus dans leur réhabilitation et leur retour en société libre. Les connaissances qui en découlent, en particulier relativement au processus d'adaptation personnelle en milieu de contrainte et à l'approche multifactorielle de la récidive et de la

---

70 J. Savolainen, 'Work, Family and Criminal Desistance: Adult Social Bonds in a Nordic Welfare State', 49 *British Journal of Criminology* 3 (2009), p. 285-304.

71 J. Savolainen, 'Work, Family and Criminal Desistance: Adult Social Bonds in a Nordic Welfare State', 49 *British Journal of Criminology* 3 (2009), p. 285-304.

72 M. DeLisi, 'Criminal Careers Behind Bars', 21 *Behavioral Sciences and the Law* 5 (2003) p. 653-669; L. Kazemian & M. Le Blanc, 'Differential Cost Avoidance and Successful Criminal Careers', 53 *Crime & Delinquency* 1 (2007), p. 38-63.

73 G. Robinson, 'Implementing OASys: Lessons from Research into LSI-R and ACE', 50 *Probation Journal* 1 (2003), p. 30-40.

74 M. Maguire & P. Raynor, 'How the Resettlement of Prisoners Promotes Desistance from Crime: Or does it?', 6 *Criminology and Criminal* Justice 1 (2006), p. 19-38.

75 D. Healy, *The Dynamics of Desistance. Charting Pathways through Change*, Cullompton: Willan Publishing, 2010.

réhabilitation, sont susceptibles non seulement de combler certaines lacunes actuelles propres à la préparation de l'exécution de la peine, mais aussi de dynamiser le système d'individualisation de la sanction.

7. DISCUSSION

En conclusion, les finalités contemporaines de l'exécution de la peine reposent essentiellement sur une idée de réhabilitation et de prévention de la récidive, voire dans les cas réputés de « dangereux » de neutralisation. Suivant ces objectifs, les professionnels œuvrant en les murs sont amenés à composer avec des visées potentiellement contradictoires, entre réhabilitation et protection de la collectivité. Si l'on s'intéresse toutefois de près aux politiques et pratiques professionnelles auprès de personnes judiciarisées, il semble que ces objectifs pénologiques tendent aujourd'hui à s'effacer progressivement derrière une rationalité de type managérial gouvernée par un fort principe de précaution.[76] Le mouvement fondé sur les données probantes en particulier, tout investi à asseoir l'importance de la réhabilitation sur des données scientifiques et démontrer ses preuves aux décideurs, semble avoir alimenté la propension des autorités carcérales, probablement sous l'influx de leurs instances politiques, à investir la « Nouvelle gestion publique ».

La nouvelle pénologie nous offrait déjà une grille de lecture susceptible de nous mettre en garde. Pour Feeley et Simon au début des années 90 aux Etats-Unis, le modèle correctionnel privilégié tendait non plus à transformer/traiter les individus, mais plutôt à gérer les risques qu'ils représentent.[77] Au tournant du 21ème siècle, il semble que cette tendance se soit renforcée à l'aune d'une « version néolibérale de l'expérience carcérale »[78], soutenue par des stratégies de prise en charge des détenus fondées sur des modèles probabilistes et des outils

---

76 M. Barry, 'The Mentor/Monitor Debate in Criminal Justice: « What Works » for Offenders', 30 *British Journal of Social Work* 5 (2000), p. 575-595; N. Rose, 'At Risk of Madness', in: T. Baker & J. Simon (eds), *Embracing Risk: The Changing Culture of Insurance and Responsibility*, Chicago: University of Chicago Press, 2002, p. 209-237; S. Lewis, 'Rehabilitation: Headline or Footnote in the New Penal Policy?', 52 *Probation Journal* 2 (2005), p. 119-135; A. Liebling, 'Prisons in Transition', 29 *International Journal of Law and* Psychiatry 5 (2006), p. 422-430; F. McNeill, N. Burns, S. Halliday, N. Hutton *et al.*, 'Risk, Responsibility and Reconfiguration: Penal Adaptation and Misadaptation', 11 *Punishment and Society* 4 (2009), p. 419-442; S. Pollack, 'Labelling Clients « Risky »: Social Work and the Neo-liberal Welfare State', 40 *British Journal of Social* Work 4 (2010), p. 1263-1278; M. Jendly (à paraître), 'Performance, transparence et accountability: une équation (dé)responsabilisante des professionnels exerçant en prison?', *Déviance et société*.

77 M. Feeley & J. Simon, 'The New Penology: Notes on the Emerging Strategy of Corrections and its Implications, 30 *Criminology* 4 (1992), p. 449-474; P. Mary, 'Pénalité et gestion des risques. Vers une justice « actuarielle » en Europe?', 25 *Déviance et société* 1 (2001), p. 33-51.

78 D. Robert & S. Frigon, 'La santé comme mirage des transformations carcérales', 30 *Déviance et société* 3 (2006), p. 305, 308.

managériaux de plus en plus proches d'une logique méritocratique de marché. Si cette tendance coïncide avec d'autres transformations économiques, politiques et culturelles actuelles de l'ordre social occidental, nous osons toutefois douter que ce soit là la voie la plus pertinente, à tout le moins pas en terme de prétendue humanisation du vécu carcéral, et ce tant pour les détenus que les intervenants.

Dans ces conditions, il importe de rester vigilants et peut-être renverser certaines perspectives. Le modèle fondé sur les bonnes vies, de même que les travaux portant sur le désistement semblent constituer des avenues fécondes. Ils investissent une approche plus compréhensive, au-delà de facteurs explicatifs tirés des théories criminologiques de la maturation, du choix rationnel ou encore du contrôle social.[79] Il ne s'agit ici pas tant d'expliquer, mais de tenter de comprendre, du point de vue des principaux intéressés, les différentes étapes qui jalonnent leur processus de changement en laissant libre cours à leurs réflexions et projections.[80] Dans cette perspective, l'important n'est pas seulement d'identifier les composants ou les motivations qui participent à la cessation des activités criminelles, mais plutôt de voir « comment ces éléments interagi[ss]ent ensemble, à travers le temps, et pourraient conduire à un désistement criminel durable ».[81] Les travaux de chercheurs qui s'intéressent au processus de désistement criminel à partir des *récits de vie* de personnes condamnées sont particulièrement saisissants lorsqu'ils sont mis en relation avec d'autres éléments contextuels.[82] Ils présument l'importance de restituer au cœur de la prise en charge l'expression de la parole du sujet. Ils renvoient en filigrane à la possibilité pour le praticien de tenter d'entrer dans le cadre de référence de ce dernier pour amorcer ensemble le travail, dans la durée et dans une approche d'inspiration quasi phénoménologique.[83] Donner du temps au récit, restituer le sujet au cœur de son processus de changement, adopter une démarche compréhensive plutôt qu'explicative ou responsabilisante, loin, très loin de la standardisation précédemment invoquée, des cotes aux grilles actuarielles et des impératifs de rentabilité, serait-ce ici que résident les clés d'un horizon réhabilitatif prometteur ?

---

79 D. Casoni, 'L'étude du processus de changement chez des hommes condamnés à de longues peines', 43 *Criminologie* 2 (2010), p. 351-372.

80 M. Barry, 'The Mentor/Monitor Debate in Criminal Justice : « What Works » for Offenders', 30 *British Journal of Social Work* 2 (2000), p. 575-595.

81 D. Casoni, 'L'étude du processus de changement chez des hommes condamnés à de longues peines', 43 *Criminologie* 2 (2010), p. 351, 354.

82 S. Maruna, *Making Good*, Washington, DC: APA Press, 2001; S. Farrall & A. Calverley, *Understanding Desistance from Crime. Theoretical Directions in Resettlement and Rehabilitation*, London : Open University Press, 2006; B. Weaver & F. McNeill, 'Travelling Hopefully : Desistance Theory and Probation Practice', in : J. Brayford, F. Cowe & J. Deering (eds), *What Else Works ? Creative Work with Offenders*, Cullompton : Willan Publishing, 2010, p. 36-60; D. Casoni, 'L'étude du processus de changement chez des hommes condamnés à de longues peines', 43 *Criminologie* 2 (2010), p. 351-372.

83 C. Debuyst, *Essais de criminologie clinique. Entre psychologie et justice pénale*, Bruxelles : Éditions Larcier, 2010; C. Adam, *Délinquants sexuels et pratiques psychosociales. Rester clinicien en milieu carcéral*, Bruxelles : Larcier, 2011.

BIBLIOGRAPHIE

Adam, C. (2011). *Délinquants sexuels et pratiques psychosociales. Rester clinicien en milieu carcéral*. Bruxelles: Larcier.

Adam, C. (2007). 'Innovation «thérapeutique» en milieu carcéral: du «ver dans le fruit» au «levain dans la pâte»', *Champ pénal/Penal field* (En ligne: http://champpenal.revues.org/2522).

Andrews, D.A. (2001). 'Principes des programmes correctionnels efficaces', in: L.L. Motiuk & R.C. Serin (eds), *Compendium 2000 des programmes correctionnels efficaces*, Ottawa: Ministère des Approvisionnements et Services Canada, p. 10-19.

Andrews, D.A. & J. Bonta (2010). *The Psychology of Criminal Conduct*. New Jersey: Anderson Publishing.

Andrews, D.A. & C. Dowden (2006). 'Risk Principle of Case Classification in Correctional Treatment: A Meta-analytic Investigation', 50 *International Journal of Offender Therapy and Comparative Criminology* 1, p. 88-100.

Allen, F. A. (1981). *The Decline of the Rehabilitative Ideal: Penal Policy and Social Purpose*. New Haven: Yale University Press.

Balier, C. (1996). *Psychanalyse des comportements sexuels violents*. Paris: PUF.

Barry, M. (2000). 'The Mentor/Monitor Debate in Criminal Justice: "What Works" for Offenders', 30 *British Journal of Social Work* 5, p. 575-595.

Besozzi, C. (1998/1999). *Die (Un)fähigkeit zur veränderung*. Berne: Office fédéral de la justice.

Birgden, A. (2002). 'Therapeutic jurisprudence and "Good Lives": A Rehabilitation Framework for Corrections', 37 *Australian Psychologist* 3, p. 180-186.

Bolle, P.-H. (sous la dir. de) (1992). *Droits fondamentaux et détention pénale*, Actes du septième Colloque international de la Fondation internationale pénale et pénitentiaire, Neuchâtel/Suisse, 3-7 octobre.

Bushway, S. *et al.* (2001). 'An empirical framework for studying desistance as a process', 39 *Criminology* 2, p. 491-516.

Casoni, D. (2010). 'L'étude du processus de changement chez des hommes condamnés à de longues peines', 43 *Criminologie* 2, p. 351-372.

Chantraine, G. (2006). 'La prison post-disciplinaire', 30 *Déviance et Société* 3, p. 273-288.

Christie, N. (2003). *L'industrie de la punition. Prison et politique pénale en Occident*. Paris: Autrement.

Combessie, P. (2000). 'Ouverture des prisons, jusqu'à quel point?', in: C. Veil & D. Lhuilier (sous la dir. de), *La prison en changement*, Ramonville Saint-Agne: Erès, p. 69-99.

Cortoni, F. & D. Lafortune (2009). 'Le traitement correctionnel fondé sur des données probantes: une recension', 42 *Criminologie* 1, p. 61-89.

Cullen, F.T. (2005). 'The Twelve People who saved Rehabilitation: How the Science of Criminology made a Difference. The American Society of Criminology 2004 Presidential Address', 43 *Criminology* 1, p. 1-42.

Cullen, F.T. & K.E. Gilbert (1982). *Reaffirming Rehabilitation*. Cincinnati: Anderson.

DeLisi, M. (2003). 'Criminal Careers Behind Bars', 21 *Behavioral Sciences and the Law* 5, p. 653-669.

De Wree, E., T. Vander Beken & G. Vermeulen (2009). 'The Transfer of Sentenced Persons in Europe. Much ado about Reintegration', 11 *Punishment and Society* 1, p. 111-128.

Debuyst, C. (2010). *Essais de criminologie clinique. Entre psychologie et justice pénale.* Bruxelles: Éditions Larcier.

Digneffe, F. & C. Adam (2004). 'Le développement de la criminologie clinique à l'Ecole de Louvain', 37 *Criminologie* 1, p. 43-70.

Dumont, H. (1993). *Pénologie: le droit canadien relatif aux peines et aux sentences.* Montréal: Thémis.

Favard, J. (1987). *Des prisons.* Paris: Gallimard.

Farrall, S. & A. Calverley (2006). *Understanding Desistance from Crime. Theoretical Directions in Resettlement and Rehabilitation.* London: Open University Press.

Farrall, S. (1995). 'Why Do People Stop Offending?', 1 *Scottish Journal of Criminal Justice Studies* 1, p. 51-59.

Farrall, S., A. Bottoms & J. Shapland (2010). 'Social Structures and Desistance from Crime', 7 *European Journal of Criminology* 6, p. 546-570.

Feeley, M. & J. Simon (1992). 'The New Penology: Notes on the Emerging Strategy of Corrections and its Implications', 30 *Criminology* 4, p. 449-474.

Garland, D. (2007). 'Adaptations politiques et culturelles des sociétés à forte criminalité', 31 *Déviance et société* 4, p. 387-403.

Garland, D. (2001). *The Culture of Control. Crime and Social Order in Contemporary Society.* Oxford: Oxford University Press.

Gendreau, P. & R. Ross (1979). 'Effective Correctional Treatment: Bibliotherapy for Cynics', 25 *Crime and Delinquency* 4, p. 463-489.

Gendreau, P. & R. Ross (1987). 'Revivification of Rehabilitation: Evidence from the 1980s', 4 *Justice Quarterly* 3, p. 349-407.

Gottfredson, M.R. & T. Hirschi (1990). *A General Theory of Crime.* Stanford: Stanford University Press.

Hannah-Moffat, K. (2005). 'Criminogenic Needs and the Transformative Risk Subject: Hybridations of Risk/Need in Penality', 7 *Punishment and Society* 1, p. 29-51.

Hannah-Moffat, K. (2000). 'Prisons that Empower. Neo-liberal Governance in Canadian Women's Prisons', 40 *British Journal of Criminology* 2, p. 510-531.

Hannah-Moffat K. & M. Shaw (2001). 'Situation risquée: le risque et les services correctionnels au Canada', 34 *Criminologie* 1, p. 47-72.

Healy, D. (2010). *The Dynamics of Desistance. Charting Pathways through Change.* Cullompton: Willan Publishing.

Huesmann, L.R., L.D. Eron & E.F. Dubow (2002). 'Childhood Predictors of Adult Criminality: Are all Risk Factors reflected in Childhood Aggressiveness?', 12 *Criminal Behaviour and Mental Health* 3, p. 185-208.

Jendly, M. (2012). 'Performance, transparence et accountability: une équation (dé) responsabilisante des professionnels exerçant en prison?', 36 *Déviance et société* 3, p. 243-262.

Jendly, M. (2005). *La coexistence des secrets en exécution de peine privative de liberté. Vers un modèle de partage des informations confidentielles en milieu carcéral*, Thèse en droit, Université de Neuchâtel.

Kaminski, D. (2009). *Pénalité, Management, innovation.* Namur: Presses universitaires de Namur.

Kaminski, D., S. Snacken & M. Van de Kerchove (2007). 'Mutations dans le champ des peines et de leur exécution', 31 *Déviance et société* 4, p. 487-504.

Kazemian, L. & M. Le Blanc (2007). 'Differential Cost Avoidance and Successful Criminal Careers', 53 *Crime & Delinquency* 1, p. 38-63.

Killias, M. (2001). *Précis de criminologie*, 2e éd. Berne: Stämpfli.

Lalande, P. (2006). 'Punir ou réhabiliter les contrevenants? Du «Nothing Works» au «What Works» (Montée, déclin et retour de l'idéal de réhabilitation)', in: P. Lalande & O. Lamalice, *La sévérité pénale à l'heure du populisme*, Québec: Ministère de la sécurité publique du Québec, p. 30-77.

Laub, J.H. & R.J. Sampson (2001). 'Understanding Desistance form Crime', in: M. Tonry (ed), *Crime and Justice: a Review of Research*, vol. 28., Chicago: University of Chicago Press, p. 1-69.

Lewis, S. (2005). 'Rehabilitation: Headline or Footnote in the New Penal Policy?', 52 *Probation Journal* 2, p.119-135.

Liebling, A. (2006). 'Prisons in Transition', 29 *International Journal of Law and Psychiatry* 5, p. 422-430.

Liebling, A. & S. Maruna (2005). 'Introduction: the Effects of Imprisonment Revisited', in: A. Liebling & S. Maruna (eds), *The Effects of Imprisonment*, Cullompton: Willan Publishing, p. 1-29.

Lindsay, W.R., T. Ward, T. Morgan & I. Wilson (2007). 'Self-regulation of Sex Offending, Future Pathways and the Good Lives Model: Applications and Problems', 13 *Journal of Sexual Aggression* 1, p. 37-50.

Lipsey, M.W. & D.B. Wilson (1993). 'The Efficacy of Psychological, Educational, and Behavioral Treatment: Confirmation from Meta-analysis', 48 *American Psychologist* 12, p. 1181-1209.

Lynch, M. (2000). 'Rehabilitation as Rhetoric. The Ideal of Reformation in Contemporary Parole Discourse and Practices', 2 *Punishment & Society* 1, p. 40-65.

MacKenzie, D., R.B. Layton, D. McDowall & C. Souryal (1995). 'Boot Camp Prisons and Recidivism in eight States', 33 *Criminology* 3, p. 327-357.

Maguire, M. & P. Raynor (2006). 'How the Resettlement of Prisoners Promotes Desistance from Crime: Or does it?', 6 *Criminology and Criminal Justice* 1, p. 19-38.

Marshall, W.L. *et al.* (2005). 'Working Positively With Sexual Offenders: Maximizing the Effectiveness of Treatment', 20 *Journal of Interpersonal Violence* 9, p. 1096-1114.

Martinson, R. (1974). 'What Works? Questions and Answers about Prison Reform', 35 *The Public Interest* (spring), p. 22-54.

Martinson, R. (1979). 'New Findings, New Views: A Note of Caution Regarding Sentencing Reform', 7 *Hofstra Law Review* 2, p. 243-258.

Maruna, S. (2011). 'Reentry as a Rite of Passage', 13 *Punishment and Society* 1, p. 3-28.

Maruna, S. (2001). *Making Good.* Washington, DC: APA Press.

Mary, P. (2001). 'Pénalité et gestion des risques. Vers une justice «actuarielle» en Europe?', 25 *Déviance et société* 1, p.33-51.

Mathiesen, T. (1990). *Prison on Trial: a Critical Assessment.* London: Sage Publications.

McCulloch, T. (2005). 'Probation, Social Context and Desistance: Retracing the Relationship', 52 *Probation Journal* 1, p. 8-22.

McCulloch, T. & L. Kelly (2007). 'Working with Sex Offenders in Context: Which Way forward?', 54 *Probation Journal* 1, p. 7-21.

McGuire, J. (2001). 'What Works in Correctional Intervention? Evidence and Practical Implications', in: G.A. Bernfeld, D.P. Farrington & A.W. Leschied (dir.), *Offender Rehabilitation in Practice. Implementing and Evaluating Effective Programs*, Chichester: John Wiley & Sons, LTD, p. 25-44.

McMurran, M., E. Theodosi, A. Sweeney & J. Sellen (2008). 'What Do Prisoners Want? Current Concerns of Adult Male Prisoners', 14 *Psychology, Crime & Law* 3, p. 267-274.

McNeill, F. (2003). 'Desistance-focused Probation Practice', in: W.H. Chui & M. Nellis (eds), *Moving Probation Forward: Evidence, Arguments and Practice*, Edinburgh: Pearson Longman, p. 146-162.

McNeill, F. *et al.* (2009). 'Risk, Responsibility and Reconfiguration: Penal Adaptation and Misadaptation', 11 *Punishment and Society* 4, p. 419-442.

Milburn, P. (2007). 'La fin du disciplinaire? Rationalité pénale et processus de normalisation au 21ème siècle', in: M. Cicchini & M. Porret (eds), *Les sphères du pénal avec Michel Foucault*. Genève: Antipodes.

Morris, N. & D. Rothman (eds) (1995). *The Oxford History of the Prison*. New York: Oxford University Press.

Nadeau, L. & C. Biron (2002). *Pour une meilleure compréhension de la toxicomanie*. Laval: Presses universitaires de Laval.

Palmer, T. (1975). 'Martinson revisited', 12 *Journal of Research in Crime and Delinquency* 2, p. 133-152.

Pires, A. (2008). 'La formation de la rationalité pénale moderne au XVIIIe siècle', in: C. Debuyst, F. Digneffe & A. Pires, *Histoire des savoirs sur le crime et la peine: Tome 2, La rationalité pénale et la naissance de la criminologie*, Bruxelles: Larcier, p. 21-247.

Petersilia, J. (2003). *When Prisoners come Home. Parole and Prisoner Reentry*. Oxford: Oxford University Press.

Petersilia, J. & S. Turner (1993). *Evaluating Intensive Supervision Probation/Parole: Results of a Nationwide Experiment*. Washington, DC: National Institute of Justice.

Pollack, S. (2010). 'Labelling Clients "Risky": Social Work and the Neo-liberal Welfare State', 40 *British Journal of Social Work* 4, p. 1263-1278.

Quirion, B. (2009). 'Le détenu responsable et autonome: la nouvelle cible de l'intervention correctionnelle au Canada', 7-8 *Revue de droit pénal et de criminologie* (juillet), p. 818-835.

Quirion, B. (2006). 'Traiter les délinquants ou contrôler les conduites: le dispositif thérapeutique à l'ère de la nouvelle pénologie', 39 *Criminologie* 2, p. 137-164.

Raynor, P. & G. Robinson (2005). *Rehabilitation, Crime and Justice*. Basingstoke: Palgrave Macmillan.

Rex, S. (1999). 'Desistance from Offending: Experiences of Probation', 38 *The Howard Journal of Criminal Justice* 4, p. 366-383.

Robert, D. & S. Frigon (2006). 'La santé comme mirage des transformations carcérales', 30 *Déviance et société* 3, p. 305-322.

Robinson, G. (2003). 'Implementing OASys: Lessons from Research into LSI-R and ACE', 50 *Probation Journal* 1, p. 30-40.

Robinson, G. (2008). 'Late-modern Rehabilitation: The Evolution of a Penal Strategy', 10 *Punishment and Society* 4, p. 429-445.

Robinson, G. (1999). 'Risk Management and Rehabilitation in the Probation Service: Collision and Collusion', 38 *The Howard Journal of Criminal Justice* 4, p. 421-33.

Rodrigues, A.M. (1999). 'Consensualisme et prison', in: *Nouvelles orientations du régime pénitentiaire*, Actes des Journées internationales de la Fondation internationale pénale et pénitentiaire, Lisbonne/Portugal, 21-25 mai 1999, p. 147-171.

Rose, N. (2002). 'At Risk of Madness', in: T. Baker & J. Simon (eds), *Embracing Risk: The Changing Culture of Insurance and Responsibility*, Chicago: University of Chicago Press, p. 209-237.

Rose, N. (2000). 'Government and Control', 40 *British Journal of Criminology* 2, p. 321-339.

Rose, N. (1998). 'Governing Risky Individuals: The Role of Psychiatry in New Regimes of Control', 5 *Psychiatry, Psychology and Law* 2, p. 177-195.

Rotman, E. (1990). *Beyond Punishment: A New View on the Rehabilitation of Criminal Offenders*. New York: Greenwood Press.

Sampson, R. & J. Laub (2003). 'Desistance from Crime over the Life Course', in: J. Mortimer & M. Shanahan (eds), *Handbook of the Life Course*, London: Springer.

Savolainen, J. (2009). 'Work, Family and Criminal Desistance: Adult Social Bonds in a Nordic Welfare State', 49 *British Journal of Criminology* 3, p. 285-304.

Seligman, M.E.P. (2008). 'Positive Health', 57 *Applied Psychology: An International Review* 1, p. 3-18.

Serin, R.C. & C.D. Lloyd (2009). 'Examining the Process of Offender Change: the Transition to Crime Desistance', 15 *Psychology, Crime & Law* 4, p. 347-364.

Sherman L.W. *et al.* (1997). *Preventing Crime: What Works, What Doesn't, What's Promising. A Report to the United States Congress*. MD: University of Maryland, Department of Criminology and Criminal Justice.

Stanford, S. (2010). '"Speaking Back to Fear": Responding to the Moral Dilemmas of Risk in Social Work Practice', 40 *British Journal of Social Work* 4, p. 1065-1080.

Tonry, M. & R. Frase (eds) (2001). *Sentencing and Sanctions in Western Countries*. Oxford: Oxford University Press.

Vacheret, M. & G. Lemire (2007). *Anatomie de la prison contemporaine*. Montréal: Presses de l'Université de Montréal.

Vess, J. (2009). 'Fear and Loathing in Public Policy: Ethical Issues in Laws for Sex Offenders', 14 *Aggression and Violent Behavior* 4, p. 264-272.

Vigour, C. (2008). 'Ethos et légitimité professionnels à l'épreuve d'une approche managériale : le cas de la justice belge', 50 *Sociologie du travail* 1, p. 71-90.

Vincent, G.M., M.J. Vitacco, T. Grisso & R.R. Corrado (2003). 'Subtypes of Adolescent Offenders: Affective Traits and Antisocial Behavior Patterns', 21 *Behavioral Sciences and the Law* 6, p. 695-712.

Ward, T. & M. Brown (2004). 'The Good Lives Model and Conceptual Issues in Offender Rehabilitation', 10 *Psychology, Crime & Law* 3, p. 243-257.

Ward, T., R.M. Collie & P. Bourke (2009). 'Models of Offender Rehabilitation: The Good Lives Model and The Risk-Need-Responsivity Model', in: A. R. Beech, L. Craig, K. D. Browne (eds), *Assessment and Treatment of Sex Offenders: A Handbook*. Chichester: Wiley-Blackwell, p. 293-310.

Ward, T. & T. Gannon (2006). 'Rehabilitation, Etiology, and Self-regulation: The Comprehensive Good Lives Model of Treatment for Sexual Offenders', 11 *Aggression and Violent Behavior* 1, p. 77- 94.

Ward, T. & R. Mann (2004). 'Good Lives and the Rehabilitation of Offenders: A Positive Approach to Sex Offender Treatment', in: P.A. Linley, S. Joseph (eds), *Positive Psychology in Practice*. New Jersey: Wiley, p. 598-616.

Ward, T., R. Mann & T. Gannon (2007). 'The Good Lives Model of Offender Rehabilitation: Clinical implications', 12 *Aggression and Violent Behavior* 1, p. 87-107.

Ward, T. & S. Maruna (2007). *Rehabilitation: Beyond the Risk Paradigm*. Abingdon: Routledge.

Ward, T. & C.A. Stewart (2003). 'The Treatment of Sex Offenders: Risk Management and Good Lives', 34 *Professional Psychology: Research and Practice* 4, p. 353-360.

Weaver, B. & F. McNeill (2010). 'Travelling Hopefully: Desistance Theory and Probation Practice', in: J. Brayford, F. Cowe & J. Deering (eds), *What Else Works? Creative Work with Offenders*, Cullompton: Willan Publishing, p. 36-60.

Whitehead, P.R., T. Ward & R.M. Collie (2007). 'Time for a Change: Applying the Good Lives Model of Rehabilitation to a High-Risk Violent Offender', 51 *International Journal of Offender Therapy and Comparative Criminology* 5, p. 578-598.

THE VALUE OF REHABILITATION TO PRISONERS

Tim Dalton*

1. INTRODUCTION: THE PRINCIPLE TERMS

The specific theme which I have been invited to address is "the value of rehabilitation to prisoners" and I think it's perhaps best to begin at the beginning: to look a little more closely at the principal terms "value", "rehabilitation" and "prisoner".

Value

Value is a term which has tended to bother the philosophers, particularly moral philosophers through the centuries. I knew from past experience that if I were to delve into the works of the great philosophers and attempt to synthesize what they meant by the term "value" it is probable that this contribution would go on for pages without reaching any conclusions. I decided therefore to leave the philosophers aside and to opt instead for the less complex definition I expected to find in the Oxford English Dictionary. Unfortunately, I found that the dictionary definition could us rapt in discussion for long too. The dictionary definition includes words like "worth", "desirability", "utility", "principles or standards", "subjective estimate of quality" and so on.

Apart from the opportunities for debate which the differences between each of these words might present, there is of course the very fundamental question as to whose values we're talking about in the first place. Are we really talking about the value, utility or worth of rehabilitation from the prisoner's perspective or are we talking about our views as to what the prisoner should consider to be worthwhile in life? I suspect that we're really talking about the latter, but you may of course disagree with me on this.

* T. Dalton is former Secretary General of the Department of Justice and Equality in Ireland, was a member of the European Committee for the Prevention of Torture and a member of the Criminal Law Mental Health Review Board.

Rehabilitation

When it came to the term "rehabilitation" I decided to avoid the philosophers and proceed directly to the English Dictionary. Here, again, there was a variety of definitional words and concepts presenting considerable room for debate. For example, the dictionary includes the following: "restoration of privileges, reputation or proper condition". More pertinently, there was the statement that, in the case of ex-prisoners, rehabilitation means "restore to effectiveness or normal life by training". But how can one restore to "normal" life a person who has never had what most of us might consider to be a normal life? Are we talking about reintegration into the prisoner's own community and his own ethnic grouping, with appropriate post-release interventions and support systems, and is that what we mean by "rehabilitation"?

Prisoner

Finally, when it came to the term "prisoner" I avoided both the philosophers and the dictionary. After all, it's pretty clear – or so I thought – that a prisoner could be defined as a person deprived of his liberty for a prescribed period on the basis of a decision by a judge that this was warranted because the person concerned had been in breach of the criminal law.

Again, of course, this definition doesn't give the full picture. For example there isn't always clarity about the period of detention – in some jurisdictions there is provision for preventive detention following expiry of the initial sentence which can, in practice, convert what initially looks like a determinate sentence into a whole life sentence. And of course it isn't invariably the case that imprisonment will follow upon a trial – in this jurisdiction, for example, there is provision for internment without trial in certain circumstances – basically where the security of the State is under serious threat. It is the case also that imprisonment can involve much more than deprivation of liberty – in some cases it can extend to additional forms of deprivation such as limited family contact and, sometimes, even solitary confinement. Imprisonment, it is true, generally results from breaches of the criminal law but it is also true that many people end up in prison because they cannot pay their civil debts.

2. SPECIAL CATEGORIES OF PRISONERS AND EX-PRISONERS

So far I've been talking in rather general terms, and you may feel that the drift of what I'm saying is that it is virtually impossible to say anything at all on the subject of the rehabilitation of prisoners that isn't so full of exceptions and caveats as to be hardly worth saying in the first place. But that is not my point –

my point is that the subject we are dealing with is quite a complex one and that it would require much more time than is now available to us to deal with it comprehensively. To illustrate the point, I discuss three categories of prisoners and ex-prisoners I've had experience of dealing with.

Travelling Community

The first are those who belong to the Travelling Community. Irish Travellers traditionally lived a nomadic lifestyle. Life in caravans on the roadsides of Ireland was difficult and it has been the policy of successive governments to encourage Travellers to settle in houses and at halting sites specially provided for that purpose.

Sensible though this policy approach may seem to be, many Travellers were far from happy with the policies pursued by Governments. Their spokespersons – and many others besides – argued that they were and are members of a separate ethnic grouping, that this should be formally recognized and that the effect of Government policy was to ignore and undermine their separate cultural identity.

This topic is not one that we are likely to resolve this morning. The point I want to make is that there were and are features of Traveller culture that raise rather complex questions when it comes to deciding what actions can be considered appropriate – and indeed permissible – when attempting to "rehabilitate" Travellers who happen to become prisoners.

It is well recognized that Traveller women, for example, who are married have traditionally placed high value on the concept of loyalty and fidelity to their husbands. While this, I suppose, should be considered a commendable attribute in all married women – and indeed in all married men also – it is very often the case that Traveller women will tend to put up with domestic violence and remain in the family home in circumstances where many – though by no means all – women in the settled community, undergoing a similar experience, would look for external help and for legal remedies.

A report published in 2009 found that, in proportional terms, Traveller women were 30 times more likely to suffer domestic violence than were other women in Ireland. However, determination to remain in the family home tended to be seen as a duty – something which was valued and respected by mothers and other members of that community.

It is by no means clear (certainly not clear to me) exactly what form of rehabilitative action should be taken by Prison authorities in such cases; how does one ensure protection from abuse while at the same time acknowledging and respecting the prisoner's own deeply held values and the expectations of the community to which she will return? Again it would appear that the requirement is reinstatement in their own community – but with necessary post-release supports in place – rather than attempting conversion to a value system that accords with majority thinking as to what a citizen requires to be "normal".

Detainees in Mental Hospital

A second category of detainees I want to mention – and I've briefly referred to them earlier – are those detained in the Central Mental Hospital in Dublin. People held at this Institution fall into three broad categories. First, there are those who are charged with criminal offences, sometimes very serious offences but were deemed by a Court to be unfit to plead to those charges due to mental illness. Second are those who were tried but were found at the conclusion of the trial not guilty by reason of insanity. The third category are those who, while serving imprisonment terms at other penal institutions, were found to be suffering from a mental illness which had not be diagnosed – or may not have been present – at the time of the original trial.

The task of the Review Board, of which I am a member, is to assess on a regular basis whether the detention of those concerned continues to be warranted and to grant conditional or unconditional release where the Board judges it right to do so. It goes without saying that the concept of rehabilitation in the case of these detainees is inseparable from the provision of specialized treatment. Here, again, some very important issues arise as to what constitutes appropriate rehabilitative action on behalf of the authorities.

Psychiatrists will, quite often, recommend and apply pharmacological remedies – and this indeed may be the only valid course of action to take, depending on the illness involved. However, we need to be sure that mechanisms are in place to guarantee that patient consent to treatment is valid. We need to be sure that sufficient weight has been given to non-pharmacological forms of intervention. And before all of this, of course, we need to ensure that all prisoners suffering from mental illness are receiving treatment. This is certainly not the case in Ireland – nor is it the case in many other jurisdictions – though genuine efforts have been made here in recent years to improve access to treatment for those in need. Mentally ill prisoners who are denied access to treatment are, by definition, also denied the opportunity for rehabilitation.

Politically Motivated Prisoners

The third prisoner and ex-prisoner grouping that I want to mention are those I encountered when involved as a frontline negotiator in the Northern Ireland Peace Process. These were quite different to other prisoners but may not be very different to politically motivated prisoners elsewhere. Most people associate the Northern Peace Process with the arrival of leading politicians including the British Prime Minister and Ireland's Taoiseach at castles and great houses where they engaged, sometimes for days on end, in negotiations with the Northern Ireland political parties.

What is less fully understood is that the groundwork for these major engagements was prepared by small teams of British and Irish civil servants who, in the periods between these major get-togethers, engaged directly with the Northern Ireland political parties and others at all sorts of venues and all hours of the day and night. Michael Mellett, who is a member of the IPPF, was also involved in this process.

My focus, as one of the senior officials on the Irish side, tended to be on security-related matters – arms decommissioning, prisoners, demilitarization, policing as well as generally attempting to work out what might or might not persuade the IRA to bring violence to an end. With that particular menu, I suppose it could be said that, in some ways, I ended up with the rough end of the stick.

The main players on the republican side (*i.e.* the Sinn Fein negotiating team) were, in many cases, either convicted members of the IRA or, at the very minimum, carried strong IRA credentials. Some had been released from prisons in the recent past and others, who were influential persuaders for peace, were still serving time in prison.

Now, the first thing that I can absolutely confirm was that there was no point whatsoever in attempting to engage with these interlocutors on the basis of any preconceived notion as to what their "rehabilitation" might require. It was absolutely essential to try to get into their way of looking at the world and it very quickly became clear that, in their worldview, the people who needed rehabilitation where not sitting on their side of the negotiating table. Their viewpoint was that our deep misunderstanding of the course of Irish history was proof positive that we were the ones who needed rehabilitation. They would have seen the need for rehabilitation as being particularly acute in the case of our British colleagues because the British understanding of Irish history was even more seriously off course than ours.

And the only actions on our part which had any prospect of initiating rehabilitative engagement – either for our benefit or theirs – was serious political discussion which would address issues such as the totality of relationships between Ireland and the UK and between the North and South of Ireland, would address the respective rights of the majority and minority communities in Northern Ireland, address the concepts of equality and parity of esteem, the release of prisoners, the case for a new policing service and so on.

In return for this, of course, they recognized that the two Governments would wish to introduce a few rehabilitative topics also, such as an unambiguous guarantee that the IRA would end its violence campaign, would decommission all illegally held weapons and recognize the principle of consent. All in all, I'm sure you will agree, not the kind of program that immediately springs to mind when one talks about the rehabilitation of prisoners.

3. A PROPOSITION WITH WHICH IT SEEMS DIFFICULT TO DISAGREE

So, to go back to a question I raised earlier – accepting that there are bound to be various caveats and exceptions and acknowledging the opportunities for debate which individual terms may present, what if anything, can one say generally about the "value of rehabilitation to prisoners"? If we want to boil it down to a single proposition I suppose we could say that in general terms, it is a good thing to try, as best we can, to bring prisoners to appreciate that it will be to their own benefit and the benefit of society if, upon release, they subscribe to the widely accepted norms and values of society by obeying its laws and respecting the rights of their fellow citizens. Here we have a proposition with which it seems difficult to disagree in principle. Sadly, however, we also have a proposition which many might, not unreasonably, regard as something of a pious platitude.

In saying this I want to acknowledge, first of all, that there is no doubting the sincerity and the enormous efforts made by a great many people – Prisons, Management and Personnel, Visiting Committees, Probation Officers, Educators, Spiritual Advisors and others, who devote their time and expertise day-in day-out towards the care and rehabilitation of prisoners.

Acknowledging – and indeed lauding – the extremely valuable contribution of the various professionals concerned is not the sole preserve of former public servants, like me, whose views on the subject might well be considered somewhat biased. Independent commentators have also acknowledged the value and importance of the work of those concerned and have acknowledged the contribution of Governments who have supported this work.

But that is not the whole story and, in saying this, I am taking account of experiences I've had as a member of the Committee on the Prevention of Torture and Inhuman or Degrading Treatment or Punishment (CPT) and otherwise. The creation of the Committee is provided for in a Council of Europe Convention of the same name which has now been ratified by all 47 Council of Europe States. It is one of the more powerful human rights protection bodies functioning at international level and provides for visits by Committee Delegations to all participating jurisdictions with a right to visit all places of detention, to talk privately to prisoners and examine all records without impediment.

Those of you who are familiar with the Committee will be aware that most of its Reports are published and that what they show is that, while detention conditions within Council of Europe States are improving – attributable in no small measure to the work of the CPT – there is still much about the way in which we treat prisoners to suggest that my reference to platitudes is not out of place.

Before I go any further I want to stress that the views I'm expressing are personal and that I'm not here speaking on behalf of the CPT. And I want to stress also that I'm not talking only about conditions in less developed or less affluent States nor am I talking only about States that would have been categorized, in the past, as totalitarian in character. Some of the States to which the following comments can be applied are so-called first world Western democracies. You will know, for example, that certain aspects of the way in which prisoners in this country have been treated has been the subject of quite strong criticism by the CPT.

It is still the case, in all too many jurisdictions, that prisoners are physically ill-treated. While instances of what might be considered as torture are uncommon, prisoners in many cases are beaten with batons, punched, kicked and humiliated by law enforcement personnel. In some cases this is taking place not only with the knowledge of State authorities but sometimes, apparently, with their tacit approval.

4. HOW TO EXPECT TO CONVINCE PRISONERS?

How can we really expect to convince prisoners who are directly undergoing or are immediately aware of experiences of this kind that there is merit in rehabilitation? How can we convince them of the need to respect the rights of their fellow citizens?

Apart from violence, it is the case that, all too often, prisoners are held in overcrowded, filthy conditions for up to 23 hours a day where those who are vulnerable are left, unprotected by staff, to the mercies of so-called crime overlords and other violent prisoners. Again there is the question – how do we expect a prisoner who has suffered in this way to trust anybody in authority upon his release from prison?

If he has been malnourished, provided with limited access to education or work opportunities during his time in prison, if he has had limited access to his immediate family members, if he is sent from the prison gates with little or no money, no place to live, depending for friendship, support and contact on former associates in crime, can we be shocked if he finds himself in trouble with the authorities and back in prison time and time again? Can we be surprised if he regards rehabilitation as a middle class preoccupation devoid of any meaning, relevance or value in his life?

The shortcomings and failures to which I've just been referring are by no means exceptional. They are commonplace and they raise a real doubt as to whether societies and their Governments are genuinely serious or fully appreciate the implications of saying that it is valuable for prisoners to undergo rehabilitation.

Rehabilitation requires considerable commitment not only inside the Prison walls but – perhaps more importantly – upon release from Prison. It is unlikely, in most cases, that rehabilitative endeavours will result in a Pauline conversion while the prisoner is still behind bars. The aim should be to return the prisoner to his own community but with post-release supports in place which are well coordinated and readily accessible to the ex-prisoner so that if he finds himself again tempted towards a criminal escapade, if he loses his accommodation, loses a relationship or whatever has somewhere to turn for help.

I've probably raised far more questions than I've answered and that this, in turn, may prompt you to raise even more questions which I will not be able to answer. But I suppose I only have myself to blame for putting myself in this position and I will do my best to answer any questions you may wish to raise.

THE VALUE OF REHABILITATION TO THE PRISONER'S FAMILY

Emilia Bouzón de Terzano*

1. THE PRISONER AS A HUMAN BEING

This article asserts that the best stategy for rehabilitation of prisoners and for crime prevention is the protection and strengthening of the family. In order to understand this it is important to acknowledge the prisoner as a human being. The individual who has been deprived of his freedom due to the violation of legal rules that regulate social life is a free and responsible human being, who has intelligence and freedom; in short, a person who has decided on his own – to a greater or lesser extent – what he did or failed to do. Unless essentially related to the human being, guilt and punishment have no sense. Even when the prisoner's acts have been influenced by diverse circumstances, guilt and punishment cannot be addressed without acknowledging a conscious and voluntary determination in him.

On this concept lies the reason of his guilt and from this fact the legitimacy of his punishment and the possibility of his moral recovery and social re-adaptation arise simultaneously. The wrongdoer does not lose his human condition due to the offence he committed, although he is limited on the exercise of some rights in order to achieve the inseparable aims of social order defence and re-adaptation of the wrongdoer to society.[1] From this concept, based on a

* Dr. E.B. Bouzón de Terzano is professor and the Director of the Institute of Criminological Studies of Argentina, President of the Secretariado de Ayuda Cristiana a las Cárceles (Secretariat of Christian Aid to Prisoners), Researcher from Conicet (Consejo Nacional de Investigaciones Científicas y Tecnológicas (National Council of Scientific and Technological Research) and Member of the Executive Board of ISPAC (International Scientific and Professional Advisory Council of the United Nations Crime Prevention and Criminal Justice Program).

1 E. Bouzón de Terzano, *Las Naciones Unidas y los Derechos Humanos del Preso* (The United Nations and the Prisoner's Human Rights), Buenos Aires, Argentina (in print), p. 2–3. See with further references to literature also P.H.P.H.M.C. van Kempen, 'Positive obligations to ensure the human rights of prisoners. Safety, healthcare, conjugal visits and the possibility of founding a family under the ICCPR, the ECHR, the ACHR, and the AfChHPR', in Peter J.P. Tak & Manon Jendly (eds), *Prison policy and prisoners' rights. The protection of prisoners' fundamental rights in international and domestic law*, IPPF volume 42, Nijmegen: Wolf Legal Publishers, 2008, p. 21–26, 43–44.

personalist and non-determinist anthropology, several and serious practical consequences arise.

The road to culpability is, hence, usually as follows: when faced with a compulsory act or omission, man makes a personal decision, he decides to disobey. His decision is followed by an external element. In order to measure the internal or subjective element of guilt, not only the external act should be taken into account but also the internal influences which have cooperated in the decision-making process of the offender, such as innate or acquired characteristics, impulses and obstacles, the influence of his education, the people and things among which he has grown, what comes from circumstances and particularly from the usual and current intensity of will, also known as the "Criminal Energy" that has contributed to committing the crime.[2] In this sense, Socrates said:

> "Under no circumstances should we be angry with offenders. On the contrary, we should teach them how to avoid committing crimes since crime is the result of ignorance and not every human being has been lucky enough to receive instruction, whether because of the loss of his parents, or otherwise."[3]

Human freedom is always present in the criminal's behaviour, although in some circumstances the offence may not be totally charged to the wrongdoer. Therefore, the prisoner still has an intimate and peculiar force in his personality, which must transform him into the leading actor of his own moral restoration. In order to achieve this, repentance for his delinquent conduct and assumption of the criminal consequences, as a step towards his future relocation in society, are essential. And here comes the function of prisons, a role of justice, a justice that is not limited to pronouncing judgment or verifying the service of a sentence but that seeks to accompany the convict in his difficult road towards regeneration, with a guardian, conscious, humane and understanding spirit.[4] Moreover, in order to achieve this aim, reintegration into society, treatment demands for a clear symptomatic and aetiological diagnosis, an individual adapted therapy, a cautious prognosis and a suitable complementary prophylaxis. Otherwise, punishment will only produce cunning convicts or resigned individuals unwilling to change or rebels resentful of society.

---

2 I. De Azpiazu, 'Concepto cristiano de la pena y características del tratamiento penitenciario' (Christian Concept of Penalty and Characteristics of Correctional Treatment), lecture delivered at the First Latin American Congress on Correctional Study and Action, Talleres Gráficos del Atlántico, Buenos Aires, 1958, p. 5–6.

3 J. Pinatel, *Traité élémentaire de science pénitentaire et de Défense Sociales: législation pénitentiaire, administration pénitentiaire, régime pénitentiaire, problèmes de défense sociale*, Melún: Recueil Sirey, 1950, Introduction, p. XXII, quoted by E. Bouzón de Terzano, *Las Naciones Unidas y los Derechos Humanos del Preso* (The United Nations and the Prisoner's Human Rights), Buenos Aires, Argentina (in print), p. 1–2.

4 I. De Azpiazu, *Mensajes* (Messages), Buenos Aires: Talleres Gráficos del Atlántico, 1958, p. 276.

It stands out clearly that the inmate cannot be left alone in this task. The above mentioned objective must be pursued by justice and community organizations created by society in its legitimate fight against crime and in favour of the social re-education of the prisoner.[5] Besides, the prisoner's family plays an essential role that will be discussed in the following section.

2. THE PRISONER AND HIS FAMILY

Under this heading we can deal with different issues: positive influence of the prisoner's family; the family's influence on criminal's genesis; the offender's influence on his own family; the influence of crime on society in general and, especially, on its basic cell, the family, and finally the family as a key factor in the prevention of crime.

2.1. POSITIVE INFLUENCE OF THE PRISONER'S FAMILY

The memory of his or her family acts upon the imagination and feelings of the lonely person incarcerated. They are usually distanced from their family as a result of their crime. In such a case, it is easy to observe the beneficial influx that the prisoner has on the restructuring of the family relations.

As stated by the VI United Nations Congress in Caracas:

> "The family was universally regarded as the most effective medium of social control normally having the strongest influence on the lives of young people. The normal family provided physical and emotional security for the child, the necessary tools for his maturation and developmental needs, as well as emotional and personality stability. Socio-economic transitions occurring in consequence of the rapid developments taking place in the developing countries had generally been observed as resulting in the decrease in the role of the family in socialization and value transmission, mainly because increased urbanization, migration and industrialization created conditions conducive to a weakening of family ties, while poverty weakened family authority and autonomy. Experiences of some countries, however, demonstrated that urbanization, industrialization, and migration/population growth *per se* were not precursors to delinquency. It was observed that efficient management, proper orientation and careful vigilance, coupled with comprehensive family assistance welfare programmes, side by side with educational

5 I. De Azpiazu, 'Concepto cristiano de la pena y características del tratamiento penitenciario' (Christian Concept of Penalty and Characteristics of Correctional Treatment), *Lecture delivered at the First Latin American Congress on Correctional Study and Action,* Talleres Gráficos del Atlántico, Buenos Aires, 1958, p. 12.

programmes, would ensure, as it had indeed ensured for some Member States, socio-economic changes without concomitant growth in juvenile delinquency. The maintenance of the family as a stable supportive unit, irrespective of development changes, was generally exhorted."[6]

The proposal on the future work in this regard to be concentrated first and foremost on the family and its central function in the prevention of crime as the main factor behind social stability was granted strong and wide support at the United Nations Congress.

2.2. THE FAMILY'S INFLUENCE ON THE CRIMINAL'S GENESIS

Delinquency and a dismantled family are closely related. This relationship is shown in numerous research projects. For instance, in the United States, more than 70% of youngsters who are in juvenile detention centres belong to families with a damaged core.[7] Similar statistics we find in different countries.

It is quite evident that the existence of deficiencies in family functions will lead to tensions, distortions and problems in family life. Duties within a family can be altered by an intolerable environment, by the physical or mental illness of one or more of its members or by serious conflicts among its members, particularly between husband and wife. One of the main duties of a family is to meet its basic needs. When these tasks cannot be satisfied, it is more difficult to maintain family integrity and a negative repercussion in society is unavoidable.[8]

The very frequent offender is the criminal result of a society unfairly organized. It is not hard to guess the moral imbalance present in the families many inmates come from. The circumstances surrounding the delinquents could not be more sombre. Illegitimate households, incomplete following the abandonment of the progenitor, violently and frequently shaken by the problems and brutally disintegrated due to the parents' separation. A moral environment which generates impulsive and rebellious attitudes, not leading to the ruling of ethical regulations. A childhood gone in exploitations.

---

6 Sixth United Nations Congress on the Prevention of Crime and the Treatment of Offenders, *Report on the Sixth Congress containing a summary of proceedings, conclusions and recommendations as adopted by the Congress*, A/CONF.87/14/Rev.1, par. 143, p. 63.

7 B. Kliksberg, 'Hacia una nueva visión de la política social en América Latina: desmontando mitos' (Towards a New Vision of Social Policy in Latin America: Destroying Myths), 8 *Revista Venezolana de Gerencia* 21 (2003), p. 21.

8 See also B. Kliksberg, 'Capital social y cultura, claves esenciales del desarrollo', *Revista de la CEPAL* 69 (1999), esp. p. 89, and Center for Research on Child Wellbeing, Princeton University, 'Parental Incarceration and Child Wellbeing in Fragile Families', *Fragile Families Research Brief* 42 (April 2008) (see further www.fragilefamilies.princeton.edu) (last visited: 1 September 2013).

This background represents valuable decision-making material to state that inmates' lives could have been different and that their criminality is originally linked to the moral imbalance of their family. This way, it is possible to explain in part, given exogenous factors, the criminal formation of their personality.[9]

2.3. THE CRIMINAL'S INFLUENCE ON HIS OWN FAMILY

If we concentrate on the prisoner, it is easy to imagine the family problems that imprisonment causes. According to a report by the United Nations[10]:

> "La encarcelación del padre o de la madre puede muchas veces desorganizar a la familia y plantear serios problemas emocionales y materiales" (Imprisonment of the father or mother may, many times, disorganise the family and cause serious emotional and material problems).
>
> We should always bear in mind that the moral and material abandonment the family is left in following the incarceration of their head is pernicious to the wife and children specially, who lacking their care and food, leave the homes and obstruct the streets... who wander around as informal salesmen or beggars and are to become due to the strength of an inexorable fatality, the future army of offenders."[11]

When the head of the family is put in prison, there is generally a grave mental and economic crisis within the family group. At these times, well-organized help could prevent many problems: severe economic problems, lack of orientation in child education, abandonment of children, general degradation, prostitution, etc.[12] Research shows that children of incarcerated parents also face considerable family instability: they are significantly less likely to live with both their parents, and are significantly more likely to experience material hardship.[13] Moreover, the economic and family challenges faced by children whose parents have been incarcerated suggest that they are also at great risk for adverse

9 I. De Azpiazu, *Mensajes* (Messages), Buenos Aires: Talleres Gráficos del Atlántico, 1958, p. 278, 282.

10 Cf. Second United Nations Congress on the Prevention of Crime and the Treatment of Offenders, London, England, August 8–19, 1960, A/CONF. 17/19, p. 13.

11 I. De Azpiazu, *Mensajes* (Messages), Buenos Aires: Talleres Gráficos del Atlántico, 1958, p. 278.

12 E. Bouzón de Terzano & J.C. García Basalo, *Realidad Post-Penitenciaria Argentina* (After Prison Reality in Argentina), Buenos Aires: Instituto de Estudios Criminológicos. Secretariado de Ayuda Cristiana a las Cárceles, 1980, p. 36. See, *e.g.*, also the contributions in Katherine Gabel & Denise Johnston (eds.), *Children of Incarcerated Parents*, New York: Lexington Books, 1995; and in Yvette R. Harris, James A. Graham & Gloria J. Oliver Carpenter (eds.), *Children of Incarcerated Parents: Theoretical Developmental and Clinical Issues*, New York: Springer Publishing, 2010.

13 Amanda Geller *et al.*, *Parental Incarceration and Child Wellbeing: Implications for Urban Families*, Annie E. Casey Foundation, 2008 (at: www.f2f.ca.gov/res/pdf/Parental_Incarceration.pdf) (last visited: 1 September 2013).

developmental outcomes.[14] These children are also significantly more likely to display anxious/depressive behavior.[15]

2.4. THE INFLUENCE OF CRIME ON SOCIETY IN GENERAL

The prisoner is part of a family, of a social, professional and/or civil community, of a State, of a municipality, and possibly also of a cultural and/or religious community. "The inmate is not only an individual but also a member of society".[16] Even if the prisoner has no active contact with people from those groups, he still maintains, at least, a legal and social bond with them. It is important that such contacts are maintained and developed in a constructive way, and do not hinder further welfare. The inmate as well as his relatives, who are often more unfortunate than the prisoner himself and are sometimes even more in need, call for assistance. Therefore, when he is set free, society should prepare itself to welcome him and facilitate his reintegration into social life. Criminality is a highly complex phenomenon of social life from the viewpoint of both its causes and its consequences. Society as a whole is affected, although sometimes indirectly, by criminal acts. An offence is a complex phenomenon as it implies a clear interdependence among the different aspects that form part of it: those issues related to the perpetrator of the crime, to the victim and, finally, to society as a whole.

2.5. THE FAMILY: A KEY FACTOR IN THE PREVENTION OF CRIME

In this day and age when ecology, *i.e.* the study of the relations that living organisms have with respect to each other and their natural environment, constitutes an undeniable value, the importance of "human ecology" cannot be forgotten. Well then, the family is the essential structure of human ecology. It may be appropriate to outline the main texts and International declarations on the subject. So first, the Universal Declaration of Human Rights, which, in its Article 16 §3 states:

> "The family is the natural and fundamental group unit of society and it is entitled to protection by society and the State".

---

14 Idem.

15 Idem.

16 Pius XII, Address to Italian Jurists on 5 December 1954.

Furthermore, Article 10 of the 1966 International Covenant on Economic, Social and Cultural Rights holds:

> "The widest possible protection and assistance should be accorded to the family, which is the natural and fundamental group unit of society, particularly for its establishment and while it is responsible for the care and education of dependent children."

Similarly, Article 23 §1 of the 1966 International Covenant on Civil and Political Rights provides:

> "The family is the natural and fundamental group unit of society and is entitled to protection by society and the State."

Moreover, the 1989 Convention on the Rights of the Child in its Preamble considers that

> "the family, as the fundamental group of society and the natural environment for the growth and well-being of all its members and particularly children, should be afforded the necessary protection and assistance so that it can fully assume its responsibilities within the community", and it recognizes that "the child, for the full and harmonious development of his or her personality, should grow up in a family environment, in an atmosphere of happiness, love and understanding".

These texts reflect a reality: the family is a natural reality and not merely a legal or religious invention.

If the life of a human being darkens, marriage and family darken as well, and this brings about negative consequences for society. "The human being-family interaction is so deep that the act of giving up man's personal dignity leads to a dehumanized and dehumanizing society. In the same way, when man meets the natural demands of his dignity as a human being he is in the right way towards a personalized and personalizing society".[17]

Family is a complex reality because it presents an interrelated group of duties on which the survival of society depends, as it provides it with members and takes care of its integral formation and its gradual integration into the social body.[18] In one word, it can be said that the family humanizes and is a key factor within the family-juvenile delinquency frame.

Socialization is just one aspect of this humanization process in which both intrinsic and extrinsic factors take part. Well then, the role of the family, which

---

17 C. Martínez de Aguirre y Aldaz, *Diagnóstico sobre el derecho de familia: análisis sobre el sentido y los contrasentidos de las transformaciones contemporáneas del derecho de familia* (Diagnosis on family law: analysis of the meaning and contradictions of contemporary transformations of family law), Madrid: Ediciones Rialp, 1996, p. 92.

18 Idem, p. 101.

is unique in spite of the many attempts to replace it with other human resources, is central. In the family, we find strong emotional as well as ideological factors that are backed by values which imply great sacrifices and efforts, which not many people (outside the family) are willing to make as regards the first socialization (that of the children).

The family life cycle tends to promote the growth and development of the human being as well as favour progress and unleashing of potential. The fundamental task of a family with teenage children is to achieve their socialization; that is to say, their incorporation to social life according to regulations, values and traditions.[19]

It is quite clear that it is essential to society that there exists a natural institution that has the necessary resources to provide society with healthy members. Why? Because, as has been mentioned above, a family is a community of love (cf. the preamble of the 1989 Convention on the Rights of the Child); it has the capacity to love each one of its members as unique and individual human beings and to love them for what each one is and not for what each one has.

This first of all means that it is of great importance that family ties with the prisoner are protected and developed. As research in Canada shows: Private family visit programs represent one of the best ways of preserving social, family and conjugal ties between incarcerated individuals and their intimates. This fact is viewed as undeniable in Canada.[20] However, family visits are not only of factual importance, they are also normatively required. As the Human Rights Committee states in its General Comment No. 09 on Humane treatment of persons deprived of liberty (Article 10 ICCPR):

> "3. In a number of cases, the information appearing in reports with respect to paragraph 3 of the article has contained no concrete mention either of legislative or administrative measures or of practical steps to promote the reformation and social rehabilitation of prisoners, by, for example, education, vocational training and useful work. Allowing visits, in particular by family members, is normally also such a measure which is required for reasons of humanity."

Furthermore, it might be necessary to learn prisoners how to repair and maintain their family relationships. Research shows that prisoners who know how to do this, have lower recidivism rates and reduced disciplinary problems within the prison system, and are moreover less likely to accept the norms and

19 C. García Francisco *et al.*, *La familia del menor infractor* (The family of the minor offender), Mexico: Ediciones Reintegra, 2004, p. 15, 19.

20 M. Vacheret, 'Private Family Visits in Canada, Between Rehabilitation and Stricter Control: Portrait of a System', *Penal Field, new international journal of criminology*, 2005, Vol. II (at: http://champpenal.revues.org/document2322.html) (last visited: 1 January 2013).

behaviour patterns of hardened criminals.[21] This illustrates that the family is not only of the utmost importance to the rehabilitations of prisoners, but that it also works the other way around: rehabilitation of prisoners is necessary to protect the family and family ties.

And last but not least, the family needs direct protection and assistance. Its function is irreplaceable. So, why don't we invest our resources in order to help, to the necessary extent, families perform their duties? Society as a whole is involved in this matter: the State, which should provide integral family policies without leaving aside the principle of subsidiarity; the different institutions and private organizations; and the families themselves, which must be conscious of the key role they play and must, therefore, assert their rights by means of the mechanisms within their reach.

Wouldn't a healthy family lead to a healthier society? A dismantled family is the root cause of different pathologies such as the offences carried out by one or several of its members.

2.6. AN ARGENTINE EXPERIENCE: AFTERCARE SERVICES

Previously, the execution of a criminal sentence was centred on repressive purposes by means of the offender's expiation and the intimidation of the global society. However, it's possible positive influence on this convict is now not enough to ensure him an acceptable social reintegration, on the part of both the prisoner and the community, when he is released.

What is needed is aftercare, which is more than an auxiliary or complement to the penitentiary regime; it is the integral and essential part of penitentiary treatment. As Rule 64 of the 1955 Standard Minimum Rules for the Treatment of Prisoners of United Nations state:

> "The duty of society does not end with a prisoner's release. There should, therefore, be governmental or private agencies capable of lending the released prisoner efficient after-care directed towards the lessening of prejudice against him and towards his social rehabilitation."

And with respect to social relations and after-care Rule 79 en 80 hold:

> "Special attention shall be paid to the maintenance and improvement of such relations between a prisoner and his family as are desirable in the best interests of both."

---

21 D.J. Bayse, S.M. Allgood & P.H. Van Wyk, 'Family Life Education: An Effective Tool for Prisoner Rehabilitation', 40 *Family Relations* 3 (1991) p. 254–257.

> "From the beginning of a prisoner's sentence consideration shall be given to his future after release and he shall be encouraged and assisted to maintain or establish such relations with persons or agencies outside the institution as may promote the best interests of his family and his own social rehabilitation."

The increasing introduction of methods that imply the serving of a sentence involving personal restraint, not in a closed, semi-open or open institution but in the ordinary social environment itself, contributes to strengthening the need of integrating penitentiary treatment with post-institutional assistance. The most widely spread of these methods is release on parole, which was incorporated some time ago into our legislation.

Nowadays in Argentina, the need for institutions providing aftercare is grounded on two facts:

- to provide effective assistance to those coming out from prisons and penitentiary institutions who may require help in their social reintegration.
- to supervise and assist those released on parole or conditional discharge.

Moreover, institutions providing aftercare must offer social assistance to the inmates, especially as regards the prisoner's relation with his family, through preservation and improvement of family relationships or by means of moral and material assistance and the necessary protection.

In Argentina there are various services that provide after care for prisoners and for prisoners' families. One of these is the Secretariat of Christian Aid to Prisons, which was founded by P. Iñaki de Azpiazu in 1954. The Argentine government recognizes the Secretariat as a qualified agency that provides services to prisoners, former prisoners and their families, regardless of their creed. Welfare assistance and criminological research are the dominant concerns of the agency. In terms of direct assistance to the needy, the Secretariat offers aid in the form of medical care, employment, literacy programmes, education, clothing allowances and meals. The activities of the institution are mainly focused on Buenos Aires but they are developed all over the country. The staff includes social workers, psychiatrist, criminologists who along with lawyers instruct college students. Volunteers visit prisoners and the inmate's relatives who are ill or in need of their services. At the World Congress on Victimology, the Secretariat of Christian Aid to Prisons presented the prisoner's family as a victim of crime too. The Secretariat has an Assistance and Family Therapy Centre that provides social assistance, medical, psychological and pedagogical assistance: family adaptation problems; behaviour problems; learning problems; and visits to families. Services given to former prisoners, prisoners and their families: lodging, documents, clothing, food, medical assistance, employment agency, assistance to obtain retirement documents, old people's homes lodging, visits to prisons, and visits to families of prisoners and former prisoners.

This is just one example of a service for prisoners' families. There are many more in Argentina. To name a few others: Prevention on the Use of Alcohol, Drugs and Aids Center; Assistance Centre for the Victim, and the Assistance Centre for Malvinas War Veterans. Also worth mentioning here is the Institute of Criminological Studies, which was set up at the beginning of the SACC. It has wide experience in the organization of seminars, conferences, day debate seminars and day study seminars, as well as in the preparation of research papers which focus mainly on the Argentinean penitentiary and post-penitentiary reality and on other related studies. Of particular importance is the project of Declaration of the Prisoner's Human Rights written and submitted by Dr. Emilia Bouzón de Terzano as Official Argentine Delegate before the United Nations Congress on Crime Prevention and Criminal Justice, Milan 1985.

2.7. PREVENTION AND TREATMENT

Prevention and treatment are the key words here. Prevention demands strengthening of family ties, especially generational ties, but also detection of violence and mistreatment problems. This is a task that also involves integration and coordination which can be very fruitful and that, clearly, calls for a relaxed atmosphere and specialized staff. In this regard, schools for parents which allow for active participation and for reflexion possibilities are of the utmost use. These programmes should be complemented with others referred to education, health and even food education, along with entities capable of offering employment possibilities in the face of hunger and unemployment.

Treatment should include the helping of families of prisoners. For such help interdisciplinary teams (doctors, lawyers, sociologists, psychologists, social anthropologists, social workers, etc.) are necessary, in the context of an ample criterion; professionals who are always willing to learn, especially about the understanding of failure. Treatment in these cases starts with the relationship. There is a strong need for trust to achieve a thorough expression of the problems, based on personal trust. People, even aggressors, need to have the opportunity to go back to the family and have an active participation in the management of their roles. What needs to change is their mentality, their qualities which should become increasingly harmonious. It is important to detect and remark, in all cases, on healthy ties and try to further them.

3. CONCLUSION

State help to marriage and family has gained great importance, especially in recent years. The State exercises influence on the family in different ways: by means of legislation, with its direct intervention and through the granting of subsidies. The concern to solve the housing problem is closely related to family aid: sanitary assistance, protection through appropriate means and above all, social aid institutions.

As the basic unit of society, families in all their formats have the right to receive greater protection from the multiple tensions derived from social and economic changes which compromise their feasibility.

These tensions have been particularly acute in the last few years in those countries where Governments have adopted measures towards reducing social expenses as part of their efforts to balance their income and public expending and to execute structural adjustment programmes. In many urban areas, millions of children and youngsters are immersed in a delicate situation given the disintegration of their families and other essential elements of the social fabric of communities; as a result of this disintegration, a great number of children and youngsters drop out of school, are abandoned in the streets or exploited in the labour market and are therefore exposed to a high incidence of unwanted pregnancies and sexually transmitted diseases. The greater employment migration is another source of tension and lack of family integration which has contributed to increasing women's responsibility. There are increasingly more vulnerable families; not only families headed by destitute women but also families with scarce resources where there are handicapped members or old age pensioners, families sheltered and moved and families whose members are affected by AIDS, drug addiction, domestic violence, violence towards children and other types of problems.

There is no doubt that from the very moment a problem is detected, solid assistance to the inmate's family should be granted, in those cases when such assistance is required. This is a particularly difficult situation given the family dismemberment that such situation usually causes. In this regard, two aspects should be mentioned: family aid to the inmate and family aid to who is released.

Governments, nongovernmental organizations and other interested parties at all levels should find innovative ways to provide a more effective aid to the family with specific problems, such as domestic violence, drug addiction and alcoholism, sexual abuse, mistreatment and neglected children.

The State is to comply with its duty and it will find by its side public and private institutions born from the noble feelings of people and driven by a strong feeling of social solidarity. For their action to be fully implemented, we simply need humanistic legislation and a healthy environment of freedom.

Consequently, we state that the best strategy to prevent crime is the protection and strengthening of the family.

THE VALUE OF REHABILITATION TO SOCIETY

Charl CILLIERS*

1. INTRODUCTION

It is well known that crime is a major social problem in society. Over the last decade it has become self-evident that the criminal justice system has not coped with crime despite huge increases in police resources, despite processing more people through the courts and locking up more people than ever before. The sheer volume of crime has continued to grow. Indeed crime, far from being unusual, is now a very common phenomenon. Over the last decade it has become self-evident that crime and its related problems can only be tackled effectively if society is involved and co-operative. For far too long we have relied on the police and the courts to deal with crime and for too long we have relied on the belief that deterrence – both the fear of being caught and the fear of punishment – will regulate criminal behaviour. Now it is generally accepted that if we are to contain and control crime, the co-operation and involvement of both individuals and society in both partial and societal sense are vital. Increasingly we are looking to find ways of managing the crime problem as well as processing individuals through the criminal justice system. In this presentation the value of rehabilitation to society will be explained and valuated. What is rehabilitation?

2. WHAT IS REHABILITATION?

Rehabilitation seeks to bring about fundamental changes in offenders and their behaviour. As in the case of deterrence, the ultimate goal of rehabilitation is a reduction in the number of criminal offences. Whereas deterrence depends upon a "fear of the law" and the consequences of violating it, rehabilitation generally works through education and psychological treatment to reduce the likelihood of future criminality.

* Prof. C. Cilliers is a Professor at the Department of Penology, University of South Africa.

It is a belief that something positive should be accomplished during the period of incarceration that forms the basis of the rehabilitation approach. Rehabilitation advocates maintain that criminal sanctions should be used as an opportunity to make some type of positive change in the offender. As George Bernard Shaw once pointed out, "if you are going to punish a man retributively, you must injure him. If you aim to reform him, you must improve him. And men are not improved by injuries."

3. SOCIETY AND REHABILITATION

Crime and delinquency are symptoms of failure and disorganisation in society as well as in individual offenders. The old criminological saying that society breeds the criminal it has holds true and it is only proper that the same society becomes part of the solution when reintegrating the ex-offender. This is a major task.

As we ponder on this task, let us review what the purpose of keeping offenders in prison is. It can be reasonably assumed that the incarceration/treatment in prison is meant to accomplish change, *i.e.* from anti-social to pro-social behaviour; from maladjustment to favourable adaptations to social norms; from being a burden and a threat to being a stable and productive member of society. Contained in this rehabilitation assumption is the possibility that the offender might develop insight into reasons for and causes of his criminality as well as attitudinal changes towards social norms and value systems and 'respect' the laws. Societal vengeance for the "sins" of the offender (he must be punished by taking away his freedom), and the protection of society are among the numerous purposes of incarceration. Let us also assume that these purposes were met through imprisonment.

It is well and good while the offender is in prison, but when the time comes for his release, how ready is society to reintegrate him with society? Communities are not fully mobilised for this mammoth task.

Ex-offenders, whether released conditionally or unconditionally, earned their release by demonstrating some form of "favourable adaptation" within the prison institution. This often means adaptation to an artificial world which involves conforming to the rules and regulations of prison life, paying lip service to the authorities for reasons for expediency, and adapting to the vicious criminal subculture of the most powerful inmates who rule by power, violence and intimidation, and therefore reinforce illegal violent values.

This kind of adaptation does not, however, mean favourable adaptation to life outside prison, which is (family, school, work, community), because the offender is cut off from these vital life processes. A major part of his rehabilitation is learning to adjust to life outside prison.

In order for the society to get involved in the rehabilitation of offenders, a needs test must be conducted. The needs are many and varied and depend on the family support networks that ex-offenders have on release. They include:

- establishing social networks that will help them to adjust and deal with problems that could lead to the violation of parole conditions;
- identifying the location of relevant resource networks in the community;
- material aid to meet the basic needs of released offenders such as food, transport and clothing;
- locating their families in the unrest environment;
- finding employment and accommodation;
- upholding their self-esteem and self-awareness as released ex-offenders;
- handling relationships within the home or family that may have evolved and changed during imprisonment;
- attitudes of people around them differ from those that ex-offenders hold about themselves;
- breaking ties with the criminal subculture that may have played a contributory part to their criminality and anti-social behaviour; and
- illiteracy and lack of adequate skills to compete in the open labour market.

4. HOW SOCIETY CAN BE INVOLVED IN THE REHABILITATION OF OFFENDERS

Employment

The current recession prompted organisations to launch campaigns that create an awareness of the needs of ex-offenders. These campaigns must reach out to employers to change their attitudes towards 'ex-cons' and make a conscious effort to change the risk-factor attitude of bias against offenders.

Corrections is a community responsibility

Currently the responsibility of corrections is seen by the man in the street as a responsibility of justice and prisons alone. According to some observers 'corrections' simply refers to rehabilitation through the use of a variety of community resources and services. I go further and say that an active campaign to take corrections to the community needs to be mounted country-wide by all disciplines involved in corrections work. This would pave the way for the implementation of community-based treatment programmes for ex-offenders (youths and adults).

Diffusing community resistance

Often overlooked is the factor or resistance by the community to play a part in matters concerning ex-offenders. A necessity to address this factor is paramount to all reintegration programmes. It may involve establishing contact with relevant communities, explaining and securing goodwill and co-operation of residents and volunteers in the design and implementation of programmes.

Education

A majority of ex-offenders dropped out of school. The level of education they have makes it impossible to compete in the open labour market. A multifaceted life skills training and educational programme could be tailored to include elements such as:

- adult literacy and remedial teaching schools for ex-prisoners and juvenile offenders;
- job skills training and job retraining as well as employment readiness programmes;
- pro-social norm education programmes could form part of after-care treatment services to ex-offenders in order to break the criminal subculture referred to earlier; and
- vocational training.

In all these programmes, use could be made of 'rehabilitated' and established ex-offenders as 'positive peer modes' or 'buddies' that could serve as models to recently released ex-offenders.

Therapeutic training of ex-offenders at community level

One of the major adjustment problems faced by ex-offenders involves forming healthy relationships. Therapeutic training places major emphasis on methods of developing interpersonal skills, responsibility, self-reliance and self-assurance in the individual. These personal qualities go a long way in reducing problematic behaviour among ex-offenders, like easily quarrelling with workers or foremen, erratic work attendance etc., which often lead to dismissals.

Community education

The community's active role or responsibility towards ex-offender reintegration will not materialise naturally or organically. An active drive to educate the community on its responsibility towards the ex-offender needs to be launched.

Such campaigns will not only raise the level of awareness, but also lead the way to what each community could do.

Services to ex-offenders

Services to ex-offenders need to be increased and the network widened. All social service organisations can pull together and provide comprehensive services that would include:

- counselling to individual prisoners, ex-prisoners and their families;
- stress management programmes for families of offenders and the wider community;
- effective parenting skills training;
- job retraining centres;
- self-help groups for ex-offenders; and
- sport and recreational facilities.

The value of rehabilitation to society will only materialize if there is a partnership between corrections and society. The relationships between corrections and society, community based organisations, NGO's and faith-based organisations are inherent to the successful achievement of the rehabilitation and reintegration of offenders. The partnership approach that is required in this regard must be managed through formal arrangements and the ongoing monitoring and evaluation of such projects and work by such organisations in order to ensure quality service delivery to offenders. At the same time, corrections should be involved in partnerships in the community, such as in social crime prevention, moral regeneration and poverty alleviation programmes.

The role that offenders can play in building these relationships in the community should be enhanced in the manner in which corrections works. The involvement of the community in the correctional system, though representation on Community Supervision and Parole Boards, and in volunteer work in correctional centres and joint projects must be reinforced and yet be guided by the approach to rehabilitation that corrections have.

5. ESTABLISHING A POLICY FRAMEWORK FOR COMMUNITY PARTICIPATION

The rehabilitation of offenders can only be truly successful and their reintegration into the society meaningful if all stakeholders are allowed to participate in the process. To this effect the participation of the community in strengthening and enhancing rehabilitation is crucial. The needs of Corrections shall have to be marketed to the community in order that the community can source expertise and services it can provide. An environment that encourages and promotes the participation of community-based service providers must be created. Entry into the Correctional environment for purposes of rendering services must be regulated yet facilitated and thus the structures necessary to accomplish this must be established.

Correctional institutions needs to be involved in community initiatives and projects. This can be done through the utilisation of offenders and visible involvement of Correctional personnel in community projects. The forging of closer links and co-operation between corrections, the community and other state departments is crucial in the fight against crime, reparation of relationships and the rehabilitation of offenders. In this regard, it will be very important for the correctional environment to develop the necessary policy and practice framework in relation to community participation.

Finally there are certain principles to be met relating to community participation and community programmes. They are:

- community participation and programmes shall promote the restoration of relationships and bring about healing and forgiveness;
- the correctional environment shall actively participate in community initiatives and projects;
- joint management and sharing of resources shall be encouraged;
- agreements between corrections and the community shall be formalized;
- programmes rendered to offenders or staff by, and agreements entered into with, community-based service providers, shall be evaluated and reviewed from time to time to ensure continuous adherence to and promotion of the Department's core business;
- community participation shall aim to enhance effective reintegration of offenders into society as law-abiding and productive citizens;
- the needs of the corrections in respect of programmes and services to enhance rehabilitation of offenders shall be marketed to community.

THE VALUE OF REHABILITATION TO THE TAX-PAYER

Seán Aylward*

1. INTRODUCTION

Public opinion, not just here in Ireland but in many other countries, is a real force in the ongoing debate about the successful operation of domestic criminal justice systems. More specifically, and from my own personal experiences as Director General of the Irish Prison Service, from 1999–2004, I can attest that penal policy and prisons administration are areas where few, if any, mistakes go unpunished in terms of public opprobrium.

The overarching theme of the book to which this paper is a contribution is the value of rehabilitation of prisoners. Rehabilitation in that context has been defined as the process by which criminals are restored to a useful life, through education, therapy and the fostering of personal responsibility in order to enable them to contribute to themselves and to society.

In the following I will explain my own personal perspectives on the challenges faced generally by policy makers in convincing tax-payers of the relative merits of prisoner rehabilitation. I will also examine the value of rehabilitation to the tax-payer and highlight a number of evidence based studies, most of which have been conducted in the UK and the US, that have sought to determine the financial benefits of prisoner rehabilitation to the tax-payer.

2. REHABILITATION – A QUICK IRISH HISTORICAL PERSPECTIVE

The concept of prisoner rehabilitation has a long history in Ireland. The first chairman and director of the Convict Prisons Board, a three man board appointed in Ireland in 1854 to manage convict prisoners, was Sir Walter

* S. Aylward is Under Treasurer at the King's Inns, Ireland. Prior to that he had been Secretary General of the Department of Justice and Equality in Ireland, and member of the European Committee for the Prevention of Torture.

Crofton. Crofton was a leading proponent of a major programme of change and reform in the Irish prison system which occurred in the nineteenth century. Interestingly, a key tenet of his penal philosophy was to *"restore the prisoner to society with an unimpaired constitution, and with sufficient health and energies to enable him to take a respectable place in the Community"*[1] – heady stuff for the 1850's.

Many of the nineteenth century prison reformers such as Crofton really believed in the rehabilitation of the offender in the custodial setting. They endeavoured to address healthcare and substance abuse problems in prison inmates and they worked assiduously towards trying to ensure that the offender returned to a useful and law abiding role in society.[2]

3. REHABILITATION – CURRENT CHALLENGES

Fast forward to the twentieth first century and the rehabilitation of prisoners and their successful reintegration into society remains an ongoing public debate and poses a significant challenge for all administrations and policy-makers. However, it is a challenge that must be confronted and overcome in order to maintain public safety and public confidence in the criminal justice system, whilst also successfully controlling increasing prison populations and maximising the efficient use of public funds.

Often the central ideological debate on prisoner rehabilitation, amongst the general tax paying public and policy-makers, tends to centre around the real or perceived value of prisoner rehabilitation programmes as well as on the notion of an adequate and just punishment for the perpetrators of crime – that catchphrase *"if you do the crime you must be prepared to do the time"* comes to mind. This ideological debate has no doubt stemmed from the differing societal expectations that any prison sentence should deliver elements of, retribution, incapacitation, deterrence and rehabilitation. The concept of an appropriate tariff for serious or heinous crimes remains in my view a genuinely necessary element in any justice system which aspires to retain public respect and confidence.

Many individuals question the effectiveness of rehabilitation programmes which seek to re-educate and develop the personal capacity of prisoners before they are re-introduced to society. Tabloid reportage of spectacular relapses by released offenders cause huge problems and shape public attitudes very negatively indeed. The Willie Horton attack adds against Governor Mike

---

1 Tim Carey, *Mountjoy: The Story of a Prison*, Cork: Collins Press, 2000, cited in S. Aylward, 'The Irish Prison Service, Past Present and Future – A Personal Perspective', in: P. O'Mahony (ed.), *Criminal Justice in Ireland*, Dublin: Institute of Public Administration, 2000, p. 570 ff.

2 S. Aylward, 'The Irish Prison Service, Past Present and Future – A Personal Perspective', in P. O'Mahony (ed.), *Criminal Justice in Ireland*, Dublin: Institute of Public Administration, 2000, p. 570 ff.

Dukakis wrecked his campaign to become US president back in 1980's for instance. Horton was a released prisoner who was a member of the African American community who attached a white girl while on furlough.

Arguments against rehabilitation normally centre on two basic arguments – firstly that rehabilitation programmes are expensive and that they are, in some cases, ineffective at reducing recidivism rates and in curtailing offending behaviour. The other argument is that it is unfair and unjust that prisoners should be the recipients of such expensive rehabilitation programmes at the expense of the tax-payer and rather that they should be punished with the sentence that is appropriate to the crime which they have committed. I think many administrations and policy makers have learned the costly lesson that prisoner rehabilitation can, at times, be a politically unpopular cause. Battling public opprobrium, as a policy maker, is never an easy task.

4. REHABILITATION – BREAKING THE CYCLICAL PATTERN OF CAUSE AND EFFECT

A few years ago, The Irish Prison Service facilitated a major study of prisoner re-offending by the Institute of Criminology at University Colleague Dublin. The findings of the study were published in the May 2008 edition of the academic journal Criminology and Criminal Justice.[3] This study indicated that the demographic attributes of the Irish prison population at that time was similar to those of prison populations elsewhere in the world. The vast majority of the prisoner cohort examined as part of the study were male (93%), unmarried (82%) and were young (the average age was under 30 years of age). A majority had not sat any formal state examinations (54%) and more than half had been unemployed prior to their incarceration (52%).[4]

From these statistics alone it is evident that imprisoning individuals without attempting to address the underlying causes of their criminal behaviour, such as the individuals failure to achieve employment due to a lack of education or job skills, whilst they are in prison only serves to reinforce and crystallise the cyclical pattern of cause and effect, thereby increasing the likelihood of re-offending.

Personally from my own experience, I believe that prison must do more than simply warehouse offenders exacting retribution on behalf of outraged victims and their families. While I was Director General of the Irish Prison Service we

3 The study was based on 19,955 prisoner releases that took place between 1 January 2001 and 30 November 2004. The unique 19,955 releases in the study data represented 14,485 different persons.

4 Ian O'Donnell, Eric P. Baumer & Nicola Hughes, 'Recidivism in the Republic of Ireland', 8 *Criminology & Criminal Justice* 2 (2008), p. 123–146.

sought to expand the range of rehabilitation options through the creation of new pathways for people in prison to follow to achieve labour participation after their release from custody. We sought to address the core issues affecting prisoners such as personal decision-making capacity, coherence amongst the delivery of our support services and linkages from the "inside to the outside". Our Probation Service continues that approach to this day via a range of initiatives led directly by its staff and through civil society and business community partnerships like the Bridge project.

The Irish Prison Service has also continued to build upon this approach and prisoner rehabilitation today involves significant multi-dimensional input by a diverse range of services aimed at providing offenders with the means to avoid re-offending following their return to the community. The services provided include work skills, training and education and are matched, where possible, to individual aptitudes and abilities, sometimes unrecognised or untapped prior to imprisonment. In addition, a range of medical, psychological and other support services are available to assist those suffering from particular problems such as drug addiction.

Building on our past efforts in this area, a new Integrated Management System (ISM) is currently being rolled out by the Irish Prison Service. This approach involves the prisoner himself or herself taking greater responsibility for their own development through ongoing active engagement with the various service providers and so ensuring a prisoner centred approach. There are around 1,000 prisoners participating in ISM at present and the introduction of further initiatives by the Prison Service such as an incentivised regimes policy (which is due to come in to operation later this year) will further encourage prisoners to participate in the structured activities available to them in prison.

Approximately 35% of prisoners engage in educational activities across our 14 institutions taking part in a wide range of classes including basic literacy and numeracy, drama, creative writing, information technology and computer aided design. The aim of the Education Service is to deliver a broad, and flexible programme of education to help prisoners cope with their sentence, achieve personal development, prepare for life after release and to establish an appetite and capacity for life-long learning. There are over 220 whole time teachers involved in delivering prison education which is quite a considerable resource. The Prison Service on the recommendation of our Inspector of Prisons, your colleague Judge O'Reilly, is undergoing an independent audit of the services being provided in order to ensure that the highest possible benefits are derived by the greatest number of prisoners. There is always a concern to ensure participation is extensive and that we get the maximum benefit out of the teaching resources.

The Irish Prison Service also places a strong emphasis on the provision of vocational training activities for prisoners. Training activities are chosen to give as much employment as possible in prison and to give opportunities to acquire skills which will help secure employment on release. Over 800 prisoners participate in work training activities on any given day. In the context of labour participation after release from custody, it is worth mentioning the collaborative work which takes place between the Irish Prison Service and Business in the Community Ireland which is a unique movement of companies across Ireland committed to responsible business practices. This includes the provision of a training, education and employment placement service to prisoners in the Mountjoy and Midlands campuses and a mentoring service which operates in another of our three prisons. One to one mentoring has been shown internationally to have a positive impact on the resettlement and rehabilitation of ex-prisoners.

In the confines of this paper I can only touch on the range of services which are offered to prisoners in custody in order to help them in their endeavours to live law abiding and purposeful lives as valued members of society.

5. THE VALUE OF REHABILITATION TO THE TAX-PAYER

The imprisonment of offenders is costly – the average cost of an available staffed prison space in Ireland during the calendar year 2010 was € 70,513.[5] The figure would be higher but for severe overcrowding which is not a budgetary strategy that anyone here would find acceptable. Indeed, I was struck recently by a statement contained in the Ministry of Justice (England) Green Paper on the punishment and rehabilitation of offenders. The sentence went as follows,

> "the criminal justice system cannot remain an expensive way of giving the public a break from offenders before they return to commit more crimes."[6]

At its most basic level, the argument for the value of rehabilitation to the tax-payer runs along the following lines – If prisoners receive effective support and rehabilitation whilst imprisoned they should be in a position to positively re-engage with society upon their release and to secure employment or pursue further education, thus reducing their likelihood of re-offending and being returned to prison at the cost of the tax-payer.

---

5 The following costs are included in the calculations: accommodation related variable costs, prisoner related variable costs (*e.g.* healthcare, catering), prisoner related fixed costs (custodial pay, uniforms) and non-custodial costs (including prisoner escorts).

6 Ministry of Justice, *Breaking the Cycle: Effective Punishment, Rehabilitation and Sentencing of Offenders*, London: Ministry of Justice, 2010, p. 1 (at: http://webarchive.nationalarchives.gov.uk/20120119200607/www.justice.gov.uk/consultations/docs/breaking-the-cycle.pdf, last visited: 1 October 2012).

On the 31st May 2011 we had 3,805 sentenced prisoners in custody here in Ireland. Based on research carried out previously 49.2% (1,872) of these prisoners will be back in custody within 4 years. If this percentage of potential re-offenders was reduced by 33% through rehabilitation the number of this prisoner cohort back in custody within 4 years would be 1,267. This would represent a reduction of 605 prisoners in custody with an approximate cost saving cost of € 70,513 per prisoner to the tax-payer. That's a potential saving of € 42m per annum.

6. RATES OF RECIDIVISM AS AN INDICATOR OF THE SUCCESS OF REHABILITATION

Rates of recidivism are perceived by many commentators as the critical indicator of the performance of the prison system and of the rehabilitative measures implemented in prisons. I would agree that an understanding of the causal factors of re-offending and recidivism help policy makers design and tailor more targeted rehabilitation programmes but I believe that recidivism rates alone are a blunt tool in assessing the benefit – in personal, societal and fiscal terms – of prisoner rehabilitation.

Recidivism studies have often been used to support the "prison doesn't work" or the "rehabilitation of prisoners is expensive and doesn't work" argument. However, measuring the performance of both prison and the value of rehabilitation is by no means an easy task – it is, I would contend a complex and multi-dimensional one. Too often, recidivism studies have failed to take account of how post release factors, such as the willingness of society itself to help with the re-integration of the offenders, impact on the likelihood of whether a former prisoner will re-offend.

7. SUMMARY OF RECENT STUDIES ON PRISONER REHABILITATION AND ITS VALUE TO THE TAX-PAYER

There has been, however, a number of academic and evidence based studies that have sought to quantify the value of rehabilitation to the tax-payer. I should mention at this juncture that I have the Centre for Effective Services to thank for some of the observations which follow as they conducted a mini review on recent studies in this area for me.

As I have mentioned, there are a large number of studies in the area of prisoner rehabilitation but it is difficult to provide a definitive answer as to what the most effective means of rehabilitation are and their cost benefit. Not all the studies have the same focus or investigate the same population which makes comparison difficult. There is also evidence which suggests that pre-existing risk factors are strong predictors of later offending behaviour but studies often fail to take these factors into account. A common theme across the systematic reviews considered is the need to improve the methodological rigour of studies of the effectiveness of measures to reduce recidivism. These challenges will relate to sample size, use of randomised controlled methodologies, controls (particularly with small samples) and what constitutes good outcomes. There is also a need for common international standards when considering cost-effectiveness and cost-benefit. What then are the key messages from these studies?

Study 1 – Benefit-Cost Analyses of Sentencing, McDougall et al. (2008)[7]

This review highlights that 'only a small number of benefit-cost studies were published between 1980 and 2001'[8] and it was difficult to draw firm conclusions due to the small number of studies and methodological issues in most of the studies identified.

There was evidence to suggest that the in-prison sex offender programmes considered were cost-beneficial.

Drug treatment diversion (*i.e.* diversion from custody) and the imprisonment of high risk offenders were also found to be cost beneficial.

In this review there was evidence that intensive supervision and Youth Wilderness Training were cost-beneficial but both of these examples were contradicted by other studies.

The review reports studies that suggest that for auto theft and burglary 'the cost of imprisonment outweighed the social benefits of imprisonment.

The review urges caution in using benefit-cost or cost-effectiveness studies where research methods are weak. There is an appeal in future studies for a marriage between robust research methods (*e.g.* randomised controlled trial) and standardised benefit-cost techniques.

Study 2 – The Effects of Custodial vs. Non-Custodial Sentences on Re-Offending: A Systematic Review of the State of Knowledge Villettaz et al. (2006)[9]

- After evaluating the available evidence against a methodological standard the authors concluded that "*we are…unable to say whether non-custodial sanctions are more effective to prevent re-offending than custodial sanctions. Whether treatment and rehabilitation are more successful than mere*

---

7 C. McDougall, M. Cohen, R. Swaray & A. Perry, *Benefit Cost Analyses of Sentencing*, Campbell Systematic Reviews, 2008:10.

8 Idem, p. 29.

9 P. Villettaz, M. Killias & I. Zoder, *The Effects of Custodial vs. Non-Custodial Sentences on Re-Offending: A Systematic Review of the State of Knowledge*, Campbell Systematic Reviews, 2006:13.

surveillance and incarceration, or whether all is a matter of assigning offenders to specific sanctions has been beyond the scope of our review."

- As they say "*The results are rather discouraging for those who had argued over years that imprisonment is damaging. If weaker studies (i.e. not as methodologically robust) had been included in the meta-analysis then they might have found evidence of a damaging effect of custodial sentences but that would have been 'at the price of reaching presumably wrong conclusions."*
- The review highlights the difficulties associated with small sample size and ability to take account of variables which may have undermined the ability of less robust studies to demonstrate that non-custodial sentences are more effective at reducing offending than custodial sentences.
- The study suggests that the sentence type is not what determines the effect; rather predisposing risk factors in relation to re-offending are likely to be of more importance.

Study 3 – The Primary Factors that Characterize Effective Interventions with Juvenile Offenders: a Meta-Analytic Overview. Lipsey (2009)[10]

Rather than try to identify the programmes that are the most effective in reducing recidivism in juvenile offenders Lipsey seeks to identify 'the factors that characterize the most effective programs and the general principles that characterize "what works" to reduce the recidivism of juvenile offenders. Three factors are identified as being strongly correlated with programme effectiveness.

a. Interventions that embodied 'therapeutic' philosophies, such as counselling and skills training, were more effective than those based on strategies of control or coercion – surveillance, deterrence and discipline.
b. Interventions applied to juveniles with higher levels of delinquency risk were more effective, though that effect was offset somewhat if the juveniles had aggressive/violent histories.
c. Interventions that were implemented with high quality were more effective.

Interventions that performed well among the therapeutic interventions included cognitive-behavioural, social learning, (more generally) skill building interventions as well as mentoring and group counselling.

This overview did not include a preponderance of evidence-based programmes that Lipsey describes as 'brand name "model" programs' rather it reflected the use of more generic programmes, more typical of the real world juvenile justice

10 M.W. Lipsey, 'The primary factors that characterize effective interventions with juvenile offenders: A meta-analytic overview', 4 *Victims and Offenders* 2 (2009), p. 124–147.

system. Lipsey states '*...the findings presented here indicate that the average program of this variable generic sort can be quite effective if implemented well and targeted on high risk offenders. It does not take a magic bullet program to impact recidivism, only one that is well made and well aimed.*'

Study 4 – Evidence-Based Public Policy Options to Reduce Future Prison Construction, Criminal Justice Costs, and Crime Rates Aos et al. (2006)[11]

- This study produced for the Washington State legislature very cogently sets out what works in reducing crime with evidence based options and explicitly links this with benefits and costs. Figures are provided for programmes for adults and juveniles both in prison and in the community. A small number of prevention programmes are also considered. Having identified a number of programmes which both reduce offending and have a beneficial cost profile they set out three implementation scenarios and postulate the potential savings to the tax-payer.

The authors do offer timely caution however by stating that "*It is one thing to model these results on computer, it is quite another to find a way to make them actually happen in the real world.*"

Study 5 – Social Impact Bonds[12]

In England, Social Finance with support from the Big Lottery and the Ministry of Justice has been piloting the use of Social Impact Bonds.

At its most basic level a social impact bond is a contract with the public sector in which it commits to pay for improved social outcomes. On the back of this contract, investment is raised from socially motivated investors. This investment is used to pay for a range of interventions to improve social outcomes while the financial returns investors receive are dependent on the degree to which outcomes improve.

The first pilot is centred on reducing the re-offending rates for short term prisoners at Peterborough Prison. To achieve a return on investment the combination of services delivered must realise a reduction in re-offending of at lest 7.5%. This initiative is attracting a lot of attention, primarily for the potential to unlock alternative finance in straightened times, but it must be emphasised

11 S. Aos, M. Miller & E. Drake, *Evidence-Based Public Policy Options to Reduce Future Prison Construction, Criminal Justice Costs, and Crime Rates*, Olympia: Washington State Institute for Public Policy, 2006.

12 Social Finance, *A Technical Guide to developing a Social Impact Bond: Criminal Justice*, March 2011.

that this pilot only commenced in September 2010 and is very much about proof of concept. To fully realise savings to the tax-payer it must go to scale. Social Impact Bonds are being advocated in the Irish system as well. They are a complex concept and I will only say that the "jury is out" on them.

Study 6 – Payment by results in the criminal justice system: can it deliver? Collins (2011)[13]

Collins looks at Ministry of Justice in England and Wales Green Paper Breaking the Cycle: *Effective punishment, rehabilitation and sentencing of offenders* to which I referred earlier. This Green Paper highlights a commitment from the Ministry of Justice to make payment by results the norm within the criminal justice system. The fiscal attractions of payment by results are self evident but Collins warns:

> "Overall there is a paucity of strong evidence in support of a move towards payment by results based on outcomes, reflecting the fact that it is a relatively new service delivery model. Partly as a result of this, there are a number of challenges and unresolved issues that will need to addressed in the development of payment by results in a criminal justice context."

8. CONCLUSION

The literature on rehabilitation of prisoners is extensive, but not conclusive. The public and the political establishment is not yet convinced but the closer one gets to the experience of managing them, the more convinced one becomes of the true value not just for the tax-payer but for the whole of society in significantly investing in prisoner and general offender rehabilitation.

13 J. Collins, 'Payment by Results in the Criminal Justice System: Can it Deliver?', 10 *Safer Communities* 2 (2011), p. 18–25.

THE VALUE OF REHABILITATION TO THE PRISON ADMINISTRATION

Luís de Miranda Pereira*

1. INTRODUCTION: TIME, DOUBTS AND CONCEPTS

The subject "The value of Rehabilitation to the Prison Administration" implicitly contains the notion that inmates' rehabilitation may not be a determining goal to the efficient functioning of the prison system or, in other words, that the value of rehabilitation is something disputable and not essential for the same purpose. Prison history, in fact, shows us that, ever since the French revolution and until mid-19th century, the social rehabilitation of prisoners was not an issue apart from the religious approach to the remission of their sins. The original, long use of prisons as a place where people would be locked up in order to force them to confess or to pay a debt, or to wait for the sentence and punishment, is a profound cultural element that even nowadays impacts the value of rehabilitation as an end, an essential purpose, for the execution of a prison sentence.

The importance of rehabilitation has varied and still varies according to different criminological theoretical approaches, following social, political and economic change, development of academic research and accuracy of evaluation models, mainly in the last 50/60 years. Clinical treatment model; nothing works; just deserts; use of meta-analyses; what works; good life model – this sequence of theories is eloquent enough to illustrate what has been said above. Besides that, one should not forget the defence of prevention as general framework and the renewed idea of not imposing treatment to deal with delinquent behaviour.

---

* L. de Miranda Pereira is former Director-General of the Portuguese Prison Services. Note by author: Some parts of this text will follow the basic reasoning of the author's view on what is the definition and purpose of prison and on the role of rehabilitation in this context. Therefore, some notions and texts already used in other publications by the author will sometimes be repeated. Several contributions made in a wider and different perspective but clearly relevant to the more synthetic and focused approach used in this text are contained in the proceedings of the Lisbon meeting of the IPPF on 21–25 May 1999 'New orientations of the prison regime'.

As a rule, criminology penitentiary theories are more or less determining in each period because of their social impact. However, they may also be amplified, conditioned or even ignored by the influence of one or more crucial elements, such as: politics – conservative, or liberal, or socialist; big budgets/low budgets; social and economic crises; insecurity; unemployment; media pressure and social and political reaction to it, adequate and inadequate prison buildings, insufficient or sufficient and qualified probation and prison staff. Each one by itself, all combined, partially or totally, those are notions that in one way or another, in the last decades, and some nowadays and in the future, have been, are, or will be crucial to the real importance of rehabilitation in the Prison Administration field practice.

Over the last period of more or less ninety years of cultural human thought evolution, mainly in the latest sixty years, the notion of rehabilitation has gained in most western penal systems, in spite of those opposed to it, a quintessential status in penal and penitentiary law and was gradually regarded as an important achievement of civilization development.

No one argues that prisons should contribute, first and foremost, to public safety, by ensuring that sentences are served in compliance with the law, that offenders do not escape, and that good and consensual discipline and order prevail within the prison environment. However, today, at least theoretically, no one absolutely contests the equal importance of the other key purpose of a modern prison system: to put in place the conditions that will provide the opportunity to all prisoners willing to accept it to develop their personal, social, cultural and vocational skills and, by so doing, to improve their chances of a successful re-integration into society after their release.

2. INTENTIONS AND REALITY – PRISON MANAGEMENT AND REHABILITATION: A FILTER TO PRISON REALITY ASSESSMENT

Nevertheless, some questions may be raised whose answers often show that there is a gap between, on the one hand, the conceptual framework, the underlying philosophy, the rules and laws, administration guidelines included, and, on the other hand, what happens in the field:

The confinement, security and guard of prisoners and the purpose of keeping them away from society is indeed, or not, what is generally regarded by the public as the exclusive role of the enforcement of a prison sentence?

On the field, taking prison administration and all categories of staff as a whole, do they all see rehabilitation as an essential goal for their jobs? And for those responding yes, do they feel it as a reasonable, attainable purpose in the specific context of their jobs?

Do they all share the same notion of rehabilitation?

In this context, what is the relationship and cooperation between guards and trained specialists?

Is there a dominant notion of team work involving all kinds of staff in prison with interactive methodologies for the same goals?

As a system, how does prison administration, and each prison, deal with the rehabilitation objective as a main concern?

In case of a budgetary cut, what kinds of staff and programs will be at stake first?

The answer to these questions and others possible on the same path depends on the interaction of multiple variables, starting with national culture, philosophy of government at each moment, social and economic context and related media pressure, and ending with the resources available: leadership, number and quality of staff and the adequate penitentiary park[1] – staff and park both

1 The penitentiary park is a decisive element to assess the real application of penitentiary theories and policies. During the initial period of penitentiary doctrines, buildings were a direct response to the object aimed by the theory. Penitentiary architecture was the first instrument to the theory application. The Philadelphia and Auburn models, for instance, had a pragmatic translation on the configuration, dimension and definition of the facilities of the penitentiary complexes then built, some of those buildings still existing nowadays and functioning as prisons.
Since then the correspondence between the evolution of penitentiary thought and the penitentiary architecture has been generally maintained. Buildings – 150, 60, 40 years old – were expressly conceived and drawn according to theories and connected practical views about how to run a prison and how sentences must be served. A new specific branch of Architecture was publicly recognised and has developed tendencies and models linked to penitentiary programmes and policies with a more or less general international acceptance independently of natural national adaptations.
But what is really important is that even if some theories manage to survive contemporary walls in the penitentiary field, reality is largely the opposite.
Indeed, walls, prison buildings, remain active while seeing the underlying conceptual framework disappear, as did disappear several other theories following the former. And even where they remain in operation, in very few cases, if any, the buildings in question will be able to be a correct instrument to the specific demands of new approaches. The penitentiary model is different and even with adaptations the walls basically remain the same. And what has been said is even more real if we think about other kinds of buildings (castles, convents, military installations, etc.) that have always been and still are used as prisons.
The same reasoning applies to the cost perspective. Especially the staff costs – guards are the decisive issue – are directly related with the type of architecture. And, as we know, staff costs weren't the problem 30 and more years ago but they are today.

related to different existing tasks and programmes. In this context, how should we address the questions and differences raised between law in the book and law in action, between the archetype model[2] and its practical application?

Under a strict conceptual penal and penitentiary perspective, what is in rules, laws, academic theses and administration guidelines will be more useful to people if filtered by a no less essential knowledge of the general organisational management of the prison system. In other words, we must have a comprehensive reading of the model through an integrated knowledge of the prison system management components: staff (guards and social intervention specialists); adequate prison buildings and facilities[3]; adequate budgets, security, treatment and educational programs, and a system that is open to the community.

By using this filter, we should then be able to realise to what extent rehabilitation is something to be regarded as essential by those responsible for the implementation of a prison sentence, and we should be able to see the fluctuations of that importance at each moment and the reasons behind them. As a matter of fact, very often, we can find within the same administration different realities – the same apparent philosophy and rules and quite different degrees of application. And this normally shows an unbalanced organisational structure of the system and/or the existence of unbalanced resources and conditions of functioning. Then, a statement about the value of Rehabilitation to the Prison Administration could be, with some irony, that "it depends" and that "it varies a lot".

3. THE REHABILITATION PROCESS AND THE ADJECTIVE ROLE OF THE PRISON SERVICE – PRINCIPLES AND ELEMENTS OF THE REHABILITATION PROCESS

As said in the beginning, the title given to this paper transmits a feeling of doubt on the value of rehabilitation to the Prison Administration. But in order to have an answer to possible doubts, we need to focus the notion of rehabilitation in

---

Since the seventies, the quick succession of penitentiary theories and models turned the majority of prison buildings into poor instruments for today's desirable good practices and good management of costs. The long wings for one hundred and more inmates, the big prison factories, the high ratio guards/inmates, for instance, suddenly become problems and not suitable and useful instruments. This reality has a major importance to the discussion about the value of rehabilitation to the prison administration, as it hardens the existence of suitable conditions for the implementation of an adequate individual rehabilitation plan.

2 Even when the archetype model is not defined and presented as a management fundamental instrument, the legislation policy, as expressed through the fundamental principles and philosophy of the penal and penitentiary systems, assumes and defines that archetype model.

3 See note 1.

itself, which seems not to be an established, univocal definition. Is rehabilitation equivalent to having success in avoiding new offences by imposing rules and treatment? Or does it imply the clear notion that we are talking about a complex process in which the main, determining actor is the sentenced person and in which prison administration plays an important but only adjective role?

We can say that in an almost anecdotal and extreme perception many people expect prison to work like a washing machine: you put in the "dirty" offender, apply the right "washing powder", set the program for a suitable length of time and, when the washing cycle ends, a "clean" rehabilitated citizen, ready to lead a law-abiding life, is released into society. Others regard prison as synonymous of crime school, or as a dreadful place where society's most vulnerable citizens are serving sentences because of their cultural and social background, and then go through life marked with an erasable stigma defined by the prison sentence.

Those who, instead, know prison reality, necessarily have the clear perception of a highly complex world implying the existence of hundreds of human beings who live their own lifetime and circumstances but who are forced to share the same closed space and time in a never ending sequence of a tense balance of powers and interests within a permanent cultural turmoil.

We all agree today that when we consider prison, we should first consider the inmate's dignity and fundamental human rights and, apart from the natural restriction on freedom, we should bear in mind to what extent constraints on other fundamental rights are justifiable in the name of penitentiary discipline, order and safety. It is, in fact, the balance reached between respect for basic rights and the limitations posed by safety, order and discipline requirements that determines how a prison system evolves and how it reflects the existence and overall development of democracy in a State under the rule of law. That balance is only possible within the rehabilitation process seen as the main objective, even under an approach of safety and discipline. This is for the State the only way of granting better safety to population and also the enforcement of principles based on ethical and philosophical grounds that are essential to the modern concept of State.

As a matter of fact, the rehabilitation process is based, in particular, upon the following main principles:

- Punishment of the specific individual guilt;
- The socialisation capability of any responsible individual;
- The right of a convict to an individualised treatment plan[4];
- The right to say no to the proposed treatment plan;
- The joint responsibility of the individual, the community and the state for treatment;
- The victim's right to reparation.

---

4 Not the right to be rehabilitated. No one can rehabilitate anybody: there is no "washing machine".

This means that the inmate must be seen as an individual considered in his own circumstances that, while serving a sentence, has a possible future without committing any more crimes. A possible future depending on the interaction between the community, the state and the sentenced person when setting the conditions for implementation of a rehabilitation plan; a possible future mainly depending on the inmate's will in agreement with the prison administration regarding the rehabilitation plan; a possible future depending as well on the state and society commitment for the creation of sound community environments where crime prevention policies are active practices; finally, a possible future depending on victims' reparation.

Prison administration needs an appropriate penitentiary park and an adequate number of staff with proper training in order to serve those principles and to play its specific role when implementing them. In the same perspective, last but not least, it needs to face and grant three main components of prison life, which are essentials for the development of the rehabilitation process and for a safe prison environment, providing the inmate with:

1) Adequate nourishment and heath care;
2) Daily intense and programmed activity and occupation, meaning the existence of[5]:
   a) *Specific programmes for specific inmates' problems*
   b) *School, education, cultural and social skills programmes*
   c) *Moral and religious support*
   d) *Work*
   e) *Professional training*
   f) *Physical education and sport*
   g) *Visits and other contacts with the exterior*
3) Open regimes and programmes and interaction with the community.

You may think that a fourth component is missing. As referred to above, prisons should primarily contribute to public safety, so that security should be a component in itself. Nevertheless, granting security is difficult or impossible without any presence of the three referred main components and we have already learned, during the latest decades, that public safety is impossible to achieve just with walls, guards and security measures. Therefore, the key purpose of a modern prison system is the rehabilitation process and, as said before, it should put in place the conditions that will offer all prisoners, as a matter of principle,

5 Again the question of an adequate prison building reference model is essential. Dealing with the present kind of prison population and the problems prison administration is facing and not ignoring the contemporary trends of criminological theories, it is essential to conceive prison complexes with separated small units for 30/40 inmates allowing diversification and specialisation of treatment, at the same time obtaining the best rationalisation of means for the use of staff.

the opportunity to develop their personal, social, cultural and vocational skills and, by so doing, to improve their chances of successful re-integration into society after their release.

Prison systems have a clear obligation to use best practices and procedures, and should provide offenders with basic solutions that, for whatever reason, were missing or had failed before they were arrested. They should deliver suitable programmes for specific health and behavioural problems, and should try to discover what works best. Only when acting this way, prison administration will reach the essence of its mission: being responsible for accomplishing the obligation to adequately use the available means, rather than as an obligation to reach final results, as would traditionally be accepted as a rule.

As generally recognised, imprisonment should reduce the likelihood of reoffending, and that is sometimes probably the case.[6] But, as a principle, imprisonment in itself is known as rarely being directly responsible for reducing the number of new offences. Furthermore, imprisonment should not be judged solely on the basis of whether it reduces reoffending, because, as already said, prison shouldn't be expected to directly produce final and long term successful results to the inmates' future. And this statement is not a paradox when we reaffirm the essentiality of the rehabilitation process to the prison administration. Prison is expected to grant good use of the adequate resources in order to open a path to the inmate's rehabilitation process; therefore, the evaluation of prison system results should be centred on this. And this is the adjective role – considering the inmate's main, decisive role – played by the prison system in the rehabilitation process. The value of rehabilitation to the prison administration will be defined by its own capacity to fulfil the said adjective role.

4. INMATES' SELECTION AND TREATMENT INDIVIDUALISATION

This approach will be not complete if we ignore one of the most difficult prison administration tasks. We are talking about inmates' selection and the prognosis of their fitness for a treatment plan.

It is up to prison management to identify those who are genuinely determined to take advantage of the available opportunities, those who want to serve their sentences in an orderly, peaceful fashion and intend to have a different future. Those are the ones who need the investment of the best resources available.

But management should also detect those who have embarked on a criminal career and who use prison environment in order to exercise and develop it, or

6 It can happen notably with occasional and socially integrated offenders able to serve their time aiming at a positive return to society.

those who normally show violent behaviour. In these cases, the prison management should minimise, as much as possible, their contact with the first group and should ensure public safety, by providing for their necessary separation in compliance with the law, avoiding offenders to escape and ensuring that discipline and order prevail within the prison environment. Treatment plans for those should necessarily be conditioned and designed mainly in order to maintain an open door to wishfully positive changes that might possibly occur.

The key to successful intervention in dealing with prisoners is individualisation over the course of the offender's prison term, the through-care period, based on objective criteria, and assessing the usefulness of practices and procedures and the results achieved as sentences are served. It is essential that our efforts should always focus on the prisoner as a person and citizen who will one day leave prison, who should be regarded as a subject of rights with a role and a voice in prison, and who is free to decide whether to take advantage of the opportunities available in the prison system.

That means the existence of an organisation built and managed in order to keep sentenced persons away from society in a safe environment, providing those persons with useful tools that allow them to have a choice regarding their future outside the prison.

To manage this organization is to manage the rehabilitation process.

Thinking only in security and order as purposes for prison management is to go back a hundred years in human civilisation development.

5. THE ARCHETYPE AND THE INFLUENCE OF ENDOGENOUS AND EXOGENOUS FACTORS

Nevertheless, prison reality as a human reality is not black and white and we only aim to reach the right beacon. Reality is normally distant from the archetype. It evolves by a succession of improved stages in a scale of grey tones. And the first step to follow the path is to accept the archetype, is to believe in it, and believing in it implies the need to act accordingly. Even so, we may describe some common knowledge realities that, among others, show how difficult this task is.

In any organisation, leadership is an essential aspect and we should bear in mind that each prison, each prison administration, is an organisation. If leadership doesn't clearly show commitment for the implementation of a prison model based on the rehabilitation process, then the importance of rehabilitation will fade. Poor conditions in prison may easily lead to a reduction of prison life to the mere deterrence factor. Incapacity in reforming the prison park diminishes the possibility of using the necessary new treatment approach. Maximum security tends to avoid rehabilitation initiatives. Private prisons management can overlook rehabilitation if it is not a clear and evaluated objective for the State. Overcrowding limits the opportunity for a rehabilitation process. Military hierarchical staff organisation underlines the security factor domain. Budgetary and staff cuts first of all have impact on rehabilitation programs. Media pressure on hardening the reaction against crime turns it difficult to invest in rehabilitation policies. Public reactions to individual open regime failure will difficult new trials. Staff limitation on understanding and practice cultural mediation[7] strongly reduces the chances of implementing a rehabilitation process.

Thus, even when the archetype is fully recognised, the way to reach it is severely influenced by endogenous and exogenous factors, as we have stressed with the few sentences we have just read. To conclude, building a rehabilitation process is something always done on unstable ground, but it is an essential task only possible by people's action.

6. THE IMPORTANCE OF STAFF AND LEADERSHIP

In any organisation, success is mostly based upon staff attitude. Quality and motivation are normally linked to objectives, work conditions, training and leadership. Prison staff in general resents the idea of being just and only wall-keepers. Even guards need to look at the fulfilment of their tasks as something not only related to prisons' and public safety. The basic, not well informed, notion of the contribution given by the prison staff in order to avoid reoffending, as the good side of being part of it, is not enough as a goal. To be, as cultural mediator[8], an active participant in building and developing an individualised rehabilitation plan, to give the offender conditions for a better choice in the future, on the contrary, is an appealing objective.

The humanitarian, multidisciplinary, specialised dimension contained in the rehabilitation idea and its individualised application can give the prison staff a dignified and motivating definition for their jobs. The call to achieve the rehabilitation process and the raising of standards that goes with it is clearly

7 The expression "cultural turmoil", we have used at p. 123, translates the existing reality in the majority of prisons. Ethnic differences, different nationalities, social and religious differences, different cultural backgrounds, different ages, and so on, gives a myriad of ways of feeling and doing all together at the same time in the same closed space. It is fundamental to find out the common denominator based on which all those differences – plus the main cultural difference separating inmates and staff made by the formal and informal rules of the sub-culture existing in each prison – can be dealt with, thus creating common ground allowing communication and understanding.
To prepare staff to be specialized cultural mediators is a master key opening way to the understanding and acceptance of the rehabilitation process trough the treatment plan.

8 See previous note.

linked to the opening up of the prison system to free society, to new experiences and to synergies generated by partnership projects, as well as linked to staff training, motivation and leadership.

For the prison system and the rehabilitation process, although buildings and budgets are very important and for some programs even essential, they are secondary regarding staff and leadership. Committed leadership and proper training and evaluation will transform rehabilitation in the leading flag of the prison administration.

7. CULTURAL CHANGE AND CULTURAL MEDIATION: THE KEY FACTOR[9]

Raising standards and reforming are only possible if we embark on a cultural change process in order to convince people that:

- it is possible to combine prison service with cultural change, quality and innovation;
- it is possible as well to give a voice to staff and inmates;
- it is possible in order to integrate prisons in the community;
- it is possible to build a real system that draws on the positive synergies found in a holistic approach.

And that can be done with realism and imagination, with the resources available.

Having in mind the archetype, aiming at the attainable, trying to move forward even when things went wrong or when resistance was found, it is always possible to examine procedures and routines and to see what may be changed and improved.

"Daily intense and programmed activity and occupation" was the second of the three main components of prison life which have been referred as essential for the development of the rehabilitation process and the existence of a safe prison environment. It is mainly in this field that resides the opportunity for positive intervention even when the lack of resources reduces the chances of implementing ambitious programmes. All the possible ideas used to occupy inmates by developing their knowledge, opening up their cultural views, on applying a systematic and individualised rehabilitation plan, will never be lost and may always be positively used by them on a moment of crucial choice.

Using prison time to invest in education is probably a unique opportunity for developing a different human reality that will be able to look upon the previous

[9] See note 7.

cultural codes from a different perspective and make them evolve in a positive way based on free and more highlighted choices.

With fewer resources, apart the intensity of involvement from those called to do something out of nothing or to lead and monitor different programmes, the coordination, supervision and management, in one word leadership, as referred above, is the key factor for success of the rehabilitation approach. Hence, the selection and recruitment of those responsible for prisons is a major decision for the central prison administration, a decision where the adherence to the rehabilitation idea should be a decisive selection parameter.

Prison leadership must be aware of the complex cultural reality surrounding all and each individual in custody and should bear in mind that it is only possible to defend their basic fundamental rights and their involvement as subjects in the execution of sentences in the light of each specific case. The bases of a rehabilitation plan are rooted in that notion, knowing that we need qualified cultural mediation in order to establish platforms for joint cultural development.

In Prison Administration, if there is political and social commitment, if objective inequalities are gradually eliminated through information – that is, for example, school education, vocational training, social skills development – and if platforms for joint cultural development are put in place, then we will be experiencing the definition of rehabilitation as a progressive process and given the exact dimension of its value to the Prison Administration.

8. REMAND AND OTHER FINAL REMARKS

It is important to briefly look into the possible and natural question of the value of rehabilitation as far as custody on remand and people on remand are concerned. In such cases, there is no need for a rehabilitation plan. As a matter of fact anyone in custody being on remand is presumed innocent and conceptually speaking the expression rehabilitation is not applicable properly. But for those being in prison even on remand, sometimes for a long period, it is impossible to imagine the existence of an aseptic environment linked to the idea of presumption of innocence. Therefore, we have to accept that in the remand period prison should be run in an active and positive way and the presumed innocent be free to participate in the activities and programs existing in prison.

In fact, there is every reason to keep in mind the already mentioned second component of prison life referring to "daily intense and programmed activity and occupation" which, as we have stressed, is, as well, essential to the rehabilitation process. Hence, for those on remand who after trial are released without conviction, any knowledge, any treatment received from any programme will have been positive for their future. For those who are convicted and start serving a sentence, the building of a rehabilitation plan will have already begun.

Thus, to the prison system the value of rehabilitation in relation to custody on remand, as regards some of its pragmatic components, is as fundamental as it is when dealing with the execution of a prison sentence.

In a wider perspective, although dealing with rehabilitation and prison issues was our main purpose, it is important, however, to stress that it is not possible to slice a person as salami and look only at the offender when he or she is within the prison walls. In fact, the subject of rehabilitation linked to the prison system only envisages the individual delinquent behaviour at one of its possible phases.

This paper doesn't cover the broader question of prevention focused on the offender before and after criminal proceedings. It does neither cover all the action possible, in the case of conviction, during the enforcement of community sanctions and measures, nor does it focus the entire prevention work to be done with concerned families and the community.

Penal and penitentiary systems shouldn't separate the same person in different drawers with different treatments, ignoring each others, during the course of the same indivisible journey. That being said, is rehabilitation a phase of prevention? And the question for Society to get better answers will it not be the need for looking at delinquent behaviour in a more integrated and comprehensive way?

In any case and regardless all the possible questions, sticking to the given task, it is important to express the conviction that the seeds of the rehabilitation process grow, nevertheless, inside the prison system even when it is managed in a more conservative way, or in a period of insufficient budget, limited staff or inadequate buildings and facilities.

Open regimes, home leaves, parole, free of drug units, electronic monitoring and other programmes can be topics illustrating the importance of a rehabilitation process. A process based on the adjective role of the prison service that helps building the ultimate and decisive moment of choice (no one knows exactly when) which will define if someone who was once convicted will be, or not, a re-offender.

Another extremely important issue that also shows the relevance of the rehabilitation process and of its underlying ideology, even when difficult circumstances are conditioning the prison system, is the intervention of voluntary organisations in the prison establishments and the existing protocols between private organisations or other entities and the prison administration, allowing prisoners to have contact with the exterior environment in order to prepare their future.

9. CLOSING REMARKS

In sum, repeating something once written on another occasion, a prison system will have fulfilled its role if it provides a safe prison environment, if it achieves a good and well thought-out selection of inmates in manageable groups, if it offers all offenders real opportunities for personal improvement, if it ensures high level training, cohesion and motivation among its staff, and if it actively pursues the best possible co-operation and interaction with the free community. This will be impossible without considering the rehabilitation process as a prison system essential objective. Even so and as a result of everything that has been said, having in society as well as in the prison administration a stable and consolidated rehabilitation culture is a continuous challenge and so far an enormous and probably rare victory.

L'IMPORTANCE DE LA RÉHABILITATION DES DÉTENUS DANS L'INTÉRÊT DES VICTIMES : L'ÉVOLUTION DE LA JUSTICE RESTAURATIVE

Edmundo Oliveira*

A l'avènement de la mondialisation ont surgi de nouveaux thèmes d'études concernant le crime et son acteur. Um de ces aspects est la victimologie, qui à l'aide des concepts interdisciplinaires recherche comprendre le crime et le criminel, dans la perspective de la victime, dans le cadre des stratégies de médiation de réconciliation, activés par la Justice Restaurative. Ainsi, cette étude vise à trouver des réponses aux questions suivantes :

- Dans quelle mesure la réhabilitation du détenu est souhaitable pour la victime ?
- Comment la réhabilitation du détenu répond aux intérêts de la victime ?
- La victime peut-elle jouer un rôle majeur dans le processus de réinsertion du détenu dans la société ?

1. INTRODUCTION

Au cours des dernières décennies, la théorie pénale a oscillé entre deux extrêmes : d'un côté, le renforcement du pouvoir punitif de l'Etat, pour satisfaire le contrôle social ; tandis que de l'autre, existe la demande de réduction de cet exercice, en raison d'une confiance fragile dans la réponse pénale.

Le grand défi pour la réussite de la mission de surmonter les diverses expressions de la criminalité, réside dans le fait d'harmoniser les droits individuels et les valeurs collectives. Seuls les progrès de mesures visant la

* Dr. E. Oliveira, PhD, est Professeur Titulaire de Droit Pénal et Criminologie Université de l'Amazonie, Brésil, et Représentant au Brésil de la Fondation Internationale Pénale et Pénitentiaire.

coexistence dans la société, et le rétablissement de la primauté du Droit sur le culte de la délinquance assureront la paix sociale.

Les bouleversements permanents dans les modes de Justice Pénale sont révélés, surtout, dans les difficultés à maintenir une bonne conduite de la Police dans la réalité des prisons. Celles-ci agissent, dans de nombreux pays, comme des filtres de promiscuité. Elles sont incapables de préparer le délinquant à un avenir d'homme libre, honnête et assurant sa subsistance.

Le premier élément manifesté par le phénomène criminel est présent dans les risques auxquels la population est confrontée, en raison de l'absence de mécanismes alternatifs de dialogue entre la société et l'administration de la Justice, pour empêcher la fragmentation de la citoyenneté.[1] Dans ce contexte, la société doit faire face aux dilemmes provoqués par des crises successives, lesquelles rendent difficile à surmonter les effets causés par les violations du bien-être public.

Parmi les nombreux défis liés aux formes de croissance des villes et aux ajustements de leurs infrastructures, il convient de souligner la préoccupation résultant de la proximité entre le délinquant et la victime.[2] Il n'y a plus de doute que la prévention et la lutte contre la criminalité passent nécessairement par l'intérêt de la communauté, pour le fait que, pour comprendre le crime et le criminel, il faut aussi comprendre les relations de cause à effet qui affectent la personne victime.[3]

Cette approche s'inscrit dans les objectifs généraux du millénaire, fixés par les Nations Unies pour mener à bien, à partir de 2.015, la réduction de la pauvreté, de l'exclusion, de la discrimination et de l'insécurité qui affligent l'humanité, en raison des pressions découlant de la globalisation.[4]

2. DANS QUELLE MESURE LA RÉHABILITATION DU DÉLINQUANT EST SOUHAITABLE POUR LA VICTIME

Etant donné la grande quantité de conduites criminelles, l'idéal serait que chaque victime puisse concevoir la prison et le prisonnier en tant que cibles de la citoyenneté durable. Ces lignes directrices devraient être orientées vers un changement de comportement du délinquant, pour faire de lui un citoyen utile.[5] Il pourrait même participer à la mise en œuvre de stratégies de protection des victimes.

---

1 Healter Strang *et al.*, 'Victim Evaluations of Face-to-Face Restorative Justice Experiences: A quasi-experimental analysis.', 62 Journal of Social Issues 2 (2006), p. 281-306.

2 Elisabeth Elliott & Robert M. Gordon (eds.), *New Directions in Restorative Justice: Issues, Practice, Evaluation*, Devon, United Kingdom: Willan Publishing, 2005, p. 31-36.

3 Gerry Johnstone, *Restorative Justice: Ideas, Values and Debates*, Devon, United Kingdom: Willan Publishing, 2002, p. 139-141.

4 Voir le site de l'Oganisation des Nations Unies (www.un.org/millenniumgoals).

5 Lawrence Sherman & Healter Strang, *Restorative Justice: The Evidence*, London: The Smith Institute, 2007, p. 167-168.

Ce que nous observons, aujourd'hui, en particulier dans les régions moins développées, est que cet objectif est simplement une aspiration théorique, en raison de trois facteurs:

Le premier – les scénarios de nombreux crimes, surtout les plus graves comme l'homicide, représentent une rupture dans la relation de la victime avec son agresseur.[6]

Le deuxième – la prison, comme outil de réhabilitation, continue à être considérée avec méfiance, surtout dans les régions de faible protection des droits civils. Dans celles-ci, l'incarcération entraîne le syndrome de la personnalité antisociale.

Le troisième – en général, dans les procédures qui se déroulent dans les tribunaux, la victime se sent comme un étranger en face de policiers qui la traitent de manière rude et d'un juge qui la regarde avec indifférence, facilitant des représailles et des combines de la part de la défense de l'accusé.[7] Cette victimisation, légitimée par la société, est particulièrement sensible en Amérique Latine, où, six victimes sur dix, font toujours une évaluation du coût avant d'engager des procédures contre un délinquant. Cela se produit en raison d'un système coûteux, lent et parfois impliqué dans les scandales de corruption.

À cet égard, l'Institut Latino-Américain pour la Prévention du Crime et le Traitement des Délinquants, ayant son siège à San Jose de Costa Rica, a lancé en avril 2010, un rapport détaillé intitulé *Prison et Justice Pénale en Amérique Latine Latine et Caraïbes*. Dans ce document, on trouve une analyse qui reflète la préoccupation croissante concernant les problèmes de la prison, et le besoin de formuler de nouvelles directives pour orienter l'application des dispositions pénales, en mettant l'accent sur l'éducation et la santé du prisonnier et de ceux qui ont quitté la prison.[8] Il ne fait aucun doute que la réhabilitation du prisonnier devient souhaitable pour la victime dès lors que les avantages lui sont présenté.

Quels sont ces avantages ?[9]

1. Le prisonnier est-il capable d'effectuer une réparation minimale en fonction de la peine criminelle ?
2. Le prisonnier est-il en mesure d'assumer les responsabilités civiles pour compenser ou indemniser la victime ?

6 Ezrah Fattah & Stefaan Parmentier, *Victim Policies and Criminal Justice on the Road to Restorative Justice*, Leuven: Leuven University Press, 2001, p. 6-8.

7 Brian Williams, *Reparation and Victim-Focused Social Work*, London: Jessica Kingsley Publishers, 2002, p. 13-14.

8 Voir la site de ILANUD (www.ilanud.or.cr).

9 Andrew Von Hirsch *et al.* (eds.), *Restorative Justice and Criminal Justice: Competing or Reconcilable Paradigms?*, Oxford: Hart Publishing, 2002, p. 81-82.

3. Le prisonnier sera-t-il capable d'assumer l'engagement de rembourser une somme ou de rendre un objet soustrait à la victime ?
4. La victime peut-elle exercer une influence sur l'application des sanctions pénales appropriées au détenu ?
5. Le prisonnier reçoit-il une formation professionnelle, permettant un avenir en toute liberté ?
6. Le prisonnier reçoit-il des soins de santé et une orientation scolaire en prison ?
7. Le prisonnier est-il apte à gérer les risques et les difficultés personnelles, sans faire appel à la violence ?
8. Quelle est la relation du prisonnier avec sa famille ?
9. L'Etat développe-t-il un programme de gestions avec des moyens capables de promouvoir la réconciliation du prisonnier et sa victime, au sein des communautés ?

Il est clair que la réhabilitation du délinquant est souhaitable pour la victime. Le délinquant lui-même, analysant de façon positive ses actions, pourrait aider à prévenir des comportements victimogènes.[10] En conséquence, le taux de délinquance diminuerait dans les zones de victimisation.

Dans cette ligne, un des points les plus intéressants dans l'état actuel des connaissances scientifiques concernant la victimisation est l'élection de directives pratiques axées sur la prévention de la criminalité par la prévention de la victimisation.[11] La prévention de la victimisation passe donc, nécessairement par les indicateurs sociaux, appliqués avec transparence par le gouvernement, dans les secteurs de la santé, de l'éducation, de la sécurité publique et de l'administration de systèmes de justice.

Voici, donc, la meilleure façon de réduire ou d'éliminer les motifs ou les tendances de la criminalité : mise au point de nouvelles méthodes de prévention de la victimisation, c'est-à-dire, que les victimes soient protégées par le succès[12] des objectifs de prévention de la criminalité.

En conformité à cet objectif, l'Organisation des Nations Unies dispose de quatre instruments pertinents pour assurer la participation de la victime au processus de réhabilitation du délinquant.

1. Les Règles Minimales des Nations Unies pour l'administration de Justice à des enfants et des jeunes, connues comme Règles de Beijing (Résolution de l'Assemblée Générale des Nations Unies n°40/33 du 29 novembre 1985) attirent

10 Howard Zehr & Barb Toews, *Critical Issues in Restorative Justice*, Monsey, New York: Criminal Justice Press, 2004, p. 16-18.

11 Carolyn Hoyle, *Restorative Justice: Critical Concepts in Criminology*, New York: Routledge Publications, 2009, p. 4-5.

12 Lode Walgrave, *Restorative Justice and the Law*, Devon, United Kingdom: Willan Publishing, 2003, p. 14-15.

l'attention sur l'importance des programmes de bien-être, à être implantés dans les communautés concernées. Ces règles se rapportent à des initiatives d'accords entre les parties, dans le cas d'indemnisation des pertes subies par les victimes, afin de faciliter la réinsertion sociale et familiale de jeunes contrevenants.

2. La Déclaration des Nations Unies sur les Principes Fondamentaux relatifs aux victimes de crimes et d'abus de pouvoir (Résolution de l'Assemblée Généale des Nations Unies n°40/34, du 29 novembre 1985) est très positive. Ces principes vont influencer les programmes des gouvernements, pour surmonter les adversités et les injustices qui frappent les victimes moralement et physiquement. Il est à noter que cette Déclaration des Nations Unies (Résolution n° 40/34), n'a pas abordé, spécifiquement, les procédures opérationnelles nécessaires à la politique de prévention de la victimisation, visant à assurer la liaison politique avec la réhabilitation du détenu.

Toutefois, l'annexe de la présente Déclaration, également adopté par l'Assemblée Générale des Nations Unies, dans la Résolution 40/34, aux points 7 et 8, contient des recommandations pour les États Membres, conformément à la législation nationale, fournissant les moyens d'exécuter la prévention de la victimisation. Ainsi, le délinquant devrait réparer équitablement le préjudice causé à la victime, en y incluant la réconciliation entre les parties, même si le contrevenant est soumis à prison ou servant des mesures non privatives de liberté.

3. Tenant compte de la pluralité des systèmes existants de la Justice Pénale dans toutes les régions, les Règles Minimales des Nations Unies pour l'Élaboration de Mesures Non Privatives de Liberté, connues sous le nom de Règles de Tokyo (de l'Assemblée Générale des Nations Unies, Résolution 45/110, du 14 décembre 1990), même si concentrées sur la gestion des mesures non privatives de liberté, elles apportent au point 1.4, le trait caractéristique de la prévention de la victimisation. Ce point souligne les préoccupations de la société concernant la sécurité publique et la prévention de la criminalité, tout en reconnaissant la préoccupation essentielle avec la victime d'un crime. Cette préoccupation démontre la nécessité d'une réinsertion sociale du délinquant incarcéré ou soumis à une mesure non privatives de liberté.

4. De son côté, les Principes de Base des Nations Unies sur l'Utilisation des Programmes de Justice Restaurative en Matière Criminelle (Résolution du Conseil Économique et Social des Nations Unies – ECOSOC, n° 2002/19, du 24 Juillet 2002) sont venus renforcer les principes précédents des Nations Unies qui donnent un sens aux initiatives de négociation de la Justice Communautaire, qui visent à assurer une plus grande assistance matérielle et psychologique aux victimes de la criminalité. Cette emphase sur l'action de la Justice Communautaire souligne le soutien à accorder à la réconciliation de la victime

avec les contrevenants, même quand ils sont soumis au régime de privation de liberté.

Les Notions de Base de l'ECOSOC énumèrent six règles et clauses explicatives qui appellent les États Membres à coopérer et à échanger des expériences sur les programmes, les recherches et la formation communautaire de négociation dans le contexte de la Justice Restaurative, en matière criminelle. L'échange d'expériences fructueuses ouvrira de nouveaux horizons pour le caractère pédagogique de réinsertion sociale du contrevenant, selon la formule de traitement définie lors de sa condamnation pénale.[13]

Cet idéal, s'inscrit dans le cadre ou la politique des options concrètes, en tenant compte de la personnalité du contrevenant et de son comportement. Et ainsi, dans la relation coût-efficacité de la réinsertion sociale ciblé, qui doit s'ajuster à l'intérêt de la victime, émergera la réalité d'envisager l'impact de cinq conséquences positives :

- Préservation du sens de justice ;
- Autonomisation de la communauté dans la résolution des conflits ;
- Restauration de la coexistence pacifique ;
- Redynamisation de la sécurité publique ;
- Formation d'obstacles au retour de relations conflictuelles similaires.

3. COMMENT LA RÉINSERTION DU PRISONNIER PEUT S'AJUSTER AUX INTÉRÊTS DE LA VICTIME ?

La réponse à cette question sera axée sur la démonstration de ce qui est le plus développé en termes de résolution de conflits entre les parties dans le Continent Américain. Dans ce continent, se distinguent des programmes qui ont connu un grand succès, grâce à la visibilité des méthodes alternatives susceptibles d'abréger les tragédies des victimes et leurs familles.[14] Dans ce contexte, il y a deux entités privées dignes de mention, les deux à New York City, Etats-Unis :

- Vera Institute of Justice[15]
- Safe Horizon Agency[16]

---

13 Elmar G.M. Weitekamp & Hans-Jürgen Kerner, *Restorative Justice In Context: International Practice and Directions*, Devon, United Kingdom: Willan Publishing, 2002, p. 21-24.

14 Caronline M. Angel, *Crime victims meet their offenders: Testing the Impact of restorative justice. Conferences on victims' post-traumatic stress symptoms*, Doctoral Dissertation, University of Pennsylvania, Philadelphia, 2005, p. 19-21.

15 Www.vera.org.

16 Www.safehorizon.org.

Les performances de ces deux entités, considérées comme les meilleures institutions en Amérique, sont des exemples concrets que la science, dans le domaine du Droit, c'est un agent de changement social pour améliorer le fonctionnement de la société, sans avoir besoin de perdre plus de temps avec les procès judiciaires qui surchargent les tribunaux traditionnels.

S'appuyant sur la Justice Réstaurative, le Vera Institute of Justice et le Safe Horizon Agency s'utilisent de la médiation criminelle, à la fois pour soulager la violence physique ou moral subi par les victimes et leurs familles, ainsi que pour élever les solutions de conflits qui renforcent la culture de pacification sociale. C'est précisément dans le travail auprès de la population, visant à la pacification sociale, qui correspond l'objectif de réinsertion du détenu: cette réhabilitation doit s'ajuster à l'intérêt et à la satisfaction de la victime. Ce travail de pacification sociale ouvre des espaces pour l'administration des désaccords ou des litiges et pour surmonter l'adversité, grâce à l'amélioration personnelle qui mène à la réconciliation des personnes impliquées dans des situations de divergences avec petit, moyen ou même un fort pouvoir offensif.[17]

Un bon exemple de ce but est le modèle du «Système Multi-Portes», qui favorise la combinaison de méthodes alternatives de valorisation personnel, renforçant les liens de confiance entre la victime et le contrevenant, avec le soutien de la famille et des amis, même dans des circonstances extrêmes, telles que celles impliquant la drogue, vols, lésions corporelles et tentative d'assassinat. Le «Système Multi-Portes» qui est déjà en cours de mis en place dans divers pays, a été conçu par Frank Sander, Professeur Émérite de l'École de Droit de l'Université Harvard.[18]

Grâce au soutien continu de Gouvernement de New York, la Cour de Justice de l'État de New York, les Cliniques de Droit de l'Université de New York et l'Université de Colombie, les performances de Vera Institute of Justice et de Safe Horizon Agency ont obtenu des succès notables dans les objectifs suivants:

1. Consolidation des politiques d'harmonisation dans les relations entre l'auteur et la victime, afin d'éviter la victimisation future;
2. Diminution de la demande dans la procédure judiciaire;
3. Résolution de 68 % de cas réglés sans recours aux processus de Justice traditionnels;
4. Les solutions de conflits caractérisés par le pardon de la victime sur la scène de la repentance et la démonstration de remords du contrevenant, même quand il est soumis à la privation de liberté;

---

17 Mark S. Umbreit, Betty Vos, Robert B. Coates & Katherine A. Brown, *Facing Violence: The Path of Restorative Justice and Dialogue*, Monsey, New York: Criminal Justice Press, 2003, p. 12-13.

18 Frank E. Sander, Nancy Rogers & Stephen Goldberg, *Dispute Resolution: Negotiation, Mediation and other Processes*, Frederick, Maryland: Aspen Publishers, 2007, p. 9-23.

5. L'émergence d'une Justice Préventive basée sur une méthode d'intervention rapide et efficace ;
6. Construction de « territoires de paix » dans les régions auparavant entourées de violence ;
7. Diminution de la dynamique de représailles et de se faire justice avec leurs propres mains.

Les actions visées ci-dessus ont attirés la bonne volonté de nombreuses victimes de crimes à des activités communautaires pour la réinsertion sociale des délinquants en cours de Stage de Probation (Convict Released on Parole), contrevenant en Régime Ouvert (Convict in a Minimum Security Prison), le délinquant en Régime Pénitentiaire Semi-Ouvert (Convict in a Medium Security Prison) et contrevenant ayant Suspension Condicionelle de la Peine (Probation).

4. LA VICTIME PEUT-ELLE EXERCER UN RÔLE PRÉPONDÉRANT DANS LA DYNAMIQUE DE LA RÉADAPTATION DU DÉTENU DANS LA FAMILLE ET LA COMMUNAUTÉ ?

Sans nul doute oui.

La médiation rituel différenciée de la Justice Restaurative, par les expériences de réconciliation, a mis le Droit Pénal et la Criminologie Experimental[19] au premier plan des débats globale sur la meilleure façon de faire face aux conséquences de la criminalité et ses implications pour l'avenir.

L'expérience innovante de la Justice Restaurative non seulement en Amérique, mais aussi en Europe, Asie, Afrique et Océanie a effectivement démontré que la réadaptation du délinquant est souhaitable pour la victime chaque fois que possible. Mais cela dépend de la diversité des procédures de nature à faire le succès des interventions sur des problèmes spécifiques dans chaque domaine de la criminalité et de chaque zone de victimisation.[20]

Ce portrait des progrès en matière de Justice Restaurative dans le traitement du binôme délinquants – victimes est largement perceptible dans l'effectif que nous vous présentons dans la Bibliographie mise à jour annexé à la présente exposition.

---

19 John Braithwaite, *Restorative Justice and Responsive Regulation*, Oxford: Oxford University Press, 2002, p. 71-72.

20 Hema Hargovan, 'Knocking and Entering: Restorative Justice Arrives at the Courts', 21 *Acta Criminologica Crimsa Conference Special Edition* 1 (2008), p. 24-40.

5. CONCLUSION

Le monde de la modernité met le Droit chargé de la mission d'assurer la paix dans le centre des principes fondamentaux de l'humanité. Cette suprématie dépend, en grande échelle, de savoir accorder une plus grande dimension sociale aux sentiments de la victime et aux réactions du délinquant, surtout quand il fait face ou s'il a fait face à la stigmatisation de la prison.

Considérant ce qui précède, on s'attend à ce que le colloque à Dublin travail comme un catalyseur. Espérons que chaque Gouvernement développe de meilleures pratiques en ce qui concerne les critères de la réhabilitation du délinquant. Et que cette réadaptation se présente chaque foi plus étroitement liée à ce qui est souhaitable pour la victime.

Cela signifie que la Fondation Internationale Pénale et Pénitentiaire nous permet de vivre l'espoir d'initiatives prometteuses sur divers aspects des systèmes pénaux, Cela exige une coopération entre les pays pour assimiler les expériences de vie avec les changements en faveur des valeurs d'une mondialisation plus saine.[21]

Le Colloque de Dublin a eu la sagesse de stimuler notre raison pour une redéfinition cohérente du rôle des régimes d'application pénale qui doivent être en harmonie avec l'étendue des droits et des intérêts de la victime.

Il s'agit d'une nouvelle carte avec de réelles perspectives, de récolte de bons fruits, de sorte que toutes les communautés bénéficient d'une prospérité, avec moins de criminalité et plus de fraternité dans les liens de la complexité de la nature humaine.

---

21 Christiaan Bezuidenhout, 'Restorative Justice with an Explicit Rehabilitative Ethos: Is this the Resolve to Change Criminality?', 20 *Acta Criminologica* 2 (2007), 43 at p. 43-48.

PART THREE

MEASURES TO DEAL WITH HIGH RISK OFFENDERS DURING AND AFTER THEIR SENTENCE

3ème PARTIE

LA GESTION DES DÉLINQUANTS À RISQUE ÉLEVÉ PENDANT ET APRÈS L'EXÉCUTION DE LEUR SANCTION

THE JUSTIFICATION FOR TAKING MEASURES TO PREDICT OFFENDING AND REOFFENDING AND TO MANAGE RISK

Warren Young*

1. INTRODUCTION

This volume is considering a single overall theme – a theme which constantly emerges in the development of criminal justice policy both in New Zealand and overseas. That theme is how the risk of reoffending should be taken into account, and what weight it should be given, when criminal justice decisions are made.

This contribution is intended to provide an overview of the issues and how they should be addressed. It therefore provides a theoretical and conceptual framework against which the subsequent papers in this volume can be assessed.

2. CHANGING CONCEPTIONS OF RISK

It is by no means a recent phenomenon that decisions in the criminal justice system take into account the risk posed by offenders. That has been done for a long time – certainly back as far as the 19th century.[1]

There have, however, been shifts in political and public perceptions of the nature of the populations who have been thought to pose a risk requiring particular or special consideration. In the first half of the 20th century, at least in Anglo-American jurisdictions, the focus of preventive measures tended to be on the persistent or habitual offender. Moreover, the mere fact of their persistence was seen to be enough to justify special treatment, including indeterminate sentences. The concept of dangerous (that is, high-risk serious) offenders received

---

* Dr. W. Young BA LLB (Hons) PhD is a policy and law reform consultant in Wellington, New Zealand. He has been Deputy President of the New Zealand Law Commission, a Deputy Secretary for Justice and a Professor of law.

1 John Pratt, *Governing the Dangerous: Dangerousness, Law and Social Changes*, Sydney: Federation Press, 1997.

relatively little attention, either in policymaking or in the academic literature, and there were few if any penal measures or other legislative provisions specifically directed towards them.

In the 1970s, that began to change. Notions of dangerousness and risk emerged as a major theme in policy-making, and have been the catalyst for a great deal of legislative activity ever since.[2] In particular, there have been three fundamental shifts in thinking.

First, greater attention has begun to be paid to those who are not necessarily convicted with great frequency but, when they do offend, cause substantial harm. In the first instance, this was confined to sexual offenders – particularly paedophiles. But more recently there has been an almost equal preoccupation with violent offenders.

Secondly, recognition of the difficulty of making accurate predictions has led to a substantial body of work designed to improve the science of risk prediction, and to develop systematic and empirically validated tools to support it. That work has largely been seen as a technical exercise, rather than (as I will come on to discuss) an exercise which ought also to be fundamentally concerned with notions of justice.

Thirdly, at least to some degree, there has been recognition of the need for responses to risk to include some notion of proportionality. Although the rationale for this has been poorly articulated, it is implicitly based on the view that preventive measures that substantially curtail freedom cannot be justified to prevent minor harm to others, in terms of both individual rights and public costs and benefits. To put it another way, it is now a little clearer that the debate needs to be not merely about *risks,* but about *unacceptable risks i.e.* dangers.

So where has this new preoccupation with risk led us, and what issues and difficulties has it given rise to? Before I attempt to answer that question, I need to discuss two fairly self-evident points: that assessment of risk now underpins nearly all aspects of decision-making; and that the need to take risk into account in that decision-making is unavoidable and that objections to it are misconceived. I will discuss each of these points in turn.

3. ASSESSMENT OF RISK NOW UNDERPINS ALMOST ALL STAGES OF CRIMINAL JUSTICE DECISION-MAKING

Risk assessment pervades all aspects of criminal justice decision-making. To take some examples:

---

2 Arie Freiberg, 'Guerrillas in our Midst? Judicial responses to governing the dangerous', in: Mark Brown & John Pratt (eds), *Dangerous Offenders: Punishment and Social Order*, London: Routledge, 2000, p. 51–69.

1. It informs the way in which the police exercise their discretion whether or not to charge a suspect, to issue a warning or (in New Zealand) to offer informal diversion from the formal criminal justice system.
2. It is the primary factor in determining whether a person charged with an offence is released on bail or remanded in custody pending trial or sentence.
3. It underpins the way in which those found insane or unfit to stand trial because of mental impairment are disposed of. In New Zealand, for example, offenders found not guilty by reason of insanity are held indefinitely as special patients if the court is satisfied that this is necessary to protect the public.[3]
4. It informs the selection of the type and length of sentence. It is obviously the primary consideration when sentences of indefinite imprisonment for public protection (*e.g.*, sentences of preventive detention or their equivalent) are being imposed. But it is more generally one of the primary rationales for taking previous convictions into account as an aggravating factor, or for treating the absence of previous convictions as a mitigating factor.[4]
5. In New Zealand it is the factor that dictates whether someone is to be released on parole and if so, the nature of the conditions attached to their release.[5]
6. In recent years it has begun to be used to justify the imposition of ongoing restrictions after the end of a sentence. In New Zealand this has taken the form of Extended Supervision Orders that enables the compulsory supervision, sometimes with restrictive conditions, of certain types of sex offenders for up to 10 years.[6] At the time of writing legislation is before Parliament to create Public Protection Orders that will permit the ongoing indefinite detention beyond the end of their sentence of a small number of high-risk individuals who pose a very high risk of imminent serious sexual or violent offending.[7]
7. Finally, it is now being used to justify civil orders to curtail freedom or prevent specified activities. These take a variety of forms in different jurisdictions but they include domestic protection orders, harassment orders and anti-social behaviour orders. In New Zealand the Vulnerable Children Bill,[8] currently before Parliament, also proposes the establishment of a child abuse prevention order, discussed in more detail below.

---

3 Criminal Procedure (Mentally Impaired Persons) Act 2003, s 24.

4 See, in the New Zealand Context, s 9(1)(j) of the Sentencing Act 2002 and J.B. Robertson, F.B. Adams & C. Browning (eds), *Adams on Criminal Law – Sentencing*, Wellington: Brookers, 2007.

5 Parole Act 2002, s 28.

6 Parole Act 2002, ss 107A-107Z.

7 Public Safety (Public Protection Orders) Bill 2012.

8 Vulnerable Children Bill 2013.

4. CRITICISMS OF THE RISK PREDICTION ENTERPRISE

It should be obvious from the list set out above that it would be both unrealistic, and publicly unacceptable, to suggest that risk should never be taken into account in criminal justice decision-making. We therefore cannot escape deciding how we can apply risk considerations in a fair and principled manner.

There is by no means universal agreement with that view. Some argue that it is impossible to assess risk and take it into account in a fair and principled manner. Their arguments generally fall into three categories.

First, it is argued that imposing any sort of coercive measures on people on account of their risk of offending (or reoffending) is tantamount to punishing them for crimes they have not yet committed and that it is therefore contrary to the presumption of innocence. I do not agree. The presumption of innocence is a legal presumption that dictates the procedures that ought to be followed in determining whether a person is to be convicted and subject to criminal sanctions for their offending, and that underpins the requirement that their offending be proved beyond reasonable doubt. It is wholly inapt to the nature and purpose of risk prediction, which is inherently uncertain. The debate should be about whether and when it is appropriate to take pre-emptive action to prevent certain sorts of behaviour in the future when one cannot be certain that it will occur. Concepts developed for different purposes do not enable us to answer that question.

Those who argue that risk prediction is a violation of fundamental rights and freedoms implicitly seem to acknowledge this, because they are generally willing to accept its use in some contexts such as decisions about bail or remand in custody, and generally also acknowledge that there are extreme outlier cases where protective measures are justified. But that points to a real inconsistency in their argument: if risk prediction is in itself a violation of fundamental rights and freedoms, exceptions allowing it cannot be made.

Secondly, it is argued that risk prediction, and preventive measures on the basis of it, represent a denial of individual free will and autonomy, because they are based on who people are perceived to be (*i.e.* what their characteristics and dispositions are), rather than on what they have done. Again, this is an overly simplistic analysis. Decisions on the basis of judgements about the characteristics and dispositions of others are made routinely in a variety of social contexts. This is simply a recognition of the fact that people demonstrate by their previous conduct a greater or lesser likelihood of acting in particular ways. It does not deny free will or the ability of people to change or to act contrary to their disposition (*e.g.* to act generously when they are widely known to be mean). It simply says that if a person's past behaviour is such that it demonstrates an ongoing willingness to act on his or her disposition, society is justified in responding accordingly.

Thirdly, risk prediction results in a large number of "false positive" mistakes – for example, the prolonged detention of people who, if released, would not have gone on to commit the predicted offending – so that, even if protective measures could otherwise be justified, they are based on judgements that are too uncertain and inaccurate to be capable of doing justice.

This is the objection with the most force. As has already been noted, any risk assessment is inherently uncertain, and measures based on it will inevitably capture a significant number of people who, in the event, would not have acted in accordance with the prediction in the absence of that measure (so-called "false positives").

But the objection is overstated. The fact that risk prediction results in "errors" is not a good enough reason to abandon the enterprise altogether. The fact that the risk does not materialise does not necessarily mean that the prediction was unjustified. Predictive error is inevitable, because people may fail to act in accordance with a justified prediction for many reasons, including a change in life circumstances or the absence of opportunity. But that is in the nature of risk prediction; it does not in itself make it unjust.

More importantly, methods of risk prediction have improved dramatically in the last 20 years. In relation to at least some types of reoffending we have pretty good information on the factors that demonstrate ongoing risk, so that some predictive tools have a high degree of accuracy.

I acknowledge the reality of the "base rate phenomenon": the fact that, if the likelihood of the predicted behaviour amongst the group being assessed is relatively low, even highly accurate predictive tools will still make many more mistakes than correct predictions. This does not make risk prediction in itself unjust. It is simply one of the factors that must be taken into account in determining whether or when to employ preventive measures. It is likely to mean, for example, that coercive "early intervention" measures can never be justified to manage the risk, because the number of unnecessary interventions and their associated harm would be too high.

These responses to the objections to risk prediction may not satisfy critics. In my view this is largely because, in public and political discourse, the basis for taking preventive measures in criminal justice has been poorly thought through and poorly articulated. Jurisdictions have not relied upon good risk prediction tools or adapted them to the situations in which risk prediction in criminal justice decision-making is required. Rather, the assessment of risk has often been done in an unstructured, intuitive and subjective way that has lacked any empirically validated foundation.

It is true that in some instances (*e.g.*, in relation to sentences of preventive detention, other protective measures imposed at the end of a sentence, or parole decision-making) the degree of risk and the types of factors that must be taken into account in determining whether it exists have been articulated, and actuarial risk "scores" have sometimes been provided to the decision-maker. Even then, the relative weight to be placed respectively on actuarial and individualized information has not been spelt out; it has been left to the decision-maker to weigh up the available information in an intuitive way.

More often, not even this degree of structure is applied to the decision-making task. In many instances (*e.g.*, when bail decisions are being made) the nature of the risk may be identified but there has typically been little specification of the threshold that must be reached; and in others (*e.g.*, when previous convictions are taken into account on sentence), the relevance of risk is implicit rather than explicit. It is in no small part due to the unstructured and intuitive nature of risk prediction that it has often been described as no better than flipping a coin.

The injustice here (and undoubtedly there is injustice) lies in the way in which we are engaging in the risk prediction enterprise, rather than in the fact that we are undertaking it. It does not mean that we should not employ measures based on predicted risk at all. Rather, it points to the fact that it is vital to the integrity and justice of those measures that the circumstances in which preventive measures are employed, and the nature of those measures, conform to a coherent conception of preventive justice and properly utilize available knowledge about how to maximize its effective application.

5. THE NEED FOR A PRINCIPLED AND CONSISTENT BASIS FOR THE IMPOSITION OF PREVENTIVE MEASURES

I turn, then, to consider what a coherent theory of preventive justice would look like. In 1981 I co-authored a book[9] with Jean Floud that represented the thinking of a Working Party on the Dangerous Offender that had been set up by the Home Office in England and Wales. In the book, we attempted, in a fairly rudimentary way, to develop a theory of preventive justice.

In essence, we suggested that the objective of preventive justice is the just redistribution of risk. Because any prediction is inherently uncertain, preventive justice necessarily subjects an offender to the risk of unnecessary measures in order to avert the risk of harm to an innocent person. Justice requires that this risk-shifting be done in a just and principled way. The starting point is that, by analogy with the presumption of innocence, everyone has the right to be treated as harmless. Risk-shifting is justified only if a person has forfeited that right. The critical question is when the right can be regarded as having been forfeited, and what measures we are entitled to employ when it is.

---

9 Jean Floud & Warren Young, *Dangerousness and Criminal Justice*, London: Heinemann, 1981.

In order to answer this question, it is perhaps useful to take a practical example of the nature of this sort of risk-shifting.

In the Vulnerable Children Bill currently before the New Zealand Parliament, there is provision for a new civil order called a child harm prevention order. This order would not depend upon a criminal conviction. It would be able to be imposed if a person were proved on the balance of probabilities to have committed at least one "qualifying offence" (a serious violent or sexual offence against a child) and the court was satisfied that he or she presented a high risk of causing serious harm to a child or children in future. It would enable conditions to be imposed on the person subject to it in order to mitigate the risk to any child or children or any classes of children. These might include restrictions on who they could live with, where they might work or what activities they might undertake. The order would not entail any detention and would not be able to incorporate any positive obligations such as an obligation to undergo a rehabilitative programme.

How might this be justified in terms of the concept of risk-shifting? There are two types of risk with which such orders are concerned. The first is the risk that children will be harmed in the future by the actions of the person against whom the order is sought. The second is the risk that the person would not, as predicted, have harmed a child in the future and will therefore be unnecessarily exposed to and harmed by the imposition of coercive measures. These are self-evidently competing risks. Where should the burden of carrying the risk lie? In my view, a compelling case can be made for the proposition, which underpins the development of child harm prevention orders, that in properly prescribed circumstances the risk should shift from the children, who are vulnerable and unable to take steps to protect themselves, to the person who may harm them in the future.

This should not be characterized as balancing competing rights. Nor should it be seen merely as an exercise in weighing up one set of harms against the other. The question is when it is *just* to transfer the risk from the adult to the child.

It may be argued that there is a better alternative: to intervene to remove the children from the situation in which they are at risk. However, that will not always be possible. Even if it is, it is hard to see why it is just to take action to mitigate risk by intervening in the lives of children (*e.g.* by removing them from home) and perhaps causing them harm in the process, but not just to intervene in the life of the person who poses a risk to them.

What principles, then, should underpin a risk-shifting policy of this type? At least five principles can be fairly readily identified.

Prior offending behavior

First, there is justification in risk-shifting only if a person who is alleged to pose a risk is at fault on the basis of his or her past offending behaviour. Action to prevent offending by a person who has not already demonstrated by his or her behaviour a clear willingness and disposition to offend in the manner predicted cannot be justified. Apart from any other considerations, in the absence of such past behavior, it is impossible to conceive that a robust risk assessment process would reach the required threshold.

To what standard must we be satisfied that they have offended? Can we act only if the person has already been convicted, or otherwise proved beyond reasonable doubt to have offended? Or are there circumstances in which a just redistribution of risk requires us to act on the basis of a lesser standard of proof?

The proposed child harm prevention order takes the approach that proof on the balance of probabilities suffices. Without that, there would be the prospect that children would be left to carry the risk of harm from a person who has probably caused harm to children in the past and is believed to be at high risk of doing so again. In my view, that must in principle be right. Otherwise society appears to be more concerned with avoiding unnecessary intrusion into the lives of adults who have probably caused harm in the past than it is in avoiding harm to vulnerable children who are at risk.

Robust risk assessment measures

Secondly, in order to act on a prediction of risk justly, there must be robust and empirically validated measures that decisions-makers are required to use. This is not because the task of risk prediction is capable of accuracy. The issue here is not that there is difficulty in identifying the subjects of predictive error with the methods available; it is that they are in principle indeterminable. There are no hidden individuals identifiable in principle, but not in practice, who certainly would or would not reoffend. In this sense there are no innocent or guilty subjects of predictive judgments. Risk prediction is inherently uncertain.

But justice requires that interventions reduce unnecessary harm to the degree that is reasonably practicable, and that in turn requires that the nature of the competing risks and the likelihood of their occurrence be identified and weighed as systematically and fairly as possible. To this end, risk assessment measures should generally incorporate an actuarial assessment tool (based on "static" risk factors such as past conduct, age etc.) and an assessment of the "dynamic" factors that might affect their level of risk in the future.

But perhaps they need to go further than this. Static factors are generally much more reliable than dynamic factors. They ought generally to be used to screen out those who do not belong to a group with a high statistical risk. Individualised or clinical judgements may justly be used to put a person in a lower risk category that their actuarial risk. But there will only be rare instances where such judgments can justly be used to put a person in a higher risk category that their actuarial risk. That fairly basic principle is not often applied. For example, in New Zealand, although actuarial risk scores are used in parole decision-making, they are simply one of a number of factors that are taken into account in the mix; there is no clear articulation as to how actuarial information is to be weighted and used vis-à-vis individualised or clinical information. Decision-makers are reluctant to accept that statistics can do better than their own intuition. That does not do justice.

High risk

Thirdly, the threshold at which society is justified in taking protective measures – in other words, the degree of risk that must exist before protective measures are invoked – must be determined and explicitly articulated. The proposed child harm prevention orders in New Zealand have a test of "high risk" without attempting to define that term.

Perhaps the threshold is incapable of more precise definition because it will vary with the nature as well as the gravity of the predicted harm. For example, the point at which we may describe something as a "high risk" may depend not only on the nature of the harm that will be caused if the risk materializes but also on the strength of our prediction – in other words, the confidence we have that the information upon which we are basing our prediction is correct.

For example, the threshold may need to be higher if the prior offending upon which it is based has been proved on the balance of probabilities rather than beyond reasonable doubt. Conversely, there is the debatable argument that the threshold may need to be lower if there is little confidence that the level of identified prior offending is a proper reflection of the person's past behaviour. For example, in percentage terms a lower level of predicted risk is generally regarded as "high risk" in relation to sexual offending against children than a similar level of risk of violence against adults, because the former has a lower detection rate than the latter and the disposition to offend is more entrenched, so that the statistical group to which the person belongs has a higher rate of unknown offending than other groups.

Proportionality

Fourthly, the types of harm that society is entitled to prevent – in other words, what risks are *unacceptable* risks – need to be determined and explicitly articulated.

The level of seriousness of the predicted harm may depend to some extent upon the nature of the preventive measures to be employed. Some harms are so minor that there is no justification for a redistribution of risk to prevent them. But beyond that, any preventive measures need to be governed by some notion of proportionality – that is, the nature of the intervention must not be disproportionate to the gravity of the predicted harm.

The proposed child harm prevention orders in New Zealand have a test of "serious harm", but do not attempt to define that term. Rather, the proposed legislation stipulates that the terms of the order are the least restrictive necessary to mitigate the risk and are proportionate to the severity of that risk.

A link between the risk and the preventive measures

Finally, it is axiomatic that if it is justifiable to employ preventive measures, they must be clearly targeted at the risk. Otherwise they shift from prevention to arbitrary punishment. Measures should be imposed only if there are no alternative means of reducing the risk that would be equally effective and less intrusive, and there must be good reason to believe that they are capable of averting the risk of harm to which they are directed.

6. CONCLUSION

The management of the risk posed by those who come before the Courts on account of their offending is a core concern of criminal justice systems around the world. It underpins a wide range of decisions from the time of first apprehension for offending to the time of eventual release from State control.

Notwithstanding the centrality of these concerns about risk, the justification for intervention on the basis of perceived risk has been poorly articulated; generally it is simply taken for granted as a strategy that is required in the public interest.

This is not a good enough basis for public policy. If justice is to be done to those individuals who are subject to the coercive power of the State, measures that are designed for protective rather than punitive purposes must be based upon a coherent theory of preventive justice. Such a theory needs to make clear the basis upon which intervention to manage risk is justified in different contexts, and the principles that should dictate the nature and scope of that intervention.

THE JUSTIFICATION FOR TAKING MEASURES TO PREDICT OFFENDING/ REOFFENDING AND MANAGE RISK: A THEORETICAL PERSPECTIVE

The view of a human rights lawyer

Andrew S. Butler*

1. INTRODUCTION

The purpose of this chapter is to provide a human rights perspective on the justifications given for taking measures to predict (re)offending and manage risk associated arising out of such prediction. In some respects, I thought the best way to tackle the issue was to engage to the greatest extent possible with Warren Young's chapter so as to identify the areas where there is common ground (and I'll leave you to see whether you can identify any!) and the points of difference.

The task presented to me in writing this chapter has been a daunting one. I will endeavour to provide an overview of the arguments in this area. In making my points, however, I will make reference to some of the relevant case law in the area that I think will demonstrate where the contemporary debate is located. I accept, however, that the case law cannot govern completely the analysis that should apply. First, not every national system will be governed by the standards evident in some of the case law. Second, even if some of the relevant case law can be read as supporting the use of preventive detention in certain circumstances, the fact that one *can* does not answer the question, which I understand will occupy much of your attention this week, of whether one *should* put in place measures to deal with so-called high risk offenders during and after their sentence, and in particular preventive detention.

* BCL (NUI, Dublin), LLM (Osgoode), PhD (EUI, Florence), Partner, Russell McVeagh, Wellington. Many thanks to Phoebe Harrop for her research assistance and Thomas McKenzie for his editorial assistance. Thanks also are due to Warren Young in particular, and the other participants of the IPPF colloquium, for feedback on the paper as presented, which has served as the basis for this chapter. Views expressed are personal to the author.

Finally, I'm going to focus on preventive detention. In doing so, I should not be taken as wishing to ignore the plethora of other preventive measures which have been enacted over recent decades, including offender registration schemes; surveillance measures (*e.g.* GPS tracking); residence restrictions; and the like. Rather, I focus upon preventive detention as a paradigm example of preventive action within the criminal justice system.

2. CHANGING CONCEPTIONS OF LIBERTY

In his chapter, Young commences by focusing on changing conceptions of risk. I start at a different place: changing conceptions of liberty.

The readers of this volume will not find it necessary for me to rehearse in any detail the development of human rights standards at the international, regional and, for many countries, domestic level for the first time in the aftermath of World War II. That wartime experience, and the history preceding it, served to emphasise the importance of placing the individual at the heart of the polity. In turn, the heart of the conception of the individual which is protected by those human rights instruments is a conception of the individual as a full human being, with all of the complexity that being a human involves. Partly informing the conception of a human being with human rights is the conception of individual autonomy and the free will theory; the notion that individuals have a moral sense which they can voluntarily control and exercise.

It must be recalled that among the measures which caused abhorrence during the war period were so called preventive measures designed to control parts of the population based on perceived dangerousness; their deficiencies in social solidarity; and social deviancy. In short, people were being incarcerated not for acts that they had committed in breach of a code of reasonable criminal laws, but based on predictions as to the danger that their actions might pose to society in the future. And of course, in turn, such preventive measures based on a form of predictive justice caused concern for many because they marked a departure from expectations about the role and purpose of punishment in society.

Against that background it is hardly surprising that within the international human rights systems, the right not to be arbitrarily deprived of liberty quickly established itself as a core value. While the human rights systems recognised – to a greater or lesser degree of explicitness and detail – the ability for the state to deprive a citizen of his or her liberty, a significant range of requirements and qualifications was established including:

a. A list of circumstances (generally narrow) that could justify a deprivation of liberty.[1]
b. Objective criteria in respect of those circumstances were required to be established.
c. The objective criteria had to be established to an appropriate degree of satisfaction by, typically, an impartial decision-maker (typically a court).
d. Proportionality between the liberty-depriving measure and the circumstances relied upon to justify the detention.
e. The requirement to uphold appropriate procedural protections in order to ensure a fair process was followed prior to the imposition of the liberty-depriving measure (with the intensity of those procedural protections generally increasing as the extent of the deprivation and its effects on the detainee increase).

In addition to the above features of the emerging requirements of human rights systems, should be added a greater willingness on the part of actors within human rights systems to be sceptical. In creating a "culture of justification" – a term I have long borrowed from the late South African constitutional scholar Etienne Mureinik – modern human rights courts have been prepared to put a government "to the proof" when it comes to identifying a social harm at which a measure that intrudes on human rights is said to be targeted; the rationality of the connection between the measure and that problem; and the balance to be struck (*i.e.* in some cases human rights courts are prepared to take the view that the fundamental human rights values at stake are so important that interference with them will rarely if ever be justifiable).[2]

3. HUMAN RIGHTS, PREVENTIVE MEASURES AND PREDICTION

Having outlined the changing conception of liberty, which adherence to international human rights standards embody, what does human rights law have to say about preventive detention? The picture is a complex one.

1 See, for example, the exhaustive list of circumstances justifying deprivation of liberty in Art. 5 of the European Convention of Human Rights. That list can of course be contrasted with the open-ended Art. 9 of the International Covenant on Civil and Political Rights ("no-one shall be deprived of his liberty except on such grounds and in accordance with such procedures as are established by law.").

2 See generally A.S. Butler & P. Butler, *The New Zealand Bill of Rights Act: A Commentary*, Wellington: LexisNexis, 2005, at 130.

3.1. APPROACH OF THE UN HUMAN RIGHTS COMMITTEE

The UN Human Rights Committee ("HRC") has been asked to consider the preventive detention regimes in both New Zealand and Australia. In 2003 in *Rameka v. New Zealand*[3] the HRC was asked to consider the compatibility of a sentence of preventive detention imposed on an offender who had committed a number of sexual offences, had a propensity to commit sexual offences, had shown a lack of remorse and in respect of whom there was a conclusion that he was at a 20% likelihood of further commission of sexual offences. The applicant was sentenced to 14 years imprisonment for sexual violation and also to a concurrent term of preventive detention (that is indefinite detention until released by the parole board). While the HRC found certain aspects of the New Zealand system to be deficient in terms of procedural protection, a majority of the HRC accepted "the permissibility, in principle, of preventive detention for protective purposes, always provided that the necessary safeguards are available and in fact enjoyed".[4] The HRC moreover, stated that detention for protective purposes "does not offend the presumption of innocence, given that no charge has been laid".[5]

Interestingly, however, a number of dissenting views were expressed. A number of committee members were concerned that preventive detention was arbitrary. A number of reasons were advanced. First, the science behind the assessment of the possibility of the commission of a repeat offence was "unsound".[6] This was particularly so where preventive detention was justified on the basis of there being a "20% likelihood" that the offender would reoffend. On a more philosophical basis the dissenters were concerned that "to rely on a prediction of dangerousness is tantamount to replacing presumption of innocence by presumption of guilt".[7] Other dissenters were prepared to accept the possibility of preventive detention for the purpose of protecting the public against dangerous criminals as not being incompatible with the ICCPR as such, but only if the strictest procedural safeguards were in place.[8] Frequent periodic review was a minimum; and ongoing care and therapy was necessary, on the premise that any human person has the potential to change and improve, *i.e.* to become less dangerous over time.[9]

---

3 *Rameka v. New Zealand* (2003) 7 HRNZ 663 (UNHRC).
4 *Ibid.* at 679.
5 *Ibid.* at 680.
6 *Ibid.* at 681 (Mr Bhagwati, Ms Chanet, Mr Ahanhanzo and Mr Yrigoyen).
7 *Ibid.* at 681 (Mr Bhagwati, Ms Chanet, Mr Ahanhanzo and Mr Yrigoyen).
8 *Ibid.* at 682 (Mr Kalin).
9 *Ibid.* at 682 (Mr Kalin).

In the 2010 cases of *Fardon v. Australia*[10] and *Tillman v. Australia*,[11] the HRC revisited aspects of preventive detention law.[12] In those cases, the HRC was asked to consider the compatibility with the ICCPR of the imposition of preventive detention as an add-on to a finite sentence of imprisonment in circumstances where the add-on occurred many years after the finite sentence had been imposed by a court. Relevantly, the preventive detention order was imposed by a court, upon application by the State, with the onus being on the State to prove that the offender met the requisite statutory definition of dangerousness. Somewhat in contrast to the general approach adopted in respect of *Rameka*, the majority of the HRC in *Fardon* and *Tillman* more closely scrutinised the permissibility of the sentence of preventive detention. By a significant majority, the HRC held that the detention orders violated Art 9.1 of the ICCPR for a number of reasons, each of which would, by itself, constitute a violation. Those reasons included:

a. The purported detention amounted, in substance, to a fresh term of imprisonment but was based on a pre-existing conviction not a new conviction.[13]
b. Effectively the offenders were subject to imprisonment. Imprisonment, in turn is penal in character and can only be imposed upon conviction for an offence in the same proceedings in which the offence is tried. Though the continuing detention order could be nominally characterised as a civil proceeding, in substance the offenders were being subjected to a heavier penalty than the one that was applicable at the time when the underlying offence was committed.[14]
c. The procedure followed to impose an order was civil, rather than criminal, in character and failed therefore to meet the due process guarantees required by Art 14 of the ICCPR.[15]
d. The justification for detaining the offenders was that they were feared to be a danger to the community in the future. The HRC considered:[16]

---

10 *Fardon v. Australia* (2010) CCPR/C/98/D/1629/2007 (UNHRC).

11 *Tillman v. Australia* (2010) CCPR/C/98/D/1635/2007 (UNHRC).

12 For an in depth discussion of these decisions and their greater significance to Australia see Patrick Keyzer, 'The International Human Rights Parameters for the Preventive Detention of Serious Sex Offenders', in: Bernadette McSherry and Patrick Keyzer (eds), *Dangerous People: Policy, Prediction, and Practice*, New York: Routledge, 2011, 25.

13 *Fardon v. Australia* (2010) CCPR/C/98/D/1629/2007 (UNHRC) at 8; *Tillman v. Australia* (2010) CCPR/C/98/D/1635/2007 (UNHRC) at 10.

14 *Fardon v. Australia* (2010) CCPR/C/98/D/1629/2007 (UNHRC) at 8; *Tillman v. Australia* (2010) CCPR/C/98/D/1635/2007 (UNHRC) at 10.

15 *Fardon v. Australia* (2010) CCPR/C/98/D/1629/2007 (UNHRC) at 8–9; *Tillman v. Australia* (2010) CCPR/C/98/D/1635/2007 (UNHRC) at 10–11.

16 *Fardon v. Australia* (2010) CCPR/C/98/D/1629/2007 (UNHRC) at 9; *Tillman v. Australia* (2010) CCPR/C/98/D/1635/2007 (UNHRC) at 11.

> "The concept of feared or predicted dangerousness to the community applicable in the case of past offenders is inherently problematic. It is essentially based on opinion as distinct from factual evidence, even if that evidence consists in the opinion of psychiatric experts. But psychiatry is not an exact science... While courts are free to accept or reject expert opinion and are required to consider all other available relevant evidence, the reality is that the courts must make a finding of fact on the suspected future behaviour of a past offender which may or may not materialise."

Interestingly, however, having expressed these doubts about the appropriateness of preventive detention, the HRC did not suggest that preventive detention on this basis was necessarily incompatible with the ICCPR; rather, the HRC continued that "in order to avoid the label of arbitrariness" in such circumstances, a state would need to demonstrate that an offender's rehabilitation could not have been achieved by means less intrusive than continued imprisonment.[17]

3.2. THE EUROPEAN COURT OF HUMAN RIGHTS

The European Court of Human Rights has also had to consider the compatibility of preventive detention with human rights norms.[18] In particular, there have been a series of cases attacking the move by German legislature to amend its preventive detention law so that it is no longer time capped and the duration of preventive detention was vested in a so-called sentence execution court, rather than the original sentencing court.[19] Having examined the German system in detail, the European Court of Human Rights has repeatedly found the extension of the preventive detention regime to be inconsistent with the European Convention.

In reaching this conclusion, the court, after considerable detailed examination, has concluded that preventive detention is in substance a form of penalty for offending, even if its purpose is to protect society against potentially dangerous offenders. Of interest, and resonating with similar comments by the

---

17 *Fardon v. Australia* (2010) CCPR/C/98/D/1629/2007 (UNHRC) at 9; *Tillman v. Australia* (2010) CCPR/C/98/D/1635/2007 (UNHRC) at 11.

18 For a general discussion of the European Court of Human Rights case law in this area see European Committee on Crime Problems, *Discussion paper on secure preventive detention*, Strasbourg, 22 February 2010, at 11–14 (see; www.coe.int/t/dghl/standardsetting/prisons/PCCP%20documents%202010/CDPC-BU(2010)%2004rev%20preventive%20detention.pdf) (last visited: 1 January 2014); see also Claire Saas, 'Exceptional Law in Europe with Emphasis on "Enemies"', paper presented at Fourth Conference of Future Adversary Systems: Preventive Detention and Criminal Justice, Ravenna, May 2012 (see: www.law.unc.edu/documents/faculty/adversaryconference/exceptionallawsineuropewithemphasisonenemiesapril2012.pdf) (last visited: 1 January 2014).

19 See, for example, *M. v. Germany* (2009) 28 BHRC 521 and *Schummer v. Germany (27360/04 & 42225/07)* Fifth Section ECHR, 13 January 2011.

HRC in the Australian cases just referred to, in *M. v. Germany* the European Court held that "having regard to the realities of the situation of persons in preventive detention", it was not prepared to accept the submission that preventive detention serves a purely preventive, and non-punitive purpose.[20]

In addition, the European Court noted that "persons subject to preventive detention, in view of its potentially indefinite duration, are in particular need of psychological care and support...".[21] The Court considered that "persons subject to preventive detention orders must be forwarded such support and care as part of a genuine attempt to reduce the risk that they will reoffend, thus serving the purpose of crime prevention and making their release possible".[22] The absence of such measures being in place meant that classification of preventive detention as punishment, rather than preventative, will be compelling.[23]

3.3. THE GERMAN CONSTITUTIONAL COURT

The concern to more clearly distinguish between preventive detention and criminal punishment was exhibited in the even more recent decisions of the German Constitutional Court in its judgments of 4 May 2011 in *Preventive Detention I* and *Preventive Detention II*.[24] There the Constitutional Court held that the German preventive detention law was unconstitutional because the preventive detention regime failed to observe the constitutional minimum requirement that the deprivation of liberty effected by preventive detention must keep a marked distance from the execution of a prison sentence (the so-called *Abstandsgebot*). In that regard, the Constitutional Court effectively accepted the legitimacy of preventive detention aimed at preventing the commission of criminal offences in the future by those with a prognosis of future dangerousness, as distinct from prison sentences imposed on those who have been found guilty of having committed offences. The principal distinction between the two forms of liberty deprivation lay in their quite distinct objectives. Preventive detention should only be justified if, with regard to its arrangement, the legislative took due account of the special character of the encroachment that preventive detention involves and ensured that further burdens beyond the indispensible deprivation of external liberty are avoided. More concretely, this required preventive detention to have a clear therapeutic orientation, with the objective of minimising the danger emanating from the detainee thereby reducing the duration of the deprivation of liberty to the absolute minimum. In practice, the Court made it clear that where preventive detention follows a finite sentence of

20 *M. v. Germany* (2009) 28 BHRC 521 at [128].

21 *Ibid.* at [129].

22 *Ibid.*

23 *Ibid.*

24 2 BvR 2365/09, 2 BvR 740/10 *et al.*

imprisonment, therapeutic measures must have been put in place sufficiently early in the course of the finite sentence as to make it possible that the preventive detention may not need to occur. In addition, preventive detainees are required to be examined with a view to treatment complying with state of the art scientific requirements, in accordance with an individual plan and intensive therapeutic care.

3.4. CONCLUSIONS

What these developments show is that, on the whole, human rights standards do not necessarily rule out preventive detention as a form of liberty deprivation. In other words there is some room for what Young has referred to as predictive justice. But at the same time, these decisions also show a level of concern and scepticism in respect of numerous matters:

a. Keeping the boundary between detention following conviction for an imprisonable offence on the one hand and detention based on predicted dangerousness in the future. In other words, where preventative measures push against existing categorisations within the legal system, courts will be very careful to test whether the intrusion is appropriate.
b. As it is wont to do, human rights law can mean that practices and institutions that have developed over the years may need to be questioned from first principles. That, in turn, requires those who wish to preserve and/or extend forms of predictive justice to re-examine the justification for those practices and institutions.
c. The practices of national authorities need to reflect the rationale for preventive detention. Accordingly, it is important that state authorities treat preventive detainees as people who can be the subject of therapeutic intervention. The essence of such intervention measures is likely to tell against the compatibility of a preventive detention regime with human rights norms.
d. Concern to ensure due proportionality between the perceived danger being addressed and the measures imposed to address that dangerousness.
e. There is real concern about the robustness of the predictive instruments in issue.

4. AREAS OF DISAGREEMENT

Having set out the informing human rights principles, and outlined the approach of judicial authorities on the compatibility of particular forms of preventive detention with human rights law, I turn now to areas of disagreement that I have with Young. In his chapter, Young states that:

> "The debate should be about whether and when it is appropriate to take pre-emptive action to prevent certain sorts of behaviour in the future when one cannot be certain that it will occur."

In doing so Young rejects the argument that the presumption of innocence has any role to play in the analysis, considering it to be "wholly inapplicable to the nature and purpose of risk prediction, which is inherently uncertain".

For myself, I'm not quite sure what Young's point is here. First, if Young's point simply is that presuming someone is innocent is unhelpful because it prevents you from exploring the extent to which a person poses a risk in the future, then he is correct. But that entirely begs the question of whether and when predicting risk of dangerous conduct is a legitimate pursuit where the purpose to which the predictive exercise is put is to deprive a person of his or her liberty. The presumption of innocence is surely relevant to the legitimacy of that purpose because the presumption reminds us that our system so cherishes individual liberty that it will countenance a probably guilty person going unpunished so that an innocent person is not wrongly convicted. That is a very powerful statement of moral value which is absolutely relevant and indeed central to predictive justice. In my view, however, it is important for Young's position that he decouple the presumption of innocence from predictive justice; because while that relationship endures the scope for predictive justice will remain limited.

Second, of course, one can never be certain what will occur in the future; but equally one might say – albeit to a slightly lesser degree – one cannot be certain what has occurred in the past. Determinations as to whether or not an individual actually committed a crime depend much on vectors of uncertainty such as memory, perception, intuition, inferability and the like. So uncertainty is not unique to predictive justice. The question is what one does having recognised the significant degree of uncertainty that exists. That in turn means that we need to focus on the real question which is the "moral" or political (in a non-party political sense) justification for taking pre-emptive action based on what may happen in the future. The answer to that question may turn, to some degree, on the strength of the prediction that can be made, but more fundamental should be the justification for the pre-emptive action in the first place. And I accept, as Young argues, that there is no intellectual purity around the strengths of prediction as such; as he argues risk prediction is a feature of a number of aspects of the criminal justice system such as bail and parole (albeit that at least in the case of the latter a way of conceptualising the risk assessment that is undertaken is that the parole authorities seek to find reason to release a prisoner "earlier" than their finite sentence term; there will not be reason to release if they cannot be satisfied that the offender will pose no, or a negligible risk if released earlier).

Third, Young takes issue with the argument that preventive measures based on risk prediction represent a denial of individual free will and autonomy. I would like to join issue. First, I think Young understates the extent of intrusion upon the traditional understandings of when preventive detention measures are justified when he says that "if a person's past behaviour is such that it demonstrates an ongoing willingness to act on their disposition, society is justified in responding accordingly." I say that because the reality of the modern debate is that many "dangerousness" statutes can be triggered, as Young himself has recognised earlier in his chapter, by dangerousness assessments which have little to do with frequency of past offending, but rather the enormity of, perhaps, one past offence combined with the enormity of the harm that is predicted to occur. Second, I think Young wrongly states his position when arguing that preventive measures based on risk prediction do not deny free will or the ability of people to change or to act contrary to their disposition. Clearly they do; the premise is that notwithstanding that the individual target in issue could well change or act contrary to their predicted disposition, they will nonetheless be targeted for particular preventive measures based on their past behaviour. While it is true to say that in many social contexts, humans do make judgements about others based on past conduct, the moral question which arises in this particular context is the appropriateness of using such assessments in order to deprive a person of his or her liberty. In that regard, it might be said that the question is not much different from that which arises in respect of discrimination law. The fact that people make predictions based on their sense of a person's likely behaviour or characteristics because of membership of a particular group does not mean that the law or society ought to support that assessment; and why? Because fundamentally human rights law is about putting the individual at the centre. Fundamentally, human rights law says the application of coercive measures needs to be justified in *my* case, based on information about *me* and *my* conduct based on what *I* have done, not based on what others have done or might do and having regard to the impact of the coercive measure upon *me*.

Fourth, Young's analysis it seems to me proceeds upon an assumption that a certain cohort of the population (the scope of which steadily expands) will contain within it individuals who will commit crimes that will cause serious harm to their victims; when those crimes will occur and against whom is sufficiently unpredictable as to expose a good many people to that harm; in turn that exposure is said to justify detaining on a pre-emptive basis more people within that group than would actually have offended had the preventive measure not been put in place (the "false positive" concern that Young has discussed in his chapter). While Young presents the public policy decision in favour of a balancing of that type as obvious and consistent with existing practice (albeit in some cases an extension of that existing practice), I do not think it is that easy. Exceptions to general principles or rules are exactly that: exceptions. As such they need to be justified not by reference to the existence of exceptions, but rather by reference to the core value of the principles and rights from which they seek to depart. There is, after all, a very big difference between denying an accused person release or jail pending trial (subject always to a power to release pre-trial if detention has become too long) and preventive detention for dangerousness: quite simply the amount of time in detention in the case of the former will be significantly shorter than in the latter case. As we know, as exceptions accrete there is real danger that they come to overpower the principle or right to which they are meant to be an exception. While this observation can be easily castigated as a "slippery slope" argument, the danger is nonetheless a real one. And so as each new development is sought to be justified it is quite proper and legitimate to remember that it is the exception that needs to be justified, not the underlying right or principle. And if there is a real risk (to use the language of this volume) that damage will be done to the underlying right or principle then society ought to deny the accretion.

5. TOWARDS A COHERENT THEORY OF PREVENTIVE JUSTICE

Notwithstanding my comments above, I think there is real value in using Young's final paragraphs as a way of thinking about how we would frame a coherent theory of preventive justice.

If we put to one side our disagreement about the applicability of the presumption of innocence (which Young would replace by his principle of harmlessness), I agree it is useful to consider the question of when the right to be treated as a harmless can be regarded as justifiably subject to limit.

Young has used the example of Child Harm Prevention Orders ("CHPOs"), a proposed child protection measure contained in the Vulnerable Children Bill (currently before the New Zealand Parliament), to illustrate how his theory of preventive justice would work in application. I will critique his schema in the light of this example. My comments on his schema follow.

a. First, I agree that risk-shifting can only be justified where a person has demonstrated by their behaviour a clear willingness and disposition to offend in the way predicted. That has got to be a minimum requirement. But equally we must accept that to properly honour that base criterion, the past offending must bear close relationship to the predicted offending; a general association would not be sufficient. Young suggests that it is appropriate, at least in the CHPO context, for risk shifting to be justified when, on the balance of probabilities, a person has caused harm to children in the past and is believed to be at high risk of doing it again. I do not agree. The balance of probabilities is a significantly lower standard than the beyond reasonable doubt threshold required for a criminal conviction. Yet the restrictions placed on a person subject to a CHPO have similar consequences to a conviction. CHPOs deprive people of their liberty; their freedom of movement and freedom of association is affected. CHPOs could also adversely affect a person's employment opportunities. Furthermore, the stigma associated with CHPOs would likely be the same as that associated with conviction for a sexual offence against a child. Moreover, Young's conclusion that the balance of probabilities standard appropriately sends the message that society cares more about protecting vulnerable children than unnecessarily intruding into the lives of probable sex offenders is concerning. That is because it undersells the importance of protecting individual liberties. After all, we know that if a person is detained against his or her will, he or she will suffer a range of harms; it seems a miscalibration to permit that certain harms occur based on a prediction of *possible* harm to another person, which prediction need only be assessed by reference to the balance of probabilities standard.

b. Second, the mandatory use of robust and empirically validated tools is clearly important. I am no expert in this area, but have read enough in preparation for this chapter to have a sense that there are legitimate concerns that much is left to the intuition of decision-makers as to what offenders might do in the future, and perhaps not enough reliance is placed on the use of tools that have at least some predictive quality. But again I would go further and suggest that we must be rigorous in our assessment of the quality of predictive tools.
c. Real concerns are being raised in the United States about the utility of static 99, the leading actuarial risk assessment tool used to make predictions of sex offenders. Recent studies suggest that notwithstanding that static 99 is the most thoroughly researched tool for predicting sexual recidivism, it does not predict recidivism well enough to meet the relevant legal standard for sex offender commitment.[25] Furthermore, the data sets from which conclusions about likely future conduct will be drawn are of highly contestable validity. To draw upon concerns that are frequently being heard in respect of border protection assessments of travellers, the problem with predictive tools is that the tool is often less directed toward individuals as such than it is directed towards their personal data, or their "data double", meaning the information collected in the database systems which is seen as representing a "real" identity with that so-called "real" identity being assessed as "the truth of the body, the person".[26] While some may say that all that can be expected is for decision-makers to use the best tools available to them, whatever the deficiencies of those tools, bearing in mind the risk of false positives and the impact on the

25 See F.E. Vars, 'Rethinking the indefinite detention of sex offenders', 44 *Connecticut Law Review* (2011), 161 at 193.

26 See 'The state and surveillance: fear and control', a conversation between Didier Bigo and Mireille Delmas-Marty, *La Clé des Lanques*, 23 september 2011 (see: http://cle.ens-lyon.fr/anglais/the-state-and-surveillance-fear-and-control-131675.kjsp?RH=CDL_ANG100100) (last visited: 1 January 2014).

affected individuals of a decision to detain them for preventative reasons, we must be more vigorous in the rigour we apply to assessing such tools.

d. However, I do welcome Young's suggestion that individualised or clinical judgements may justly be used to put a person in a lower risk category than his or her actuarial risk. This approach reinforces the idea that an individual is a full human being with all the complexities that come with being a human being. These complexities cannot be expressed through statistics.

e. Third, clearly in agreement with Young, there will be a spectrum of dangers that legitimately identifies as ones which it is not prepared to run the risk of occurring. We need to be very clear about what those risks are and why they are worthy of singling out. For example, the threshold for the proposed CHPOs is reached when a person is at "high risk" of committing a qualifying offence. This is inappropriately unclear because, as Young admits, "high risk" is incapable of precise definition. As noted, preventive detention statutes typically focus on sex and/or violence offences. To respect the underlying human rights values, we need to interrogate ourselves as to why these offences are of particular singling out and examine the counterfactual; that is, if preventive detention measures were only available in highly restricted circumstances, how would the balancing of interests play out. A further element of the modern debate on preventive detention measures is the wider context in which the debate is occurring. One of the challenges which supporters of preventive detention face, particularly as the reach of preventive detention statutes appears to expand, is what the nature of the crime problem is that is being targeted. Without being in a position to comment authoritatively on the correctness of the observations, it is interesting to note that critiques of recent sex offender preventive detention regimes in places as different as the US and Germany,[27] suggest that "moral panic"[28] may explain why such measures were thought appropriate.[29]

f. Fourth, the threshold at which we are justified in taking protective measures is a particularly important issue. I agree with Young that statutes which set out to establish a threshold need to better state what is required to be shown before the preventive measure can be imposed. This is something that the Vulnerable Children's Bill fails to do. The proposed CHPOs set a threshold of "serious harm" to children. The Law Society in its submission to the select

---

27 Compare C.R. Yung, 'Sex offender exceptionalism and preventive detention', 101 *The Journal of Criminal Law and Criminology* 3 (2011), at 973 et seq and A. Dessecker, 'Dangerousness, long prison terms and preventive measures in Germany', 6 *Champ pénal/Penal field* (2009), varia at para 36 (see: http://champpenal.revues.org/7508) (last visited: 1 January 2014).

28 Dessecker at para 36.

29 In that regard, there may be a New Zealand precedent in the case of the recently mooted public protection orders ("PPOs") which may be able to be traced to perceived lack of ability to deal with Stewart Murray Wilson – dobbed with the media as the "Beast of Blenheim" – and the fear of several communities in New Zealand that Wilson would be resettled in their community, without restriction and free to predate: (17 September 2013) 693 NZPD 13441.

committee responsible for the Bill expressed concern at the fact that "serious harm" was not defined. It picked up on the fact that it is not clear whether the harm has to be physical harm, or whether psychological harm would be enough. It further noted that it is not clear what the qualification "serious" adds to the meaning of "harm".[30]

g. Returning to the facts of the *Rameka* case before the Human Rights Committee, is a 20% likelihood of sexual reoffending sufficiently high to justify potentially indefinite detention. We wouldn't punish somebody by conviction and imprisonment if all we could say about them was that there was a 1 in 5 chance that had actually done the crime; so on what basis is it legitimate for us to say that a 1 in 5 chance that that person will at some stage commit such an offence in the future justifies depriving them of their liberty potentially indefinitely?
h. Fifth, the preventive measures must be targeted at the risk and be as minimally intrusive as possible in light of that risk. This is an area where I suspect national practices will require some re-examination and scrutiny. A lesson to be taken from the German Constitutional Court's decisions in *Preventive Detention I* and *II* is that where states do adopt detention measures which are explicitly premised on a preventive goal, rather than a punishment, then it is incumbent on them to put in place proper measures which actively pursue the preventive policy objectives. That can mean the expending of considerable time and resource on offenders who, quite frankly, are unlikely to be regarded with sympathy by their general populous. But if the integrity of the values which inform our conception of liberty is to be maintained, then that is the price which may need to be paid.

6. CONCLUSION

In this chapter, as stated at the outset, I've focused on preventive detention. But hopefully I've been elaborate enough to indicate that the approach of courts in this area is to combine principle with granularity; to state the broad values that animate human rights concerns in this area and then to examine in detail the particular scheme in issue for its compatibility with those broad values. More broadly then for the predictive justice project that Young has outlined in his chapter, that means accepting that there will be room for prediction about dangerousness within the criminal justice system – broadly defined – but how much room must turn on the appropriateness of the particular measure. And in determining whether a particular measure is appropriate it's not simply enough to say we can; human rights norms ask whether we should.

30 New Zealand Law Society, *Submission on the Vulnerable Children Bill* (6 November 2013) at [58] (see: www.parliament.nz/resource/0002032435) (last visited: 1 January 2014).

L'IMPORTANCE DE LA NOTION DE RISQUE DE RÉCIDIVE DANS LA DÉTERMINATION DU TYPE ET DE LA DURÉE DE LA SANCTION

André VALLOTTON*

« Les gens commencent à croire qu'ils peuvent réussir à changer leur vie lorsque ceux qui les entourent commencent à croire qu'ils en sont capables. »
Shadd Maruna et Thomas P. Le Bel

1. INTRODUCTION

La prévention du crime est devenue depuis quelques décennies une préoccupation importante dans nos sociétés. Et le problème est particulièrement aigu en ce qui concerne la délinquance violente, qui entraîne des réactions émotionnelles et des intolérances de plus en plus exacerbées.

Mais lorsque nous examinons les modes de fixation et d'exécution des peines frappant les délinquants perçus comme dangereux, nous devons hélas constater qu'aucun des courants pénologiques modernes, de la rétribution kantienne à la défense sociale en passant par leur combinaison, n'offre de réponse cohérente et globale à leur passage à l'acte.

Outre le fait que la notion de dangerosité ne peut être clairement précisée et que l'évaluation du risque présente encore de nombreuses incertitudes, aucun des concepts actuels ne peut à la fois donner du sens à la sanction et répondre aux besoins liés à la réinsertion du coupable et aux préoccupations sécuritaires.

Ce constat montre la difficulté de la problématique que nous allons examiner et l'impossibilité qui existe, en l'état, de disposer de solutions totalement

* A. Vallotton est Président du Conseil de coopération pénologique (PC-CP), Ancien délégué du Conseil d'Etat aux Affaires pénitentiaires Canton de Vaud, Suisse, et Chef de projet, Unité d'appui au Programme d'appui de la réforme du Système pénitentiaire Ministère de la Justice, Alger.

satisfaisantes, tant dans le domaine de la fixation de la peine que dans celui de son exécution et de son contrôle.

Nous nous bornerons donc à porter un regard critique sur les réponses apportées actuellement à la dangerosité avant de proposer quelques pistes qui devraient nourrir les réflexions à venir.

2. QU'EST-CE QUE LA DANGEROSITÉ ?

La première partie de la réflexion nous conduira à nous intéresser au concept même de dangerosité.

Une société peut à la fois admirer le free ride et le base jumping, considérer les accidents de la route comme un risque peu souhaitable, mais inévitable, et n'accepter parallèlement ni des inondations en zone naturellement inondable, ni les atteintes à la personne. Le port d'armes létales, prohibé dans un Etat, peut être considérée comme normal dans l'Etat voisin. De même, des abus sexuels dont la révélation était autrefois taboue pourront faire l'objet au même endroit, quelques décennies plus tard, de dénonciations quasi systématiques. La notion de dangerosité est donc difficile à préciser dans le temps[1] et dans l'espace.

Dans le cadre d'une étude faite en 2010, le Conseil de Coopération Pénologique du Conseil de l'Europe (PC-CP) a tenté d'élaborer une définition du délinquant dangereux. Après de nombreuses discussions, il a défini ce dernier comme « *an offender, who has caused very serious physical or psychological harm and who presents a high probability of re-offending causing similar (i.e. very serious) harm* ».[2]

Cette définition met en relation trois paramètres: un premier acte délictueux, particulièrement dommageable (i), *révélateur* d'une personnalité ou de troubles (ii) *susceptibles* d'entraîner leur auteur à commettre des actes du même type (iii).

Nous ne pouvons que mettre en doute, sur le plan scientifique, l'exigence d'un premier délit particulièrement dommageable: certains actes mineurs peuvent également être le révélateur de troubles qui pourront générer des récidives particulièrement graves. Mais à partir de quel moment octroyer la

---

1 La notion de dangerosité est donc difficile à préciser dans l'espace et dans le temps. Dans une de ses dernières études: *Libertés et sûreté dans un monde dangereux*, Mireille Delmas Marti stigmatise, par exemple, «le récent passage, dans le monde occidental, de la vision d'un délinquant responsable de ses actes et ré-humanisé par le jugement à celle d'un ennemi dont il faut se protéger», ainsi que le virage «d'une anthropologie humaniste vers une anthropologie guerrière», qui fait ré-émerger des courants pénologiques que l'on croyait en voie de disparition.

2 Nicola Padfield, *The sentencing, management and treatment of 'dangerous' offenders*, PC-CP (2010) 10 rev 4.

priorité à la défense sociale dans une société de droit ? Peut-on intervenir avant la commission du premier délit ? Nous sommes ici au cœur d'une question cruciale, mais non résolue.

Il convient, enfin, pour être complet, de signaler un quatrième paramètre non mentionné dans le définition mais qui sera pris en compte lors de l'évaluation du risque : le contexte environnemental (iiii), qui peut faciliter ou empêcher la commission des actes délictueux et influencer positivement ou négativement l'évolution de la personne.

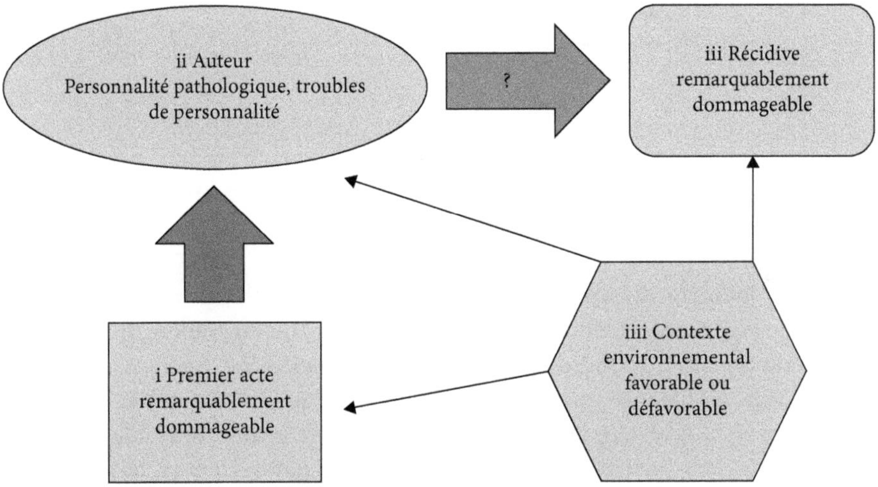

La définition du PC-CP présuppose donc la définition d'un seuil de tolérance et l'établissement d'un lien solide entre la qualification du premier dommage et un désordre de personnalité susceptible de favoriser une réitération.

Restent donc à fixer le degré de gravité et de répétition socialement admissible et à établir des liens pertinents entre un premier acte, une personnalité et des actes futurs.

Le tableau imaginé par Rob Canton, sur lequel il répartit les actes délictueux en fonction de la gravité du préjudice subi et selon la probabilité d'un nouveau passage à l'acte[3] peut nous aider à traiter la première question.

[3] Rob Canton, *Dangerosité et risque. Un document de discussion préparé par le Conseil de coopération pénologique*, PC-CP (2010) 02.

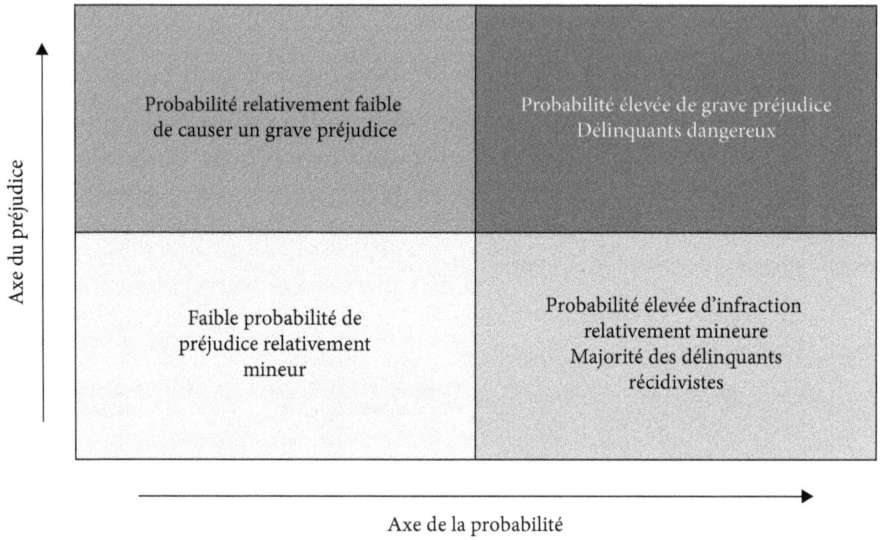

Utilisé de manière dynamique, ce modèle est particulièrement intéressant. Il permet de mettre en évidence les seuils de tolérance tant en matière de fréquence de réitération qu'en terme de gravité. Plus une société est tolérante, plus elle élèvera vers le haut le curseur des dommages qu'elle assume et plus elle repoussera vers la droite la limite qu'elle fixe entre risque tolérable et risque inadmissible. Une société sécuritaire ou paralysée par ses peurs, au contraire, agrandira le carré supérieur droit et y inclura un nombre plus important de délinquants considérés comme dangereux.

Mais si ce modèle est particulièrement utile pour illustrer la problématique, il ne permet pas de définir le risque admissible.

Il ne nous reste donc qu'à tenter d'inventorier les infractions spécialement réprimées, dans le but d'identifier les facteurs d'intolérance qui pourraient constituer un dénominateur commun.

Les atteintes directes à la personne, physiques ou psychologiques, sont proscrites dans la majorité des pays.[4] Viols, meurtres, blessures graves, incendies intentionnels ou séquestrations sont présents dans l'ensemble des catalogues d'infractions impliquant le prononcé d'une mesure de sûreté[5] ou prescrivant une aggravation de la peine. La récidive ou la réitération sont également considérés par de nombreux codes pénaux comme des facteurs légitimant une plus grande sévérité.[6] La criminalité organisée et le terrorisme

4 Nicola Padfield, *The sentencing, management and treatment of 'dangerous' offenders*, PC-CP (2010) 10 rev 4.

5 Voir à ce sujet, par exemple, l'art. 64 du code pénal suisse et l'art. 66 du code pénal allemand.

6 Les peines plancher, par exemple, introduites en France par la loi du 10 août 2007.

font eux aussi l'objet de mesures spéciales dans tous les pays qui y ont été particulièrement confrontés.[7]

De nombreux facteurs de risque graves restent cependant relativement ignorés des législateurs. Certaines formes de criminalité économique, qui causent des dégâts directs ou indirects considérables, comme l'inconscience de chauffards irréductibles donnent souvent lieu à des peines moins sévères que celles qui sanctionnent les atteintes directes à la personne. Et les risques de pollution volontaire, qui pourraient constituer d'ici quelques décennies un risque majeur, ne sont encore que faiblement pris en compte.

Cet inventaire ne permet donc pas non plus de définition cohérente de la dangerosité. Il autorise au mieux de relier cette notion à un risque d'agression physique ou psychologique communément admis et qui a des conséquences particulièrement dommageables, mais sans permettre plus de précision.

La notion de dangerosité est donc tout, sauf un énoncé scientifique. Le degré d'acceptation du risque est un fait individuel et social qui évolue d'une période à l'autre[8] et d'un endroit à l'autre, et les seuils de tolérance et les modes de prévention et de répression mis en place pour protéger la société du danger sont des réponses politiques[9] à un niveau d'intolérance.

À chaque représentation consciente ou inconsciente de la délinquance correspond une conception spécifique du crime et de sa régulation.[10]

3. LA FIABILITÉ DE L'ÉVALUATION

Le fait de s'entendre sur une définition minimale devrait cependant permettre une certaine qualité de prédiction des comportements dangereux.

Mais établir un lien objectif entre un acte passé, un type de personnalité et un acte futur n'est pas aussi évident qu'il ne paraît.

Certains actes atroces, commis sous l'effet d'une émotion violente et dans des circonstances particulières, ont très peu de chance de se reproduire[11] alors que

---

7 A titre d'exemple, il Codice delle leggi antimafia e delle misure di prevenzione.

8 La seule constante actuelle, du moins dans le monde occidental, est une intolérance toujours plus grande à toute forme d'agression qui se fonde sur un mélange de sentiment d'insécurité et une insécurité réelle, mais locale ou sectorielle. Certes, certaines sociétés sont en pleine mutation, mais les risques réels correspondent rarement aux risques imaginaires.

9 André Vallotton, *Dangerosité, un document de discussion*, PC-CP (2010) 3.

10 Les discussions concernant l'application rétroactive de mesures de sûreté en Allemagne ou en France sont la meilleure démonstration d'une notion de dangerosité qui suit la courbe des tolérances. Voir à ce sujet l'affaire M. contre Allemagne, 2009, ou la décision du Conseil constitutionnel français du 21 février 2008 (no 2008-562 DC).

11 Trente coups de couteau assénés dans un état de rage paroxystique n'auront pas forcément la même signification, en terme de dangerosité, qu'un coup mortel unique, mais décrit froidement et minutieusement à une future victime maintenue dans l'incapacité de se défendre.

quelques actes mineurs peuvent être les prémisses de comportements beaucoup plus graves.[12]

La qualité de la prédiction en matière de délinquance violente, d'ailleurs contestée en tant qu'acte scientifique par de nombreux corps professionnels et en particulier par la psychiatrie, reste donc encore moyennement fiable, en dépit des progrès réalisés. Et les meilleures méthodes ont une capacité de prédiction relative.

Examinons les possibilités et les limites de chacune.

3.1. L'OBSERVATION

Un premier outil auquel il est possible de recourir dans l'évaluation est l'observation qui est, et reste, une des bases du métier pénitentiaire. La répétition ou la non répétition d'actes quotidiens, la relation à l'autre, les fréquentations, la capacité d'autonomie, la réaction à la frustration, la capacité d'appeler à l'aide et la relation avec le personnel constituent une mine d'informations pour l'observateur.

Mais les résultats des observations peuvent être entachés d'erreurs. Les observateurs sélectionnent, occultent, oublient, amplifient, sont attirés par certains détails qui leur en dissimulent d'autres, projettent et mélangent les constats et les interprétations.

Damasio, par exemple, montrait déjà clairement en 1994 la subjectivité des images de rappel et la reconstruction imprécise en mémoire de travail des perceptions d'événements stockées dans les diverses zones du cerveau.[13]

L'utilisation de l'observation comme outil d'évaluation nécessite donc certaines précautions, même si certaines grilles d'observation, focalisant leur regard sur des comportements strictement codifiés et corrélés, ont de bons résultats dans des domaines délimités.[14]

3.2. L'EXPERTISE CLINIQUE

L'expertise du psychiatre ou du psychologue est également un instrument fréquemment utilisé dans le cadre de la procédure pénale. L'observation, l'étude

---

12 La précocité, la diversité ou la répétition et le sens d'actes mineurs peuvent être la manifestation de troubles qui pourront s'exprimer ultérieurement de manière plus spectaculaires. L'escalade est une des caractéristiques de certains types de délinquance.

13 Antonio R. Damasio, *L'erreur de Descartes*, Paris: Odile Jacob, 2010, p. 139-141 et 144-145.

14 Par exemple, le VIAOT, développé par Andre Mckibben, à Montréal, qui montre un bon niveau de corrélation entre le décodage de certains comportements sociaux et les progrès en thérapie.

de l'anamnèse du délinquant et les entretiens qui lui servent d'outils s'appuient souvent sur la passation de tests complémentaires.

De nombreux tests ont été développés spécialement pour la population délinquante ou morbide. Échelles de psychopathie, inventaires de personnalité et tests projectifs apportent aux expertises des compléments indispensables. Les MMPI[15], MCMI[16], HCR20[17], PCL-R[18] ou échelle d'agression de Bus et Perry peuvent permettre de préciser les diagnostics[19] en matière de dangerosité.

Le but premier de l'expertise légale est d'abord de définir le degré de responsabilité de l'auteur au moment de l'acte. Mais l'expertise s'appuie sur un diagnostic des affections ou des troubles psychiques ou des traits de personnalité pathologiques qui sera utile à tous les intervenants. Elle propose également un pronostic sur le futur du délinquant et suggère des solutions quant à sa problématique. Et elle sera utile avant le jugement, en début de prise en charge, comme à chaque étape charnière ultérieure.

Mais l'expertise n'est pas une science exacte. Elle est faite par des êtres humains qui ont leurs compétences, leur formation, leur niveau d'expérience et leurs faiblesses. La réaction, la sincérité, la collaboration ou la non collaboration de l'expertisé peuvent également influencer le résultat.

3.3. L'APPROCHE CRIMINOLOGIQUE

Le criminologue trouvera dans l'analyse du crime, de son processus de déclenchement et du mode opératoire ainsi que dans celle de la criminalité antérieure une source d'informations utiles à la compréhension du criminel et à la mise en place du traitement correctionnel.[20]

Âge du premier délit, fréquence des actes délictueux, diversité des infractions, influence du milieu et des valeurs sociales, analyse de la répétition des modes opératoires et de leurs modes de déclenchement permettront de donner du sens aux passages à l'acte, de comprendre le mode de fonctionnement de l'auteur, d'inventorier les facteurs de risque et de proposer des solutions d'assistance, de contrôle et d'accompagnement.

Mais comme en ce qui concerne l'expertise clinique, on a affaire dans l'expertise criminologique à deux subjectivités : celle de l'auteur du délit et celle de l'examinateur, et à la confrontation de leurs deux expériences.

Pas plus que l'expertise clinique, le recours à une expertise criminologique ne pourra apporter de certitudes.

---

15 Minnesota Multiphasic, Personnality Inventory.
16 Million Clinical Multiaxial Inventory.
17 Historical Clinical Risk Management 20 item scale.
18 Hare Psychopathy Checklist.
19 Gérard Niveau, *Evaluation de la dangerosité et du risque de récidive*, Paris : L'Harmatan, 2011.
20 Jean Proulx, *Profession Criminologue*, Montréal : Presses de l'Université de Montréal, 2006.

3.4. L'ÉVALUATION ACTUARIELLE

La méthode la plus récente utilisée dans le domaine de la prédiction de la récidive est l'évaluation actuarielle. La découverte de la présence de facteurs de risques de récidive a facilité la réalisation de grilles d'analyse informatisées[21], fondées sur l'étude statistique des risques et sur la répétition de leur combinaison. L'usage de la statistique a permis de constater des corrélations élevées entre certaines caractéristiques antérieures ou présentes et la récidive. Les questionnaires élaborés permettent d'isoler ces facteurs, d'en quantifier l'impact et d'intégrer leur poids dans l'élaboration du pronostic. A la fin de l'introduction des données, le logiciel calcule automatiquement la probabilité d'un ou de plusieurs types de récidive après un certain nombre d'années.

La première génération de ces logiciels ne tenait compte que de facteurs de risque statiques, de critères non influençables tels que l'âge ou la délinquance antérieure. Les générations actuelles permettent également d'inventorier les risques dynamiques (les besoins criminogènes) sur lesquels une intervention correctrice est possible. Les derniers intègrent non seulement l'ensemble des facteurs de risque actuellement recensés, mais ils tiennent également compte de la réceptivité du criminel au traitement et permettent de poser des diagnostics sur l'efficacité de la prise en charge.

Ces outils sont séduisants : ils sont simples, systématiques, identiques pour tous, au contraire de l'examen clinique, et le degré de corrélation entre le pronostic et les récidives est indiscutable. La majorité des programmes de 3e et de 4e génération assure une fiabilité du pronostic de près de 75 %. Reste cependant un risque d'erreur de 25 % qui est non négligeable. A ce niveau de fiabilité, on est seulement à mi-chemin entre les résultats d'un pile ou face et la certitude absolue.

Et que faire des données ? Si le risque de récidive est de 40 % après 5 ans, aucun logiciel ne dira si le condamné testé fait partie des 40 % de futurs récidivistes ou des 60 % qui ne récidiveront pas. L'application mécanique de cette méthode sans autres examens, qui se répand malheureusement toujours davantage, risque donc de produire de nombreux faux dangereux dont le destin risque d'être influencé négativement par leur étiquetage.[22]

Enfin, un résultat n'est valide que si on dispose de toutes les informations nécessaires pour alimenter le programme de données pertinentes. Un tel processus implique donc la standardisation des méthodes de travail de la police, de la magistrature, des services sociaux et des thérapeutes.

---

21 Risk Matrix 2000, OASys, FOTRESS, VRAG, SORAG, etc.

22 Un condamné suisse, souffrant de troubles de personnalité, mais avec lequel un contact était auparavant possible, bien que difficile, est récemment mort en haute sécurité après un régime qui s'est durci au fur et à mesure que ses réactions et son intolérance au régime se renforçaient.

3.5. COMBINER LES APPROCHES

L'usage mécanique d'une seule procédure d'évaluation risque donc de faire considérer comme dangereuses des personnes qui ne le sont pas, et inversement.

Le processus le plus fiable reste par conséquent la combinaison de plusieurs méthodes.[23] L'analyse croisée de certains indicateurs relevant des observations et des expertises, tels que la précocité, la diversité et l'intensité de la délinquance, le sens de l'activité délictueuse, le mode de déclenchement, la présence d'une pathologie ou d'un trouble du comportement durable en lien avec le crime, la prise de conscience de sa pathologie par le patient, les compétences sociales, la compliance au traitement ou à une prise en charge, l'accessibilité aux modes d'intervention existants et la qualité et la fiabilité du cadre de vie à venir sera plus fidèle qu'une méthode unique, aussi sophistiquée soit-elle.[24]

3.6. UNE PRÉDICTION FIABLE À COURT TERME

Enfin, aucune méthode d'évaluation ne peut assurer une prédiction à long terme. L'âge, qui est un facteur de risque statistiquement prépondérant[25], évolue indépendamment de toute intervention institutionnelle. Et la prise de conscience de ses troubles ou l'envie de réaliser de nouveaux objectifs existentiels peut surgir dans la vie d'un délinquant au moment où on s'y attend le moins.[26]

Il sera par conséquent nécessaire de procéder à des réévaluations et à des réajustements périodiques qui tiennent compte du vécu récent et de l'évolution personnelle du délinquant.[27] Mais de telles sanctions et modalités d'exécution ne font que rarement partie de l'arsenal sécuritaire.[28]

---

23 Le processus de réflexion mise au point par le prof. Dittmann, à Bâle, ou les parties du HCR 20 ne permettent pas de définir un seuil de dangerosité, mais ces instruments ont tous deux l'avantage de s'obliger à se poser les questions essentielles dans les domaines de la pathologie, de la prise de conscience et de la compliance à la prise en charge et de l'environnement social, soit en ce qui concerne le passé délinquant, le présent et le futur du criminel.

24 Suite aux commissions mises en place au Canada au début des années 1990, nombre d'Etats ont instauré des comités d'évaluation de la dangerosité, interdisciplinaires, qui évaluent avec du recul le travail des intervenants et servent d'intermédiaires entre ceux-ci et les décideurs.

25 L'âge du délinquant est le facteur de risque le plus important. Statistiquement, le taux de délinquance croît rapidement pour atteindre son plafond entre 18 et 24 ans et décroître rapidement avec le vieillissement.

26 Et il y a peu de cas pour lesquels on peut affirmer que le changement est le résultat d'une intervention déterminée. Même l'auteur du délit n'est pas toujours capable de discerner les causes du changement.

27 Voir les chapitres suivants consacrés à l'examen de la peine rétributive et de la mesure.

28 La période de sûreté ou la peine plancher, de durée fixe ne permettent pas de tenir compte d'une évolution de la personne.

4. LES RÉPONSES PÉNALES À LA DANGEROSITÉ

Après avoir examiné les problèmes liés à la définition de la dangerosité et à son évaluation, nous analyserons, toujours à travers le prisme de la dangerosité, les réponses pénales les plus importantes mises en œuvre depuis le Siècle des lumières : la peine rétributive et la défense sociale ainsi que leurs formes modernes afin de vérifier dans quelle mesure elles sont capables de couvrir les besoins de rétribution et de prévention.

4.1. LA RÉPONSE RÉTRIBUTIVE

A la peine rétributive née au 18e siècle sont rattachés les concepts philosophiques[29] de culpabilité, de responsabilité et de libre arbitre.

La sanction, proportionnelle à la culpabilité de l'auteur, a à la fois pour but de rétablir l'équilibre de la loi transgressée et de restaurer le coupable dans sa dignité. Le fait de juger ce dernier et de le sanctionner le reconnaît en effet comme un être raisonnable, honneur « qui ne lui serait pas accordé », comme le dit Hegel, « s'il n'était considéré que comme une bête nuisible qu'il faut mettre hors d'état de nuire ou qu'on cherche à effrayer ou amender[30] ».

Cette approche présuppose la reconnaissance de l'existence du libre arbitre du coupable et celle de sa responsabilité personnelle.

La reconnaissance de la responsabilité de l'auteur est d'ailleurs un préalable, ou était encore un préalable il y a quelques années[31] à l'ouverture de la procédure de jugement.

La peine prononcée constitue donc une réponse à un acte passé, exécuté de manière volontaire et consciente.

Or, la rétribution d'un acte intentionnel est difficilement associable avec la prévention de risques futurs. Comment, en effet, juger simultanément un acte passé et prévenir un acte à venir dont on ne peut que présupposer l'avènement[32] ? Nos constats nous ont montré, comme les études longitudinales, que certains auteurs d'infractions mineures ou moyennes pouvaient se révéler, à l'occasion de passages à l'acte ultérieurs, d'une dangerosité extrême alors qu'une large partie des auteurs d'actes gravissimes ne recommençait pas. Faire coïncider les deux approches sans transiter par l'examen de la personnalité de l'auteur relève donc du pur hasard.

---

29 Kant, Hegel.

30 G.W.F. Hegel, *Principes de philosophie du droit,* trad. A. Kahn, Paris : Gallimard, 1940.

31 L'introduction, en France, de la distinction entre l'imputabilité matérielle et l'imputabilité psychologique à travers la loi de 2008, qui a pour conséquence l'organisation d'un débat sur l'expertise devant les parties avant le prononcé d'un non lieu, a modifié cette approche.

32 Voir les limites du processus d'évaluation dans le chapitre qui y est consacré.

D'autre part, la prise en compte stricte de la responsabilité entraîne dans de nombreux cas des décisions correspondant mal aux besoins de prise en charge. Les expertises psychiatriques concluent souvent à une irresponsabilité partielle qui rend impossible une stricte séparation des compétences entre la médecine et l'appareil pénal, alors que c'est dans cette zone grise, entre acte voulu et acte inconscient, que se concentrent les récidives les plus spectaculaires et que la conjugaison des approches et des traitements est la plus nécessaire et la plus efficace.[33]

Cette vision cartésienne de l'intention correspond également de moins en moins aux découvertes des neuro-sciences.

Damasio, dans *L'erreur de Descartes*, montre par exemple, que le cerveau et le reste du corps constituent une entité globale qui interagit avec son environnement et dont la partie évolutive se constitue à travers chaque interaction. Il y décrit également les raccourcis aux processus de raisonnement et de décision qui sont facilités par des marqueurs somatiques. Il montre enfin que le processus de choix fait souvent appel à des mécanismes de sélection plus rapides que ceux qui sont gérés par la raison.

Dennett[34], pour sa part, montre le fractionnement d'une conscience, parfois principe d'identité, parfois sentiment d'exister, parfois pensée réfléchie, qui n'est que la conjonction momentanée d'images venant de différents endroits du cerveau, et qui ne se combinent qu'à de rares moments pour former un sentiment de conscience plein et achevé.

Il est donc difficile de rattacher la notion de libre arbitre à l'action d'un appareil cérébral qui se construit en permanence et fait des choix souvent influencés par ses expériences.

La stricte rétribution d'une infraction passée ne permettant ni de traiter clairement les situations marginales, ni de prendre en compte les risques futurs, la majorité des pays a dû imaginer des possibilités de prolongement de la peine de base permettant de répondre à une dangerosité qui ne peut être prévenue par la seule rétribution.

Examinons donc dans quelle mesure ces peines complémentaires permettent d'atteindre cet objectif.

La période de sûreté incompressible, le rallongement de certaines sanctions ou la fixation d'une durée de peine plancher correspondent plus à un souci de prévention du risque qu'à une réponse à la culpabilité.

Aux Etats Unis, par exemple, les évaluations actuarielles contribuent désormais à la définition de profils de risque intégrés dans les *sentencing guide lines* qui président à la fixation de la peine.

---

33 Voir à ce sujet *The Pyramid Framekork, Adapted from WHO Mind Project*, modèle sous forme de pyramide étageant les responsabilités en fonction du niveau de soins et du niveau de sécurité nécessaires: www:who.int/mental_health/policy/services/2_Optimal%20MIX%20 of%Services_Infosheet.pdf.

34 Daniel C. Dennett, *La conscience expliquée*, Paris: Odile Jacob, 1991.

Et dans le domaine de la lutte contre la récidive, la peine plancher française[35] ou le *three strikes and you are out*[36] de certains Etats américains ont pour seul but de faire disposer d'une période de neutralisation que la réponse rétributive n'offre pas.

Et malheureusement, aucun de ces «suppléments de peine» prononcés lors du jugement initial ne prend en compte les évolutions possibles de la personne délinquante.

Ils risquent donc de faire maintenir en prison des détenus bien au-delà des besoins d'une rétribution équitable, et au-delà de ce qui serait nécessaire en fonction de leur évolution personnelle.

Si le concept de rétribution ne permet ni de prendre en compte en soi la notion de dangerosité ni une classification pragmatique des délinquants, les peines complémentaires qui ont été créées présentent donc également des inconvénients. Leur mise en œuvre sans nuance risque à la fois d'étiqueter durablement, et avec des effets négatifs, une population qui ne nécessite pas de telles mesures, et de confirmer dans la population des sentiments d'insécurité qui ne demandent qu'à croître.

L'approche rétributive, même corrigée par des mesures complémentaires, ne répond donc pas entièrement aux besoins.

4.2. LA RÉPONSE DE LA DÉFENSE SOCIALE

La mesure de sûreté, propre à l'Europe continentale et initiée par les positivistes italiens, serait-elle plus efficace que la peine en matière de prévention de la récidive violente ?

L'idée de protection contre l'ennemi public n'est pas née avec l'école italienne. Parallèlement à une sanction considérée comme la médecine de l'âme par Platon[37], reprise par St. Thomas D'Aquin (poena medicinalis)[38] et par toute la pénologie moderne, existe depuis tout temps l'envie de mettre hors d'état de nuire la personne irrécupérable ou nuisible. On retrouve déjà cette idée chez Aristote.[39] Et cette volonté de protection, reprise par de nombreux penseurs tels que Saint-Thomas, et même Beccaria, s'est traduite tout au long de l'histoire des peines par l'élimination, le bannissement, les galères, le bagne ou la relégation.

---

35 Il s'agit de fixer une peine minimale plus élevée pour les récidivistes.

36 Certains Etats du Sud des Etats Unis ont introduit, pour lutter contre les «prédateurs» à répétition, la possibilité d'une condamnation d'au moins 25 ans ou à perpétuité dès la troisième condamnation, quelle que soit la gravité de l'infraction commise.

37 Platon, *Gorgias* 525b.

38 Saint Thomas d'Aquin, La *Somme Théologique*, IIaIIae, question 66.

39 Aristote, *Ethique à Nicomaque*.

Mais ce sont les positivistes italiens[40] qui sont à l'origine des mouvements de défense sociale qui se sont traduits au 20e siècle par la mise en place de mesures de sûreté dans un certain nombre de pays européens, et plus particulièrement initialement dans les régimes fascistes de l'Allemagne et de l'Italie. L'internement de sûreté allemand de 1933 est l'expression absolue de la volonté de se protéger et d'écarter les criminels jugés dangereux ou non tolérables.

La mesure de sûreté, justifiée par la probabilité que l'auteur commette à nouveau une infraction particulièrement dommageable a également été introduite en Belgique, à travers les lois de 1930, de 1964 puis de 2007. La Hollande possède elle aussi un tel instrument avec le TBS.

L'Allemagne a introduit l'internement de sûreté dans son code pénal en 1933. Maintenu après guerre par la commission alliée, l'internement fut abrogé en RDA en 1952, mais maintenu en RFA avec une connotation plus thérapeutique, allant dans le sens de la défense sociale nouvelle.[41] Les conditions de prononcé ont été restreintes en 1969, puis à nouveau durcies en 1998, 2002, 2004 puis 2008 avec l'introduction d'une possibilité de prononcé rétroactif. La particularité de ce modèle est la coexistence dans le droit pénal de la peine et de la mesure, le juge pouvant prononcer à la fois une peine correspondant à un acte criminel et une mesure visant à la prévention de nouveaux crimes. Si la peine est rétributive, tournée vers un acte passé, la mesure est destinée à la prévention d'un acte potentiel, hypothétique. La mesure est donc subsidiaire à la peine, et elle s'y substitue dès que la peine ne suffit plus pour prévenir la récidive.

La Suisse, qui s'inspire largement de l'Allemagne en matière de droit pénal, a également introduit dans son arsenal pénal, à côté de la peine, un traitement ambulatoire, un internement institutionnel à fin thérapeutique, qui peut être exécuté en prison ou dans une institution spécialisée et un internement de sûreté prononcé lors du jugement, mais dont la mise en œuvre est décidée en fin d'exécution de peine. Elle a de plus introduit dans sa constitution un vrai internement à vie, dont l'exécution ne peut être réexaminée que si une commission scientifique constate qu'un nouveau traitement pourra réduire le risque de réitération. Le premier prononcé d'internement à vie fait actuellement l'objet de recours au niveau national et il sera intéressant de voir ce que la Cour Européenne fera de cette décision.

Parmi les pays disposant également du système des mesures, la Cour européenne cite également dans son arrêt de 2009 *M. contre l'Allemagne* l'Autriche[42], le Danemark[43], l'Italie[44], le Liechtenstein[45], Saint-Marin[46], et la

---

40 Ferri, Garofalo.

41 M. Ancel inclut dans la défense sociale le traitement du condamné.

42 Art. 23 et suiv. et 47 et suiv. du code pénal autrichien.

43 Art. 70 et suiv. du code pénal danois.

44 Art. 199 et suiv. du code pénal italien.

45 Art. 23 et suiv. et 47 du code pénal du Liechtenstein.

46 Art. 121 et suiv. du code pénal saint-marinais.

Slovaquie.[47] La dangerosité des détenus est réexaminée périodiquement et les internés sont libérés sous condition s'ils ne constituent plus un danger pour la collectivité.

Les personnes qui y sont soumises sont incarcérées dans des établissements ou sections spécialisés en Autriche au Liechtenstein à Saint-Marin[48], en Slovaquie et en Suisse. Même si la législation italienne exige la même disposition, les rares personnes concernées par cette mesure en désuétude sont accueillies en Italie dans des prisons ordinaires dans le cadre d'un régime de détention spécial. Il en est de même au Danemark.

Au Danemark, en Italie, à Saint-Marin, en Allemagne et en Suisse, les dispositions applicables ne fixent pas de limite de durée à la détention de sûreté. En Autriche et au Liechtenstein, en revanche, ce type de détention ne peut dépasser dix ans, comme dans l'ancien code pénal allemand.

D'autres pays, tels que la Norvège, connaissent également le principe de la détention préventive.[49]

Dans la majorité des cas, même si ce n'est pas toujours réalisé de manière adéquate, les mesures de sûreté doivent être accompagnées d'un traitement visant à réduire les risques[50]de réitération.

Une libération conditionnelle est en général prévue dès que la mesure, dont la portée doit être proportionnelle au risque, n'est plus nécessaire. L'examen de son maintien ou de sa levée doit être effectué périodiquement.

L'utilisation de la mesure répond donc aux constats que nous avons faits lors de l'évaluation du risque. Proportionnelle à ce dernier, elle est prononcée dès que la peine en soi n'est pas suffisante. Elle permet un réajustement des restrictions et des traitements en fonction de l'évolution du condamné, ainsi que la prise en compte de la fiabilité relative et du manque de durabilité des pronostics.

Mais elle souffre de deux défauts majeurs.

Elle tient mal en compte de la rétribution du délit initial, la levée de la mesure étant uniquement conditionnée par le risque de récidive. Et le lien entre le risque et la culpabilité s'estompe au fur et à mesure de la durée de l'exécution.

D'autre part, le moment où la mesure doit supplanter la peine – le moment où la défense sociale l'emporte sur la rétribution – dépend de la définition donnée à la dangerosité. Et dans une ambiance de recherche du risque zéro, la tentation est grande de privilégier la sécurité publique et d'exclure une composante de risque calculé pourtant nécessaire à une bonne prise en charge.[51] La pratique montre

---

47 Art. 81 et 82 du code pénal slovaque.

48 Ces deux pays font exécuter les peines dans le pays voisin.

49 « Preventive detention » prise dans le sens anglais du terme, et non dans le sens de pre trial detention.

50 Les insuffisances en matière de possibilité de traitement sont souvent dénoncées par le CPT et par la Cour.

51 Voir chapitre suivant.

que les mesures de sûreté risquent d'être utilisées, dans ce cas, plus souvent, et plus longtemps que nécessaire.

L'Allemagne a été condamnée par la Cour Européenne en 2009[52] en raison d'une violation à l'article 5 et à l'article 7 CEDH. Certes il s'agissait de l'application rétroactive, bien après le jugement initial, d'un rallongement de la durée de la mesure de sûreté, mais cet arrêt introduit deux brèches dans le concept de la mesure.

La Cour constate tout d'abord que la mesure constituerait une détention arbitraire et ne rentrerait dans aucune des hypothèses prévues par l'article 5 de la Convention si elle ne résultait pas directement de la condamnation pénale initiale. De plus, l'internement constitue à ses yeux une peine, au sens de l'article 7 de la Convention.

Il n'est donc pas exclu que les pays qui disposent du même système dual que l'Allemagne doivent procéder à certains aménagements, et ceci d'autant plus que de nouvelles condamnations ont été prononcées par la Cour Européenne depuis 2009.

Comment donc concilier la répression d'un acte, à laquelle la sanction doit être liée selon les normes européennes, et la prévention d'un danger potentiel? Comment concilier ou prioriser rétribution et défense sociale? Ni la peine rétributive, ni une mesure contestée ne semblent pouvoir assurer pleinement ces deux exigences.

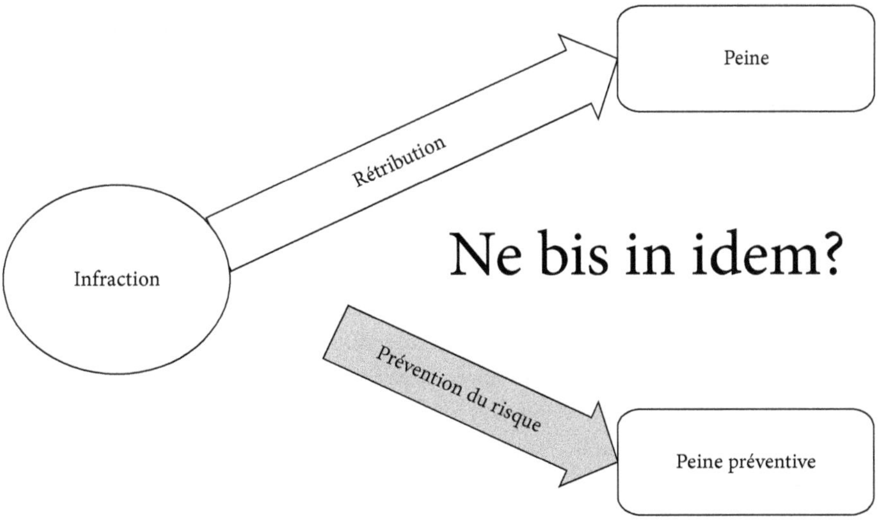

52 Affaire M. C. Allemagne, 2009.

5. LE TRAITEMENT CORRECTIONNEL

Notre analyse ne serait pas complète si nous n'examinions pas pour terminer dans quelle mesure l'exécution pratique des peines et des mesures correspondent aux objectifs précités.

Nous achèverons donc notre parcours en examinant de quelle manière, et dans quel cadre, les deux pratiques confondues peuvent effectivement contribuer à la prévention du risque.[53]

La prise en charge des délinquants repose sur une recherche d'équilibre subtile entre garantir la sécurité à court terme (éviter les incidents immédiats) et assurer la sécurité à long terme (éviter la récidive à la libération). Il s'agit de prendre ici et maintenant les mesures de sécurité nécessaires, mais sans nuire au traitement amorcé ni hypothéquer les possibilités d'évolution de la personne par des contraintes supérieures aux besoins du moment et contraires aux besoins de traitement.

Les tensions existant entre les exigences de la sécurité immédiate et celles de la sécurité à long terme impliquent un dosage subtil et constamment réadapté entre le contrôle et l'incitation au changement. Trop de sécurité peut nuire au processus d'évolution personnelle alors qu'une absence de prise en considération des risques peut conduire à la réitération d'actes inadmissibles ou à l'opacité du parcours de réinsertion.

Tout en gardant une lucidité et une distance suffisante, il est donc nécessaire de croire au potentiel de développement du criminel et de créer un cadre propice, mais maîtrisé, à l'apprentissage de la vie sociale, à l'acquisition des outils et compétences nécessaires à la vie externe et à la construction d'un nouveau mode de vie.

La gestion du parcours du condamné consiste donc en une succession de prises de risques calculés, jalonnant les étapes de la prise en charge, et adaptées à son niveau d'évolution.

Les approches les plus efficaces seront celles qui se concentrent sur les cas les plus graves et qui nécessitent un traitement intensif. La pluridisciplinarité des approches dans la cohérence, voire leur interdisciplinarité, offrira la meilleure garantie de résultats. Les recherches semblent également montrer que les approches cognitives sont celles qui ont le plus de chance de succès.[54] Elles soulignent aussi l'efficacité plus grande des prises en charges dans la communauté.[55]

---

53 La majorité des codes pénaux inscrivent la prévention de la récidive comme but de l'exécution de la peine.

54 Quelques réserves semblent pouvoir être émises en ce qui concerne l'apprentissage de processus qui ne seront pas forcément répétés dans les situations de stress.

55 Services Correctionnels du Canada, *Compendium 2000 des traitements correctionnels.*

Mais le processus de prise en charge exige un doigté, une souplesse et un degré d'individualisation que la rigidité des procédures rend souvent difficile. Chaque condamné réagit subjectivement à la sanction et progresse à sa vitesse et en fonction de ses propres objectifs et non en fonction des exigences légales.

Et la tension entre les exigences formelles et la préparation du changement est particulièrement importante en ce qui concerne le suivi des détenus dangereux. L'incident, qui peut être banalisé dans les autres cas, prend dans leur cas une importance toute particulière.

Les règles les concernant visent par conséquent essentiellement à protéger la société. Elles rigidifient les processus[56], rallongent les examens, et multiplient les obstacles là où une souplesse éclairée devrait être la règle. Mais cette formalisation compréhensible par rapport aux enjeux est difficilement contournable. Elle exige de la part des intervenants des trésors d'imagination pour faire comprendre à des personnes, initialement peu enclines à la patience, la nécessité de passer à chaque étape sous les fourches caudines et de vivre dans l'incertitude jusqu'à la libération finale.

6. CONCLUSION

Ce rapide panorama met en évidence de nombreuses difficultés et tensions. La notion de dangerosité ne peut être clairement définie, son évaluation est incertaine, et aucune approche pénologique, souvent difficile à concilier avec ses voisines, n'offre encore de solution idéale.

L'exécution de la mesure semble cependant autoriser, malgré des risques de mise en œuvre sécuritaires, une plus facile progression dans les régimes alors que les peines minimales et les périodes de sûreté, tout comme une libération conditionnelle dont le prononcé manque souvent de souplesse, rendent difficile l'individualisation de l'exécution.

Mais si l'usage de la mesure semble séduisant, cette dernière se fonde sur une analyse prospective qui n'a qu'une relation indirecte avec le premier délit commis.

C'est pourquoi notre examen ne peut aller au-delà du constat que les approches actuelles ne permettent qu'imparfaitement de tenir compte à la fois des exigences d'une juste rétribution et de celles de la sécurité publique.

Il semblerait donc utile de réformer le système des peines, et de le rendre plus pragmatique, plus souple, plus individualisé, afin qu'il puisse concilier les deux objectifs.

---

[56] Commissions spéciales d'évaluation du risque, double examen, limites temporelles, etc.

Nous n'aurons pas la prétention d'achever cette démarche. Mais les quelques principes qui suivent devraient contribuer à guider la réflexion.

- Préciser la définition de la dangerosité en y décrivant plus précisément le seuil de tolérance de manière à limiter les interventions préventives et répressives à celles qui sont nécessaires à la gestion des risques réellement intolérables.
- Définir clairement la place de la rétribution et celle de la défense sociale et à quel moment doit s'enclencher entre elles un mécanisme de subsidiarité.
- Inscrire dans les textes légaux des critères tenant mieux compte de la diversité et de l'individualité des situations.
- Prendre en compte les possibilités d'évolution de la personne et les intégrer dans la fixation de la peine et dans la gestion de son déroulement, tout en garantissant à la victime et à la société une rétribution équitable.
- Créer un système dynamique, orienté vers la réintégration, fondé sur le principe du risque calculé et non sur l'interdiction du risque.
- Favoriser les approches pluridisciplinaires et les regards croisés pour compenser les difficultés d'évaluation et de prise en charge.

Souhaitons que ces quelques pistes nous aideront à nous diriger vers une gestion de la délinquance violente à la fois efficace vis à vis de la société et respectueuse des Droits de l'Homme.

THE RELEVANCE OF THE RISK OF REOFFENDING IN DETERMINING THE TYPE AND THE LENGTH OF SENTENCES – A COMPARATIVE CRIMINAL LAW PERSPECTIVE

Peter J.P. TAK*

1. INTRODUCTION

Let me start with some semantics. In this chapter I will speak about dangerous offenders instead of high risk offenders. The term high risk offender seems to be much more appropriate than the term dangerous offender. Nevertheless, I will use the term dangerous offender as a synonym because this term is much used in policy papers and in legislation within Europe and is furthermore quite common used in public debate and popular discourse.[1] Dangerous offenders are like high risk offenders those who pose a substantial risk of further serious offending and include sexual and violent offenders, terrorists, and members of organized criminal groups.

The management of high risk or dangerous offenders during and after their sentence is of major concern for governments in Europe because reoffending by these offenders may cause unrest amongst the population and may lead to public outcry. Therefore, recently new legislation in order to manage dangerous offenders has been proposed or adopted in various West-European countries. In some countries this legislation was focused on a serious increase of the maximum statutory sentence for the most serious crimes or on the adoption of mandatory sentences in cases of recidivism.

* Dr. P.J.P. Tak is an em. Professor of law at Radboud University Nijmegen, The Netherlands. Email: p.tak@jur.ru.nl.

1 The topic has been on the agenda of the European Committee of Crime Problems since 2007. An impressive report for the committee was written by N. Padfield: *The Sentencing, Management and Treatment of 'Dangerous' Offenders*, PC-CP(2010) 10 rev 5, Strasbourg 20 December 2010.

In France and England new legislation adopting or extending mandatory sentences in case of recidivism came into force recently.[2] One cannot deny that the 'three strikes and you are out' rule as applied in a number of American States was taken as a motive for that legislation.[3] What was the core element of this new legislation?

Under the French 2007 'Loi Dati', the law named after the then Minister of Justice, the court has to impose a listed mandatory minimum sentence in case of a reconviction for all crimes that carry a statutory prison sentence of three years and more. The sentence is compulsory and courts hardly have any discretion to impose a sentence below the mandatory minimum.

In Chapter 15 on Dangerous Offenders in the 2012 Legal Aid, Sentencing and Punishment of Offenders Act, England adopted rules that the court has to impose life imprisonment for serious sexual and violent offences committed by repeat offenders unless the court believes that it would make it unjust to do so in all the circumstances (Section 122). In fact this is not even three strikes and you are out, but rather two strikes.

In the Netherlands very severe mandatory sentences in case of recidivism have been proposed in an MP Bill. The statutory maximum sentences for violent and other serious crimes would have been increased with 250%. Furthermore, the MP Bill proposed a mathematic strict and compelling system of mandatory minimum sentences. The system intentionally did not take into account the variety of forms a crime can manifest itself.[4] Adoption of the Bill would have caused serious problems for the judiciary because courts would have been compelled to impose draconian sentences. Due to a change in the government the Bill will not be adopted. A new less strict Bill on mandatory minimum sentences is pending in Parliament.

In many legal systems the dangerousness of the offender has an impact on the determination of the sentence as well as on the execution of the sentence. On the one hand, prison sentences are increased in the light of offenders' dangerousness, when he is reconvicted or when his reoffending is considered by the court to be a probable risk after the expiry of the sentence. On the other hand, offenders' dangerousness generally has an influence both on their conditions of detention and on their chances of benefitting from a reduction of their sentence or from early release. So dangerousness of the offender concerns both his behavior in the past as his probable behavior in the future.

---

2 See for the French *Loi Dati* of August 10 the 2007, J. Pradel, *Enfin des lignes directrice pour sanctionner les délinquants récidivistes*, Dalloz 2007 p. 2247–2256.

3 R. Ward & O. Davies, *The Criminal Justice Act 2003, A Practitioner's Guide*, Bristol: Jordan Publishing, 2004, p. 206.

4 See Peter J.P. Tak, *De minimumstraf opnieuw bezien. Een geactualiseerde beknopte rechtsvergelijking* (The mandatory minimum sentence revisited. An updated concise comparative law report for the Dutch Council for the Judiciary), Research Memorandum 4/2010, Raad voor de rechtspraak, Den Haag: SDU, 2010.

2. OUTLINE OF THE CHAPTER

This chapter will talk about the impact of probable future crimes on sentencing by courts and about the actual time of the imposed prison sentence a prisoner has to serve and consists of three parts.

The first part will deal with sentencing of dangerous offenders who are considered sane and fully criminal responsible for the crime they have to stand trial for. Three questions will be answered:

- What possibilities does the court have to take into consideration the dangerousness of the offender when sentencing?
- In what ways is early release and parole influenced by the future dangerousness of the offender?
- What measures can a court impose after the full service and expiry of the sentence that in fact extend the duration of the deprivation of liberty due to the dangerousness of the offender?

In the second part I will change my scope and I will concentrate on the possibilities courts have to sentence an offender who is dangerous due to a mental disorder or insanity. Do special security measures exist for these offenders? Can these measures last as long as the dangerousness exists and who decides on the dangerousness?

In the last part I will answer some major questions in relation to the management of dangerous offenders. These questions concern the effectiveness of compulsory minimum sentences, the reliability of risk assessment methods and instruments and the risk avoidance criminal policy.

Since this chapter is of a comparative criminal law nature, it will discuss some specific rules which laws on sentencing in Denmark, England, France, Germany, the Netherlands and Norway contain that are focused on the management of dangerous offenders by courts.

3. PART I. POSSIBILITIES THE COURT HAS IN ORDER TO TAKE INTO ACCOUNT THE FUTURE DANGEROUSNESS OF THE OFFENDER WHEN SENTENCING

There are many ways for criminal courts to take into account the future dangerousness of offenders. One way is to impose prison sentences of substantial length. The penal codes of many countries know life sentence as its longest prison sentence but a life sentence is rarely a deprivation of liberty for life.

3.1. LIFE SENTENCE

In most countries courts may impose life sentences for offences that carry a statutory life sentence when the offender is considered to be a risk for the community and will probably commit new serious offences. He is a dangerous offender who must be kept out of free society for a long time.

In most of the countries, however, a life sentence is not a real life sentence. After years the prisoner can apply a conditional release or parole. The release systems in the European countries vary enormously,[5] but as a rule life prisoners may be released after having served a substantial part of their sentence. Whether he will be released, however, is in some countries highly influenced by the assessment of the risk that the offender will reoffend. I will explain this for Germany and England.

After the abolition of capital punishment in 1965 life sentence is the most severe penalty that can be imposed by English courts. Murder is the only crime that carries a mandatory life sentence, all other life sentences are discretionary sentences. As a rule life imprisonment does not last until the prisoner's death. Mandatory lifers serve an average of fourteen years and discretionary lifers around nine years.

In 2005 the Criminal Justice Act 2003 came into force which introduced the concept of dangerous offenders. Indeterminate sentences of imprisonment for public protection (IPP) and extended determinate sentences of imprisonment for dangerous sexual or violent offenders were introduced. Rules were adopted for mandatory sentences for specified offences that carry a statutory imprisonment for life or for a determinate period of ten years or more. In 2012 a number of the provisions creating indeterminate sentences for public protection and extended sentences were repealed by the Legal Aid, Sentencing and Punishment of Offenders Act and replaced with provisions for life sentences to be imposed on conviction for a second serious offence and with new provision for extended sentences.

Core of the new rules is that the court must impose a life sentence for a specified crime[6] that is serious enough to justify a sentence of imprisonment of ten years or more, if that person has previously been convicted of an offence and was sentenced to a relevant life sentence or a relevant sentence of imprisonment in respect to that previous offence. A life sentence is relevant when the offender was not eligible for release during the first five years of his sentence. A prison sentence is relevant if the custodial term was ten years or more. However, the court is not obliged to impose a life sentence where it is of the opinion that there

---

5 N. Padfield, D. van Zyl Smit & F. Duenkel (eds.), *Release from prison: European policy and practice*, Cullompton: Willan Publishing, 2010.

6 That is a crime listed in Part 1 of Schedule 15B of the CJA 2003, such as manslaughter, the possession of a firearm with the intention to endanger life, armed robbery, rape, sexual activity with a child and terrorism.

are particular circumstances which relate to the offence, the previous offence or the offender which would make it unjust to do so in all the circumstances (Article 224A, life sentence for the second listed offence).

The impact of dangerousness of the offender on the sentence is expressed in the new Article 226A. That section created new extended sentences in respect of sexual and violent crimes that may be imposed for specified offences when the court considers that the offender presents a risk of causing serious harm to members of the public through reoffending. One further condition has to be met. Either the court must consider that the current offence is serious enough to merit a determinate sentence of at least four years or at the time the present offence was committed the offender must have previously been convicted of a specified offence. Where these conditions are made out the court imposes an appropriate custodial term and determines an extended period for which the offender is to be subject to a license. Upon release the offender during the extended period has to observe the rules set in the license. This period is up to five years for violent offences and up to eight years for sexual offences (Article 226A(8) CJA). The appropriate custodial term and the extension period must not exceed the maximum prison term permitted for the offence.

This in fact implies a risk assessment by the court. The court must assess whether the offender is dangerous. How does this work and what matters the court has to take into account when assessing the risk? Before 2008 the risk assessment for future offences was mainly based on previous convictions. The existence of previous convictions for specified offences was a presumption of dangerousness. That no longer is the case but previous convictions still are very relevant for the assessment of dangerousness. According to Article 229(2) CJA as amended by Article 17 Criminal Justice and immigration Act 2008 the court must take into account all available information on the nature and circumstances of the offence and may take into account information about the nature and circumstances of offences the offender has been previously convicted for. Furthermore, the court may take into consideration information about the pattern of behavior of which any of the offences forms part and any information about the offender.[7]

In Germany life sentence is the mandatory sentence for murder. That is the only mandatory life sentence known in the German Penal Code. All other life sentences are discretionary life sentences which courts can impose for around twenty very serious offences which have led to the death of the victim, like rape, kidnapping or arson followed by the death of the victim. Unlike in England, whole life sentences are unknown. All life prisoners in Germany are in principle eligible for early release, however, early release is not always granted, as we will see hereafter.

---

7 See the website of the Crown Prosecution Service (www.cps.gov.uk/legal/s_to_u/sentencing_and_dangerous_offenders/#a01) (last visited: 1 September 2013).

In the Netherlands a life sentence in fact is a whole life order because it means imprisonment until death. The Dutch Penal Code contains a set of rules on early release (Articles 14a ff Criminal Code (CC) (Wetboek van Strafrecht (WvSr))[8] but those rules are not applicable in case of a life sentence. Although the number of life sentences in the Netherlands is still rather low, the lack of any perspective for the life convict and the lack of any possibility for courts to review a life sentence or to assess the need to continue with the execution of the life sentence should be of concern, the more because in the previous decades a number of life sentences have been imposed because the court was of the opinion that the maximum fixed term sentence at that time, twenty years, was not an appropriate sentence. Since the maximum fixed term sentence has been increased to thirty years the number of life sentences imposed has considerably decreased.

In a number of cases where Dutch courts have imposed a life sentence or very long sentences sometimes in combination with penal measures because of the diminished criminal responsibility of the offender, courts expressed their concern on the risk of reoffending and reasoned the decision to impose the life sentence or long-term sentence on that concern.

Now we have dealt with the statutory framework of sentencing of dangerous offenders, it is time to deal with parole and release from custody of those offenders who were assessed dangerous by the court. Are there any specific rules in the Netherlands, Germany and England concerning the release of dangerous offenders?

3.2. THE IMPACT OF FUTURE DANGEROUSNESS ON EARLY RELEASE OR PAROLE IN CASE OF A LIFE SENTENCE

The German Federal Constitutional Court has found life imprisonment without the mere possibility of parole to be antithetical to human dignity as expressed in Article 3 of the Basic Law (Grundgesetz). This doesn't mean that all lifers have to be released after serving a considerable number of years but they must at least have a realistic chance for eventual release, provided that they are not considered dangerous any longer.[9]

In Germany all prisoners sentenced to life imprisonment can apply for parole after having served fifteen years (Article 57a CC) (Strafgesetzbuch (StGB)). The decision-making process on whether to grant parole is rather complex and is made by the Strafvollstreckungskammer, the parole court. This court has to decide whether 15 years of imprisonment has been sufficiently severe to punish

8 See in detail, Peter J.P. Tak, *The Dutch Criminal Justice System. Organization and Operation*, Nijmegen: Wolf Legal Publishers, 2008, Ch. 11.

9 Constitutional Court, Judgment of 21 June 1977, BVerfGE.Bd 45, p. 187 ff.

offenders for the specific conduct of which they were guilty and whether the offender continues to pose a risk for society as expressed in Article 57(1,2) CC.

On what basis must the parole court decide whether 15 years of imprisonment is sufficient? The Federal Constitutional Court has ruled that the court which imposes the initial sentence has to make a finding about whether or not the offender was particularly blameworthy.[10] When that court did not find the guilt of the offender particularly blameworthy, the parole court may concentrate its decision solely on the risk to society. When that court did find that the offender was particularly blameworthy, the parole court must furthermore take into account whether the offender already got his just desert and whether further incapacitation of him is required. If the parole court rejects the request a reapply is possible within two years (Article 57 (IV) CC). When declining the first request for parole the parole court determines in the light of the severe gravity of guilt (besondere Schwere der Schuld) and the development of the prisoner how many additional years the inmate has to serve before he is eligible to apply for early release. There is no legal limit on that term. Usually, however, it is five years.

Who decides on whether the offender continues to pose a risk for society? Does the Justice Minister or the prison governor have a say in the release of the prisoner? According to Article 2(2) of the Constitution, read with Article 104(2) only a judge may rule upon the permissibility or continuation of any deprivation of liberty. In its judgment of 30 April 2009 the Federal Constitutional Court ruled that: 'the parole court alone must decide on the continuation of imprisonment after the minimum term has been served. That is only guaranteed if the court clarifies the prognostic basis of its decision independently and does not leave it to third parties (like the prison governor or the expert psychiatrist, P.T.). In particular, it prohibits the executive from exercising untested and possibly illegal influence on the judicial decision by predetermining its content and outcome'.[11]

In England the Criminal Justice Act 2003 set out guidelines for how long murderers should spend in prison before they are eligible for parole. The court, when imposing a life sentence, can set a minimum term in order to meet the requirements of retribution and deterrence, the so-called tariff, the offender has to spend in prison before parole is possible. For some crimes such as multiple murder involving sexual abuse, recidivism of murder and grave high treason, the court can decide that the offender should never become eligible for parole. That is known as a whole life order. A whole life order means that the offender remains in prison until his death unless there are exceptional circumstances such as compassionate grounds due to great age or infirmity.

A whole life order, also known in England, has recently been challenged before the European Court in the case of *Vinter and others vs the United*

10 Constitutional Court, Judgment of 3 June 1992, BVerfGE.Bd 86, p. 288 ff.

11 Constitutional Court, Judgment of 30 April 2009, *NJW* 2009, p. 1941ff.

Kingdom. The Strasbourg court ruled that 'because the whole life orders were imposed by a court only after consideration of the facts of each case and because the life prisoner could apply for compassionate release, a whole life order is not in conflict with his human rights'.[12]

3.3. THE IMPACT OF DANGEROUSNESS ON EARLY RELEASE OR PAROLE IN CASE OF EXTENDED OR DETERMINATE SENTENCES

The Legal Aid, Sentencing and Punishment of Offenders Act 2012 set out the release arrangements for the new extended sentence. Different release arrangements will apply depending on the seriousness of the offence in respect of which the sentence was imposed. Offenders who have committed an offence listed in parts 1 to 3 of Schedule 15 B or whose offending merits a custodial term of ten years or more will be considered for release on license by the parole board once the offender has served two thirds of the appropriate custodial term and will be released automatically at the end of the appropriate custodial term. Offenders who have not committed a schedule 15 B offence but have committed an offence meriting an appropriate custodial term of less than ten years, will be released automatically after two thirds of the appropriate custodial term (Article 246A CJA). Although the release for determinate sentences as a rule is at half term, in the release arrangements based on the Legal Aid, Sentencing and Punishment of Offenders Act 2012 the dangerousness of the offender plays an important role and leads to a postponed release and a longer period of probation.

In Germany the dangerousness of the offender may have an impact on his early release. As a rule early release is granted by the parole court after the offender has served two thirds of the prison sentence and the release is justified with regards to the interest of the public safety. The parole court has to consider *inter alia* the personality of the offender, his prior life, the circumstances of the criminal act and the seriousness of the criminal offence in case of recidivism. The prognosis of the offender after having been released must be favorable but a degree of risk of reoffending has to be accepted. The court, when granting early release, may attach behavioral conditions to the release. Non-compliance will as a rule lead to revocation.[13]

In case the offender, after having served the full term of his prison sentence, still constitutes a danger for society, the offender can be kept in preventive detention. That measure is highly controversial in Germany and has given rise to

---

12 ECtHR 17 January 2012, Appl. Nos 66069/09, 130/10 and 3896/10.

13 See for further details, F. Dünkel & I. Pruin, 'Conditional release in Germany', in: N. Padfield, D. van Zyl Smit & F. Dünkel (eds.), *Release from prison: European policy and practice*, Cullompton: Willan Publishing, 2010, p. 185–212.

bookshelves of publications and large series of judgments of the highest federal court in criminal cases, the Bundesgerichtshof, of the highest federal court in constitutional cases, the Bundesverfassungsgericht and finally, of the European Court on Human Rights. Let us therefore look somewhat closer at the measure of preventive detention.

3.4. SECURE PREVENTIVE DETENTION

In many European countries there are specific rules regulating the detention of dangerous offenders for public security reasons. There is one measure for public protection that asks for further elaboration: the so-called secure preventive detention which is know in many countries such as Austria, Belgium, Denmark, France, Germany and Norway, and may be an indeterminate sanction, despite the regular reviews and possibility of release. I will deal with the secure preventive detention in Denmark, France, Germany and Norway.

In Denmark offenders who are considered dangerous can be sentenced to security detention and can be kept in prison until they no longer are considered to be dangerous.[14] After being released they remain under probation for five years. Security detention is an indeterminate sentence. In practice security detention is mainly used for offenders who suffer from a mental disorder.[15]

Security detention can only be used when three conditions are met:

- the offenders must have been convicted for (attempts to) homicide, robbery, rape and other serious sexual offences, or serious violent crimes, serious threats and arson;
- the offenders pose an obvious danger to health, life, body and freedom of others which is apparent from the nature of the offence committed and from the information on his character with special reference to his criminal record, and
- preventive detention is considered necessary in order to avert this danger (Article 70 CC).

The majority of security detention sentences are served in Herstedvester prison, where the prisoners receive psychological and psychiatric treatment. Serious sex offenders receive psychotherapy and may be treated with anti-hormone medicine.[16]

---

14 See H. Hansen, 'Treating the "Untreatable" in Denmark: past and present', in: T. Millon and others (eds.), *Psychopathy. Antisocial, Criminal and Violent Behavior*, New York: Guilford Press, 1998, p. 458–477.

15 See for more details L.B. Langsted, P. Garde & V. Greve, *Criminal Law in Denmark*, Copenhagen: DJØF Publishing, 2004, p. 106–107.

16 H. Hansen & L. Lucke-Olesen, 'Treatment of dangerous sexual offenders in Denmark', 8 *Journal of Forensic Psychiatry* 1 (1997), p. 195–199.

In Norway the situation is slightly different. Norway has abolished the life sentence in 1985 and the maximum prison sentence a court may impose is 21 years. When the offender has committed a very serious offence, a prison sentence is considered not to be a sufficient protection of the society, and if there is an imminent risk for a new serious offence, the court may sentence the offender to secure preventive detention (Forvaring, Articles 39c ff CC 1902, art. 40 ff CC 2005).[17] The rules on preventive detention have been recently reviewed by the Act of 20 January 2012[18] as far as it concerns the application of secure preventive detention for juvenile offenders. For those this reaction can only be used under extraordinary circumstances.

Anders Behring Breivik, the offender who killed 77 people in a bomb attack at the Oslo government complex and in a shooting spree on the island of Utoya was sentenced to a secure preventive detention. According to Article 39c CC (Art. 43 CC 2005) a sentence on secure preventive detention shall be fixed to a determinate period of time that should not exceed 15 years and may not exceed 21 years. The court should at the same time stipulate a minimum detention time, which may not be longer than 10 years. The secure preventive detention may, however, three months before it expires at the prosecutor's request by the court be extended for a period of five years at a time as long as the offender is considered to be at serious risk of reoffending. This means that after full service of the determinate sentence the deprivation of liberty may continue in order to prevent that the offender will commit new serious offences. A sentence on preventive detention may last for an indefinite period and in extreme cases even for life.[19]

The secure preventive detention is a penal sanction for dangerous offenders as well as a measure for public protection. Three conditions have to be met before the court can impose a secure preventive detention (Article 39c CC 1902, Article 40 CC 2005). The first condition is that a regular prison sentence has been assessed to be insufficient for the protection of the general public. The second condition is that the crime committed or attempt to commit has to be a listed serious crime, such as violent crime, sexual crime, arson or other serious crimes which violate life, health or freedom or put them at stake. The third condition is that the imminent risk exists that the offender will commit a new serious offence. This risk assessment is made by experts. For the risk assessment special attention has to be given to the behavior of the offender and his social and personal functioning.

When the law on the secure preventive detention took effect in 2002, replacing the previous outdated preventive detention system, the detention

17 The 2005 PC will not replace the 1902 PC until 2017 due to data problems.

18 At: www.Lovdata.no/all/tl-20050520-028-008.html. See the Report by the CPT to the Norwegian Government of 15 December 2011, CPT (2011) 70, p. 23–24, and the report of the USA Law library of Congress, Norwegian Criminal Law and the July 22, 2011, Massacre, p. 5–7, at: www.loc.gov/law/.

19 UN Committee against Torture, CAT/C/NOR/6–7, 30 January 2012, p. 6–8.

should serve both as a special criminal sanction and as punishment. The essential features of a special criminal sanction are its aim to protect the society for those deemed at risk of reoffending with serious crimes and the indeterminate length of the sanction. Nowadays the elements of a criminal sanction have disappeared and the secure preventive detention is considered as a mere punishment. Since the sentence to preventive detention can be prolonged and in effect can lead to a lifelong deprivation of liberty a conflict exists between the need to protect society through indeterminate incapacitation and the philosophical demands for a punishment proportional to the seriousness of the offence.[20] So far however, in Norway secure preventive detention never was applied lifelong.

According to the law commission which prepared the Bill on preventive detention the indeterminate nature of preventive detention is warranted because at the time of conviction it is not possible to estimate how long there is a danger that the offender will commit a further offence.[21] Further warrants are the high threshold for the imposition of preventive detention and for the extension of the sentence. An offender, after having served the minimum detention time, has the right to apply for provisional release once every year (Article 39f CC 1902, Article 44 CC 2005). Provisional release may be granted if it is determined that the offender is no longer a danger for society. The probation period is one to five years. The court will attach behavioral and other conditions to the provisional release (Article 39g CC 1902, Article 45 CC 2005). Non-compliance with the conditions will lead to a revocation of the provisional release.

An evaluation in 2008 of the system of preventive detention by an expert committee (The Mæland Working Group) showed that the provisional release of offenders in preventive detention is problematic because the system of gradually preparing offenders for provisional release is not satisfactory and reintegration of preventive detainees into community after release is rather difficult. Furthermore, the report from the committee had raised the question whether such people, of whom a high percentage were classified as having serious personality disorders, were capable of changing so that their behavior was no longer a risk to society.[22] In practice in a significant number of cases, courts have granted release or release on probation to offenders who were sentenced to secure preventive detention despite an advice by the prison and probation service not to decide so on the grounds that sufficient progress had not been made.[23]

20 See B. Johnson, 'Forvaring-fra saerreaktsjon og "straff" til lovens strengeste straff: Ett skritt frem eller et tilbake?' (Preventive detention – from security measure to the most serious penalty), 98 *Nordisk tidsskrift for criminalvidenskab* 1 (2011), p. 2–16.

21 Ot.prp.nr.87 (1993–1994), om lov om endringer i straffeloven m.v. ((strafferettslige utilregnelighetsregler og særreaksjoner, section 8.7.3) (measure for mental disordered offenders or sanction)).

22 CAT/C/NOR/6–7, 30 January 2012, p. 7.

23 CPT Report 15 December 2011, CPT (2011) 70, p. 24.

Anders Behring Breivik is expected to be an offender who will never be granted release. He has been sentenced to preventive detention with a determinate sentence of 21 years. In its sentencing the Oslo court reasoned the need for a preventive detention by referring to statements made by Breivik during court trial and by referring to reports of behavioral experts. Breivik has declared to be able to commit more killings like the decapitation of the former prime minister Gro Harlem Brundtland and to commit more extreme violent acts. Experts appointed by the court came to the conclusion that the risk for future violent acts by the offender was very high due to his serious personality mental disorder.[24]

3.5. CONCLUSION

The conclusion of the first part is that in a number of countries special rules and regulations have been adopted, some of them rather recent, that provide courts, when sentencing and imposing criminal sanctions, to take into consideration the risk that the offender in the future will reoffend and commit serious crimes. Also, when decisions have to be taken on requests for early release or parole courts may make their decisions dependent on their assessment of the risk for future crimes by the applicant.

4. PART II. POSSIBILITIES THE COURT HAS WHEN SENTENCING OFFENDERS WHO ARE DANGEROUS DUE TO A MENTAL DISORDER

Now I will analyze the security measures which the court may impose when it considers the offender dangerous for society due to a mental disorder. In almost every criminal law system courts have the possibility to send offenders to psychiatric hospitals because they pose a risk of reoffending. In many countries this placement in such a hospital is of limited duration but in some countries like in Germany there is no time limit (Article 63 CC). In this part, I will discuss two security measures, the preventive security measure introduced in France since 2008, and the Dutch entrustment order known in the Dutch Penal Code since 1928.

24 The verdict is published in full text in the *Aftenposten.no* (24 August 2012). See at: www.aftenposten.no/nyheter/iriks/Her-er-hele-dommen-mot-Anders-Behring-Breivik-6973988.html#.UZJCA7WeMnt (last visited 1 June 2013).

4.1. PREVENTIVE SECURITY DETENTION

In France preventive security detention has been introduced by the 2008 Act on post-sentence security detention and the diminished criminal responsibility due to mental disorder.[25] The adoption of that Act was inspired by some very serious crimes committed by offenders during the execution of their sentence. The Act is very controversial[26] because it provides the court with the power to impose a security detention that is implemented after the prison sentence has been served. This type of detention is not considered a penalty but a criminal measure that the court may order after conviction against dangerous offenders who after an examination at the end of their sentence are considered to pose a high risk of reoffending because they suffer from a serious personality disorder. The measure is of an indeterminate length because the measure can be renewed as long as the offender poses a risk of reoffending (Article 706–53–13 Code of Criminal Procedure (CCP)). A very controversial part of the Act was that the measure could be applied retroactively, which means that it could be ordered against persons convicted of offences committed prior to the publication of the Act. That part of the law was decided by the Constitutional Council to be unconstitutional.[27] The 2008 Act was supplemented by the 2010 Act on the reduction of risk of recidivism.[28] That Act ruled *inter alia* that an offender could be sentenced to a post-sentence security detention only after having had a social, medical and/or psychological treatment for his mental disorder during the execution of his sentence.[29]

Three conditions for a security detention order have to be met. The first is that the measure is limited to cases where the offender has been sentenced for designated serious crimes such as murder, rape, kidnapping of a child, crimes committed under aggravating circumstances and recidivism of serious crimes. The second is that the prison sentence is at least fifteen years and the third is that the court (Cour d'Assises) explicitly includes the measure in the sentence.

At least a year before the offender has served his sentence the multidisciplinary committee on security measures has to examine the offender

25 Loi relative à la rétention de sûreté et à la déclaration d'irresponsabilité pénale pour cause de trouble mental de 25 février 2008.

26 See J. Pradel, 'Une double révolution en droit pénal français avec la loi de 25 février 2008 sur les criminels dangereux', *Receuil Dalloz* 15, p. 1000–1012 and A. Wyvekens, 'La rétention de sûreté en France: une défense sociale en trompe-l'œil (ou les habits neufs de l'empereur)', 34 *Déviance et société* 4 (2010), p. 503–525.

27 See the decision of the French Conseil constitutionel of 21 February 2008, *Journal Officielle*, 26 février 2008, p. 3272.

28 Loi du 10 mars 2010 tendant à amoindrir le risque de récidive criminelle et portant diverses dispositions de procédure pénale.

29 See A.G. Robert, 'Loi du 10 mars 2010 tendant à amoindrir le risque de récidive criminelle et portant diverse dispositions de procédure pénale', 4 *Revue de Science Criminelle et de Droit Penal Comparé* (2010), p. 929ff.

and his dangerousness by assessing whether his personality causes a high probability of reoffending and committing a serious offence. The security preventive detention lasts for a year but may be extended. The offender has the right to challenge the measure every three months.

The German Penal Code contains one penal measure that can be seen as a means to manage dangerous offenders and to protect the public. This penal measure is called preventive detention and has been adopted by the 1933 Act against dangerous habitual offenders and on measures of correction and prevention.[30] In cases where the convict is found to pose a clear and present danger to society, the sentence may include a provision for secure preventive detention (Sicherungsverwahrung) to be served consecutive to the actual prison sentence.

Until 1988, the court had to impose preventive detention when the offender was sentenced for an intentional offence to a prison sentence of more than one year when three requirements were met:

1. the offender must have been sentenced previously twice for an intentional offence which carries a statutory prison sentence of one year or more;
2. must have previously served a prison sentence or been detained for at least two years; and
3. a comprehensive assessment of the offender and his acts must have revealed that he presents a danger to society because of his propensity (in German: Hang) to commit serious offences, notably those which seriously harm their victims physically or mentally (Article 66 CC).

The court had also the discretionary power to impose a preventive detention when the offender, due to his propensity, had committed three intentional offenses which each carry a statutory prison sentence of more than one year and the offender is sentenced with a prison sentence of three years or more. Conditional release was possible when this was considered acceptable or the risk that the offender would reoffend was not present any longer.

The regulation of the preventive detention was inspired by the ideas of Franz von Liszt on habitual offenders and the two track sanction system (penalties and measures) is still considered a necessary means to protect society against offenders who reoffend with serious crimes. The preventive detention is not executed automatically because at the end of the serving of the sentence the court responsible for the execution of sentences (Strafvollstreckungsgericht) must consult an expert on the question whether a convicted person is likely to commit serious offences when released. At the session of the Strafvollstreckungsgericht the offender is represented by a defense counsel

30 Gesetz gegen gefährliche Gewohnheitsverbrecher und über Massregeln der Sicherung und Besserung.

appointed by the court. The preventive detention after review may be prolonged every two years until it is found that the convict is unlikely to commit further crimes. Initially the total length of preventive detention was restricted to ten years.

Due to some serious cases of recidivism of violent and sexual offences and the public outcry in 1998 the Combating Sexual and Dangerous Offenders Act[31] has been adopted, which made it possible for security reasons to continue the deprivation of liberty of offenders after they had served their prison sentence. Since that Act preventive detention may be imposed when the offender has had a previous prison sentence of more than three years and is sentenced for a new serious offence (including rape and sexual abuse of children) to a prison sentence of at least two years and presents a danger for society. The maximum term of preventive detention of ten years was abolished and got a retroactive effect. So the preventive detention of all offenders who at that time served their sentence became indefinite instead of ten years maximum. The court responsible for the execution of sentences shall, however, terminate the execution of the preventive detention after ten years when there is not any longer a danger that the offender, due to his propensity, will commit serious offences that may harm the victim physically or mentally (Article 67d(3) CC).

This Act did not solve the problem in case an offender, who at the time he must be released is considered to be dangerous, has not been sentenced to preventive detention. That problem was discussed in German Parliament and Draft Bills were issued but did not get parliamentary consent.[32] In some of the German States legislation was adopted to empower the court to impose preventive detention in a separate court procedure at the end of the sentence. This preventive detention was called the nachträgliche Sicherungsverwahrung, the retrospective preventive detention.[33]

Initially preventive detention could not be imposed in combination with a life sentence but since the 2002 Act on suspended preventive detention,[34] courts may impose a life sentence and additionally a suspended preventive detention. In the meantime, the constitutionality of the retroactivity and the indefinite term of the preventive detention received serious criticisms in two sessions before the Constitutional Court. In early February 2004, the Court ruled that both the

---

31 Gesetz zur Bekämpfung von Sexualdelikten und anderen gefährlichen Straftaten of 26 January 1998.

32 In more detail, see O. Milde, *Die Entwicklung der Normen zur Anordnung der Sicherungsverwahrung in den Jahren von 1998 bis 2004*, Hamburg: Verlag Dr Kovac, 2006.

33 See for the legal scope of preventive detention, A. Boetticher & J. Feest, 'German criminal and prison policy', in: Peter J.P. Tak & Manon Jendly (eds.), *Prison policy and prisoners' rights*, Nijmegen: Wolf Legal Publishers, 2008, p. 361–365; J. Kinzig, *Die Legalbewährung gefährlicher Rückfalltäter. Zugleich ein Beitrag zur Entwicklung des Rechts der Sicherungverwahrung*, Berlin: Duncker & Humblot, 2010.

34 Gesetz zur Einführung der vorbehaltene Sicherungsverwahrung vom 7 Juni 2002.

indefinite term and the retroactivity[35] are not in conflict with any provision of the German Basic Law. One week later, the Court ruled that States do not have the legislative power to adopt legislation in respect to preventive detention and that this belongs to the legislative domain of the Federation.[36] In July 2004, the Federal Parliament adopted the retrospective preventive detention in Article 66b CC.[37] The court may order preventive detention retrospectively if prior to the end of a sentence for crimes that carry a statutory sentence of at least one year against life, limb, personal liberty or sexual self determination or other listed offences, evidence comes to light which indicates that the convicted person presents a danger to the public.

Both the retroactivity and the retrospective preventive detention have been subject to decisions of the European Court on Human Rights.

In *M v. Germany* the Court ruled that the preventive detention initially was justified under Article 5(1)(a) ECHR but after ten years could not be justified by any subsection of Article 5. More in particular not by subsection 1 under e, because the court had not established that the offender was a person of unsound mind nor by subsection 1 under c, because the danger that the offender would commit new serious offences after his release was not made concrete and specific by the Court.

Furthermore, the Court ruled that the retroactivity of the Act which replaced the maximum term of ten year preventive detention in an indefinite term violates Article 7 of the Convention that deals with the prohibition of retrospectively increasing a penalty. Despite the fact that in Germany preventive detention is considered a penal measure and not a penalty the Court comes to the conclusion that the preventive detention in effect is a penalty since it is executed in regular prisons without psychological or psychiatric care and treatment.[38]

In *Haidn v. Germany*[39] the Court ruled that the retrospective preventive detention must be justified by any of the subsections (a to f) of Article 5(1) of the Convention. For a justification by subsection a there must be a causal connection between the criminal conviction and the preventive detention based on the finding of guilt for a new offence. Retrospective detention, however, was not a preventive detention in addition to the sentence and by virtue of that conviction. It is neither justified by subsection c (preventive detention does not equal pretrial detention, the offender is not promptly brought before a judge and tried) nor by subsection e, because a true mental disorder was not established before a competent authority on the basis of objective medical expertise.

35 BVerfG Urteil 2.2.2004, BVerfGE.Bd.109, p. 190 ff.
36 BVerfG Urteil 5.2.2004, BVerfGE.Bd.109, p. 133 ff.
37 Gesetz zur Einführung der nachträgliche Sicherungsverwahrung vom 28 Juli 2004.
38 *M. v. Germany*, ECtHR Judgment of 17 December 2009, Appl. No. 19359/04.
39 *Haidn v. Germany*, ECtHR Judgment of 13 January 2011, Appl. No. 6587/04.

In that case he would have been placed in a psychiatric or mental hospital. The Court therefore came to the conclusion that the preventive detention in this case was not justified by any of the sub sections of Article 5 and therefore violates Article 5 of the Convention.

By judgment of the 4th of May 2011 the Constitutional Court declared all forms of preventive detention for unconstitutional and in conflict with Articles 2 juncto 140 and 2 juncto 20 Basic Law. The Court ordered the Government before May 2013 to reform the law on preventive detention on a concept that should be oriented on freedom and therapy.[40]

In reaction on the judgments of the ECrtHR and the Constitutional court new laws have been adopted. On 1 January 2012 the Therapieunterbringungsgesetz (Therapy Accommodation Act) came into force which justifies a retrospective preventive detention by applying Article 5(1)(1) ECHR (persons of unsound mind). This Act is only applicable to those who had to be released due to the ECrtHR decisions, but who still are considered to pose a high risk.

In June 2013 a new Act will come into force in Germany which gives the suspended preventive detention even more importance. It will become the cornerstone of the future dealing with high risk offenders in Germany. If in doubt, courts will reserve the right to impose security detention to a later point in time. By providing the courts this power, the German legislator hopes to comply with Strasbourg Court's requirement of a causal connection between the criminal conviction and the preventive detention.

4.2. ENTRUSTMENT ORDER

Like in Germany, the Dutch PC distinguishes between penalties and measures. Penalties are aiming at punishment and general prevention; measures aim at the promotion of security and safety of society against offenders. The entrustment order with nursing care[41] is the major and most severe security measure under Dutch penal law. It aims at the protection of society against dangerous offenders who are mentally disordered, by both detaining them and providing them medical, psychological and psychiatric treatment and care in view of their return into society.[42]

---

40 Constitutional Court 2BvR 2365/09.

41 Also the entrustment order without nursing care exists. That order is combined with conditions aiming to protect the safety of others (Sect. 38 PC).

42 For further details on the Dutch entrustment order, see Peter J.P. Tak, *Essays on Dutch Criminal Policy*, Nijmegen: Wolf Legal Publishers, 2002, p. 175–207; Peter J.P. Tak, 'Die "Überlassung mit behördlicher Unterbringung" – Die Niederländische Sicherheitsmassnahme gegen gefährliche Straftäter' (The entrustment order with nursing care – The Dutch security measure against dangerous offenders), 94 *Monatschrift für Kriminologie und Strafrechtsreform* 4 (2011) p. 296–314.

The entrustment order has been adopted in 1928 and is considered to be an effective means to protect society against dangerous offenders. Because of some very serious crimes committed by offenders who previously were sentenced to an entrustment order, the call for more appropriate security measures which can be imposed by a criminal court in order to protect society against dangerous offenders recently became louder. In 2005 the effectiveness of the order and the release rules were therefore discussed by a Parliamentary Inquiry Committee. The results of the inquiry have led to major reforms in the entrustment order system and in the release policy in order to improve the security effects of the order.

A major principle of Dutch criminal law is that there is no criminal liability without blameworthiness. An offender who is held not criminally liable cannot be punished, but the Court may order his committal to a psychiatric hospital in case he poses a danger for society. If the Court considers that a defendant, despite his mental defect or disorder, can be deemed criminally responsible, though diminished, it may, when the safety of other people, the general public or property require so, impose an entrustment order with compulsory nursing care additional to a prison sentence when the offender is sentenced for crimes carrying a statutory prison sentence. This is however only possible of at least four years or when the crime constitutes an offence that is specifically listed as an offence relative to which an entrustment order may be imposed, such as the offence of threatening another person or causing a lethal traffic accident by negligence. The principle that the sentence must be proportionate to the level of blameworthiness is not applied in Dutch criminal law. When sentencing, the Court may take into account the dangerousness of the offender. In cases of diminished criminal responsibility courts therefore may impose long sentences for serious crimes together with an entrustment order. There is, however, one restriction. The Court may not impose a life sentence together with an entrustment order[43] because the entrustment order's aim is to prepare the offender for his return into society which is contrary to the aim of the life sentence.

The order may only be issued after submission of opinions by two behavioral experts who have examined the offender, except when he refuses to cooperate in such an examination. The Court is not bound by the opinion of the behavioral experts and decides on its own discretion.[44] The order is carried out in a special secure private or state forensic psychiatric institution, where the person will receive psychological and psychiatric care (Article 37a CC). The offender has to serve his prison term prior to the start of the execution of the entrustment order. Due to the restricted number of places in the forensic psychiatric institutions offenders as a rule have to wait before their treatment can start. During the treatment they are called patients.

The entrustment order lasts for four years maximum. However, when the order was imposed for sexual and violent offences, the Court, at the request of

43 Dutch Supreme Court 14 March 2006, *NJ* 2007, 345 (Lucia de B).

44 Dutch Supreme Court 20 January 2009, *LJN* BF2089.

the prosecution service, may extend the order by two years at a time as often as the safety of others so requires. The governor of the forensic psychiatric institution where the offender is treated must provide the Court with a reasoned opinion on whether an extension is necessary. Every six years, a full review of the entrustment order has to take place and a recent opinion of behavioral experts has to be available to the Court.

Decisions of the Court to extend the entrustment order, or to refuse to extend, may be appealed by the psychiatric patient or by the public prosecutor to the penitentiary division of the Court of Appeal in Arnhem. The division consists of three professional judges, and two experts in behavioral sciences who are not members of the judiciary.

In recent years, the forensic psychiatric institutions have been under great pressure. The courts have increasingly imposed entrustment orders but the number of detained psychiatric patients being released has decreased. The main reason for this trend is a rise in the number of serious crimes, mainly violent crimes and sexual offences, and the increase in the number of severely mentally disordered offenders due to alcohol and drug addiction. These factors have led to an increasing average length of the term of treatment (eight to nine years). Despite long-term treatment, a number of mentally disordered psychiatric patients continue to pose a high risk to society and therefore cannot be released. For these persistently dangerous psychiatric patients, long-stay wings have been opened. In the long-stay wing, the psychiatric treatment has low priority. For psychiatric patients who are eligible for the long-stay wing, the prognosis is rather bad. Those who have been under an entrustment order for more than twelve years have a tendency to become chronic delinquent psychiatric patients. It is estimated that one third of the total population in the forensic psychiatric institutions are eligible for long-stay wings. With the establishment of long-stay wings, it is accepted by psychiatrists and by courts that the entrustment order in effect means a detention for life.

Patients who, after being treated, are considered no longer to pose a danger gradually receive leave permissions and eventually the nursing care will be conditionally terminated. The conditional termination of nursing care (Article 38g CC) offers the possibility of a smooth transition from the nursing care in the forensic psychiatric institution to complete freedom and a return to society. A gradual transition and an increase in freedom are made possible. The conditional termination runs one year and may be extended twice for one year. During the conditional termination of the nursing care, the entrustment order is still valid and may even be extended by the Court. The conditional termination is combined with behavioral instructions to comply with during the probation period that runs nine years. After the expiry of that period, the possibility no longer exists to assist, supervise or treat the patient for example in order to monitor the use of psycho-pharmacy and to reduce recidivism.

Recent research shows that recidivism of sexual offenders who have been under an entrustment order and are eventually released is substantial after nine years when supervision and control no longer takes place.[45] 30,5% after eighteen years has reoffended with a serious crime, which carries a statutory prison sentence of eight years and more.[46] So it might be a good idea to continue supervision and control even after nine years.

4.3. LIFELONG SUPERVISION

Recently, the Dutch Minister for Security and Justice issued a draft Bill that makes it possible to put offenders who are released from the entrustment order on lifelong supervision. That supervision period is now restricted to nine years. Research on recidivism under former sexual offenders who served an entrustment order showed that more than 30% of them constituted a risk to reoffend, even eighteen years later. A lifelong supervision for offenders with a mental disorder who, after they served their sentence, still are considered to pose a risk to commit new serious offences is already known in England. There exists a large variety of orders which may be imposed and aim at lifelong supervision. In England the restriction order for mental disordered offenders,[47] a life license for released offenders who served a life sentence, or a notification order for dangerous offenders and restricted patients may be of indeterminate length.[48] In the majority of the countries, supervision after release from prison is restricted to a certain period and as a rule with a maximum limit of five years.

4.4. CONCLUSION

The conclusion of the second part of my presentation is that the Strasbourg Court's case law on the German Sicherungsverwahrung may also affect similar instruments applied in Denmark, France, Norway and the Netherlands. An extension of the deprivation of liberty due to a continuous dangerousness of the offender after having served the sentence must be based on one of the grounds of Article 5 ECHR. The ground for the long stay in the Netherlands, the secure preventive detention after 21 years of imprisonment in Norway as well as the security detention in France seems to be rather questionable and might cause a conflict with Article 5 ECHR. A continued dangerousness is not such a ground.

45 H.J.M. Schönberger & C.H. de Kogel, *Kenmerken en recidivecijfers van ex-terbeschikkinggestelden met een zedendelict* (Characteristics and figures on reconviction for sexual offences by former entrustment order patients), Den Haag: WODC, 2012.

46 Idem, p. 36.

47 See Reference Guide to the Mental Health Act 1983, Dept. of Health, TSO London, 2008, p. 53 ff.

48 D. Middleton, *The requirements for notification by sexual offenders in England and Wales*, UNAFEI Resource Materials Series 72, Tokyo, 2006, p. 60–70.

5. PART III. SOME MAJOR QUESTIONS ON DANGEROUS OFFENDERS

After the presentation of a number of possibilities the courts in various countries have in order to take into account the future risk of reoffending when sentencing and delaying the release of the offender after serving his sentence because he poses a risk to reoffend, some questions immediately arise. I will now deal with three of these questions.

5.1. IS THERE ANY RESEARCH AVAILABLE ON WHETHER THE USE OF THESE POSSIBILITIES REALLY HAS LED TO A DECLINE IN (THE RECIDIVISM OF) SERIOUS CRIME?

In a previous comparative law report on mandatory sentences in Europe I have looked for research on the effects of mandatory sentences on recidivism and serious criminality. In none of the countries which recently have adopted mandatory sentences in the fight against recidivism research is available on the effects of mandatory sentences on recidivism. Criminological literature merely deals with the effect of that legislation on the significant rise in prison population, the enormous rise in costs for the implementation of prison sentences[49] and on the resistance within the judiciary against compulsory strict application of the mandatory sentence.[50]

New laws on mandatory sentences, compulsory life sentences for a second serious crime and secure preventive detention give the public at large the impression that the reduction of serious crime is manageable and that harsh laws and measures are effective to reduce criminality. That impression is not reliable and not based on proper criminological research. A public that is misled by this impression will ask for even more and harsher laws when serious criminality has been committed again. The public has to be informed that the society they live in is full of danger but that danger is much more likely to come from traffic, pollution, food and illness than from serious criminality.

49 See 'Story of the prison population 1995–2009 England and Wales', *Ministry of Justice Statistic Bulletin*, July 2009; P.V. Tournier, *L'impact de la loi 'Dati' renforçant la lutte contre la récidive des majeurs et des mineurs*, Centre d'histoire sociale du XXe siècle, UMR CNRS 8058 juillet 2007, p. 40.

50 Peter J.P. Tak, *De minimumstraf opnieuw bezien. Een geactualiseerde beknopte rechtsvergelijking* (*The mandatory minimum sentence revisited. An updated concise comparative law report for the Dutch Council for the Judiciary*), Den Haag: Raad voor de rechtspraak/SDU, 2010, p. 36–38.

5.2. DO RELIABLE METHODS EXIST TO ASSESS THE RISK THAT THE OFFENDER, AFTER HIS SENTENCE WILL REOFFEND?

There are two major ways to assess the risk of continued dangerousness. The first is the unstructured clinical judgment approach (UCJ). Psychiatrists, psychologists and other behavioral experts observe the offender prior to or during his stay in a mental hospital. Mainly based on this observation, the Court is advised on what order to impose or on release and parole decisions. This way of assessing the risk, which is widely used in Europe[51], is considered to be less reliable when compared with the structured professional judgment approach (SPJ). This risk assessment is performed by forensic experts by means of standardized checklists containing empirically derived risk factors, historical as well as dynamic, the so-called actuarial risk assessment instruments. There are various standardized checklists such as HCR-20 (The Historical Clinical Risk Management Scheme),[52] PCL-R (Psychopathy Checklist-Revised)[53] and the Violent Risk Appraisal Guide (VRAG[54]). These instruments are developed on the basis of risk factors that are empirically related to (sexual) violent behavior. Some actuarial risk assessment instruments are very specific for particular groups of offenders, such as the sexual offenders. At present, there exist more than 25 risk assessment instruments for sexual offenders. Five risk assessment instruments for sexual violence offenders are widely applied to assess the risk of reoffending such as Sexual Violence Risk 20 (SVR 20), the Sex Offender Risk Appraisal Guide (SORAG) or the Sex Offender Need Assessment Rating (SONAR).[55]

The reliability and validity of a number of assessment methods are sometimes weak and need serious improvement. The use of risk assessment instruments in predicting the risk of recidivism, however, is more preferable than the pure clinical assessment that contains many subjective elements.[56]

---

51 See the comparative research by D. Giovannangeli, J-P. Cornet & C. Mormont, *Etude comparative dans les 15 pays de l'Union Européenne: Les méthodes et les techniques d'évaluation de la dangerosité et du risque de récidive des personnes présumées ou avérées délinquants sexuels (Résumé)*, Université de Liège, 2000.

52 R.D. Hare, *The Psychopathy Checklist Revised*, Toronto: Multi Health Systems, 2003.

53 C.D. Webster *et al.*, *HCR-20, Assessing Risk for Violence* (Version 2), Vancouver: Mental Health, Law and Policy Institute, Simon Fraser University, 1997.

54 V.L. Quinsey *et al.*, *Violent Offenders: Appraising and Managing Risks*, Washington DC: American Psychological Association, 2005.

55 R.K. Hanson & A. Harris, *The Sex Offender Need Assessment Rating (SONAR): A Method for Measuring change in risk levels*, Ottawa: Dept of the Sollicitor General of Canada, 2000.

56 See *e.g.* M. Rettenberger & R. Eher, 'Predicting Reoffence in Sexual Offender Subtypes: A Prospective Validation Study of the German Version of the Sexual Offender Risk Appraisal Guide (SORAG)', 2 *Sexual Offender Treatment* 2 (2007); M. Rettenberger, S.J. Hucker, D.P. Boer & R. Eher, 'The Reliability of the Sexual Violence Risk-20(SVR-20): An International Review', 4 *Sexual Offender Treatment* 2 (2009).

5.3. WILL IT EVER BE POSSIBLE TO AVOID THAT SERIOUS CRIME WILL BE COMMITTED AND HOW CAN ONE AVOID THAT THE SECURITY MEASURES ARE NOT ONLY ADOPTED TO APPEASE THE PUBLIC OPINION?

There are many reasons to ask this question. One important reason to do so is that a number of legislative actions aiming to reduce criminality and in particular recidivism, neglect the outcome of major researches on the effects of harsher sentencing on the reduction of criminality and recidivism. Two major research reviews which summarize the results of numerous empirical researches in this field come to the conclusion that lengthier prison sentences and more punitive alternatives to imprisonment do not lead to a reduction of recidivism. Cognitive behavioral programs, however, are successful in the reduction of criminality and recidivism.[57]

Another important reason to ask this question is that it is impossible to predict with accuracy who will commit future dangerous acts. Poor predictions not only mean that many people may be detained unnecessarily but also fail to protect the public and may lead to greater anxiety.

6. CONCLUSIONS

The general conclusion is that it is possible to reduce the risk of reoffending by dangerous people but from literature and research it is made clear that new and harsh laws hardly contribute to the reduction of that risk. That conclusion does not mean that policymakers should not do their utmost to keep criminality within acceptable limits by providing dangerous offenders during the service of their sentence with education, social and psychological care as well as medical and psychiatric care aiming to improve their social reintegration. For those who pose a risk for society due to mental disorders, punishment should not be the last resort but treatment. In the exceptional cases that despite treatment proper psychological and psychiatric examinations give rise to serious indications that there is a clear and present danger that the offender will reoffend a continuation of the deprivation of liberty is only possible by taking into account the

57 D.L. MacKenzie, *What Works in Corrections-Reducing the Criminal Activities of Offenders and Delinquents*, Cambridge: Cambridge University Press, 2006, p. 331–346; and J. McGuire, 'Integrating Findings from Research Reviews', in: McGuire (ed.), *Offender Rehabilitation and Treatment-Effective Programmes*, Chichester: Wiley series in forensic clinical psychology, 2003, p. 3–38. See also H. Kury, M. Brandenstein & T. Yoshida, 'Kriminalpräventive Wirksamkeit härterer Sanktionen-Zur neuen Punitivität im Ausland (USA, Finnland und Japan)', 121 *Zeitschrift für die gesamte Strafrechtswissenschaft*, 1 (2009), p. 190–238.

requirements of the European Convention of Human Rights for such a continuation.

I have dealt with the Human Rights court decisions more extensively because the Strasbourg case law seems to be very important for security measures to be applied against dangerous offenders. From the ECrtHR decisions against Germany concerning secure preventive detention one can draw some conclusions:

- Secure preventive detention imposed by the Court in addition to or instead of a prison sentence is considered to constitute a 'detention after conviction by a competent court' (Art. 5 (1) (a) ECHR).
- Secure preventive detention imposed by a court not being the sentencing court is not in compliance with the requirement of conviction for the purpose of Article 5(1)(a) ECHR.
- At a certain moment the causal link between the initial conviction and the further deprivation of liberty due to a continuation of the secure preventive detention may become weak and may become inconsistent with the objectives of the initial detention. In such a situation the continuation of the deprivation of liberty may become arbitrary.
- Secure preventive detention that consists of deprivation of liberty without any substantive difference in treatment as compared to regular prisoners is of punitive nature and is not to be considered as a penal measure. The prohibition of retroactivity (Art. 7 ECHR) applies.

THE "OTHER" DEATH PENALTY: LIFE IN PRISON IN THE UNITED STATES

Emilio C. VIANO*

ABSTRACT

The sentence of life in prison, with or without possibility of parole, is imposed quite frequently in the United States, differently than in most developed countries. This chapter examines the historical and cultural reasons behind such practice. Then it critically examines why the reasons used to justify such penalty do not work and why this penalty is actually counterproductive and deeply damaging to society. The chapter also examines recent correctional trends in the United States, pointing out powerful forces and interests that support the harsh and punitive correctional system generally operating in the country.

1. INTRODUCTION

Recently, a woman in California, Catherine Kieu, was sentenced to life in prison for cutting off the penis of her ex-husband and destroying it by throwing it into the garbage disposer in the kitchen. This is one of the latest examples of the obsession of the United States criminal justice system with tough, "life in prison" sentences.

Outside of the United States, life sentences actually lasting a lifetime in prison are rare, especially in European countries, but in the United States they are fairly common. While the California court was sentencing Catherine Kieu to life in prison, a British court also sentenced Dale Cregan to the same penalty for murdering four people, including two policewomen. Thus he will never be eligible for release. This makes him one of 50 persons serving a similar sentence in the United Kingdom. If he had been sentenced in the U.S., it would have been quite routine and actually expected.

In the United States, at least 40,000 people are confined for life without hope of parole, including 2,589 minors under 18 years of age that Human Rights Watch

* Dr. E.C. Viano is a Professor of Law at the American University and at Washington College of Law in Washington DC, USA.

found serving life sentences in 2009.[1] In 2010, the United States Supreme Court, in the case of *Graham v. Florida*, ruled that sentencing minors to automatic sentences of life without parole for crimes other than homicide (generally, first-degree murder, and usually with aggravating factors and/or accompanying felonies) violates the Eighth Amendment's prohibition on "cruel and unusual" punishment. In finding that the United States Constitution prohibits as cruel and unusual punishment a sentence of life without parole for a juvenile in a non-homicide case, the American Supreme Court stated that "the overwhelming weight of international opinion against" juvenile life without parole "provide[s] respected and significant confirmation for our own conclusions".[2]

The numbers cited above are just a fraction of those who are sentenced to life imprisonment but with a difference: they may be paroled, that is go free, one day. The Sentencing Project, a nonprofit organization that studies sentencing in the U.S., estimated that in 2009 at least 140,000 prisoners in the country were serving life sentences.[3]

The figure does not include offenders with extremely long sentences for a fixed period or with consecutive sentences, such as an Alabama man sentenced to 200 years for kidnapping and armed robbery. The majority of those sentenced to life in prison have a chance of parole, although in reality only a few will actually receive it. For example, in California, where the lifer population has increased, as a percentage of the overall prison population, from 8% in 1990 to 20% in 2010, a lifer has only an 18% chance of being granted parole by the Board of Parole Hearings. This rate has fluctuated widely over the last 30 years, at times approaching zero percent and never going over 20% of those petitioning for release. At the same time the length of time a petitioner must wait before being heard again has also increased. The likelihood of a prisoner sentenced to life in prison to receive parole from the Board of Parole Hearings and not have that decision reversed by the Governor of California is quite slim. In 2010 it was only 6%.[4]

2. HISTORICAL AND CULTURAL FOUNDATIONS FOR HARSH SENTENCES

There are several factors that explain the high number of Americans receiving life sentences. In great part, these punishments reflect the overly punitive nature of the criminal justice system in the United States. Some analysts trace this

---

1 Human Rights Watch, State Distribution of Youth Offenders Serving Juvenile Life Without Parole (JLWOP), 2009.

2 *Graham v. Florida*, 130 S. Ct. 2011 (2010) at 2034.

3 Sentencing Project, *The State of Sentencing 2009*, Washington, DC, 2009 (at: www.sentencingproject.org/doc/publications/s_ssr2009Update.pdf; accessed on June 29, 2013).

4 Robert Weisberg, Debbie A. Mukamal & Jordan D. Segall, *Life in Limbo: An Examination of Parole Release for Prisoners Serving Life Sentences with the Possibility of Parole in California*, Stanford: Stanford Law School, 2011.

general attitude to the Puritan origins of the first English colonies on the northeastern coast of today's United States, notorious for their stern religious upbringing; unforgiving religious intolerance; tight control of people's lifestyle; the Salem, Massachusetts witch hunts and numerous executions; and harsh punishment for a large variety of behaviors. The westward expansion of the United States, where for decades the law of the strongmen and the survival of the fittest ruled, the so-called "Wild West", also influenced the perception and understanding of crime and punishment in the country. Rough, quick, violent retribution was the norm of the day, given the circumstances. Slavery and the need to control the slaves, and harshly punish any attempt at insurrection or escaping and the subsequent deeply rooted racism in the country, also contributed to a tradition of severe penalties as the rule.

It is not only that life sentences, with or without possibility of parole, are applied more extensively in the United States than in other developed nations. Even when the criminal event is less dangerous or severe, like, for example, a theft or a car theft, the convict will be imprisoned for a longer time than in other industrialized countries, especially Canada and Europe.

The overly punitive criminal justice system of the United States was also justified in the last decades of the twentieth century by a major and at times violent social change; rapid urbanization; political upheaval, especially in relation to the Vietnam war; the civil rights and the women's liberation movements; the so-called "sexual revolution" marching on at the sound of the Beatles and hard rock music, laced with the aroma of marijuana and other drugs; and the fragmentation of social and cultural understandings due to the massive increase of non-European immigration into the country.

All of these factors and American society's conflictual reaction to them led to the "inflation in sentences" that began in the 1980s, when crime rates in the United States were high and being tough on crime became a major prerequisite for political office, including the presidency. For decades, there was definitely a competition between Republicans and Democrats about which party was best suited to combat crime and was going to be tougher on crime and better able to convince the voters accordingly.

Significantly, for example, in 1988 the candidacy of the Democratic Party nominee for the Presidency of the United States, Michael Dukakis, was not successful in part because of his more liberal correctional policies, especially his support for a prison furlough program, and because of his opposition to the death penalty. This was highlighted in the debate of October 18, 1988 with George H.W. Bush when Dukakis was asked if he would support an irrevocable death penalty for someone who had, hypothetically, raped and killed his wife. His negative response was a significant factor, among others, in sinking his chances to win election.

3. BEING SOFT ON CRIME: POLITICAL SUICIDE

Moreover, many believe that a severe sentence sends a powerful message about the moral stance against and the reprobation of the criminal behavior on the part of society. Especially in jurisdictions that have abolished the death penalty, harsh sentences are its moral equivalent. Politicians and state officials dislike being seen as soft against crime, and worry the most about the risk of granting parole to an offender, only to have him or her promptly commit another crime upon release. The loss by Michael Dukakis of his presidential bid as the nominee of the Democratic Party in 1988 was due in part to his veto of a Massachusetts law prohibiting furloughs for people convicted of first-degree murder. This allowed the release of convicted murderer William "Willie" Horton, who committed a rape and assault in Maryland shortly after being furloughed, causing a torrent of criticism against Dukakis. This sent a clear and unequivocal message to politicians nationwide not to be or appear to be "soft on crime" if they wanted a chance at a successful political career. For years politicians in the United States, especially at the presidential and state governorship levels, keenly competed in attempting to show the voters who would be harshest and unforgiving on criminals and miscreants.

4. 'THREE STRIKES AND YOU ARE OUT' LAWS

The 1993 kidnapping, sexual assault and murder of twelve-year-old Polly Klaas by a young man with a long criminal record who had recently been paroled, caused California to adopt the "three strikes" rule, requiring a sentence of 25 years to life for anyone guilty of three felonies. Eventually, twenty-five other States also adopted different versions of this law. The stated objectives for the different States to implement three strike laws is to ensure that repeat offenders are constantly imprisoned to guarantee the safety of the public. The simple and seemingly convincing logic is that while a criminal is in prison, he or she cannot be on the streets, hurting anyone. Since three strike laws apply to defendants who commit multiple crimes in succession, it is maintained that these laws ensure that the criminals most likely to repeat their offenses will remain in prison.

This rule has been amply criticized in the media and public arena and challenged in the courts for many reasons. The most serious criticism of the three strikes laws is that the punishment is often very disproportional to the crime that led to the arrest and can be arbitrarily applied. For example, in *Lockyear v. Andrade*, the U.S. Supreme Court considered the case of Leandro Andrade, who in late 1995 was a repeat offender who committed thefts of trifling value, some $150, and some residential burglaries, but no violent crimes or crimes against the person.[5] Under

---

[5] *Lockyear v. Andrade*, 536 US 63 (2003).

California law, the thefts could be classified as felonies or misdemeanors. In his case the prosecutor charged Andrade with felonies and Andrade received two consecutive 25-year in prison sentences. Since Andrade was 37 at the time of the offences, the 50-years-to-life sentence was in reality a penalty of life without parole. Thus he was effectively condemned to die in prison for petty crimes that, differently categorized, might have earned him a brief stay in prison, especially if the three strikes law was not in place (The U.S. Supreme Court by a 5–4 vote decided that Andrade's punishment was not excessive or grossly disproportionate and therefore did not violate the Eighth Amendment of the Constitution).

The difference between the punishments is based on the different way in which the punishment is determined. The novel and important factor is that the three strikes law permits the courts to take into account the convict's previous record and then impose a more serious sentence for those previous crimes, even if the convict has already paid his price to society. Thus, under the three strikes system, a person's criminal past can be brought back to haunt the person over and over again, each and every time the person is convicted of a felony.

Another major criticism of three strikes laws is that judges often apply the laws unequally. Racial differences and injustices in prison sentences, already a problem before the introduction of three strikes laws, have been exacerbated under the three strikes system. An additional reason to question the three strikes laws is that the definition of a felony does not always and necessarily include violent or serious crimes. For many convicts the third strike was actually a non-violent and relatively minor crime, like shoplifting or drug possession. It has been estimated that about one-third of the 3,000 "third strikers" held in California prisons had committed a relatively minor crime as their third strike. This aspect of the law, perceived to be unfair and misguided, led to a softening of the "three strikes and you are out" law in 2000, when 69% of California voters approved Proposition 36, six years after the enactment of the law. Beside the symbolic impact and interpretation of the three strikes law, it has also had important substantive impacts. Since three strikes laws have been adopted in California and in 25 other states, sentences have become harsher, particularly in politically conservative jurisdictions, and black or other minority felons receive longer prison sentences.[6]

5. ABOLITION OF THE DEATH PENALTY AND LIFE SENTENCES

Ironically, the movement for the abolition of the death penalty has unwittingly given support and justification to the imposition of life sentences, especially without possibility of parole. It is an option offered as a stern alternative to

6 John R. Sutton, 'Symbol and Substance: The Effects of California Three Strikes Law on Felony Sentencing', 47 *Law and Society Review* 1 (2013), p. 37–72.

execution, ensuring that the convict will not return to society and have a chance to repeat his or her crimes. This argument is also further supported by calculating the cost of an execution versus that of life in prison. One of the main arguments against the death penalty is that an execution costs considerably more than confining someone to prison for the rest of his life because of the extensive appeals, mandated or discretionary; security requirements in death row; the maintenance and use of the death chamber; and the execution itself.

6. THE VICTIM-WITNESS MOVEMENT

Another movement that has provided support for increased penalties, lengthy stays in prison and increased difficulties in obtaining parole is the victim-witness movement. Victim advocates have correctly pointed out how at times sentences for heinous crimes were relatively light and most of all, that a "life sentence" in the United States might mean at most twelve years or so in prison, assuming "good behavior." The "truth in sentencing" demands by victim advocates created pressure for a tightening up of the actual serving out of life and other sentences, for granting fewer petitions for probation and parole, and in the end, for longer periods of incarceration, including life without possibility of parole. But now, both the U.S. as in the UK, the sentence of life imprisonment without parole is being questioned.

7. QUESTIONING THE RATIONALE FOR LIFE IN PRISON: SAFER STREETS?

One of the main rationales for a life sentence, especially without possibility of parole, is that imprisoning criminals for life makes society safer for others. Supporters of tougher sentences like to equate "life in prison" to "safer streets". There is some truth to this, of course. If we can eliminate the risk of a convict re-offending in the larger society, then we have eliminated a risk of more crime occurring. This approach is being questioned from different angles.

In England, for example, three convicts sentenced to a life sentence, meaning they cannot be released other than at the discretion of the Secretary of State on compassionate grounds (for example, if they are terminally ill or seriously incapacitated), have been fighting it in the courts all the way to the European Court of Human Rights.[7] They are a double murderer, Douglas Vinter, who killed his wife shortly after being released on parole for a previous murder; Jeremy Banter, who killed his adoptive parents, his sister and her two children to

7 ECtHR, 9 July 2013, *Vinter and others v. the United Kingdom*, Appl. 66069/09, 130/10 & 3896/10.

become the sole inheritor of the family's assets; and Peter Moore, a serial murderer, who killed and dismembered four gay men.

These individuals argued first in front of the U.K. courts and then of the European Court of Human Rights that sentencing them to die in prison is cruel and inhumane punishment and that the refusal to give them the parole option does not allow them to prove that they have changed. They also asserted that meting out these sentences is arbitrary: they are imposed on some but not other convicted murderers. After examining the three cases and how they were sentenced, in January 2012, the European Court of Human Rights ruled that there had been no violation of Article 3 (prohibition of inhuman or degrading treatment) of the European Convention on Human Rights in the case of any of the applicants by giving them a life sentence. According to the Court, the whole life orders were justified. The case is now on appeal before the Grand Chamber of the European Court of Human Rights.

In the United States too, a life sentence without possibility of parole has been called "The Other Death Penalty". Even worse, it is seen by some as a long, slow, destructive death sentence lacking the legal or administrative protection correctly provided to those sentenced to the traditional forms of execution. It reveals society's hidden belief that redemption and personal transformation are not possible for every human being, and that it is fair and just to forever define an individual by his worst act. From this point of view, life without the possibility of parole is wrong and should be eliminated. Their ultimate objective is the permanent abolition of this type of state-sanctioned execution (along with all other forms), with all life term prisoners having, at least, possible access to parole.

8. LIFE SENTENCES AND THE DECLINE OF CRIME RATES

In the United States sentences of life in prison, especially without possibility of parole, and the general toughness in sentencing have been hailed by some as one of the major reasons for the steady overall decline in crime rates in the country in the last 20 years or so. The same is true in Canada where crime rates have reached the lowest point since the 1970s. Ironically, lower crime rates seem to make politicians ever more determined to be tough on crime, to avoid being accused of weakening a system that works in preventing crime. Clearly, in many politicians' mind there is a strong connection, even causation, between high rates of imprisonment and lower rates of crime, a link that many scholars and policy analysts question. The Sentencing Project study on the issue states that "Increasing incarceration while ignoring more effective approaches will impose a heavy burden upon courts, corrections and communities, while providing a marginal impact on crime. The common sensical notion that, if we imprison more people, they cannot commit more crimes" is too simplistic. The connection of crime and imprisonment is more complex than that.[8]

9. DIMINISHING RETURNS OF INCARCERATION

Diminishing returns is one of the first and major reasons for the limited impact of incarceration on crime. Frequent and violent offenders will normally be incarcerated, even if the rate of incarceration in a country is relatively limited. As the rate of incarceration increases, more and more people convicted of lesser crimes will be sent to prison. This means that the return on incarceration, relative to reducing crime rates, is not diminishing. The tenet, "Fewer criminals on the street, fewer crimes" continues to hold true, at least in the mind of politicians and many citizens. However, in reality, the cost-to-benefit ratio changes as the same amount of resources is invested in imprisoning offenders whose potential to commit serious crime may be considerably different. In the case of low-level offenders, the state is getting a lower return on its investment. As a way to illustrate this, it is like a group of people renting an expensive boat with a crew to go fishing for a week. Initially they catch all the big fish in the lake; thus, their investment is producing a high return. However, once all the big fish are caught, they now have only small fish to catch while the expensive boat, crew, hotel, food and other expenses remain the same. Thus, their return on investment is now much smaller. For them catching a small fish is just as costly as catching a big one, but the return on their investment is obviously quite different. There are analysts who use the same reasoning evaluating the effectiveness of growing imprisonment numbers that inevitably must include increasing numbers of "smaller fish." This is especially true with the dramatic increase of people incarcerated in the United States for drug offenses.

10. WAR ON CRIME/WAR ON DRUGS

The war on crime has produced a large number of low-level offenders arrested, tried and imprisoned. It has been one of the main criticisms especially of the war on drugs that kingpins and major dealers are rarely arrested and prosecuted while it is the foot soldiers, the drug peddlers on the street corner that are most frequently arrested, tried and incarcerated.

Of the 1.6 million prisoners in the United States at the end of 2011, some 330,000 were doing time for drug offenses, including nearly 95,000 doing federal

8 Sentencing Project, *Incarceration and Crime: A Complex Relationship*, Washington, DC, 2005 (at: www.sentencingproject.org/doc/publications/inc_iandc_complex.pdf; accessed on July 3, 2013).

time. In 1980 there were 40,000 incarcerated drug offenders. "Drug war" prisoners have largely driven the growth in the federal prison population. As of May 25, 2013, drug offenders constituted almost 48% of all federal inmates, or some 94,600 inmates.[9] By contrast, only 7.6% of federal inmates are doing time for violent crimes.

Among state prisoners, drug offenders at the end of 2011 accounted for 17%, or slightly fewer than one out of five. But this adds up to some 235,000 doing state prison time on drug charges, bringing the combined state and federal total to 330,000. Of the 3,971,319 adults on probation in the US at the end of 2011, 25% (approximately 992,830 people) were drug offenders; of the 853,852 people on parole at the end of 2011, 33% (approximately 281,771 people) were drug offenders.[10]

11. THE REPLACEMENT EFFECT

The main drawback to connecting these growing rates of incarceration to less drug activity in the country is the so-called "replacement effect," Removing a murderer or an armed robber from the community may somewhat impact the crime rate. However, drug markets are demand driven. Thus, arresting one drug seller simply means that another will promptly take his or her place. For as long as there is demand, there will be a supply network in operation. Thus, the effort of society should not be so much on arresting and incarcerating the supplier, promptly replaced at the street level, but on dampening the demand. The almost tenfold increase of drug offenders in prison has seemingly had no impact on the continuing trafficking, sale and use of drugs in the country.[11] Among the key findings of a study by John Schmitt, Kris Warner, and Sarika Gupta were that, in 2008, one of every 48 working-age men was in prison or jail.[12] Non-violent offenders made up over 60 percent of the prison and jail population while non-violent drug offenders were 25 percent of all incarcerated offenders. Importantly, the total number of violent crimes in the United States was only about three percent higher in 2008 than it was in 1980. During the same time span, the U.S. population increased by 33 percent while the prison and jail population

9 Federal Bureau of Prisons, Quick Facts About the Bureau of Prisons, Washington, DC, 2013 (at: www.bop.gov/news/quick.jsp; accessed on July 2, 2013).

10 Laura M. Maruschak & Erika Parks, Bureau of Justice Statistics, *Probation and Parole in the United States, 2011,* Washington, DC: US Department of Justice, November 2012, NCJ 239686, Appendix Table 2, p. 26, and Appendix Table 3, p. 17 (at: www.bjs.gov/content/pub/pdf/ppus11.pdf).

11 Justice Policy Institute, *Substance Abuse Treatment and Public Safety,* Washington, DC, January 2008, p. 1 (at: www.justicepolicy.org/images/upload/08_01_REP_DrugTx_AC-PS.pdf).

12 John Schmitt, Kris Warner & Sarika Gupta, *The High Budgetary Cost of Incarceration,* Washington, DC: Center for Economic Policy Research, 2010 (at: www.cepr.net/documents/publications/incarceration-2010–06.pdf; accessed on July 8, 2013).

mushroomed by more than 350 percent. At the same time, police continued to arrest and courts to convict with no visible effect on criminal activity leading to arrest and conviction, the "replacement" effect working at its best.

12. NEGATIVE IMPACT ON THE COMMUNITY

Another major shortcoming of the increasing imprisonment rate on the fight against crime is the negative impact that it has on the community with the consequence of continuing to breed crime. For example, the United States has five percent of the world population but 25 percent of its prisoners. In another example, with the fourth highest prison population in the world, Brazil's incarceration rate is alarming with as many as 3,000 new prisoners each month. Even more serious is that almost 50 percent of those sitting in Brazilian prisons have never been tried and some will wait for years to see a judge. Sadly, this situation is very common in Central and South America and other parts of the world. Many arrestees spend years in pre-trial detention or remain in prison after the expiry of their sentence, due to bureaucratic incompetence or systemic failings. Severe overcrowding, poor sanitary conditions, gang violence and torture are commonplace.

13. NEGATIVE IMPACT ON THE ECONOMY

The historic, sustained rise in incarceration in many countries has broad implications, not just for the criminal justice system, but also for the larger economy. Record incarceration rates can have long term negative economic impacts by contributing to increased income inequality, more concentrated poverty, and arrested development. The employment prospects of people released from jail or prison are quite poor, adding to the financial strain on their families, communities and public assistance systems. Research indicates that individuals who serve prison terms have lower lifetime earnings and that they and their families are far less likely to move out of poverty than their peers who never went to prison.

Western and Pettit analyze in detail the financial damage incarceration does to prisoners and the broader economic potential trapped in America's prisons.[13] The United States currently jails a little more than one in every 100 adults – the highest rate in the world. To start with, that costs one of every 15 state general fund dollars, more than $50 billion a year. But incarceration is not only costly for

13 Bruce Western & Becky Pettit, *Collateral Costs: Incarceration's Effect on Economic Mobility*, Washington DC: Pew Charitable Trusts' Economic Mobility Project and its Public Safety Performance Project (PSPP), September 2010 (at: www.pewstates.org/research/reports/collateral-costs- -85899373309; accessed on July 8, 2013).

the taxpayer. It also represents a major cost for the inmate. Time spent in confinement diminishes the earnings of a prisoner by an average of 40 percent. It also greatly reduces their future economic mobility. And it greatly damages the financial standing of many children given that 1 in every 28 has a parent behind bars (for Afro-Americans this becomes one in nine children).

On average, imprisonment eliminates more than half the earnings a white man would otherwise have made through age 48, and 41 and 44 percent of the amount Hispanic and Afro-American men would have earned. It must be noted that these losses are not limited to the time when they were in prison. They represent instead a major earning gap for a lifetime between former prisoners and those never so confined. Western and Pettit also point out that the United States incarcerates so many working-age people – over 2.300.000 of them – that it causes a distortion in the employment and unemployment data.[14] The traditional ways of measuring employment do not include men and women behind bars, thus generating a partial picture. The most obvious and largest impact is on the employment-to-population ratio (EPOP), a way of measuring how economically productive the workforce is. When prisoners are included in the standard calculation, the EPOP changes significantly. According to Western and Pettit, it falls from 67 to 61 percent in the case of working-age African-American men.[15] When this is controlled for age, for 20 to 34-year-old Afro-American men, it falls from 66 to 58 percent. Jail has become so common for black men, in fact, that they are more likely to be in jail than at work, if they are young and don't have a high-school diploma.

14. DESTRUCTIVE EMOTIONAL IMPACT ON THE FAMILY

Another impact of imprisonment is clear: prisons separate people from their families and communities. Almost every individual sent to jail or prison leaves behind a network of family and community relationships. In the United States a record 1.7 million children younger than 18 years of age have an imprisoned parent.[16] Possibly millions of additional children have a parent incarcerated in jail. Many affected children experience increased risk for developing behavior problems, academic failure, and substance abuse.[17]

14 *Idem.*

15 *Idem.*

16 Emily Sanders & Rachel Dunifon, *Children of Incarcerated Parents*, Ithaca NY: Cornell University, 2011.

17 J. Poehlmann, D. Dallaire, A.B. Loper, & L.D. Shear, 'Children's Contact with Their Incarcerated Parents: Research Findings and Recommendations', 65 *The American Psychologist* 6 (2010), p. 575–98.

Parent-child contact during the imprisonment period is a key issue. Imprisonment places a severe burden on the relationship between these parents or caretakers and their children with many negative consequences. Incarceration of parents and pregnant women, which is quite common in the United States, creates major problems for the incarcerated individuals' children. Research on human attachment shows the negative effects on children of having their parents incarcerated and the probability of future crime and incarceration for both the adults and their children. Among various consequences are the intergenerational transmission of attachment insecurity, the need for having the parent of an incarcerated adult take custody of the children, and the many problems associated with the attachment insecurity of incarcerated adults (including perpetrated and received abuse, drug and alcohol problems, a history of educational and employment difficulties, and inadequate models of parenting). Parental incarceration is a strong risk factor for long-lasting psychopathology, including antisocial and internalizing outcomes.[18] It destabilizes children's attachment security because of parent-child separation, confusing explanations about parental absence, limited contact with imprisoned parents, and unreliable caregiving provisions.

Parental incarceration also brings about economic difficulties, less supervision, stigma, home and school moves, and other negative and destabilizing life events for children. Thus, there are many ways in which parental incarceration can increase the risk for child psychopathology. Generally, the incarceration of the mother causes more disruption for children than that of the father and a greater possibility of insecure attachment and psychopathology.[19]

15. PRISONS AWAY FROM POPULATED CENTERS AND BREAK-UP OF THE FAMILY

Sadly, these impacts are worsened by the increasing practice of imprisoning convicts far away from populated centers or the cities of their normal residence. Distances even within the same state or province can be considerable, in the hundreds of miles or kilometers, especially in large countries like the United States, Canada, Brazil, Australia and others. Federal prisoners may be confined very far from their families or loved ones, at times more than 500 miles (800 km.) away and even in a different region of the country, requiring costly and time-consuming long distance travel, even by air, to visit them. The lack of public

18 L. Aaron & D.H. Dallaire, 'Parental Incarceration and Multiple Risk Experiences: Effects on Family Dynamics and Children's Delinquency', 39 *Journal of Youth & Adolescence* 12 (2010), p. 1471–84.

19 J. Murray & L. Murray, 'Parental Incarceration, Attachment and Child Psychopathology', 12 *Attachment & Human Development* 4 (2010), p. 289–309.

transportation in rural areas exacerbates the problem. The National Council on Crime and Delinquency found that 60% of mothers in the United States are incarcerated 60 miles (100 km.) or more away from their children, making even occasional visitation difficult to organize and financially onerous or impossible.[20] It has been found that inmates serving their sentence more than 50 miles (80 km.) away from their place of residence are much less likely to receive phone calls or visits from children, family and friends.[21] An added obstacle are the administrative rules and days/hours of visitation that are at times unreliable, frustrating, unpredictable and arbitrarily applied. This can result in not being successful in visiting an inmate, after the time and expense of traveling there, and/or in additional hotel and other costs for people often of limited means. The distance, the difficulty and cost of "getting there", and the administrative obstacles that may deny or shorten the visit or make it a stressful experience, result in diminished or no visitation. Differently from the outside world, the cell phone and electronic revolution have not reached prisons yet. Communications with family, friends, lawyers and other in the United States is still generally by phone. Phone calls from prison are limited to local, collect calls or calls charged to the inmate's account and they are monitored. Such phone calls are quite costly to start with and often more so because the rates are inflated by the private contractor handling phone communications by the inmates. It also presupposes that family or friends regularly deposit funds for the inmate to have credit in order to use the phone. Economic, cultural, and language difficulties and lack of a bank account or access to financial institutions by many families make this seemingly easy operations difficult and even unachievable. This, in effect, adds a major element of punishment to the penalty of incarceration with consequent negative effects for everyone involved and especially the family unit, if there is one. Especially for women, lack of contact with their children is the most punitive aspect of their incarceration. Lack of contact with their children and the family is tied to a considerable loss of self-esteem and identity for women in prison.[22]

16. FINANCIAL IMPACT ON FAMILY, CHILDREN AND THE COMMUNITY

Additionally, many incarcerated or jailed parents were previously breadwinners. Their imprisonment results in economic instability and more poverty impacting

---

20 Kelly Bedard & Eric Helland, *The Location of Women's Prison and the Deterrent Effect of 'Harder' Time*, December 2002, p. 7 (at: http://econ.ucsb.edu/~kelly/prison.pdf; accessed on July 3, 2013).

21 *Idem*, p. 2.

22 George E. Conklin, 'Family Ties, Depression and Adjustment of Women in Prison in North Carolina', 26 *Sociation* 3 (2000), p. 2.

their family's health, educational, emotional and career prospects. It also impoverishes other relatives, often grandparents on limited income, or the community, who must care for the children left behind. People in jail and prison are the children, parents, siblings, kin, neighbors and employees of an untold number of individuals and businesses who are negatively affected in different ways when they are arrested, removed, jailed or incarcerated, and eventually returned home with dimmed employment and earning futures. Schmitt, Warner and Gupta, on the basis of data of the Bureau of Justice Statistics, estimated that, in 2008, the United States had between 12 and 14 million ex-offenders of working age.[23] The record of a felony conviction and of imprisonment dramatically diminish an ex-offender's ability to secure employment and re-join the labor market upon release. Schmitt, Warner and Gupta calculated that this large population of ex-offenders depressed the total male employment rate in 2008 by 1.5 to 1.7 percentage points.[24] While this may not seem much, in Gross Domestic Product (GDP) terms, this loss of employment cost the U.S. economy between $57 and $65 billion in lost output.

The ripple effects on their communities are obvious. Unfortunately, the impact of incarceration on the community, its economy and development has received little attention. The long term impact on the children of imprisoned parents, their diminished chances for academic and career success, and the likelihood that they will be swept up in a life of unstable relationships, family violence, deviance and crime constitute enormous costs for any society. Examining the economic impact of incarceration on human capital and, by extension, on the family and on the micro and macro communities show how destructive imprisonment, and especially lengthy imprisonment, can be not only on the inmate but on his or her family, the economy and the community. It is essential that we shape public policy to minimize the loss of human potential and community development not only to crime and its consequences, but also to the harshness, inefficiencies, injustices, and failures of the criminal justice system.

17. THE COST OF LIFE IMPRISONMENT

Another reason to question the clear preference, if not obsession, of the United States criminal justice system with life sentences is their cost. Just as the victim's rights movement demanded "truth in sentencing", others ask "truth in the cost", the real cost, of the tough-on-crime laws and use the issue of "true cost" to argue

23 John Schmitt, Kris Warner & Sarika Gupta, *The High Budgetary Cost of Incarceration*, Washington, DC: Center for Economic Policy Research, 2010 (at: www.cepr.net/documents/publications/incarceration-2010–06.pdf; accessed on July 8, 2013).

24 *Idem*.

against the excessive use of prison sentences, especially long term ones. Imprisonment by the States in the United States has increased 700% since 1970.[25]

For example, *One in 100,* a 2008 report by Pew's Public Safety Performance Project has detailed how, for the first time in history, more than one in every 100 adults in America are in jail or prison – a fact, the report says, that significantly impacts state budgets without delivering a clear return on public safety.[26] Another report by the Pew's Public Safety Performance Project aptly entitled *High Cost, Low Return,* points out that while 1 in every 33 adults is under correctional supervision in the United States (to include non incarcerated offenders on probation or parole), 1 in 2.3 offenders returns to prison with three years of release, hardly an indication that imprisonment deters.[27] This confirms the criticism voiced by some that confining more people in prison generally decreases the chance of them perpetrating offenses affecting the general public while imprisoned but it increases the probability of them committing crimes once they are out of prison and in the community. The prison appears indeed to be the premier "school of crime".

Even when it comes to jails, supposedly meant to briefly hold suspects – presumed innocent until proven guilty – until trial, communities are bearing the cost of a massive explosion in the jail population, which has nearly doubled in less than two decades. Research found that jails are now warehousing more people – who have not been found guilty of any crime – for longer periods of time than ever before.[28] Due to the rising costs of bail, people arrested today are more likely to serve jail time before trial than twenty years ago, even though crime rates are at the lowest levels in years. Consequently, the jail population has exploded. To calculate as correctly as possible the cost to the States of imprisoning offenders, the Vera Institute of Justice Center for Sentencing and Corrections and Cost Benefit Analysis Unit in collaboration with the Pew Center on the States developed a specific methodology. On this basis, it was found that the total cost to taxpayers for the correctional systems of the 40 States that took part in the survey was $39 billion, $5.4 billion more than what was budgeted.[29]

---

25 Pew Center on the States, *Prison Count 2010: State Population Declines for the First Time in 38 Years*, Washington, DC: The Pew Charitable Trusts, 2010.

26 Pew's Public Safety Performance Project, *One in 100*, Washington, DC: The Pew Charitable Trusts, 2008 (at: www.pewstates.org/research/reports/one-in-100–85899374411; accessed on July 4, 2012).

27 Pew's Public Safety Performance Project, *High Cost, Low Return*, Washington, DC, 2012 (at: www.pewstates.org/research/data-visualizations/the-high-cost-of-corrections-in-america-85899397897; accessed on July 4, 2013).

28 Amanda Petteruti & Nastassia Walsh, *Jailing Communities: The Impact of Jail Expansion and Effective Jail Expansion and Public Safety Strategies*, Washington DC: Justice Policy Institute, 2008 (at: www.justicepolicy.org/uploads/justicepolicy/documents/08–04_rep_jailingcommunities_ac.pdf; accessed on July 4, 2013).

29 Christian Henrichson & Ruth Delaney, *The Price of Prisons. What Incarceration Costs Taxpayers*, New York: Vera Institute of Justice, January 2012, p. 6 (at: www.vera.org/sites/default/files/resources/downloads/Price_of_Prisons_updated_version_072512.pdf).

This still does not calculate all the real costs. For example it does not include "collateral" costs like welfare costs, supplemental income assistance, medical insurance, education costs etc. for the family and the children left behind. When it comes to individual cost, among the 40 States surveyed, the average yearly per-inmate cost was $31,286, with a range from a low of $14,603 in Kentucky to a high of $60,076 in New York.[30] These amounts are often compared for maximum effect to the cost of sending a young person for a year to a university as good as Harvard or Yale or a similar. They represent only spending in itself; they do not represent how well planned or effective the spending is or the quality of the correctional system and its services to the inmates. There are also regional variations in the cost of living to be taken into account. Thus, it would not make sense for New York to aspire to lower its cost to Kentucky's level. While there is room to cut back on correctional expenses, it is imperative that it be done safely, wisely and prudently while providing decent services to the inmates and acceptable wages for the staff. For example, it would not be acceptable to drive down costs by increasing overcrowding of inmates.

It is not only in the United States that the issue of the increasing cost of correctional institutions is debated and criticized. In neighboring Canada there has been criticism that there is no evidence to justify the mega-costly, mega-prisons construction projects by the Government. There has also been a call for all Canadians to know all the costs associated with mega-prisons. According to press reports the cost of the federal prison system has gone up 86% since 2006, a budget hike of over a billion dollars each year. Some call this approach an outdated American model, and a very large cost to the taxpayers.[31]

Many in Canada, the United States and elsewhere state that to combat crime, it is much better to fund crime prevention initiatives, support front-line law enforcement, introduce youth programs, offer rehabilitation programs inside the prisons and provide jobs and training than build larger prisons. Strong and effective prosecution of the worst offenders like gang leaders, drug and people traffickers, sexual predators and their recruiters, naturally, must accompany this, in order to ensure safe communities.

18. THE ECONOMIC CRISIS AND ITS IMPACT ON CORRECTIONS

One powerful argument to reduce new prison construction projects and downsize the inmate population has been the economic crisis and the falling revenues for various governments beginning in 2008. Budget problems and

30 Christian Henrichson & Ruth Delaney, *The Price of Prisons. What Incarceration Costs Taxpayers*, New York: Vera Institute of Justice, 2012, p. 11.

31 National Post, 'Crime Rates Continue to Drop Across Canada', *National Post*, 21 July 2011.

shortfalls definitely lead politicians to reconsider their priorities. However, this has been tempered by strong financial and political interests in keeping prisons open and full, for example to provide revenue and employment in depressed or economically challenged areas of a State where often prisons have been built. Also private companies that own and manage prisons in the United States constitute an influential lobby against any measure that would soften laws, introduce alternative sentencing, reduce prison terms and downsize prison construction in order to continue guaranteeing these private companies large profits. Ten years ago there were only 5 private prisons with 2,000 prisoners. Now there are over 100 with 62,000 inmates. It is projected that in the coming decade that number will grow to 360,000. There have also been accusations that, once large prisons have been built, there has been tremendous pressure to keep them full by sentencing more people, especially non-violent offenders, to prison terms and by increasing the severity and length of the sentences. Another element that has been identified as supporting full prisons are the prison industries where inmates work full shifts for minimal pay producing goods for various industries, with the large profits divided between the State and the private firms. Given the large presence of African-Americans in the United States correctional system, some have described prison industries as a "legalized" continuation of slavery.[32] Thus, stopping prison construction, closing prisons, or reducing the inmate population runs afoul of powerful vested interests, even when budget shortfalls make it compelling to consider downsizing.

19. COURT DECISIONS LIMITING LIFE IMPRISONMENT

There have been also some limited Court victories. In 2012 the United States Supreme Court ruled in *Miller v. Alabama* that for juvenile *homicide offenders*, a sentence of life without possibility of parole automatically imposed and without individualized consideration of the defendant's status as a child or of the child's life circumstances contravenes Constitutional safeguards against cruel and unusual punishment.[33] It is unconstitutionally disproportionate. It is still possible to impose a life sentence without possibility of parole on juveniles' homicide offenders under certain circumstances, for example if the youth is "irretrievably depraved" or "irreparably corrupted". The Supreme Court refused to rule that under a certain age, *e.g.* 15 years of age, it would be unconstitutional under any circumstance to impose such sentence on a juvenile.

32 Vicky Pelaez, 'The Prison Industry in the United States: Big Business or a new Form of Slavery?', *Global Research*, January 31, 2013 (at: www.globalresearch.ca/the-prison-industry-in-the-united-states-big-business-or-a-new-form-of-slavery/8289; accessed on July 9, 2013).

33 *Miller v. Alabama*, 132 S. Ct. 2455 (2012).

20. PRISON OVERCROWDING AND THE COURTS

The U.S. Supreme Court in 2011 in the case, *Brown v. Plata*, No. 09–1233, affirmed a 2009 order by a special three-judge federal court requiring state officials to reduce the prison population to 110,000, which is 137.5 percent of the system's capacity.[34] There have been more than 160,000 inmates in the system in recent years. The overcrowding has been especially harsh on inmates who are seriously or terminally ill and on those with mental health problems, often confined to cells so small to be described as "telephone booths without toilets". For more than 10 years, the State of California has been the defendant in lengthy litigation over the consequences of the extreme overcrowding at its prisons. Conceding early on that this overcrowding constituted cruel and unusual punishment under the Eighth Amendment for prisoners with serious medical or mental conditions, the State has been under various forms of court supervision due to its inability to rectify the constitutional violations. The April 11 opinion was the latest attempt of the courts to bring California into constitutional compliance.

The Court stated that prison overcrowding in California, partially the outcome of harsh sentences, mandatory minimums and the three strikes rule, violates the same Constitutional protections. With that decision, the Court ordered the State to free some 40,000 prisoners. But in reality, even after these verdicts, action has been slow, and State officials continue to fight in court against downsizing prison populations. The Governor of California, Jerry Brown, is ignoring the courts orders, engaging in intentional delays, and shows no desire to comply with the court orders.

21. ISOLATION OF INMATES

The cruel and unusual punishment aspect is especially strong when it comes to "isolation" of the inmates. According to a study by Kim, Pendergrass and Zelon, every day, nearly 4,500 prisoners across New York State are confined in extreme isolation, lacking any meaningful human interaction or mental stimulation, boxed into small, barren cells where they live 23 hours a day.[35] Their meals are delivered through a slot in the cell door by disembodied hands without any human interaction or conversation. "Recreation" provides no real outlet or relief. It consists of an hour, alone, in an empty, outdoor cage, no larger than the cell, totally closed in by high concrete walls or heavy metal grates. There are no activities, programs or classes to break the monotony of each and every day.

---

34 *Brown v. Plata*, 131 S. Ct. 1910 (2011).

35 Scarlet Kim, Taylor Pendergrass & Helen Zelon, *Boxed in: The True Cost of Extreme Isolation in New York*, New York ACLU, October 2012 (at: www.nyclu.org/files/publications/nyclu_boxedin_FINAL.pdf; accessed on July 9, 2013).

There are no phone calls allowed. Very few personal possessions are permitted. These prisoners are rotting in isolation for days, weeks, months and even years on end. Perversely, New York State also uses a different model of solitary confinement in half of isolation cases, mostly because the ever-increasing use of segregation and isolation means that there are not enough single cells for each inmate. Two inmates are locked up 23 hours of the day together in the same cell for days, weeks, and months… It is called "double celling." The potential for conflict, aggression, exploitation, and sexual and other violence is very high, given the circumstances. Privacy of any kind is obviously totally absent. Forcing two strangers into such an intimate, close proximity is certainly part of cruel treatment. The impact of this situation on the physical, mental and emotional health of the inmates is extremely negative and may lead to illness, premature death, deep depression, mental illness, and suicide. It conveys a very negative message about how the correctional system even minimally values and protects human dignity. It is degrading for everyone, including the staff working under these inhumane conditions.

New York State is not the only State with ample use of isolation in the 1000s. The Federal system and all States do it with increasing frequency. The so-called "Supermax" prisons (Super-maximum security prisons) are notorious for this pattern of treatment with destructive consequences on the inmates so confined. Even worse is the accusation often voiced that some inmates, who really do not belong to Supermax institutions, are sent there anyway to keep them full and justify their existence and the connected expenditures.[36]

22. LIFE IN PRISON AND THE ELDERLY

The high cost and the meager benefits of incarceration are nowhere so obvious than with the imprisonment of the elderly. With ever increasing numbers of people sentenced to long prison terms or to life in prison, it follows that the elderly prison population is growing every day. It is projected that by 2030, 33 percent of the United States prison population will be over 65. This will amount to more than 400,000 elderly inmates. In 1981, there were less than 9,000 state and federal prisoners. The elderly are expensive inmates given their declining physical and mental health and frequent illnesses, at times chronic or terminal. To provide a comparison, in 1988 the entire U.S. correctional system did cost some $11 billions. Today, $16 billion are spent just imprisoning elderly convicts. It has been calculated that the cost per year to house an average inmate is $34,135; for a prisoner older than 50 it goes up to $68,270. There is no question

---

36 Caroline Isaacs and Matthew Lowen, *Buried Alive: Solitary Confinement in Arizona's Prisons and Jails*, AFSC Arizona, May 2007 (at: https://afsc.org/sites/afsc.civicactions.net/files/documents/Buried%20Alive.pdf; accessed on July 9, 2013).

that the increase in the elderly population in prison is due not so much to older people committing crimes but rather to longer and harsher sentences. For comparison, it has been calculated that in 1979 only 2 percent of older inmates had been in prison 20 years or more. Today, that percentage can be as high as 15 percent in Mississippi to 25 percent in Ohio. The irony is that all research shows that older inmates are the least likely to perpetrate new crimes. Only between five and ten percent of older released convicts return to prison having committed new crimes. Yet, according to a Vera Institute of Justice study, most States that actually have measures on the books allowing for the release of elderly inmates do not use them, regardless of the low risk posed by their release and the obvious savings, especially in health costs.[37]

23. CONCLUSION

In the United States, once someone has been sentenced to life, even with the possibility of parole, it's hard to go free. The harsh sentences that imprison millions for long periods of time and even for life, even when the inmate is elderly, in poor health or with mental problems, are common in the United States criminal justice system. They have been enshrined as necessary to control the surge in crime; provide security, especially in urban areas; and ensure the utmost longevity of the political careers of legislators and governmental officials whose major claim for election or re-election is being tough on crime, mostly by being harsh on convicts, regardless of their age, juvenile or elderly, and of their crime, with many non-violent offenders or minor drug offenders being sentenced to lengthy stints in prison. This political and cultural orthodoxy, fiercely guarded and enforced by various interest groups, keeps going strong and unyielding, regardless of the fact that a large number of reasons and factors addressed in this paper clearly prove that it is not a correct, effective and humane policy to pursue. The public thirst for revenge, retribution, and incapacitation and its desire to use the criminal law and its sanctions to prove that their specific cause is worthy of attention and of societal rejection and disapproval also fuel this punitive, harsh, costly and demonstrably ineffective policies and measures. All activists championing a cause that involves criminal behavior want the State to intervene and support them by making the proscribed behavior a crime with harsh consequences. The more severe the sentence is, the more vindicated and supported they feel.

Socio-economic, racial, ethnic, educational level and other considerations also influence and impact the assessment of guilt and culpability and the

---

37 Tina Chiu, *It's About Time: Aging Prisoners, Increasing Costs, and Geriatric Release*, New York: Vera Institute of Justice, April 2010 (at: www.vera.org/sites/default/files/resources/downloads/Its-about-time-aging-prisoners-increasing-costs-and-geriatric-release.pdf; accessed on July 9, 2013).

imposition of harsh sentences. Convicts from lower socio-economic levels, pertaining to racial, ethnic or religious minorities, often with a broken family's background and a poor education, are most often sentenced to harsh sentences than the powerful, upper class, well connected convict.

Strong and exploitative interests in creating and maintaining high rates of incarceration and prison labor, especially in the private prison sector, also support the continuation of an approach to crime characterized by very punitive approaches and outcomes, even when the transgressions are minor and non violent and their impact on the affected party and society at large is mitigated by insurance policies and other remedies. There is an urgent need to bring concrete, reasoned, empirically based innovative policies and approaches to the fore for consideration and adoption, revolutionizing our approach to crime and its aftermath. It is clear that the current system does not work; is costly, cruel, abusive, and inefficient; and often represents institutionalized violence, exploitation, and obvious violations of human dignity and human rights. The excesses and most patent injustices of the system can be minimized and eventually eliminated only when passion, preconceptions, stereotypes, prejudice and racism are brought under control and a truly rational, positive and proactive approach is adopted that stresses rehabilitation, reintegration, training and short and long term support and fosters the involvement of the family and of the community in this enterprise.[38] Overspending in police, prisons, and security and under-spending in prevention, treatment and communities will not produce long term positive change for the better in society and will actually cause ever increasing costs for the States.[39] Augmenting law enforcement expenditures while decreasing, for example, juvenile justice investments and community support is exactly the contrary of what is needed to produce a positive long term impact on public safety and a substantial, overdue decrease in the number of people incarcerated in the United States.

REFERENCES

Aaron, L. & D.H. Dallaire (2010). 'Parental Incarceration and Multiple Risk Experiences: Effects on Family Dynamics and Children's Delinquency', 39 *Journal of Youth & Adolescence* 12, p. 1471–84.

American Civil Liberties Union (ACLU) (2012). *At America's Expense: The Mass Incarceration of the Elderly* (at: www.aclu.org/files/assets/elderlyprisonreport_20120613_0.pdf; accessed on July 9, 2013).

38 Catholic Bishops, *Challenges for the Criminal Justice Process in the South*, 2010 (at: www.catholiclabor.org/church-doc/CBS-1.htm; accessed on July 9, 2013).

39 Justice Policy Institute, *Department of Justice 2010 Budget Likely to Increase Incarceration in U.S.*, Washington DC, 2010 (at: www.justicepolicy.org/news/1936; accessed on July 7, 2013).

Bedard, K. & E. Helland (2002). *The Location of Women's Prison and the Deterrent Effect of 'Harder' Time* (at: http://econ.ucsb.edu/~kelly/prison.pdf; accessed on July 3, 2013).

Catholic Bishops (2010). *Challenges for the Criminal Justice Process in the South* (at: www.catholiclabor.org/church-doc/CBS-1.htm; accessed on July 9, 2013).

Chiu, T. (2010). *It's About Time: Aging Prisoners, Increasing Costs, and Geriatric Release.* New York: Vera Institute of Justice (at: www.vera.org/sites/default/files/resources/downloads/Its-about-time-aging-prisoners-increasing-costs-and-geriatric-release.pdf; accessed on July 9, 2013).

Conklin, G.H. (2000). 'Family Ties, Depression and Adjustment of Women in Prison in North Carolina', 26 *Sociation* 3, p. 2.

Federal Bureau of Prisons (2013). Quick Facts About the Bureau of Prisons. Washington, DC (at: www.bop.gov/news/quick.jsp; accessed on July 2, 2013).

Henrichson, Christian & Ruth Delaney (2012), *The Price of Prisons. What Incarceration Costs Taxpayers*, New York: Vera Institute of Justice (at: www.vera.org/sites/default/files/resources/downloads/Price_of_Prisons_updated_version_072512.pdf).

Human Rights Watch (2009). State Distribution of Youth Offenders Serving Juvenile Life Without Parole (JLWOP).

Isaacs, C. & M. Lowen (2007). *Buried Alive: Solitary Confinement in Arizona's Prisons and Jails.* Arizona: AFSC (at: https://afsc.org/sites/afsc.civicactions.net/files/documents/Buried%20Alive.pdf; accessed on July 9, 2013).

Justice Policy Institute (2008). *Substance Abuse Treatment and Public Safety.* Washington, DC (at: www.justicepolicy.org/images/upload/08_01_REP_DrugTx_AC-PS.pdf).

Justice Policy Institute (2010). *Department of Justice 2010 Budget Likely to Increase Incarceration in U.S.* Washington, DC (at: www.justicepolicy.org/news/1936; accessed on July 7, 2013).

Kim, S., T. Pendergrass & H. Zelon (2012). *Boxed in: The True Cost of Extreme Isolation in New York*, New York: ACLU (at: www.nyclu.org/files/publications/nyclu_boxedin_FINAL.pdf; accessed on July 9, 2013).

Makariev, D.W. & P.R. Shaver (2010). 'Attachment, Parental Incarceration and Possibilities for Intervention: An overview', 12 *Attachment & Human Development* 4, p. 311–31.

Maruschak, L.M. & E. Parks, Bureau of Justice Statistics (2012). *Probation and Parole in the United States, 2011.* Washington, DC: US Department of Justice, NCJ 239686 (at: www.bjs.gov/content/pub/pdf/ppus11.pdf).

Murray, J. & L. Murray (2010). 'Parental Incarceration, Attachment and Child Psychopathology', 12 *Attachment & Human Development* 4, p. 289–309.

National Post (2011). 'Crime Rates Continue to Drop Across Canada', *National Post.*

Pelaez, V. (2013). 'The Prison Industry in the United States: Big Business or a new Form of Slavery?', *Global Research* (at: www.globalresearch.ca/the-prison-industry-in-the-united-states-big-business-or-a-new-form-of-slavery/8289; accessed on July 9, 2013).

Petteruti, A. & N. Walsh (2008). *Jailing Communities: The Impact of Jail Expansion and Effective Jail Expansion and Public Safety Strategies.* Washington DC: Justice Policy Institute (at: www.justicepolicy.org/uploads/justicepolicy/documents/08-04_rep_jailingcommunities_ac.pdf; accessed on July 4, 2013).

Pew Center on the States (2010). *Prison Count 2010: State Population Declines for the First Time in 38 Years.* Washington, DC: The Pew Charitable Trusts.

Pew's Public Safety Performance Project (2008). *One in 100.* Washington DC: The Pew Charitable Trusts (at: www.pewstates.org/research/reports/one-in-100–85899374411; accessed on July 4, 2012).

Pew's Public Safety Performance Project (2012). *High Cost, Low Return.* Washington DC (at: www.pewstates.org/research/data-visualizations/the-high-cost-of-corrections-in-america-85899397897; accessed on July 4, 2013).

Poehlmann, J., D. Dallaire, A.B. Loper, & L.D. Shear (2010). 'Children's Contact with Their Incarcerated Parents: Research Findings and Recommendations', 65 *The American Psychologist* 6, p. 575–98.

Sanders, E. & R. Dunifon (2011). *Children of Incarcerated Parents.* Ithaca NY: Cornell University.

Schmitt, J., K. Warner & S. Gupta (2010). *The High Budgetary Cost of Incarceration.* Washington, DC: Center for Economic Policy Research (at: www.cepr.net/documents/publications/incarceration-2010–06.pdf; accessed on July 8, 2013).

Schmitt, J. & C. Warner (2010). *Ex-Offenders and the Labor Market.* Washington, DC: Center for Economic Policy Research (at: www.cepr.net/documents/publications/ex-offenders-2010–11.pdf; accessed on July 4, 2013).

Sentencing Project (2005). *Incarceration and Crime: A Complex Relationship.* Washington, DC (at: www.sentencingproject.org/doc/publications/inc_iandc_complex.pdf; accessed on July 3, 2013).

Sentencing Project (2009). *The State of Sentencing,* 2009, Washington DC. (at: www.sentencingproject.org/doc/publications/s_ssr2009Update.pdf; accessed on June 29, 2013).

Sutton, J.R. (2013). 'Symbol and Substance: The Effects of California Three Strikes Law on Felony Sentencing', 47 *Law and Society Review* 1, p. 37–72.

Weisberg, R., D.A. Mukamal & J.D. Segall (2011). *Life in Limbo: An Examination of Parole Release for Prisoners Serving Life Sentences with the Possibility of Parole in California.* Stanford: Stanford Law School, 2011.

Western, B. & B. Pettit (2010). *Collateral Costs: Incarceration's Effect on Economic Mobility.* Washington, DC: Pew Charitable Trusts' Economic Mobility Project and its Public Safety Performance Project (PSPP) (at: www.pewstates.org/research/reports/collateral-costs- -85899373309; accessed on July 8, 2013).

CASE LAW

Brown v. Plata, 131 S. Ct. 1910 (2011)

ECtHR, 9 July 2013, *Vinter and others v. the United Kingdom,* Appl. 66069/09, 130/10 & 3896/10

Graham v. Florida, 130 S. Ct. 2011 (2010)

Lockyear v. Andrade, 536 US 63 (2003)

Miller v. Alabama, 132 S. Ct. 2455 (2012)

MANAGING THE RISK POSED BY OFFENDERS AFTER THE EXPIRY OF SENTENCE: THE BRITISH EXPERIENCE

Stephen C. SHUTE*

1. INTRODUCTION

There is a widely-held belief that it is possible to cut crime and better protect the public by making changes to the criminal justice system. That fundamental tenet has formed the centre-piece of penal policy in many different parts of the world for some time and has driven governments of all political persuasions to introduce a kaleidoscopic palette of reform with the focus often placed on new sentencing legislation. The United Kingdom has been no exception to this trend. In the document which preceded its formation in the early summer of 2010, the current Coalition government promised 'a full review of sentencing policy to ensure that it is effective in deterring crime, protecting the public, punishing offenders and cutting reoffending'.[1] Six months' later, in December 2010, the then Secretary of State for Justice, Mr Kenneth Clarke, produced a Green Paper, *Breaking the Cycle: Effective Punishment, Rehabilitation and Sentencing of Offenders*,[2] in which he explained the Coalition government's plans. Subsequently, these proposals – which included reform of existing sentencing legislation – were incorporated into the Legal Aid, Sentencing and Punishment of Offenders Act 2012.[3] At the same time, the Coalition government moved forward with its commitment to create a 'rehabilitation revolution' by setting in train a process through which the provision of a body of criminal justice work in England and Wales could be transferred to Non-Governmental Organisations (NGOs). These organisations would then be charged with delivering improved penal services for

* Dr. S.C. Shute is a Professor of Criminal Law and Criminal Justice and Head of the School of Law, Politics and Sociology, The University of Sussex, United Kingdom.

1 *The Coalition: Our Programme for Government*, 2010.

2 Cm 7972. In June 2011, the Ministry of Justice published its response to the consultation: see *Breaking the Cycle: Government Response*, Cm 8070.

3 The provisions on dangerous offenders were introduced by the Secretary of State for Justice, Mr Kenneth Clarke, at the report stage of the Bill: see HC Debs Col 626 31 October 2011 and HC Debs Col 784 1 November 2011.

which they would be paid only if their interventions were demonstrably effective: a system known as 'payment by results'.[4]

As part of the package of reforms introduced by the Legal Aid, Sentencing and Punishment of Offenders Act, the heavily-criticised sentence of Imprisonment for the Protection of the Public (IPP), created by the previous Labour Government in the Criminal Justice Act 2003, was prospectively abolished.[5] The IPP is an indeterminate sentence akin to a life sentence which brings with it similar release procedures. Prior to its abolition, the Labour Government attempted to control its use. The original list of more than 150 trigger crimes was heavily cut back and a threshold requirement was introduced restricting the availability of an IPP to cases where the sentencing court concluded that a four-year minimum determinate sentence (or 'tariff') was warranted.[6] Despite these attempts to rein the sentence in, however, almost 5,500 offenders are currently serving IPPs in prisons in England and Wales and almost two-thirds of these offenders are post-tariff.[7] Indeed, since the sentence was introduced some 10 years ago, only around 500 offenders serving IPPs have actually been released. The IPP also survived a challenge before the European Court of Human Rights in *James, Wells and Lee v. United Kingdom*. The Court concluded that the

4 See *Competition Strategy for Offender Services*, Ministry of Justice, July 2011; *Punishment and Reform: Effective Probation Services*, Cm 8333, March 2012; *Transforming Rehabilitation: A Revolution in the Way we Manage Offenders*, Cm 8517, January 2013; and *Transforming Rehabilitation: A Strategy for Reform*, Cm 8619, May 2013. The underpinning legislation, The Offender Rehabilitation Bill, was introduced into the House of Lords on 9 May 2013. A commitment to a 'rehabilitation revolution' was also incorporated into the Coalition Agreement.

5 See section 123 of the 2012 Act. IPPs could be imposed where an offender had committed a serious offence – listed in a Schedule to the Act – which carried a determinate sentence of 10 years or more, so long as the court also concluded that there was a significant risk from the offender to members of the public. For reviews and criticisms of the IPP see, for instance, *Indefinitely Maybe? How the indeterminate sentence for public protection is unjust and unsustainable*, Prison Reform Trust, July 2007; *Service review – Indeterminate Sentence Prisoners (ISPs)*, 'The Lockyer Review', Ministry of Justice, 17 August 2007; *Securing the Future: Proposals for the Efficient and Sustainable Use of Custody in England and Wales*, 'The Carter Review', Ministry of Justice, December 2007; *Towards Effective Sentencing*, Justice Committee, 2007–08, 22 July 2008, HC 184; *The Indeterminate Sentence for Public Protection*, HM Inspectorate of Prisons, September 2008; *Indeterminate Sentences for Public Protection: A Joint Inspection by HM Inspectorate of Prisons and HM Inspectorate of Probation*, March 2010; and *Unjust Deserts: Imprisonment for Public Protection*, Jessica Jacobson and Mike Hough, Prison Reform Trust and the Institute for Criminal Policy Research, July 2010.

6 These reforms were achieved by amendments made by the Criminal Justice and Immigration Act 2008 which inserted a new section 225(3A) and 3(B) and the new Schedule 15A into the Criminal Justice Act 2003.

7 The figure for 30 September 2013 was 5,468: see *Offender Management Statistics: Quarterly Bulletin, April to June 2013, England and Wales*, p. 8. Of these, 3,548 had passed their tariff, 1,893 had not yet reached their tariff, and for 23 the tariff expiry date was not yet available, see Table 1.4: 'Indeterminate sentence prisoner population, by tariff length and tariff expiry date, 30 September 2013, England and Wales'.

continued detention of post-tariff offenders was unlawful because of the absence of training programmes in British prisons while ruling that the fundamental structure of the IPP was Convention compliant.[8]

The abolition of the IPP did not, however, indicate a loss of faith by the Coalition government in indeterminate sentencing. As a counter-weight to the IPP's removal, and as a way of a responding to the continuing need to protect the British public from dangerous offenders, the Coalition introduced a 'two strikes' policy which required (subject to a residual discretion) a life sentence to be passed on any offender aged 18 or over when four conditions were met: the offender had been convicted of a second listed serious sexual or violent offence; that offence was deemed serious enough to justify a sentence of imprisonment of 10 years or more; the offender had previously been convicted of a listed offence; and that earlier offence had produced a sentence of imprisonment for life or imprisonment for a period of 10 years or more.[9] In addition to this 'two strikes' provision, a further risk-based measure was introduced, a reformed 'extended sentence' for certain violent and sexual offenders.[10] This sentence is available when an offender has been convicted of a specified serious sexual or violent offence and the court concludes that there is 'a significant risk to members of the public of serious harm occasioned by the commission by the offender of further specified offences'. (The test for 'significant risk' is the same as that which was used for IPPs under the 2003 Act.) The sentencing judge must also be satisfied that one of two further alternative conditions has been met: either the offence must have been serious enough to warrant a determinate sentence of at least four

---

8 [2013] 56 EHRR 12. The current Secretary of State for Justice, Mr Chris Grayling, told Parliament that he was 'very disappointed' by the ruling, adding that this was 'not an area' where the government welcomed the Court seeking to make rulings. He said that the United Kingdom government intended to appeal: see HC Debs col 764 18 September 2012. For the decision of the House of Lords in this case, see *R. (on the application of James) v. Secretary of States for Justice; R. (on the application of Lee) v. Secretary of States for Justice; R. (on the application of Wells) v. Secretary of States for Justice* [2009] UKHL 22, [2010] 1 AC 553, [2009] 4 All ER 255, [2009] 2 WLR 1149.

9 See section 122 of the Legal Aid, Sentencing and Punishment of Offenders Act 2012 which inserted a new section 224A into the Criminal Justice Act 2003. The listed offences are contained in Part 1 of Schedule 15B to the Criminal Justice Act 2003 which was inserted by Schedule 18 to the 2012 Act. The effect of the two strikes policy is not retrospective; the second trigger offence must therefore have been committed after the section came into force. The residual discretion not to impose the life sentence arises if, in the opinion of the judge, there are particular circumstances that relate to the current offence, the previous offence, and the offender which, in all the circumstances, make the sentence unjust.

10 See section 124 of the Legal Aid, Sentencing and Punishment of Offenders Act 2012 which inserted a new section 226A into the Criminal Justice Act 2003. Sentencers had been able impose a 'longer than commensurate sentence' under sections 79(2)(b) and 80(2)(b) of the Powers of Criminal Courts (Sentencing) Act 2000 but this power was repealed by Schedule 37 to the Criminal Justice Act 2003. A previous version of the extended sentences had been created by sections 227 and 228 of the Criminal Justice Act 2003 but this was also repealed by the 2012 Act.

years or the offender must previously have committed one or more listed offences.[11] The sentence is 'extended' because it allows the judge to impose an extra five years' licence period for violent offenders, and an extra eight years' licence period for sexual offenders, beyond what would otherwise be available.[12] The sentence precludes an offender's release from the custodial part of the sentence until two-thirds of that has been served rather than the usual halfway.[13]

It is notable that all the changes discussed above have sought to control the risk posed by dangerous offenders *within* the envelope of the sentence itself. The intention has been to develop the sentencing framework in a way which better allows for public protection but does not undermine its traditional punitive function. Over the last 15 or so years, however, criminal justice policy makers in the United Kingdom have also sought to bolster public protection by designing measures which operate *outside* of the boundaries of a standard penal sentence.

11 The requirement that the offence for which the sentence is imposed must have been serious enough to warrant a sentence of at least four years was not a feature of the version of the extended sentence contained in the 2003 Act. The latter alternative condition is not available for those aged under 18 and the arrangements for those under the age of 18 are set out in a new section 226B.

12 Again, these provisions mirror those in the repealed parts of the 2003 Act. Section 226A(9) limits the length of the appropriate custodial term and the extension period: together they can be no longer than the length of the maximum term of imprisonment that may be imposed for the offence. Apart from this restriction, the extension period must be of such a length that the court considers 'necessary for the purpose of protecting members of the public from serious harm occasioned by the commission by the offender of further specified offences'.

13 The Parole Board's authorisation is required for the release up to the end of the sentence rather than automatically at the two-thirds point. The arrangements for release from an extended sentence vary according to the seriousness of the offence in respect of which the extended sentence was imposed. If the sentence was imposed for an offence listed in Parts 1 to 3 of Schedule 15B, or whose offending merits a custodial term of 10 years or more, the offender will be considered for release on licence by the Parole Board once the offender has served two-thirds of the appropriate custodial term, and will be released automatically at the end of the appropriate custodial term if the Parole Board has not already directed released. If the sentence was imposed for an offence not listed in Schedule 15B which merited an 'appropriate custodial term' of less than 10 years, then that offender will be released automatically after two-thirds of the appropriate custodial term and will be considered by the Parole Board for release at the halfway point. These provisions are more restrictive than for the old extended sentence introduced under the 2003 Act where the offender became eligible for release by the Parole Board at the halfway point irrespective of the offence for which they had been sentenced. The release test is the same as that used for IPPs and Life Sentences (see section 8 of the Crime (Sentences) Act 1997). The Board must not direct release of an extended sentence prisoner unless it is 'satisfied that it is no longer necessary for the protection of the public' that the offender should be confined. For an offender convicted of an offence listed in Schedule 15B, if the Board is not so satisfied, the prisoner will be required to remain in custody until he or she has served the 'appropriate custodial term'. Only at that point will the Home Secretary be under a duty to release the offender on licence into the community. A further change (see section 128 of the 2012 Act) gives the Secretary of State the power, by order, to set additional conditions around the release test for the Parole Board in respect of extended sentence prisoners. Where the prisoner is released automatically, it is the Secretary of State who sets the conditions; where the prisoner is released by the Parole Board, it is the Parole Board that sets the conditions (see Schedule 20, para 6.3).

Drawing on the structure of the long-standing application to 'bind over' a person to keep the peace, the roots of which lie so deep in the common law that they have rightly been described by the English Law Commission as 'lost in history',[14] policy makers in the United Kingdom have attempted to achieve this goal by introducing a sophisticated range of new 'civil preventive orders' many of which have been explicitly designed to enhance public protection. Examples from the late 1990s include 'restraining orders' which were created by the Protection from Harassment Act 1997 and 'sexual offences orders' (SOOs) which were created by the Crime and Disorder Act 1998.[15] The development of these orders has not been universally welcomed. Some have even questioned their constitutionality.[16] Nonetheless, further similarly-structured orders were introduced in the United Kingdom in the 2000s to control, amongst other things, sexual offending, offending by organised and so-called 'life-style' criminals, and violent offending. The shape of each of the major orders that have been created to provide protection in these areas will now be discussed.

2. CONTROLLING THE RISK OF SEXUAL OFFENDING

The Sexual Offences Act 2003 introduced three new 'civil preventive orders' to manage the risk presented by certain sex offenders: Sexual Offences Prevention Orders (SOPOs); Foreign Travel Orders (FTOs); and Risk of Sexual Harm Orders (RSHOs).[17]

---

14 See *Binding Over*, Law Commission Report No. 222, 1994, para. 21.

15 See also 'disqualification orders' under section 1 of the Company Directors Disqualification Act 1986; 'orders prohibiting trespassory assemblies' under section 70 of the Criminal Justice and Public Order Act 1994; 'occupation orders' and 'non-molestation orders' under sections 33 and 42 of the Family Law Act 1996; injunctions against anti-social behaviour under sections 152 and 153 of the Housing Act 1996; 'anti-social behaviour orders' (ASBOs) under section 1 of the Crime and Disorder Act 1998; 'parenting orders' under sections 8 to 10 of the Crime and Disorder Act 1998; banning orders under section 14 of the Football Spectators Act 1989, as amended by section 1 of, and Schedule 2 to, the Football (Disorder) Act 2000; 'travel restriction orders' for drug trafficking offenders under sections 33 to 37 of the Criminal Justice and Police Act 2001; and 'drinking banning orders' which were made available from 31 August 2009 under sections 1 to 14 of the Violent Crime Reduction Act 2006. Compare also 'exclusion orders' under section 1 of the Licensed Premises (Exclusion of Certain Persons) Act 1980 and 'closure orders' for premises used for certain activities related certain sexual offences which were introduced into the Sexual Offences Act 2003 by section 21 of the Policing and Crime Act 2009.

16 See, for example, the House of Lords Select Committee on the Constitution, *Report on the Serious Crime Bill*, HL 41, 2006–07, para. 17.

17 SOOs (along with 'restraining orders' (ROs) which had been created by section 66 of, and Schedule 5 to, the Criminal Justice and Court Services Act 2000, inserting a new section 5A into the Sex Offenders Act 1997) were abolished by the Sexual Offences Act 2003. The 2003 Act also created 'Notification Orders' (NOs) under sections 97 to 103. In the seven-year

Sexual Offences Prevention Orders

A SOPO is available to the courts either when a defendant has just been convicted of a qualifying offence or on receipt of an application from a Chief Officer of Police regarding a person living in the community who has a previous conviction for such an offence. They can be imposed on both adults and offenders under the age of 18. The purpose of a SOPO is to protect the public from serious sexual harm. It is available to the courts not just upon proof of criminal activity by the defendant but also upon proof of non-criminal activity. The order, which can be made to last indefinitely but cannot last less than five years, may prohibit an offender from 'doing anything described in the order' so long as the court regards the restriction as 'necessary for the purpose of protecting the public or particular members of the public from serious sexual harm'. A common prohibition, for example, would be to proscribe the offender from contacting his or her victims or from living in a household with children under the age of 16. If, without reasonable excuse, the person subject to a SOPO does anything which the order prohibits, then that person is liable, on conviction on indictment, to a term of imprisonment not exceeding five years.

SOPOs have proved to be very popular with the courts. The annual number imposed in England and Wales has increased every year since 2006/2007 and in 2012/2013 it reached 3,064. Across the seven-year period from 2006/2007 until 2012/2013 more than 14,000 SOPOs have been made on offenders in England and Wales; and of these, 8,160 (58%) have been made in the last three years.[18]

It is important to recognise of course that the context in which SOPOs have been created can vary considerably. A recent case, albeit at the serious end of the spectrum, provides an example. The case came before HH Judge Patrick Thomas QC at the Crown Court in Stafford in 2012. It involved two brothers, Ahdel Ali and Mubarek Ali, who were convicted, after entering not guilty pleas, for a series of very serious sexual crimes perpetrated in Telford from 2008 to 2010. The offences were against four girls, aged between 13 and 17.[19] Married and of Pakistani origin, the two brothers had deliberately sought out vulnerable young white girls who had been 'gravely damaged by their experience of life'. They then

period from 2006/2007 until 2012/2013, 522 NOs have been made on sex offenders in England and Wales; of these, 253 (48.5%) have been made in the last three years: see *Multi-Agency Public Protection Arrangements Annual Report 2012*/13, Ministry of Justice, 31 October 2013, p. 13, Table 6: 'Sexual Offences Prevention Orders (SOPOs), Notification Orders (NOs) and Foreign Travel Orders (FTOs) imposed by the courts. 2006/07–2012/13.'

18 See *Multi-Agency Public Protection Arrangements Annual Report 2012*/13, Ministry of Justice, 31 October 2013, p. 13, Table 6: 'Sexual Offences Prevention Orders (SOPOs), Notification Orders (NOs) and Foreign Travel Orders (FTOs) imposed by the courts. 2006/07–2012/13.' The figure for the seven-year period is 14,088.

19 See *The Times*, 6 October 2012, p. 20.

used and abused those girls. Two were sold to friends or acquaintances for sexual purposes as 'sexual commodities'. The brothers' purpose 'went beyond profit'. It 'involved sheer, gratuitous pleasure in the power [they] exercised' over the girls: for them, the judge said, it was 'fun'; for the girls, it was 'degradation'. The evidence was that the two brothers had targeted, groomed and then pimped the children to immigrant workers who had 'queued' to have sex with them 'in the back rooms of restaurants and takeaway food outlets' in Telford.[20] It was, the jury was told, a world of 'alcohol, cigarettes, car rides, and cannabis' followed by 'brute contempt' and then abuse. One of the victims, a 13-year-old girl, told the jury that she thought she was in love with Ahdel Ali, a fast food delivery driver, even though he had raped her in a car the first time they had sex. She told the court she was 'just lonely' and 'wanted that extra bit of loving, someone that cares about me'. Ahdel Ali, who was aged 24, was convicted of rape, 11 counts of sexual activity with a child, three counts of controlling child prostitution, one count of inciting child prostitution, one count of inciting a child to engage in sexual activity, and one count of meeting a child after sexual grooming. For these offences he received a total sentence of 18 years' imprisonment. His elder brother, Mubarek, who was aged 29, was convicted of four counts of controlling child prostitution, two counts of trafficking a child within the United Kingdom for sexual exploitation, and one count of causing child prostitution. He received a sentence totalling 14 years' imprisonment. As part of an extended sentence, both were required to a serve a further period of eight years on licence in the community at the end of their sentence. In addition, and outside of the framework of the criminal sentences, each of the brothers was made subject to a SOPO for an indeterminate period. The fact that the two men would not be released for many years did not stand in the way of the SOPO being made nor prevent it coming into effect immediately.

Foreign Travel Orders

Unlike SOPOs, FTOs cannot be imposed by a sentencing court. They enable restrictions to be placed by the magistrates' courts on overseas travel by those convicted, either in the UK or overseas, of qualifying sexual offences committed against a person under the age of 18.[21] FTOs also differ from SOPOs in that they cannot be made to last for a period longer than five years (originally six months

20 See *The Times*, 6 October 2012, p. 20. See also *R. v Ahdel Ali and Mubarek Ali* [2014] EWCA Crim 140.

21 Originally the age limit was set at 16 but that was raised to 18 in England and Wales by sections 23 and 116(1) of the Policing and Crime Act 2009 which were brought into force on 1 April 2010 by The Policing and Crime Act 2009 (Commencement No. 4) Order 2010, S.I. 2010/507, Art. 5(j). In Scotland, the change was made by sections 101(2) and 206(1) of the Criminal Justice and Licensing (Scotland) Act 2010 which were brought into force by S.S.I. 2010/413, Art. 2.

but raised in 2010[22]). Like SOPOs, breach of the order may result in a sentence of up to five years' imprisonment. In comparison to SOPOs, the number of FTOs imposed by the courts in England and Wales has been small: just 80 in the whole of the seven-year period from 2006/2007 until 2012/2013. However, 49 (61%) of those were in the three-year period from 2010/11 to 2012/13, so their use is becoming more frequent.[23]

Risk of Sexual Harm Orders

RSHOs may be made against persons aged 18 or over (but not against persons under the age of 18), irrespective of whether they have been convicted of a sexual offence, or indeed any offence at all. The order cannot be shorter than two years but can last indefinitely. It can only be imposed if magistrates are satisfied that the police have proved that the defendant has, on at least two previous occasions, engaged in sexually explicit conduct or communication with a child or children (defined as persons aged under 16) and the magistrates are satisfied that the order is 'necessary to protect a child or children from harm from the defendant'.[24] Again, breach of the order is a criminal offence punishable by up to five years' imprisonment.

3. CONTROLLING THE RISK CREATED BY ORGANISED AND 'LIFESTYLE' CRIMINALS

Both the current Coalition government and the last Labour government have been concerned to develop a robust response to the problem of organised crime in the United Kingdom. In March 2004, the Labour government published a White Paper, *One Step Ahead: A 21st Century Strategy to Defeat Organised Crime*, which set out a changed approach.[25] The central idea in the White Paper was to move beyond merely increasing the chances of the major players in organised

22 In England and Wales and Northern Ireland, the change was effected by an amendment made by sections 24 and 116(1) of the Policing and Crime Act 2009. That change was brought into force on 1 April 2010 by The Policing and Crime Act 2009 (Commencement No. 4) Order 2010, S.I. 2010/507, art. 5(k). In Scotland, the change was made by sections 101(4) and 206(1) of the Criminal Justice and Licensing (Scotland) Act 2010 which was brought into force by S.S.I. 2010/413, art. 2.

23 See *Multi-Agency Public Protection Arrangements Annual Report 2012*/13, Ministry of Justice, 31 October 2013, p. 13, Table 6: 'Sexual Offences Prevention Orders (SOPOs), Notification Orders (NOs) and Foreign Travel Orders (FTOs) imposed by the courts. 2006/07–2012/13.'

24 See section 123(4)(b) of the Sexual Offences Act 2003.

25 Cm 6167. The White Paper was introduced by the then Home Secretary, David Blunkett. The Coalition Government has now announced its cross-Government strategy for tackling serious and organised crime (the announcement being timed to coincide with the launch of the new National Crime Agency (NCA)): see *Serious and Organised Crime Strategy*, Cm 87, 15 October 2013.

crime being apprehended and convicted to a broader strategy which sought to disrupt their activities at an earlier stage and hence sought to reduce the likelihood that the crimes would occur at all. To achieve this, the White Paper floated the idea of a new type of civil preventive order which could be used against those serious acquisitive criminals whom the authorities believed posed the most significant long term threat. It was envisaged that the orders would enable the financial affairs of these people to be monitored by the authorities. Every six months they could be required to file a detailed return which set out their income, assets and expenditure. They could also be obliged to report all the bank accounts and credit cards that they used and forbidden from carrying out financial transactions by any other route. One year after the publication of the White Paper, the Labour government brought in legislation to turn the idea of a new civil preventive order into a reality. Accordingly, the Serious Organised Crime and Police Act 2005 made provision for Financial Reporting Orders (FROs). These could require 'lifestyle' criminals to provide the relevant authorities with details of their income, assets and expenditure on a regular basis.

Then, in July 2006, the Labour government's strategy of continuing to bear down on organised crime was taken a stage further with the publication of a follow-up Green Paper entitled *New Powers Against Organised and Financial Crime.*[26] That document proposed the introduction of yet another civil preventive order, the Serious Crime Prevention Order (SCPO). The intention behind this order was to move beyond financial reporting and protect the public from known organised and 'lifestyle' criminals by allowing limitations to be imposed on both their travel and their communications. Even if these restrictions failed in their primary aim of deterring continuing criminal activity, the Green Paper argued that there would be other beneficial effects. The orders would force those subject to them to change their ways of working, thus leaving them open to easier law enforcement scrutiny. In the case of a 'stubborn refusal' to comply, they would render the person liable to breach proceedings. Additionally, the Green Paper observed that a 'unique feature' of the order was that it could be imposed not only on individuals but also on organisations. The Green Paper explained some of the circumstances in which these orders might be used: where, although there was a strong evidence of criminality, it was not sufficient for a prosecution; where there was sufficient evidence but a prosecution was deemed inappropriate on public interest grounds; where known criminal activity could not be prosecuted because, for example, it had taken place overseas; and where a prosecution was

26 Cm 6875, July 2006. See also *New Powers Against Organised and Financial Crime – A Summary of Responses*, November 2006; and *Powers Against Organised and Financial Crime – responses received to the consultation document*, 17 May 2007 (issued following an FOI request).

planned but additional measures were needed to prevent harm from occurring in the interim period. The following year saw the introduction of these SCPOs with the enactment by the Labour government of Part 1 of the Serious Crime Act 2007.

We will now consider both these orders, FROs and SCPOs, in more detail.

Financial Reporting Orders

The power to make an FRO was, as we have just seen, introduced by the Serious Organised Crime and Police Act 2005. Under section 76 of that Act, which came into effect as of 1 April 2006,[27] a court is able to make an FRO when sentencing or otherwise dealing with a person convicted of a specified offence if, but only if, that court is satisfied that the risk of the offender committing another specified offence is 'sufficiently high' to justify the order being made.[28] Section 76 also provides an exhaustive, but lengthy, list of the specified trigger offences. These now include certain offences under the Fraud Act 2006; conspiracy to defraud; false accounting; any of the so-called 'organised crime lifestyle offences' specified in Schedule 2 to the Proceeds of Crime Act 2002 (which include 'drug trafficking', 'money laundering' offences contrary to section 327 and 328 of the Proceeds of Crime Act 2002, 'directing terrorism', 'people trafficking', 'arms trafficking', 'counterfeiting', certain 'intellectual property offences', offences relating to pimping and brothels, and blackmail); certain offences under the Bribery Act 2010; 'money laundering offences' contrary to sections 93A, 93B, and 93C of the Criminal Justice Act 1988; offences under the Drug Trafficking Act 1994; offences under the Terrorism Act 2000; offences under section 329 of the Proceeds of Crime Act 2002 ('acquisition, use and possession of criminal property'); cheating in relation to the public revenue; fraudulent evasion of duty under the Customs and Excise Management Act 1979; offences relating to VAT under the Value Added Tax Act 1994; fraudulent evasion of income tax under the Taxes Management Act 1970; and tax credit fraud under the Tax Credits Act 2002.[29] If an FRO is made in a magistrates' court it must not exceed five years but if made by one of the higher courts the order may last for 15 years or, where the person is sentenced to imprisonment for life, 20 years. The extent of the obligations created by an FRO is explained in section 79. In essence, these require persons subject to the orders to make a report on their financial affairs.

---

27 See SI 2006/378.

28 Section 76 applies to England and Wales; sections 77 and 78 make similar provision in respect of Scotland and Northern Ireland.

29 Under section 76(4) the Secretary of State may, by order, add or remove offences from the list. Many new offences were added to the list of trigger offences by an order which took effect as of 4 May 2007: see The Serious Organised Crime and Police Act 2005 (Amendment of Section 76(3)) Order 2007 SI 2007/1392 3 May 2007.

Reports must include 'any specified documents' required by the court and must be made to a specified person, at specified periods, and in a specified format. Under section 79(10), failure to comply with the requirements of the order 'without reasonable excuse', or including false or misleading information in a report, is an offence which is liable on summary conviction in England and Wales to imprisonment for a period not exceeding 51 weeks.[30]

A number of cases on FROs have now reached the appellate courts but thus far no offender has been successful in their attempt to have an FRO quashed. The first case to come before the Court of Appeal was *R. v. Adams (Terence George)* in April 2008.[31] The FRO, which was to run for 10 years, had been made on 21 May 2007 in the Crown Court after Adams, who was aged 52, had pleaded guilty at an earlier hearing to one count of conspiracy to conceal the proceeds of criminal conduct contrary to section 93C of the Criminal Justice Act 1988, a 'money laundering' offence for which he had received a sentence of seven years' imprisonment.[32] In addition, a confiscation order for £750,000 had been imposed. The Court of Appeal described Adams as someone who had been for a significant period of time a highly successful career criminal and was well known as such. He had, the Court stated, amassed a considerable fortune from his criminal activities. This was expended on a lavish lifestyle which involved, according to the prosecution, 'significant numbers of first class flights to different destinations around the world, expensive jewellery, private education for his child, and the acquisition of antiques, works of art, and other property'. He had paid no income tax for a long period. The Court dismissed Adams' appeal against both the sentence of seven years' imprisonment and the FRO, which had required him to make reports on his financial position every six months while he remained in custody and every four months after his release.[33] Giving the judgment of the Court, Latham LJ, the Vice-President of the Court of Appeal (Criminal Division), held that the requirements of the FRO were 'proportionate to the problem presented by the fact that this Appellant had for so long manipulated his financial activities to hide the proceeds of crime'. Latham LJ also expressed the opinion

30 Or in Scotland a period not exceeding 12 months or in Northern Ireland a period not exceeding six months.

31 [2008] EWCA Crim 914, [2008] 4 All ER 574.

32 Originally this particular 'money laundering' offence was not included as a specified offence in section 76(3) of the Serious Organised Crime Police Act 2005 and so was not a trigger offence. It was, however, added by The Serious Organised Crime and Police Act 2005 (Amendment of Section 76(3)) Order 2007 SI 2007/1392 3 May 2007 which took effect as of 4 May 2007.

33 The focus in the White Paper was on the value an FRO might provide after an offender was released from custody. Indeed, it was considered that these obligations might usefully run for between five and 10 years after that happened. Under the terms of the Serious Organised Crime and Police Act 2005, however, (and as *Adams* illustrates) an FRO can run while a prison sentence is being served.

that an FRO was not a 'penalty' under the terms of article 7(1) of the European Convention on Human Rights. Rather, it was a 'preventive measure' which was designed to enable the courts to 'keep control over those in respect of whom there is the risk that they may indulge in criminal activity'.

Six months later, in December 2008, another major case involving an FRO came before the Court of Appeal in *R. v. Wright (Brian Brendon).*[34] This case again involved a career criminal who operated on 'an enormous scale'. Wright, who was 61, was described by the sentencing judge as 'a master criminal, manipulative, influential and powerful'. He had at various times been 'the controlling mind and financial backbone' behind an international drug smuggling ring operating in South America, particularly Columbia, through the Caribbean to the United Kingdom. The benefit Wright had obtained from his drug trafficking activity was colossal. It was assessed in confiscation proceedings as amounting to no less than £45 million. Wright was said to be a man who throughout his adult life had lived 'outside the system'. There was, it was observed, 'no or virtually no recorded trace of his existence'. He gave evidence in his trial, which lasted three months, that he owned no property, paid no tax, had no social security or National Insurance, no bank accounts, and no car registered in his name. Yet he maintained a lavish lifestyle which was supported almost entirely by cash. At the conclusion of his trial he was convicted of offences of importing and supplying cocaine over a period of about three years in the late 1990s and was sentenced to a total of 30 years' imprisonment. In view of the length of that sentence, it is not surprising that the risk which the FRO was designed to confront was money laundering rather than further drug offences. The FRO was made to last 10 years and Wright appealed against this order. That appeal was dismissed. Giving the judgment of the Court, Hughes LJ, as he then was, observed that it was a case in which the temptation on the defendant to deal with his enormous assets in a way which constituted an offence of money laundering was so great that 'any, even limited, prospect of restraint' by means of a Financial Reporting Order justifies that order being made'.[35]

A third case to have reached the Court of Appeal, *R. v. Bell (Kevin John) and Burgess (Carl Richard Ian)*, also involved men who were described by the Court

---

34 [2008] EWCA 3207.

35 Hughes LJ added that while 'the paradigm case' for an FRO was the defendant who had a history of unsatisfactory business or financial dealing and, at some stage in the future, was likely to be 'at large and engaged in business, commercial or financial activity which would otherwise be unsupervised or unmonitored', there was no doubt that the FRO also embraced persons such as Brian Wright. He also stressed that judges who were asked to make FROs 'should give careful consideration' to whether the order 'would actually achieve anything' and should 'look at alternative powers which are available to financial investigators if they would have much the same effect'.

of Appeal and the sentencing judge as 'career criminals of a very serious calibre'. They had been involved in a large-scale conspiracy to supply Class A drugs which had generated them more than £1 million. FROs were imposed by HH Judge Wide QC at the Crown Court in Northampton in July 2011. Bell's FRO was ordered to run for 12 years and Burgess' for the maximum period available of 15 years. These orders sat alongside long prison sentences which had been imposed on the two men following guilty pleas. Bell, aged 28, had received a sentence of nine years' imprisonment for conspiracy to supply cocaine, two sentences of nine years' imprisonment concurrent for two counts of offering to supply diamorphine, and a sentence of two-and-a-half years' imprisonment consecutive for conspiracy to handle stolen goods, making a total sentence of 11-and-a-half years' imprisonment. Burgess, aged 26, had received a sentence of 12 years' imprisonment for conspiracy to supply cocaine, two sentences of 18 months' imprisonment consecutive for two counts of delivering a counterfeit currency note with intent (which were ordered to run concurrent with each other but consecutive to the 12-year sentence), and a consecutive sentence of 18 months' imprisonment for handling stolen goods, making a total sentence of 15 years' imprisonment. Both men appealed against their FROs, arguing that they should not have been made in the circumstances of their cases. The Court of Appeal dismissed their appeals but did agree to reduce the duration of the FRO that had been imposed in Burgess' case from the maximum period of 15 years to 12 years.[36]

That outcome can be compared with *R. v. Baybasin and others* which also involved a very substantial conspiracy to import cocaine and other Class A drugs.[37] There the Court of Appeal (in a judgment given by Lord Judge CJ) refused one of the appellants, Anthony Geraghty, leave to appeal against a 15-year FRO which had been imposed alongside a 20-year prison sentence for his role in the conspiracy, a conspiracy which was described as involving 'highly organised drug trafficking on a vast scale', which had been planned and executed for a considerable time. Geraghty, who was 43, argued that an FRO for the maximum period of 15 years was 'manifestly excessive'. The Court of Appeal took a different view. Given the risk of future offending that Geraghty presented,

---

36 See *R. v. Bell (Kevin John) and Burgess (Carl)* [2011] EWCA Crim 2728, [2012] 2 Cr App R (S) 5. The Court of Appeal (*per* Kenneth Parker J) noted that the sentencing judge had, 'on relevant and cogent material', concluded that both Bell and Burgess 'were career criminals of a very serious calibre' who had been 'able to conceal the proceeds of their criminal activities effectively and on a substantial scale'. Both were regarded as at high risk of committing further offences on release. The Court of Appeal agreed that there was 'no good reason in their cases to believe … that any licence conditions would effectively, in the circumstances, either eliminate or reduce very substantially the risk of such offending'. In confiscation proceedings, it was concluded that Carl Richard Ian Burgess had benefited from the crimes in the amount of £777,193 and Kevin John Bell had benefited in the amount of £378,695.

37 [2013] EWCA Crim 2357.

it concluded that the order was necessary, proportionate and of the appropriate length. It did not impose any particularly onerous demands and its duration took account of the fact that the appellant would be in prison for some time and that important parts of the order would not 'effectively bite' until he was released.[38]

Serious Crime Prevention Orders

The aim of the SCPO, which draws its inspiration from the introduction of provisions relating to Civil Racketeer Influenced and Corrupt Organisations (Civil RICO) in the United States of America and took effect as of 6 April 2008,[39] is to render it much more difficult for serious criminals to operate by imposing conditions on them. As with the other orders discussed above, SCPOs are designed to be preventive not punitive. Furthermore, it is a requirement of their imposition that the conditions they contain are tailored to, and

---

38 For other appellate cases on FROs, see (i) *R. v. Bagnall and another* [2012] EWCA Crim 677, [2012] All ER (D) 98, [2013] 1 WLR 204. This was an appeal against an FRO imposed on Bagnall, a wealthy businessman who claimed he had made his money from the wholesale distribution of mobile telephones. He had been convicted of a money laundering offence contrary to section 328 of the Proceeds of Crime Act 2002 (entering into or becoming concerned in an arrangement involving criminal property) after he was found in possession of a bag containing £99,200 in Bank of England notes. For that offence, he was sentenced in March 2007 to 15 months' imprisonment by HH Judge Atherton at the Crown Court in Manchester. Three years' later, in February 2010, after a process described by the Court of Appeal as 'tortuous and lengthy', the same judge made a confiscation order against Bagnall for £1,818,619.97 and an FRO. The appeal against the order was dismissed by the Court of Appeal. (ii) *R. v. Mullen (Kenneth Ross), Davison (Adrian), and Bingham (Andrew)* [2012] EWCA Crim 606. This case involved what are known as 'boiler room frauds' (so-called because of the pressure put on victims) where the victims, often retired people, were persuaded to buy either shares in companies that did not exist or worthless shares in companies that did exist. All received prison sentences and four of those convicted for participating in this fraud also received FROs, two of which were ordered to run for 15 years, one for seven years, and one for five years. Permission to appeal requested by Davison and Bingham, who were subject to the two 15-year FROs, was refused by the Court of Appeal. (iii) *R. v. Peacock (Michael)* [2011] EWCA Crim 844. This was an appeal against a 15-year FRO imposed by HH Judge Brown at the Crown Court in Preston on 20 October 2010 on Peacock, a 45-year-old man who despite not being a qualified accountant had run an accountancy business and had become involved in a money laundering operation for a brothel in Preston called Brazilia. He was sentenced to a total of four years three months' imprisonment for a number of offences. Leave to appeal against the sentence and the FRO was refused. (iv) *R. v. Davies (Jonathan Robert)* [2010] EWCA 2720. In this case, a 14-year FRO was imposed on Davies who was involved in a conspiracy to supply heroin, controlling and directing the movements of others. He was convicted on one count of conspiracy to supply a class A drug (diamorphine) and was sentenced on 17 August 2009 by HH Judge Gilmour at the Crown Court in Liverpool to 17 years' imprisonment and made subject to the FRO. His appeal against the sentence and the FRO was dismissed by the Court of Appeal. Judge Rook QC, sitting as a judge of the Court of Appeal, held the sentencing judge was 'entitled to conclude', given the appellants' 'history of drugs and financial dealings', that the statutory requirements for the making of the FRO were made out.

39 USC §1964.

proportionate to, the end of preventing harm. SCPOs are limited to adults.[40] They cannot be imposed on persons who are aged less than 18 years. The period across which an order can be in force is limited to five years. Like many of the other orders, the maximum penalty for breach of a SCPO is five years' imprisonment.[41]

Section 19 of the Serious Crime Act 2007 Act gives the Crown Court in England and Wales the power to impose a SCPO on an individual, following his or her conviction for a serious offence, where the court has reasonable grounds to believe that the imposition of the order would protect the public 'by preventing, restricting or disrupting involvement by the person in serious crime in England and Wales'.[42] SCPOs in England and Wales can only be made on an application by the Director of Public Prosecutions, the Director of Revenue and Customs Prosecutions or the Director of the Serious Fraud Office.[43] They cannot be made by magistrates' courts. The definition of 'involvement in serious crime in England and Wales' is provided by section 2 of the 2007 Act. It refers to a person who has committed an offence which is 'specified' (or falls within a description specified) in Part 1 of Schedule 1 to the Act *or* is one which, in the particular circumstances of the case, the court considers to be sufficiently serious to be treated for the purposes of the application or matter 'as if it were so specified'. The latter alternative gives the court the power to extend the reach of the list of trigger offences for a SCPO where it deems that appropriate. The list of 'specified' offences is long. It includes offences relating to 'drug trafficking', 'people trafficking', 'arms trafficking', 'prostitution and child sex', 'armed robbery', 'money laundering' (contrary to section 327 and 328 of the Proceeds of Crime Act 2002), 'fraud', the 'public revenue', 'corruption and bribery', 'counterfeiting', 'blackmail', 'intellectual property', and the 'environment'. The list has a certain degree of overlap with the specified offences which can trigger an FRO.

Where they are available, SCPOs – unlike, for example, SOPOs – can be used to impose positive as well as negative obligations on an offender. Section 5 offers examples of the types of 'prohibitions, restrictions or requirements' that may be imposed. But it does not limit the orders to these examples. A list of some of the persons subject to SCPOs as of May 2013 is included in the National Crime Agency's website. The names of more than 80 persons are given there, along with, *inter alia*, their dates of birth, offences committed, order start dates, the duration

[40] See section 6 of the Serious Crime Act 2007.
[41] See section 25(2).
[42] The High Court is given the power to make these orders by section 1.
[43] See section 8.

and terms of the order, and whether the person is in prison or has been released from custody.[44]

As with the other orders, a number of cases where SCPOs have been imposed has now reached the Court of Appeal. These give a flavour of the issues that arise, the sorts of circumstances in which these orders may be made, and the types of conditions – positive and negative – that the Crown Court may include within them. Two cases, both involving frauds, will be offered as examples.

R. v. Batchelor (Andrew John)[45]

In this case Batchelor, who was a 'professional criminal', appealed against a five-year SCPO and sentences of five years' imprisonment which had been passed at the same time for 29 counts of offences of fraudulent trading, obtaining property by deception, and fraud by false representation. These offences involved jewellery scams that had been perpetrated by Batchelor. His crimes involved an abuse of the trust that had been placed in him by his victims. The SCPO contained six detailed clauses which, inter alia, prohibited Batchelor from working within a business engaged in the jewellery trade, being in possession of any article for use in the jewellery trade, or entering a pawnbroker's establishment in England and Wales without leave of the court. On appeal, the Court of Appeal upheld both the sentences and the SCPO. The judgment of the Court was given by the Lord Chief Justice, Lord Judge, who said it was clear that SCPOs were not restricted to violent or sexual offences. They could also apply to crimes of dishonesty. The test for their application was also clear: 'The single test is whether there are reasonable grounds to believe that the order would prevent, restrict or disrupt the applicant's involvement in serious crime'. In the circumstances, Lord Judge concluded that it was 'entirely reasonable and utterly proportionate' for the sentencing judge to have imposed a SCPO to disrupt the possibility of Batchelor committing these kinds of offences again.

R. v. Deeds (John)[46]

This case also involved an appeal against the making of a SCPO. Deeds had been convicted, following a guilty plea, of 12 offences of fraud, two offences of doing an act tending and intended to pervert the course of justice, and one

44 Details are also given of persons subject to FROs and Travel Restriction Orders. See *Publication of Ancillary Orders: May 2013*. The list, though, is not a complete list of those subject to any of these orders. Of the 88 SCPOs listed there, one is for two years, two are for three years, one is four years, 83 are for five years, and one (apparently in excess of jurisdiction) for 10 years.

45 [2010] EWCA Crim 1025.

46 [2013] EWCA Crim 1624.

offence of dishonestly obtaining wrongful credit. He was sentenced to a total of 40 months' imprisonment and a SCPO was made. Deeds was 43 years old and had appeared before the courts on 13 previous occasions for some 60 different offences, all of which were offences of dishonesty and fraud and the majority of which were offences of obtaining property by deception. He had served several previous prison sentences, the longest being three years. The current offending had involved obtaining high value items, mainly computers, by deception using false names; obtaining fuel cards from different suppliers by deception, thereby enabling Deeds to obtain fuel and other items; and, finally, what were described by the sentencing judge as a series of 'ingenious' frauds in which 'streamline' facilities were obtained in different names and used to secure bogus credits for transactions which never took place. The total value of the frauds was said to be in excess of £288,000. The SCPO contained four clauses and was timed to last for five years from the day upon which Deeds was ultimately released from prison. The restrictions in the SCPO included a prohibition on his using or being known by any other name than John Deeds without his first notifying the police; a prohibition on his making any application for credit without his first notifying the police; and a prohibition on his operating a bank account or building society account without his first notifying the police. While agreeing to a slight change of wording in one of the clauses, the Court of Appeal rejected the suggestion made by Deeds' counsel that the order was unnecessary or disproportionate or oppressive. Nor was the Court impressed by the argument that the order would unduly restrict Deeds' freedom. Roderick Evans J, who gave the judgment of the Court, said there was 'ample evidence, perhaps one can say overwhelming evidence' of the need for a SCPO in the circumstances of the case.

4. CONTROLLING THE RISK OF VIOLENT OFFENDING

In addition to all the preceding orders, the last Labour government also established a parallel regime for violent crime: Violent Offender Orders (VOOs). These orders were the result of a joint initiative between the Home Office and the Association of Chief Police Officers. They were created with the enactment of Part 7 of the Criminal Justice and Immigration Act 2008 and their declared purpose is to protect the public from the risk of serious violent harm caused by the offender. They seek to achieve this by targeting offenders who continue to pose a risk of committing a serious violent offence after they have been released from prison or once their licence has expired.

Violent Offender Orders

VOOs, which took effect from 3 August 2009, have the same basic structure as SOPOs. But there are also some important differences. A qualifying offender is a person over 18 who has committed a specified offence and received a sentence of at least 12 months. VOOs are not available for persons under the age of 18. Applications for a VOO may be made by a Chief Officer of Police to a magistrates' court but, unlike SOPOs, VOOs are not available on conviction. Nor, in a further marked contrast to SOPOs, can VOOs come into force while an offender is in prison or subject to a supervision order (or a hospital order) or while the offender is subject to statutory licence conditions made in relation to any offence.[47] A magistrates' court may impose a VOO if it concludes that the offender has acted in such a way as to make an order necessary for the purpose of protecting the public from the risk of serious violent harm.[48] Serious violent harm is defined as serious physical or psychological harm caused by the offender committing one of a limited list of serious offences: manslaughter, soliciting murder, an offence under section 18 of the Offences Against the Person Act 1861 (for example, wounding with intent to cause grievous bodily harm), an offence under section 20 of the Offences Against the Persons Act (for example, malicious wounding), attempted murder, or conspiracy to commit murder. The restrictions that can be included in a VOO are set out in section 102 of the Criminal Justice and Immigration Act 2008. This list is exhaustive. It allows VOOs to include prohibitions from specified areas or places, prohibitions from attending specific events, and prohibitions from having any or particular kinds of conduct with specified individuals. As a result of this section, the limitations that can be included in a VOO are considerably more constrained than for SOPOs or SCPOs.[49] Furthermore, unlike SOPOs, which have a five-year minimum period and can last indefinitely, VOOs cannot run for less than two years or last longer than five years. Breach of a VOO, like breach of a SOPO or a SCPO, can lead to a maximum penalty of five years' imprisonment.

From what has been said above, it can be seen that the VOO is a much more restricted order than the SOPO. Its focus is on the top end of seriousness, 'the critical few' as they are sometimes called. For this reason, the Home Office estimated that only about 125 VOOs would be made annually.[50] The introduction

47 An example of a SCPO imposed on a prisoner before his or her release from custody is that imposed on two large-scale drug smugglers, Cavan Hanna and James Hanna, who had five-year restrictions placed upon them which required notification of prison visitors and imposed restrictions on the use by them of the prison telephone system.

48 See section 101(3)(b) of the Criminal Justice and Immigration Act 2008.

49 Sections 107 to 112 of the Criminal Justice and Immigration Act 2008 also impose a set of notification requirements on offenders who are subject to a VOO.

50 See *The Telegraph*, 5 August 2009.

of VOOs had the strong support of the police and was also welcomed by the probation service.[51] Nonetheless, VOOs have been criticised by Frances Crook, the Chief Executive of the Howard League for Penal Reform, as an 'imprecation not a solution'.[52]

Examples of VOOs that have been imposed thus far include an order imposed by Leicester magistrates' court on a 43-year-old man, Ricky Michael Simon, in February 2010. Simon was said to have a '20-year history of violence' and his VOO prohibited him from entering a large area of the City of Leicester from 6.00 pm to 6.00 am on Mondays to Fridays and at any time on Saturdays and Sundays.[53] A second example is a VOO which was imposed on Sean Aslam, a 38-year-old man from Stoke-on-Trent, in April 2013. Aslam's previous record included a sentence of eight years' imprisonment in 2005 for an offence under section 18 of the Offences Against the Person Act 1861 (wounding with intent to cause grievous bodily harm) which occurred after he picked up a prostitute in his car and then later slashed her throat. In the light of this offence, the VOO banned Aslam from specified parts of the red-light district of the city. Within weeks, however, he was reported as having breached the order by entering the area from which he was prohibited. He was spotted in a pub in the restricted area by an off-duty police officer. For this breach, he was sentenced by the Crown Court at Stoke-on-Trent to five months imprisonment.[54]

5. SENTENCES FOR BREACH OF PREVENTIVE ORDERS

Not only can the terms of preventive orders vary considerably, so can the ways in which these terms are breached. This makes the task of the sentencing court demanding, particularly as there are 'no ready guidelines' available to them.[55]

---

51 In August 2009, the Vice Chair of the Probation Chiefs Association, Steve Collett, welcomed their introduction, observing that they would provide a useful additional tool to protect the public from 'a very small group of highly dangerous offenders': see his appearance on BBC 1 Breakfast TV on 5 August 2009.

52 See the entry on her blog for 5 August 2009.

53 See *Leicester Mercury*, 27 February 2010. The newspaper report stated that Simon was 'first person in Leicestershire' to have been made subject to a VOO. As yet there seem to be no decided appellate cases on VOOs which is why these examples are taken from press reports. The first VOO to have been ordered in the West Midlands was apparently imposed on a 22-year-old man from Birmingham in April 2010; he was given a two-year order: see *Birmingham Mail*, 19 April 2010, 'Yob hit with violent offenders order'.

54 See *The Sentinel*, 16 April 2013. The police in Stoke-on-Trent indicated to the newspaper that Aslam's VOO would be 'proactively policed' when he was released from that sentence.

55 *Per* Aikens LJ in *R. v. Stephen Christopher Bell* [2012] EWCA Crim 2362. But see, for example, *R. v. Fenton* [2007] 1 Cr App R (S) 97, *per* Leveson J (as he then was): 'If the breach does not involve any real or obvious risk to that section of the public who it is intended should be

Sentencing judges in these cases must take a forward looking, crime prevention perspective as well as a backward looking, retributive perspective. They must, in other words, decide on the appropriate punishment for breaking the court order (which could incorporate a deterrent element) and decide on the preventive element that might need to be imposed to protect the public from the sort of behaviour which had led to the imposition of the order in the first place.[56] The circumstances of the breach will have a bearing on an assessment of the nature and degree of the risk posed by it and hence will be a significant factor in determining the appropriate sentence. The court will also take into account the objective of ensuring and enforcing future compliance with the terms of the order. The ultimate aim for the court will always be public protection.[57]

A review of the cases on sentencing for breach to have reached the Court of Appeal reveals just how difficult these cases can be. The following provide examples of some of the complexities that can arise. The first, *R. v. Bell (Stephen Christopher)*,[58] concerns a SOPO; the second and third cases, *R. v. Koli (Rajkumar Dattarem)*[59] and *R. v. Pitt (Michael Andrew)*[60], both involve SCPOs.

R. v. Bell (Stephen Christopher)

This was an appeal against two three-year concurrent sentences of imprisonment which were passed on a 31-year-old man, Stephen Bell, for breach of his SOPO. The SOPO had been imposed in December 2010 following Bell's conviction for four sexual offences: two of indecent exposure and two of inciting a female child under the age of 16 to engage in sexual activity not involving penetration. For these offences, Bell received a community order with a three-year supervision requirement. He was also given a SOPO which was to last indefinitely or until further order. The SOPO included prohibitions on speaking to, approaching, communicating or attempting to communicate, directly or indirectly, with any

---

protected by the Order, a community penalty which further assists the offender to live within the terms of the Order may well be appropriate although repeated breaches will necessarily involve a custodial sentence if only to demonstrate that the orders of the court are not to be ignored and cannot be broken with impunity. Any breach which does create a real and obvious risk to those whom the Order is intended to protect must inevitably be treated more seriously and multiple or repeated breaches may well justify sentences that might otherwise have been considered far higher than any specific criminal offence or misconduct would have attracted'.

56 See *R. (ex parte McCann) v. Manchester Crown Court* [2003] 1 Cr App R (S) 11 (ASBO case). For a SOPO case in Scotland which refers to this reasoning, see *Scottish Criminal Case Review Commission in Thomas Hendry Shannon Appellant against Her Majesty's Advocate Respondent* [2011] HCJAC 12.

57 See *Scottish Criminal Case Review Commission in Thomas Hendry Shannon Appellant against Her Majesty's Advocate Respondent* [2011] HCJAC 12.

58 [2012] EWCA Crim 2362.

59 [2012] EWCA Crim 1869, [2013] 1 Cr App Rep (S) 39, [2012] All ER (D) 14.

60 [2013] EWCA Crim 1846.

female under the age of 16 years. It also included a prohibition on entering any internet site for the purpose of viewing any female child under the age of 16 years.

Within a year, Bell had breached the terms of the order by starting an internet conversation, through a chat room called 'TeenChat', with a police officer who was acting covertly and posing as a 13-year-old girl. Bell used the name 'Hannah Bell' and purported to be a single mother aged 14. Bell was under the impression that he was having a conversation with a girl called 'Amy'. Bell asked 'Amy' if she was 'into spanking'. The conversation later progressed into Windows Live Messenger and in this phase Bell claimed to be a 44-year-old single mother who was involved in an 'all mother spanking club' where girls were subjected to spanking and physical abuse with a number of different implements. At this point, Bell distributed several images online, one of which was an indecent image of a female child aged approximately 11 to 13 who was posing naked from the thigh upwards on a bed. Subsequently, Bell was arrested by the police in February 2012. His home was searched and his computer was examined. He was interviewed by the police and admitted to having sexual fantasies about spanking and communicating with children under the age of 16. After guilty pleas, he was convicted on two counts of breaching his SOPO and one count of distributing an indecent photograph of a child. He received concurrent sentences of three years' imprisonment for the SOPO breaches and a concurrent two-month sentence for the offence involving the indecent photograph. The sentencing judge, HHJ Richardson QC at the Crown Court in Hull, concluded that 'there was a serious risk that [he] would indulge in sexual crimes in the future unless restrained and that the protection of the public must be the highest priority'.[61] He had three previous convictions for indecent assault on females for which he had received a conditional discharge in February 1999. He also had a long-standing sexual preoccupation with spanking and with the naked images of female children and tended to minimise his offending and displayed little victim empathy. In light of this, Judge Richardson concluded that the sentence for the breach of the SOPO must be 'a severe one'. He further noted that there had been 'a flagrant defiance of a court order'. He was of the opinion that Bell would 'almost certainly' have carried matters through if he had been talking to someone other than a police officer. Bell's pre-sentence report had concluded that he presented a high risk of further sexual offending and of causing serious harm to the public. It also said he had little motivation to stop offending.

Bell appealed against his sentence, arguing that it was manifestly excessive given that the breaches were not of the most serious kind and did not involve any actual physical contact with any child. The Court of Appeal (*per* Lord Justice

---

[61] HH Judge Richardson had also been the judge who had imposed the SOPO at the Crown Court at Great Grimsby in December 2010.

Aikens) emphasised that SOPOs were court orders which 'must be obeyed'. Any serious breach was therefore 'likely to attract a substantial custodial sentence'. There were three reasons for that: first, 'by the very nature of the order', a sexual crime had already been committed, second, the SOPO had been 'held by the court to be a necessity', and, third, it had been 'flouted by the offender'. Nonetheless, the Court of Appeal recognised that in Bell's case the two breaches of the SOPO had been part of the same incident; that these were the first breach by Bell of that SOPO; and that Bell had pleaded guilty. The Court of Appeal therefore halved the custodial terms that had been imposed at first instance, replacing the two concurrent sentences of three years' imprisonment with two concurrent sentences of 18 months' imprisonment.

R. v. Koli (Rajkumar Dattarem)

This case involved two offences of failure to comply with a SCPO. It was described by the Court of Appeal as 'ground-breaking' since no prosecution for breaches of a SCPO had come to attention of the Court before. The appellant, Koli, was 36. He drove a Ferrari with personalised number plates and tried to make out that he was a successful businessman. Following not guilty pleas and a trial, he was sentenced to 24 months' imprisonment for two breaches of his SCPO. He was acquitted by the jury of one further breach. The SCPO had been imposed in June 2009 by the Crown Court at Maidstone alongside a three-and-a-half year sentence for money laundering.[62] The terms of the SCPO, which was made to last for five years, required Koli to notify the Serious Organised Crime Agency (SOCA) of the possession, use or control by him of more than one mobile telephone, the possession, use or control of more than one computer, and the possession, use or control of more than one landline. The SCPO also included notification requirements relating to vehicles and the conditions under which they were held and notification requirements on the possession of cash. Koli's breaches related to his failure to notify SOCA of his possession of at least one mobile telephone handset and his use and possession without notification of a

62 See *R. v. Koli and another (Mee)* [2010] EWCA 715, [2010] All ER (D) 223. The sentence, which was imposed on 12 June 2009 following a guilty plea, was originally five years in length but was reduced to three-and-a-half years by the Court of Appeal. Koli pleaded guilty on re-arraignment to conspiracy to conceal, disguise, convert or transfer criminal property. At this point Koli had no previous convictions. The money laundering activity was on a large scale: about £5 million in cash was seized from various locations. See also *R. v. Koli (Raj)* [2012] EWCA Crim 555 which concerned an unsuccessful appeal against a confiscation order imposed under section 6 of the Proceeds of Crime Act 2002. In confiscation proceedings on 28 January 2011, Koli 'was found to have a criminal lifestyle' and was found 'to have benefited in the sum of £3,296,314.22 and the realisable assets were determined to be £1,600,000'. A confiscation order was made for the latter amount, payable within six months, with seven years' imprisonment consecutive to the substantive sentence in default of payment. *Koli v. Maidstone Crown Court* [2011] EWHC 2821. See also *The Independent*, 'How a black Ferrari snared the £1bn drug barons', Friday 12 June 2009.

Honda motor vehicle. There being no precedent in these cases, Moses LJ (giving the judgment of the Court of Appeal) set out the considerations which a sentencing judge ought to take into account when considering the gravity of breaches of SCPOs:

> "It must be borne in mind that Parliament has set a maximum of five years' imprisonment in respect of a breach of the order, but the court will have to take into account the lapse of time between the imposition of the original order and the date of the breach. It must take into account any history of non-compliance and the issue as to whether non-compliance has been repeated and has come in the face of warnings and requests for information. It must take into account whether the non-compliance was inadvertent or deliberate. It is of course of particular importance that the court should consider whether the breach was related to the commission of further serious offences and might lead to the conclusion that the failure to comply added to the risk that the particular subject of the order was likely to commit further offences. The court would also have to consider the harm caused by non-compliance for breach."

In the case itself, Moses J noted that most of the breaches had derived from Koli's failure to take the order seriously rather than in furtherance of new criminal activity. He therefore quashed the concurrent sentences of 24 months' imprisonment and substituted instead concurrent sentences of 12 months' imprisonment on each count.[63]

R. v. Pitt (Michael Andrew)

This was an appeal against two concurrent sentences of nine months' imprisonment which were passed in March 2013 at the Crown Court at Blackfriars by HH Judge Karsten QC. The sentences were imposed for two breaches of a SCPO and followed a guilty plea. The SCPO had been imposed on Pitt in September 2011 by the Crown Court at Hove where Pitt, also following a guilty plea, had received a total sentence of five years' imprisonment (subsequently reduced on appeal to four years' imprisonment by the Court of Appeal[64]) for three offences: being knowingly concerned in the fraudulent

---

63 See also *Koli v. Maidstone Crown Court* [2011] EWHC 2821 where Koli sought to challenge his SCPO and an FRO which had been imposed by HHJ Macdonald QC at Maidstone Crown Court on 28 January 2011. At the time of the case Koli had been released on licence and appeared in person. The Court of Appeal held that the case was 'completely hopeless' and 'totally devoid of merit'. The Court considered it an abuse of the process that it had been brought before the court.

64 See *R. v. Pitt (Michael)* [2012] EWCA Crim 583: the sentence of four year eight months' imprisonment was reduced to four years and the four-month sentence was ordered to run concurrently with that sentence. For another case involving Michael Andrew Pitt, this time for handling stolen goods (computers), see *R. v. Pitt* [1998] 2 Cr App Rep (S) 52, [1998] Crim LR 137. There Pitt was described by the Court of Appeal as 'a professional receiver' of stolen goods.

evasion of duty (four years eight months' imprisonment); making, adapting, supplying and offering to supply an article for use in fraud (no separate penalty); and controlling computer equipment and software for use in the course of or in connection with a fraud (a consecutive sentence of four months' imprisonment). That case involved the fraudulent evasion of what was estimated by the prosecution to be £546,000 of duty on the purchase of some 2.5 million cigarettes from duty free outlets located at airports throughout the United Kingdom. The offences had taken place between February 2009 and May 2010. There were seven other co-accused who either pleaded guilty or were convicted but Pitt was said to be 'the principal and the lynchpin of the fraud'.

Pitt's SCPO was ordered to run for a period of five years from his release from custody. It prohibited him from possessing a mobile phone without notification and without providing full details to the Crown. It also prohibited his presence at an airport, seaport or international rail terminal without giving seven days' written notice to the Management Unit of HM Revenue and Customs. Within six months of his release from custody in May 2012 he ignored these restrictions and went to easyJet's offices at Luton airport. His visit was motivated by a desire to seek out a particular security officer on the airline's staff to obtain that person's support in a further case that was running against him relating to the proceeds of his crimes. He was in an agitated state and during the visit revealed that he had a mobile telephone on his person, the details of which he had not notified to HM Revenue and Customs as he was required to do. As in the case of *R v Koli* above, there was no suggestion that his breaches had been motivated by an intention to commit further criminal offences.

Nonetheless, he was prosecuted and, in the proceedings in the Crown Court at Blackfriars leading up to the passing of sentence, HH Judge Karsten warned him, through his counsel, that he should hand in his telephone to Customs and Excise before leaving the court. The Judge indicated that there would be a short adjournment and if it was 'to influence [his] mind' in passing sentence for the breach, the phone would have to handed over before Pitt left the courtroom. It did not appear that it was. In passing concurrent sentences of nine months' imprisonment for each of the two breaches, Judge Karsten accepted the breaches had not been in furtherance of crime. He also made reference to the *Koli* decision in the Court of Appeal. At the same time, he emphasised the importance of Pitt's failure to comply given he had used very large numbers of mobile telephones for fraud in the past. He also emphasised the warning he had given to Pitt about handing over the phone and noted that Pitt had a long record of serious criminality and had been convicted for 44 offences on 25 different occasions, most of which had been for fraud or theft. Pitt appealed against these nine month sentences. His application was not successful. In refusing Pitt leave to appeal, the

Court of Appeal (*per* Irwin J) described HH Judge Karsten's approach to the sentence as 'impeccable'.

6. CONCLUSION

Each of the orders discussed in this chapter has the same broad three-stage structure: risky behaviour, followed by a formal legal warning, followed by the possibility of punishment if that legal warning is ignored. As a consequence, the orders straddle, in a somewhat uneasy fashion, the boundary between the civil and the criminal. Sometimes their imposition is limited to persons who have been convicted of a criminal offence. Sometimes, as we have seen, they are available for persons who have no criminal convictions of any kind. In each case, their goal is to reduce the risk of serious offences being committed in the future, whether sexual offending, violent offending, or offending committed by persons involved in serious organised criminality. They seek to achieve that in a way which is 'preventative' rather than 'punitive' in character[65] by imposing a series of legal requirements on those who are made subject to the order, usually (but not always) in the form of prohibitions. In so doing, they create what is, in effect, a new personalised criminal offence for the individual concerned. Furthermore, as we have seen, the implications for the individual of breaching the terms of that new criminal offence can be severe with many of the orders rendering the person liable to a sentence of up to five years' imprisonment.

Nonetheless, over the last 15 years, governments in the United Kingdom from both the left and the right have seen these orders as a key tool for enhancing public protection and all the indications are that their use is set to increase further. Building on the legacy created by the previous Labour government, the Coalition government's recently published cross-government strategy for tackling serious and organised crime, the release of which was timed to coincide with the launch of the new National Crime Agency (NCA), provides a clear indication of that. As part of its 'Prevent' strand, the document states that the Coalition wants to see 'wider use by the NCA and others of Serious Crime Prevention Orders (SCPOs)'.[66] There is also a promise that the Home Office 'will work with the NCA law enforcement leadership and the College of Policing to support law enforcement officers in more routinely seeking inunctions and ancillary orders to disrupt serious and organised crime'.[67]

---

65 See, for example, the speech of Lord Steyn in the House of Lords' decision in *R. (McCann and others) v. Crown Court at Manchester* [2003] 1 AC 787 at 805–806 and 808.

66 *Serious and Organised Crime Strategy*, Cm 8715, October 2013, para 1.19. The same is said about Travel Restriction Orders (TROs).

67 Para 5.37.

In addition, the Coalition has introduced late amendments to the Anti-social Behaviour, Crime and Policing Bill which is currently going through Parliament to open up yet further the courts' ability to impose restrictions on sex offenders, despite that fact that it acknowledges that the United Kingdom already has 'some of the toughest powers in the world to manage the risks posed by sex offenders'.[68] The amendments introduce changes to the system of civil orders contained in the Sexual Offences Act 2003. Their goal is to make these powers 'more flexible and effective';[69] 'to ensure that the balance is even more firmly in favour of protecting the vulnerable from the risk of sexual harm';[70] and 'to give enhanced protection to children and vulnerable adults, both in the UK and abroad'.[71] The Bill has already completed its passage through the House of Commons and at the time of writing is under consideration by the House of Lords.

Under the terms of the proposed amendments, SOPOs, FTOs and Risk of Sexual Harm Orders will be abolished. In their place two new orders will be created: a Sexual Harm Prevention Order (which replaces SOPOs and FTOs) and a Sexual Risk Order (which replaces the Risk of Sexual Harm Order). The Bill also opens up the grounds on which the two new orders can be imposed. Under the earlier legislation, SOPOs could be imposed where the risk posed by the defendant was to persons of any age but RSHOs were restricted to cases where the risk posed by the defendant was to children. Under the provisions of the new Bill, Sexual Risk Orders (SROs) will be able to be imposed to protect members of the public of any age if the potential victims are within the United Kingdom. The Bill will also extend the power to apply for an order from just the police to the new National Crime Agency (which was created to fight serious, organised and complex crime). It also widens the available prohibitions and allows both of the new orders to include a restriction on foreign travel thus rendering the FTO redundant.

Like SOPOs, Sexual Harm Prevention Orders (SHPOs) must last for a minimum of five years and will have no maximum duration. SROs, in contrast, will last a minimum of two years but again may last for life (although the travel restrictions if imposed can last no longer than five years but may be renewed). SROs, like RHSOs, will be able to be imposed on persons who have no criminal convictions so long as they are deemed to pose a risk of sexual harm. But there will no longer

68 HC Debs Col 473, 14 October 2013. *Per* the Minister, Damian Green.

69 *Anti-social Behaviour: Crime and Policing Bill Fact Sheet*: Overview of the Bill, Home Office, October 2013.

70 Damian Green, HC Debs Col 476, 14 October 2013. The Minister in the House of Lords, Lord Taylor of Holbeach, the Parliamentary Under-Secretary of State in the Home Office, explained the rationale for the amendments in this way: Part 9 of the Bill will 'seek to address serious weaknesses in the existing regime of civil preventative orders under the Sexual Offences Act 2003'. See HL Debs Col 1484, 29 October 2012.

71 HL Debs Col 1484, 29 October 2012.

be a requirement that the person have engaged on two separate occasions in the specified behaviour before the order can be imposed.[72] Lastly, the threshold for the imposition of the two new orders will be lowered. Previously, a SOPO and an RSHO could only be imposed if the order was considered to be necessary to protect potential victims from 'serious sexual harm'. Now, both the SHPO and the SRO will be able to be imposed where the order is necessary to prevent the risk of sexual harm. Nonetheless, it would appear that the magnitude of the risk must still be held to amount to 'a real, not remote, risk' of that harm occurring.

Finally, it is worth noting that, in addition to continued development of civil preventive orders in the United Kingdom, the model is being taken up in some other common law jurisdictions too. Thus in New Zealand the Public Safety (Public Protection Orders) Bill that is currently before Parliament incorporates a proposal for a new Public Protection Order (PPO). If enacted, this will create the power for the High Court to issue a PPO to allow very high risk offenders who have served their prison sentence to be kept in detention indefinitely. As Clause 4 of the Bill explains, the objective of the legislation is 'to protect members of the public from almost certain harm that would otherwise be inflicted by the commission of serious sexual or violent offences'. Both Clause 4 and Clause 5 make it clear that the measure is not designed to punish persons against whom an order is made; it will be a civil order. Nonetheless, it is a civil order with a very draconian edge, as it will authorise indefinite confinement without conviction.[73] There is also proposal for a new Child Harm Prevention Order (CHPO) in Part Two of the Vulnerable Children Bill which was given a first reading in the New Zealand Parliament on 17 September 2013. The Bill allows CHPOs to be made against persons who pose a high risk of offending against persons under the age of 18. The orders are described by the New Zealand government as allowing 'tough new restrictions on adults who present a high risk of going on to hurt more children'.[74] The proposed regime mirrors the fundamental building blocks of the SOPO regime in the United Kingdom although there are also many significant differences.

---

72 The criminal standard of proof will continue to apply but SROs will be made available both for those under 18 and those over 18.

73 See www.legislation.co.nz.

74 The government published a *White Paper for Vulnerable Children* in October 2012 which set out a 'programme of change' to provide vulnerable children 'with the protection and support they need'. This was preceded by a *Green Paper for Vulnerable Children* which was launched in July 2011. The government also published a *Children's Action Plan* (October 2012) which included a promise to introduce legislation by the end of 2013 to allow the Court to make Child Abuse Prevention Orders and by the end of 2014 to tackle and monitor persons subject to those orders through the 'Vulnerable Kids Information System' and by the end of 2019 to monitor and report on the impact of the new legislation. See also *Alternative Pre-Trial and Trial Processes: Possible Reforms*, New Zealand Law Commission, 2012, NZLC IP30, section 4F: 'Child Protection Orders'.

COMMUNITY MEASURES TO DEAL WITH HIGH RISK OFFENDERS AT THE PERIPHERY OF THE JUSTICE SYSTEM

Effi Lambropoulou*

1. INTRODUCTION: OFFENDER-RISK AND CONTEMPORARY WESTERN PENAL SYSTEMS

The present article is concerned with community-based prevention measures dealing with high risk crime groups, and persons in danger of displaying acutely antisocial behaviour and committing crimes due to their past offences and/or their personal experiences and social environment. It also examines the actual application of such measures, as well as the experience of their enforcement, their effectiveness, problems and the eventual perspectives arising from them.

The issue of how to protect the public from 'dangerous' offenders is clearly not a new one, and developments of the last decade bring to mind the relevant debate conducted in the 1970s and 1980s among criminologists and policy makers in many countries. At the same time, however, they highlight some of the major differences between then and now, as the general 'climate' of criminal justice and the ongoing discourse have a serious impact on decision making.[1]

The 1970s and 1980s sentencing reforms, including indeterminate prison sentences and long fixed-term sentences[2] to 'incapacitate' offenders judged to pose a risk of serious harm to the public, were resisted strongly and effectively by opponents, such as civil liberties groups, leading criminologists, criminal law professors and lawyers.[3] It was pointed out that the concept of 'dangerousness'

* Dr. E. Lambropoulou is a Professor of Criminology at the Department of Sociology, Panteion University of Social and Political Sciences, Athens, Greece. E-mail: elambro@panteion.gr.

1 H. Kemshall & M. Maguire, 'Public Protection, Partnership and Risk Penality: The Multi-Agency Risk Management of Sexual and Violent Offenders', 3 *Punishment & Society* 2 (2001), p. 237–264 (p. 240–241) (at: http://pun.sagepub.com/content/3/2/237). All internet sources are last visited in July 2013.

2 J. Floud & W. Young, *Dangerousness and Criminal Justice*, London: Heinemann, 1981.

3 *E.g.* L. Radzinowicz & R. Hood, 'A dangerous direction for sentencing reform', *Criminal Law Review* (December 1978), p. 713–724, according to Kemshall & Maguire, 2001, *op. cit.*, p. 240 (The article's abstract is available at: www.ncjrs.gov/App/publications/abstract.aspx?ID=55781).

is vague and subject to shifts of meaning, so that the numbers of people it is applied to can easily expand, and that laws allowing preventive detention on such grounds are potentially open to serious abuse. Some also argued that it is wrong in principle to punish people on the basis of what they might do in the future.[4] Others saw the unreliability of the 'science of prediction' as a major hindrance, regarding it as morally unacceptable basis for legislation or sentencing.[5]

However, since the 1980s objections arising from considerations of human rights and human dignity have had decreasing impact on legislators and policy makers. The number and severity of preventive measures against 'dangerous' offenders began to grow on the grounds of public protection and the common good. What was remarkable about the severity of sentences was the relatively small amount of argument among influential circles, including academics in many countries.

In parallel with these position changes towards longer or indeterminate prison terms for dangerous offenders, increasing attention has been paid to ways of monitoring and controlling their behaviour in the community – most commonly, to extend the incapacitative effect of imprisonment by lengthy periods of surveillance after release.

This trend in contemporary criminal justice discourses and the resulting legislative framework on regulating the behaviour of risk offenders reflects the central importance of risk within social and political theory in general.[6]

For criminologists, two linked claims tend to dominate the literature of the corresponding developments.[7] The first refers to the widespread acknowledgement of a fundamental failure of the modernist criminal justice and penal (or 'penal-welfare') system to deliver its implicit promises of transforming offenders and reducing crime.[8] This, as it is claimed, has undermined the credibility of penal experts (in particular, their capacity to 'change' offenders, rehabilitative ideal/ resocialization/ reintegration) and has opened the door to a new mode of penality. The second claim is that this new penality is characterized

4 A.E. Bottoms, 'Reflections on the Renaissance of Dangerousness', 16 *The Howard Journal of Criminal Justice* 2 (1977), p. 70–96; A. Bottoms & R. Brownsword, 'Dangerousness and rights', in: J.W. Hinton (ed.), *Dangerousness: problems of assessment and prediction,* London *et al.*: Allen & Unwin, 1983, p. 9–22.

5 Kemshall & Maguire, 2001, *op. cit.*; J.W. Hinton (ed.), *Dangerousness: problems of assessment and prediction*, London *et al.*: Allen & Unwin, 1983; J. Wolsfeld, *Gefährlichkeitsprognose bei Straftätern*, Norderstedt: Grin Verlag, 1994.

6 U. Beck, *Risikogesellschaft: auf dem Weg in eine andere Moderne* (1986), 21. Aufl., Frankfurt am Main: Suhrkamp, 2012; see also A. Giddens, *The Consequences of Modernity*, Cambridge: Polity Press, 1990/2007, and M. Douglas, *Risk and Blame*, London: Routledge, 1992.

7 Kemshall & Maguire, 2001, *op. cit.*, p. 243–247.

8 D. Garland, 'Penal Modernism and Postmodernism', in: T. Blomberg & S. Cohen (eds.), *Punishment and Social Control: Essays in Honor of Sheldon Messinger*, New York: Aldine de Gruyter, 1995, p. 181–210 (p. 193).

by a major shift from the emphasis laid on individual behaviour and the possibility of change, towards the management of risk distribution.[9]

A particular manifestation of this is the spread of 'actuarialism' (the mathematical calculation of levels of risk) and a consequent focus upon aggregate risk groups rather than individuals.[10] Risk management strategies are evident in various forms in several crime control approaches in many countries.[11] For example, in policing practice the 'reactive investigation of individual crimes' was replaced by a 'strategic, future-oriented and targeted approach to crime control',[12] in court decisions 'incapacitative sentencing' replaced rehabilitation, and probation service replaced 'normalization' of the offender with "classification systems for purposes of surveillance, confinement and control".[13] These approaches reflect wider changes in patterns of social regulation, whereby the production and exchange of risk knowledge is the key mechanism by which some groups control others.[14]

After all, it can plausibly be maintained that addressing offender-risk holds an important place among the rationales and legitimating principles of modern penal systems.[15] For the penal system, risk refers primarily to the likelihood of *reoffending by already convicted individuals.* Contemporary risk assessment and management procedures are directed, in the main, at people who have been convicted of serious violent or sexual offences. The catalyst for the expansion of such procedures was the issuing and implementation of legislation concerned with sex crimes against children (USA, UK), imposing various modes of registration and monitoring (*e.g.* a requirement on most convicted sex offenders to register their address with the local police).[16]

Many approaches to dealing with such risks have been developed. They include the maintenance of special databases of offenders, the regular classification of offenders into specific risk groups, the development,

---

9 N. Reichman, 'Managing Crime Risks: Toward an Insurance Based Model of Crime Control', 8 *Research in Law, Deviance and Social Control: A Research Annual* (1986), S. Spitzer (ed.), Greenwich, Conn. *et al.*: JAI Press, 1986, p. 151–172; see also J. Simon, 'The Ideological Effects of Actuarial Practices', 22 *Law and Society Review* 4 (1988), p. 771–800.

10 M. Feeley & J. Simon, 'The New Penology: Notes on The Emerging Strategy for Corrections', 30 *Criminology* 4 (1992), p. 449–474; M. Feeley & J. Simon, 'Actuarial Justice: The Emerging New Criminal Law', in: D. Nelken (ed.), *The Futures of Criminology*, London *et al.*: Sage, 1994, p. 173–201.

11 Kemshall & Maguire 2001, *op. cit.*, p. 244.

12 M. Maguire, 'Policing by risks and targets: Some dimensions and implications of intelligence-led crime control', 9 *Policing and Society* 4 (2000), p. 315–336 (p. 316).

13 K. Bullock, 'The Construction and Interpretation of Risk Management Technologies in Contemporary Probation Practice', 51 *British Journal of Criminology* 1 (2011), p. 120–135.

14 Kemshall & Maguire 2001, *op. cit.*, p. 244; J. Pratt, 'Dangerousness, Risk and Technologies of Power', 28 *Australian and New Zealand Journal of Criminology* 1 (1995), p. 3–31.

15 Kemshall & Maguire 2001, *op. cit.*, p. 241–242.

16 J. Plotnikoff & R. Wolfson, *Where Are They Now? An Evaluation of Sex Offender Registration in England and Wales*, K. Willis (ed.), London: Home Office, 2000, Policing and Reducing Crime Unit, RDSD. (at: http://library.npia.police.uk/docs/hopolicers/prs126.pdf).

implementation and monitoring of individual 'risk management plans', formal partnerships at a local level between police forces, probation services, social services and other agencies, protocols to permit the exchange of confidential information about individuals considered to be a threat to others, and the formation of civil partnerships (*e.g.* 'multiagency public protection panels') set up to monitor individual cases.[17]

The vast majority of non-residential programmes including prevention and support measures, which will be presented below, refer to high risk young offenders, and not to adults.

2. DIVERSION AND COMMUNITY-BASED INTERVENTIONS

Alternatives to formal court procedure targeting *high-risk young offenders* at the disposition stage, when custody would be the obvious next step in legal procedure, began to develop in English speaking countries in the 1990s.[18]

The main ideas were actually established on the basis of old findings indicating that community-based interventions were superior to residentially-based interventions in their ability to reduce offending. Incapacitation through custody may protect the public in the short term, but fails to do so in the long run. Community-based alternatives to custody can both protect the public in the short term and reduce recidivism in the long term. Nevertheless, it is not easy for members of the public and sentencing judges to be made aware and convinced of these findings.[19]

2.1. THE MULTISYSTEMIC THERAPY APPROACH/MST

Multisystemic therapy represents a holistic approach and was considered to be a viable alternative to custody for high-risk young offenders.[20] It adopts a *social-ecological approach to understanding anti-social behaviour.* Antisocial and

---

17 Kemshall & Maguire 2001, *op. cit.*, p. 238.

18 A.W. Leschied, *Multisystemic Therapy: Community-Based Treatment for High Risk Young Offenders, Rationale and Overview from the Randomized Clinical Trials in Canada*, UNAFEI Resource Material Series No. 59, Part II, Tokyo, Japan, October 2002, p. 54–82 (p. 61–67) (at: www.unafei.or.jp/english/pdf/RS_No59/No59_10VE_Leschied2.pdf).

19 P.J. Hofer, K.R. Blackwell, R.B. Ruback, 'Effect of the Federal Sentencing Guidelines on Interjudge Sentencing Disparity', 90 *Journal of Criminal Law and Criminology* 1 (1999), p. 239–30 (p. 250–254); P. Johnston, 'Blunkett Seeks Support for Sentencing Reform', *The Telegraph*, 30 August 2001 www.telegraph.co.uk/news/uknews/1338920/Blunkett-seeks-support-for-sentencing-reform.html); C.C. Spohn, *How Do Judges Decide? The Search for Fairness and Justice in Punishment*, 2nd edn, Los Angeles *et al.*: Sage, 2009, p. 105–122.

20 Leschied, 2002, *op. cit.*

delinquent behaviour is attributed not only to youth's personality (values and attitudes, social skills, organic factors, etc.) but also to his/her 'social ecology': the family, school, peer group and neighbourhood.

The MST process begins with the identification of the problem behaviours involving the whole family. The assessment process identifies firstly the *strengths* in the youth and his/her family, for example a trusting relationship with an extended family member or teacher. Secondly, it identifies such factors in the youth's social environment that support the *continuation of problem behaviours*, as well as factors that operate as obstacles to their elimination, for example, parental substance use, or a neighbourhood culture encouraging antisocial values, financial stresses experienced by the family, etc. By identifying the problems in relation with the broader systemic context, MST workers are defining both the targets of intervention and the indicators for the assessment of whether the measures undertaken have been effective.[21]

MST is designed to be an intense but short-term involvement that can result in the generalization of treatment gains over the long-term. An important goal in this process is to enable the parents or another caregiver to develop the necessary skills to solve the problems of their children and their own, rather than rely on professionals.[22]

Several randomized and quasi-experimental studies of MST have been carried out in the United States,[23] Canada[24] and New Zealand.[25] They found that MST has reduced rates of criminal activity (officially recorded and self-reported), institutionalization, and drug abuse. MST proved also to be successful at engaging and retaining families in treatment and encouraging completion of substance abuse programmes. Furthermore, it may improve family functioning and cohesion.

MST has been effective in inner city urban areas, among youths with serious criminal records, youths identified as at high risk to reoffend, and among economically marginal families and those with long histories of unsuccessful interventions.

A study by the Washington State Institute for Public Policy (1998)[26] rated MST as the most effective and cost-effective of the 16 programmes analysed.

---

21 Leschied, 2002, *op. cit.*, p. 65–66.

22 Leschied, 2002, *op. cit.*, p. 66.

23 Leschied, 2002, *op. cit.*, p. 67; S.W. Henggeler, 'Treating Serious Antisocial Behavior in Youth: The MST Approach', Washington, DC.: Office of Juvenile Justice and Delinquent Prevention (OJJDP), *Juvenile Justice Bulletin*, May 1997 (at: http://ncmhjj.com/resource_kit/pdfs/Treatment/References/TreatSerious.pdf).

24 A.W. Leschied & A. Cunningham, *Seeking Effective Interventions for Serious Young Offenders. Interim Results of a Four-Year Randomized Study of Multisystemic Therapy in Ontario*, Canada, 2002 (at: www.lfcc.on.ca/seeking.html).

25 See special paragraph below about 'Te Hurihanga', and at: www.centralhealth.co.nz/index.php/services/multi-systemic-therapy-services.html.

26 S. Aos, R. Barnoski & R. Lieb, *Watching the Bottom Line: Cost-Effective Interventions for Reducing Crime in Washington*, Olympia, WA: Washington State Institute for Public Policy, Evergreen State College, 1998 (at: www.wsipp.wa.gov/pub.asp?docid=98-01-1201); A.W.

Each programme followed youths until the age of 25. *None eliminated offending*, but 15 of the 16 programmes documented lower rates of recidivism among programme participants, when compared to control groups. Five of the 16 programmes reviewed did not reduce crime enough to pay for themselves and none generated the level of savings linked to the MST intervention.

Lately an MST programme has been applied in New Zealand. 'Te Hurihanga' *(The turning point)*[27] started in April 2007 and finished in June 2010. It was a nine- to eighteen-month therapeutic programme for young males (aged 14 to 16 years at entry) who had appeared before the courts and who lived within the Hamilton/Waikato region. The three-phase programme aimed to: reduce re-offending, hold young people accountable for their offending, and provide tailored, specialist support to young people and their families so they can make positive choices rather than continue on their current (offending) trajectories.

An evaluation that began in late June 2007 and was completed in July 2009 found positive intermediate outcomes for the youngsters and their families. The young people themselves and their families were generally confident about their futures. Finally, only eight of 23 young offenders who started the nine- to 18-month programme graduated; while five had pulled out entirely. The cost to date has been just over $5 million, while for each graduate was $630,000, as only eight had finished.[28] After all, and despite the praise by the government, the programme has been closed due to its high costs.

2.2. COMMUNITY INTERVENTIONS[29]

Another group of community measures also began to be applied in the late 1990s in the USA, targeting *Serious Violent Juvenile Offenders* (SVJ),[30] as well as

---

Leschied & A. Cunningham, 'Alternatives to Custody for High-Risk Young Offenders: The Multisystemic Therapy Approach', 6 *European Journal on Criminal Policy and Research* 4 (1998), p. 545–560 (p. 553).

27 J. Warren with L. Fraser, *Te Hurihanga Pilot: Evaluation Report*, Prepared for the Ministry of Justice, Centre for Research, Evaluation and Social Assessment (CRESA), Ministry of Justice, Wellington-New Zealand, October 2009 (at: www.justice.govt.nz/publications/global-publications/t/te-hurihanga-pilot-evaluation-report/documents/Te%20Hurihanga%20Pilot%20Evaluation%20Report.pdf).

28 *Otago Daily Times*, Online News, 'Closure of Te Hurihanga programme defended', 2 February 2010 (at: www.odt.co.nz/news/politics/91549/closure-te-hurihanga-programme-defended).

29 OJJDP, *Juvenile Justice Bulletin*, School and Community Interventions to Prevent Serious and Violent Offending, NCJ 177624, Community Interventions, October 1999 (at: www.ncjrs.gov/html/ojjdp/jjbul9910-1/contents.html).

30 SVJ offender is different from the typical juvenile involved in delinquent conduct. The majority of SVJ offenders tend to have multiple problems such as substance abuse and mental health difficulties in addition to truancy, suspension, expulsion, and dropping out of school. Furthermore, SVJ offenders are disproportionately victims of violence, see R. Loeber & D.P. Farrington (eds.), *Serious and Violent Juvenile Offenders*, OJJDP, U.S. Department of Justice, May 1998 (at: www.ojjdp.gov/jjbulletin/9805/contents.html).

juveniles at risk of drug use. Eight types of community interventions have been identified: citizen mobilization, situational prevention,[31] comprehensive community interventions,[32] mentoring,[33] afterschool recreation programmes,[34] policing strategies,[35] regulatory interventions (legislation and policy change), and media interventions.[36]

The eight types of community-wide interventions focused on several risk factors, including easy access to firearms and drugs (regulatory intervention),[37] community disorganization,[38] and community norms or attitudes favouring antisocial behaviour.[39] The interventions also focused on such protective factors as social bonding and clear community norms against antisocial behaviour. According to the studies and evaluations of these interventions, prevention strategies that cross multiple domains (comprehensive community interventions) and that are mutually reinforcing (regulatory interventions: legislation and policy change) and maintained for several years (after-school recreation programs) produced the greatest impact.

---

31 R.V. Clarke, 'Situational crime prevention: Its Theoretical Basis and Practical Scope', in: M. Tonry & N. Morris (eds.), *Crime and Justice*, vol. 4, Chicago, IL: University of Chicago Press, 1983, p. 225–256 (at: www.jstor.org/stable/pdfplus/1147510.pdf).

32 C.A. Johnson *et al.*, 'Relative Effectiveness of Comprehensive Community Programming for Drug Abuse Prevention with High-Risk and Low-Risk Adolescents', 58 *Journal of Consulting and Clinical Psychology* 4 (1990), p. 447–456 (at: http://dx.doi.org/10.1037/0022-006X.58.4.447).

33 J.M. McPartland & S.M. Nettles, 'Using Community Adults as Advocates or Mentors for At-Risk Middle School Students: A Two-Year Evaluation of Project RAISE', 99 *American Journal of Education* 4 (1991), p. 568–586 (at: www.jstor.org/stable/i245216). Cf. OJJDP, Report to Congress: Juvenile Mentoring Program (JUMP), December 1998 (at: www.ncjrs.gov/pdffiles1/952872.pdf).

34 M.B. Jones & D.R. Offord, 'Reduction of Antisocial Behavior in Poor Children by Nonschool Skill-Development', 30 *Journal of Child Psychology and Psychiatry and Allied Disciplines* 5 (1989), p. 737–750 (at: www.ncjrs.gov/html/ojjdp/jjbul9910-1/ref.html).

35 A.M. Pate, W.G. Skogan, with the assistance of M.-A. Wycoff & S. Annan, *Reducing the Signs of Crime: The Newark Experience*, Technical report Washington, DC: Police Foundation, 12 July 1985 (at: www.ncjrs.gov/pdffiles1/Digitization/102307NCJRS.pdf); W.G. Skogan & M.A. Wycoff, 'Storefront Police Offices: The Houston Field Test', in: D. Rosenbaum (ed.), *Community Crime Prevention: Does It Work?*, Newbury Park, CA: Sage Publications, 1986, p. 179–199.

36 P. Palmgreen & L. Donohew, 'Effective Mass Media Strategies for Drug Abuse Prevention Campaigns', in: Z. Sloboda & W.J. Bukoski, *Handbook of Drug Abuse Prevention*, New York: Springer US, 2006, Part II p. 27–43 (at: http://link.springer.com/chapter/10.1007%2F0-387-35408-5_2).

37 D. McDowall, A.J. Lizotte & B. Wiersema, 'General Deterrence through Civilian Gun Ownership: An Evaluation of the Quasi-Experimental Evidence', 29 *Criminology* 4 (1991), p. 541–560. (at: http://onlinelibrary.wiley.com/journal/10.1111/%28ISSN%291745-9125/issues).

38 R.B. Taylor & A.V. Harrell, *Physical Environment and Crime*, A Final Summary Report Presented to the National Institute of Justice, U.S. Department of Justice, Office of Justice Programs, National Institute of Justice, January 1996, p. 5, 13 (www.ncjrs.gov/pdffiles/physenv.pdf).

39 D.D. Brewer, J.D. Hawkins, R.F. Catalano & H.J. Neckerman, 'Preventing Serious, Violent, and Chronic Juvenile Offending: A Review of Evaluations of Selected Strategies in Childhood, Adolescence, and the Community', in: J.C. Howell, B. Krisberg, J.D. Hawkins, & J.J. Wilson (eds.), *Sourcebook on Serious, Violent, and Chronic Juvenile Offenders*, Thousand Oaks, CA: Sage Publications, Inc., 1995, p. 61–141.

3. RISK GROUPS AND SUPPORT OR RESTORE SCHEMES IN THE COMMUNITY

3.1. VARIOUS TYPES OF ACTIVITIES OF HIGH RISK GROUPS AND MEASURES FOR THEIR CONTROL

3.1.1. Drunk driving and hard core drinking drivers

Traffic safety research during the last decade explores driving behaviours and quantifies the risk of crash involvement for certain groups of drivers. *'Hard Core Drinking Drivers'* are regarded as the main high risk group posing exceptionally high threats to public safety due to their frequency of drinking and driving and their high level of intoxication while driving.[40] HCDDs are also at high risk for re-arrest for driving while impaired and for future involvement in a drinking-related crash.

Studies have focused on exploring the effectiveness of *license suspension/revocation* (S/R),[41] and have demonstrated that this sanction is effective for reducing the subsequent accident and traffic conviction rate of high-risk drivers only over a short term.[42]

Other research discovered that the use of multiple interventions, *e.g.*, license suspension/revocation, treatment, and criminal sanctions, is more effective than using any single intervention (*Combination Principle*).[43]

---

40 H.M. Simpson *et al.*, 'Hard Core Drinking Drivers', 5 *Traffic Injury Prevention* 3 (2004), p. 261–269 (http://dx.doi.org/10.1080/15389580490465355); about a comparison among countries see B.M. Sweedler *et al.*, 'Worldwide Trends in Alcohol and Drug Impaired Driving', 5 *Traffic Injury Prevention* 3 (2004), p. 175–184 (at: http://dx.doi.org/10.1080/15389580490465175).

41 D.I. Smith & G.E. Maisey, *CR 94: Survey of Driving by Disqualified and Suspended Drivers in Western Australia*, Research and Analysis Report, Australian Government, The Department of Infrastructure and Transport Federal Office of Road Safety, Canberra, 1991 (at: www.infrastructure.gov.au/roads/safety/publications/1991/pdf/Surv_Unlic_1.pdf); H.-L. Chang, T.H. Woo, C.-M. Tseng & I.-Y. Tseng, 'Driving Behaviors and Accident Risk Under Lifetime License Revocation', 43 *Accident Analysis and Prevention* 4 (2011), p. 1385–1391 (p. 1391) (at: http://dx.doi.org/10.1016/j.aap.2011.02.013).

42 R.E. Mann *et al.*, 'Sentence Severity and the Drinking Driver: Relationships with Traffic Safety Outcome', 23 *Accident Analysis & Prevention* 6 (1991), p. 483–491 (http://dx.doi.org/10.1016/0001-4575(91)90014-V); S.S. Brar, *Estimation of Fatal Crash Rates for Suspended/Revoked and Unlicensed Drivers in California*, Final Report, California Department of Motor Vehicles, Research and Development Branch, Sacramento, CA, September 2012 (http://apps.dmv.ca.gov/about/profile/rd/r_d_report/Section_6/S6-238.pdf); see also H.-L. Chang, T.H. Woo & C.-M. Tseng, 'Is Rigorous Punishment Effective? A Case Study of Lifetime License Revocation in Taiwan', 38 *Accident Analysis and Prevention*, 2 (2006), p. 269–276 (at: http://dx.doi.org/10.1016/j.aap.2005.09.002).

43 W.L. White, *Management of the High Risk DUI Offender*, Springfield: Illinois, Department of Transportation, August 2003, p. 82–83 (at: http://cspl.uis.edu/illaps/Research/documents/Management_of_the_High_Risk_DUI_Offender2003.pdf); see also W.L. White & D.L. Gasperin, *Management of the High-Risk Offender, Recognizing, Managing and Containing*

It is also interesting that those who are 'forced' into addiction treatment have similar outcomes to those who 'volunteer' for treatment. Lack of motivation for change does not exclude long-term positive outcomes from treatment services (*Motivation/Behaviour Principle*).

Finally, it is maintained that many HCDDs change their behaviour when the punishment for continued drinking and driving is certain, severe, and quick (*Accountability Principle*).

3.1.2. Violent extremism

The need of identifying and addressing the factors that contribute to violent radicalisation is recognised as a central issue in the fight against terrorism in all relevant documents adopted by the European Union (EU), including the declarations following the Madrid and London attacks.

A study carried out by the Change Institute (2008) for the European Commission (Directorate General Justice, Freedom and Security) and based on extensive fieldwork and collection of new empirical data, lists several examples of best practice, focusing on cooperation between authorities and civil society with a view to the prevention of radicalisation.[44] The programmes involve a wide range of actors.

Belgium

Since 2007, the Catholic University of Leuven has been offering (every three years) a special diploma within the fields of Bachelor of Theology and Religious Studies, under the title 'Religious studies components: Introduction to Islam'.[45] According to Change Institute,[46] the course is intended to provide practical training and leadership development for individuals from Muslim communities, whilst also providing education for a range of individuals such as teachers, civil

---

the "Hard Core Drinking Driver", Coordinated by the Institute for Legal and Policy Studies, Center for State Policy and Leadership, University of Illinois at Springfield, 2006, p. 10–11. (at: http://cspl.uis.edu/ILLAPS/Research/documents/Recognizing_Managing_and_Containing_the_Hard_Core_Drinking_Driver.pdf).

44 (The) Change Institute, *Study on the Best Practices in Cooperation Between Authorities and Civil Society with a View to the Prevention and Response to Violent Radicalisation*, A Study Commissioned by DG JLS of the European Commission, July 2008 (at: http://ec.europa.eu/home-affairs/doc_centre/terrorism/docs/ecvr_best_practice_core_report_en.pdf).

45 (The) Katholieke Universiteit Leuven/KU Leuven 2012–13, Faculty of Theology and Religious Studies › Student Programmes and Resources, Bachelor of Theology and Religious Studies – Bachelor of Arts (at: http://onderwijsaanbod.kuleuven.be/2012/opleidingen/e/SC_51016745.htm#bl=01,02). It is also included in other courses, such as the Study Abroad Programme in European Culture and Society (PECS), in Bachelor of Theology and Religious Studies (Abridged Programme), and the Bachelor of Philosophy (non philosophical electives). See also, KU Leuven, Theology@KULeuven – International newsletter for alumni, January 2009 (at: https://theo.kuleuven.be/apps/newsletter/view/1/).

46 The Change Institute, 2008, *op. cit.*, p. 52.

servants, police and security officials and other interested groups. Furthermore, it aims to foster cultural understanding and develop networks among the participants.

While the course has received support from the inspectors of Islamic teaching in Belgium, it has drawn some criticism from other members of the 'Muslim Executive', the official organisation representing Muslims in Belgium. However, it has been suggested that some of this criticism is also supported by resentment on the part of providers offering pre-existing rival courses.[47]

Denmark

A dialogue initiative between Danish Security and Intelligence Service with Imams in Denmark (2003) attempted to create a degree of mutual understanding and trust. According to the authors of the Report, it has not been possible to find detailed information on this project or to interview the Imams participating in this dialogue. This is because the activities carried out by the Intelligence Service are traditionally not brought to the knowledge of the public.[48]

France

The 'Muslim Scouts of France' is part of the world scouting movement and joined the Federation of French Scouting in 1994. It was set up in 1990 as a secular association of Muslim inspiration open to all faiths.

In Grenoble, an MSF branch was set up to focus on the district of la Villeneuve, a working class area predominantly populated by Algerian families. While not directly targeted at countering violent extremism, the scheme was set up by local residents in response to concerns about alienation amongst Algerian youth in the area and a lack of culturally sensitive activities being on offer to them.[49]

In particular, participants have highlighted the successful emphasis on education and the promotion of a range of political concerns of relevance to many youth – from both Muslim and non-Muslim backgrounds – that have contributed to rapid and discernible impacts on many alienated youth who had previously espoused radical views.[50]

Sweden

In December 2011 the Swedish government published an *Action plan against violence promoting extremism*.[51] Numerous measures are entailed in this effort,

---

47 The Change Institute, 2008, *op. cit.*, p. 52–55.
48 The Change Institute, 2008, *op. cit.*, p. 55–58.
49 The Change Institute, 2008, *op. cit.*, p. 59–67.
50 The Change Institute, 2008, *op. cit.*, p. 61.
51 (Swedish) Ministry of Justice, *Action Plan to Safeguard Democracy against Violence Promoting Extremism*, 8 December 2011, Government communication 2011/12:44,

such as strengthening awareness of democratic values (supporting civil society organisations and initiatives in the education system), preventing individuals from joining violent extremist groups and supporting individuals wishing to leave such groups, countering the breeding grounds for ideologically motivated violence. The first follow-up of the original Action Plan is going to be carried out in 2014.

Greece

Greece is not included in Change Institute's best practices, but was added by the author. It is the main EU entry point for undocumented immigrants coming from the Middle East and South Asia, but also still from Albania. Therefore, it could be used as a transit route, among others, for terrorists travelling to Europe and America. Since 2011, the local governments aiming to counter radicalization and violent extremism, established councils to facilitate immigrant integration, by fostering dialogue on issues such as discrimination, social benefits for immigrants, legalization, employment, and security ('immigrants' integration councils'; Law 3852/2010). The membership in them is drawn over two-thirds from representatives of the immigrant communities. Police officials met with representatives of the different immigrant communities to discuss ways to address discrimination and incidents of police abuse.[52] As the proceedings of the council in the city of Athens show, the role of the council is limited for the time being to promoting the economic and political benefits of the immigrant communities rather than their integration.[53]

For Greece, a key topic for systematic research should be the rise of terrorism during recent years (as well as the upturn of hooliganism) and the measures for its prevention and control, apart from law issuing and punishment. In particular, the prevention and monitoring of terrorism and vandalism is an important political and criminal justice issue, with the (private) media playing a catalytic role.

United States of America

US Countering Violent Extremism (CVE)[54] is a pillar of the US Administration's strategic approach to counterterrorism. Through a mix of local grants developed

---

Stockholm, 16 March 2012 (at: www.government.se/sb/d/13973/a/188700), (2012a, p. 36–48).

52 See U.S. Department of State, *Country Reports on Terrorism 2010*, Europe and Eurasia Overview, 18 August 2011 (at: www.state.gov/j/ct/rls/crt/2010/).

53 E. Lambropoulou, 'Illegal Markets in a Collapsing Economy', in: P. Saitta, J. Shapland & A. Verhage (eds.), *Getting by or Getting Rich? The Formal, Informal and Criminal Economy in a Globalized World*, The Hague: Eleven International, 2013, p. 61–93 (p. 66–67).
Cf. A. Khan, O. Uduku & C. Cripps, 'English Muslims and ghettoisation: Trends and consequences', 6 *Global Built Environment Review* 2 (2007), p. 52–66, Ghettoised perceptions versus mainstream constructions of English Muslims: The future of the multicultural built environment (at: www.edgehill.ac.uk/gber/pdf/vol6/issue2/Article5.pdf> Temporarily not available due to uploading their back catalogue, 30/07/2013).

54 U.S. Department of State, Bureau of Counterterrorism, Countering Violent Extremism (CVE) (at: www.state.gov/j/ct/programs/index.htm#CVE).

and managed by U.S. embassies and larger awards managed from Washington, the CVE programme pursues to provide positive alternatives to populations found to be most at-risk. Although this initiative started only in September 2011,[55] the USAID Lebanon programme,[56] which operates under the same logic, already begun in 2007.

The USAID/Office of Transition Initiatives (OTI) supports Lebanese organizations in offering high demand activities such as English language, information technology and vocational training, music, and theatre. USAID/OTI partners also support youth activism as a means for citizenship training. From 2007 until April 2012, 23,832 youth trained in civic participation and 237 social media sites promoting youth activism have been created. No further evaluation of the programme, which is planned to finish in 2013, appears to have been published yet.

3.1.3. Hooliganism[57]

Hooliganism is a violence-oriented subculture that mostly involves young males. Sport-related crime is regarded as displaying certain similarities with the violence perpetrated by extremist groups.[58] Cooperation among the relevant organisations on the central, regional and local level to control crime committed in relation to sport events, belongs to the main targets of several European governments.[59]

In some European countries it is believed that the prevention of football hooliganism requires the promotion of consciousness among youth and the strengthening of their ties with football clubs.[60] Football, in this sense, is viewed

55 (The) White House, *Executive Order 13584 --Developing an Integrated Strategic Counterterrorism Communications Initiative*, 9 September 2011 (at: www.whitehouse.gov/the-press-office/2011/09/09/executive-order-13584-developing-integrated-strategic-counterterrorism-c).

56 U.S. Agency for International Development/USAID, Fact Sheet, Office of Transition Initiatives/OTI Lebanon Project, April 2012 (at: http://transition.usaid.gov/lb/about_us/factsheets.html).

57 (Swedish) Ministry of Justice, Press Release: Government Communication, Action Plan to Safeguard Democracy against Violence Promoting Extremism, Stockholm, 9 December 2011 (at: www.government.se/sb/d/14233/a/182400); 2012a, *op. cit.*

58 (The) Swedish National Council for Crime Prevention (Brå) – Centre For Knowledge about Crime and Crime Prevention Measures, *Strategies against Football-Related Disorder*, English summary of Brå report No 2008: 20 (Swedish: Fotbollsrelaterade ordningsstörningar, Report nr 2008: 15), 2009 (at: www.bra.se/bra/bra-in-english/home/publications/archive/publications/2009–01–01-strategies-against-football-related-disorder.html); (Swedish) Ministry of Justice, 2012a, *op. cit.*, p. 36.

59 (Swedish) Ministry of Justice, 2012a, *op. cit.*

60 J. Nijboer & M. Althoff, 'Fußballgewalt und Hooliganismus in den Niederlanden', 87 *Monatschrift für Kriminologie und Strafrechtsreform* 3 (2006), p. 246–262; R. Spaaij, 'Football Hooliganism in the Netherlands: Patterns of Continuity and Change', 8 *Soccer & Society* 2–3 (2007), p. 316–334 (p. 5) (at: www.tandfonline.com/doi/pdf/10.1080/14660970701224566).

as an important scene for socialization and thus for crime prevention. In this context *fan projects* have been introduced by Belgium, Germany[61] and the Netherlands,[62] promoting the cooperation between local governments and football clubs.[63] A number of countries have followed by introducing similar fan projects or fan coaching.

The national emphasis of the fan projects varies considerably among countries. It is worth mentioning that the Belgian association Fan Coaching has received the UEFA-backed European Football Supporters Awards 2011 for its actions against violence in sport.[64]

Fan projects from the one hand are generally commended for their contribution to the prevention of football hooliganism, while from the other are criticized for their 'soft' approach and the difficulty in assessing their preventative effects. Certain projects have improved the relationship between hooligans, clubs, youth workers and the police, and have prevented young fans from identifying with football hooliganism as a fashionable way of life.[65] However, it is unclear to what extent fan projects can have any influence on committed hooligans. Ramón Spaaij underlines that the better organized hooligan groups distance themselves from 'regular' fans and relocate their activities to other sites. For some of these groups, violence has become an end in itself and their ties with fan communities have loosened.[66] They have developed an 'elite self conception' based on physical toughness, valour and style. This development blocks the fan projects' ability to build a fruitful relationship with these groups.

Measures against football-related disorders in Sweden are integrated into programmes aiming to prevent young people from being drawn towards violent extremist environments, as mentioned above.[67]

---

61 G. Kett-Straub, 'Hooliganismus in Deutschland: Phänomenologie, Abgrenzung zu den "Ultras", Drittortauseinandersetzung, Erklärungsansätze und Prävention', 24 *Neue Kriminalpolitik* 3 (2012), p. 98–106.

62 Spaaij, 2007, *op. cit.*

63 S. Frosdick & P.E. Marsh, *Football Hooliganism*, Cullompton *et al.*: Willan, 2005, p. 182–185.

64 *European Forum for Urban Security*, 'Belgian Fan Coaching Association Wins European Football Supporters Award 2011', Brussels, 6 February 2012 (at: http://efus.eu/en/topics/places/large-events-recreational-scenes/partners/2629/).

65 R. Spaaij, 'The Prevention of Football Hooliganism: A Transnational a Perspective', in: J. Aquesolo (ed.), *Actas del X Congreso Internacional de Historia del Deporte*, Seville: CESH, 2005, p. 1–10 (p. 5, endnote 34) (at: http://cafyd.com/HistDeporte/htm/pdf/4-16.pdf); Spaaij, 2007, *op. cit.*, p. 330; see also E. Dunning, 'Towards a Sociological Understanding of Football Hooliganism as a World Phenomenon', 8 *European Journal on Criminal Policy and Research* 2 (2000), p. 141–162 (at: http://link.springer.com/article/10.1023%2FA%3A1008773923878); Frosdick & Marsh, 2005, *op. cit.*, p. 113–123.

66 Spaaij, 2005, *op. cit.*, p. 5.

67 (Swedish) Ministry of Justice, 2012a, *op. cit.*, p. 36–48; see also The Swedish National Council for Crime Prevention [Brå], 2009, *op. cit.*, p. 20.

Section 3.1. started from various types of activities of high risk groups and continued with the measures for their control; below the analysis will focus on measures or programmes used for various risk groups (3.2., 3.3.).

3.2. NEIGHBOURHOOD WATCH SCHEMES

Local neighbourhood watch schemes in the USA inform (amongst other activities) the residents of an area, via websites connected with official government lists, about the presence of high risk offenders in the area (*e.g.* Neighbourhood Watch Association of St. Albert).[68] Moreover, official sites, such as those by the police (*e.g.* Mashpee Police Department/Massachusetts-USA) prompt the organization of neighbourhood block watches because they are regarded to be valuable resources for law enforcement and to help "integrate the community in (sex) offender management programmes".[69]

In 1997, a report was submitted by the U.S. Department of Justice to the Congress after a systematic review of more than 500 scientific evaluations of crime prevention practices. The report lists which programmes proved successful and which did not. Among those proved to be *un*successful were neighbourhood watch programmes organized with the police.[70]

On 10 January 2013 a report was published on the website of *neighbourhoodwatch.net* in the UK about a reform initiative begun by the Justice Secretary Chris Grayling in order to "tackle reoffending and manage offenders in the community". The Secretary underlined that the expertise and experience of public, private and voluntary sectors must be used to bring down the *high reoffending rates*. In particular, according to the 'new approach' private providers would only be paid in full if they reduce reoffending in their area through *Payment by Results contracts*.[71] The proposals are intended to drive innovation and efficiency through the criminal justice system. The public sector will retain ultimate responsibility for public protection in all cases.[72]

68 Neighbourhood Watch Association of St. Albert, St. Albert RCMP Crime Stoppers Release, 5 June 2012 (at: http://eyewatch.info/iWatch/iQuery.asp?WCI=CrimeStoppersRelease&WCE=OutputResult&WCD=323).

69 Town of Mashpee, Massachusetts. Sex Offender Management Empowering Communities with Knowledge (at: www.mashpeema.gov/pages/MashpeeMA_Police/SexOffender/management).

70 L.W. Sherman *et al.*, *Preventing Crime: What Works, What Doesn't, What's Promising*, Washington DC: National Institute of Justice, July 1998, p. 1, 7.

71 (UK) Ministry of Justice, *Transforming Rehabilitation – Less Crime, Fewer Victims, Safer Communities*, 9 January 2013 (at: www.justice.gov.uk/news/press-releases/moj/transforming-rehabilitation-less-crime,-fewer-victims,-safer-communities).

72 Neighbourhoodwatch.net (at: www.neighbourhoodwatch.net/index.php?func=PageHome).

3.3. OTHER MEASURES AND PROGRAMMES USED FOR VARIOUS RISK GROUPS

3.3.1. Housing high-risk offenders in the community

Individuals who are released from prison are confronted with barriers when trying to find housing. More difficult is the situation for high-risk offenders, since community safety is regarded to be considerably impacted by their release. These people in addition to the stresses of staying clear of addictive substances, managing their risk levels, and maintaining finances, they are often under stress of being homeless.

In Canada a set of best practices has been created to be used when housing high-risk offenders in the community.[73] Staff members work pro-actively while in the community with high-risk clients because they sometimes have poor life skills.[74]

3.3.2. Circles of support and accountability

Small 'circles' of volunteers in cooperation with staff of the *Mennonite Central Committee-Ontario*/Canada become new communities for men whose crimes have marginalized them from society. MCC is a worldwide organization of Anabaptist churches responding to "basic human needs and working for peace and justice". The target of the circles is to prevent re-offending by individuals who have been incarcerated for sexual offending and are returning to the community by offering them both support and the opportunity to be accountable.[75]

3.3.3. Center for human development – Adolescent re-entry services

The Center that funded by the Massachusetts Department of Youth Services/ DYS, helps youths involved with the Youth Services return to their home communities and schools. The Centre coordinates community re-entry services two sites (Holyoke and Springfield) for more than 100 juvenile offenders. Case

---

73 With funding from the Law Foundation, the John Howard Society of the Lower Mainland of British Columbia/JHSLMBC in Canada has created these practices to use when housing high-risk offenders in the community.

74 K. LeMoel & D. Wilson, *Best Practices to Use When Housing High-Risk Offenders in the Community, A Legal And Non-Profit Perspective*, File Number LRG1686, The John Howard Society of the Lower Mainland & The Law Foundation of British Columbia, March 2010, p. 56–61 (at: www.jhslmbc.ca/images/BestPracticesFinalVersion2010.pdf).

75 Mennonite Central Committee Ontario/MCC, Restorative Justice, *Circles of Support and Accountability* (at: http://mcco.ca/restorative/circlesupport); see also MCC Ontario, Annual Reports, 2011/2012 & 2012/2013 (http://mcco.ca/about/annualreport).

managers meet with youths out in the community and work to find and provide appropriate services for them and their families.[76]

3.3.4. *Restore program*[77]

The restorative justice perspective argues that those directly harmed should have decision making authority on the crime resolution. Furthermore, an important value of restorative justice is that there should be a balance among the victims, offenders, and the community that constitute the three 'customers' of the criminal justice system.[78] Usually restorative programmes involve victims, offenders, but not the community,[79] while mediation is not appropriate for application to many crimes (*e.g.* against women including sexual assault).[80]

To address these problems, a cooperation of victim services, prosecutors, legal scholars, and public health professionals has been created in Pima County, Arizona/USA in 2000, implementing and evaluating RESTORE, a victim-driven, community-based restorative justice programme for selected sex crimes. 'RESTORE' prepares victims *('survivors')*, offenders *('responsible persons')*, and both parties' families and friends for face-to-face dialogue in order to identify the harm and develop a remedy plan. Referral is made by prosecutors and participation is voluntary. Afterwards, the programme monitors the offender's compliance for 12 months. RESTORE was designed for participants over 18 years old (both victim and offender), while offenders who had previous arrests for felonies, interpersonal or domestic violence were not admitted.

The programme applied sentencing circles and family group or community conferencing.[81] RESTORE/ Arizona closed because it could not be maintained

---

76 CHD/Center for Human Development, Adolescent Reentry Services, Holyoke, Springfield, MA (at: www.chd.org/index.php/adolescent-reentry-services.html).

77 This section is drawn largely from M.P. Koss, K.J. Bachar, C.Q. Hopkins & C. Carlson, 'Expanding a Community's Justice Response to Sex Crimes through Advocacy, Prosecutorial, and Public Health Collaboration. Introducing the RESTORE Program', 19 *Journal of Interpersonal Violence* 12 (2004), p. 1435–1463 (p. 1435–1445) (at: http://jiv.sagepub.com/content/19/12/1435).

78 G. Bazemore & M. Umbreit, 'Rethinking the Sanctioning Function in Juvenile Court: Retributive or Restorative Responses to Youth Crime', 41 *Crime & Delinquency* 3 (1995), p. 296–316 (p. 304) (at: http://cad.sagepub.com/content/41/3/296).

79 Koss *et al.*, 2004, *op. cit.*, p. 1443, Victim-offender programmes originated in Kitchener, Ontario, in 1974, based on the Mennonite church traditions; see also H. Strang, *Repair or Revenge: Victims and Restorative Justice*, Oxford, UK: Clarendon, 2004.

80 Koss *et al.* 2004, *op. cit.*; cf. J.G. Brown, 'The Use of Mediation to Resolve Criminal Cases: A Procedural Critique', 43 *Emory Law Journal* (1994), p. 1273–1279 (at: https://litigation-essentials.lexisnexis.com); E. Zellerer, 'Community-Based Justice and Violence against Women: Issues of Gender and Race', 20 *International Journal of Comparative and Applied Criminal Justice* 2 (1996), p. 233–244 (at: www.tandfonline.com/doi/abs/10.1080/01924036.1996.9678575#.UfJ5Hqz-TRs).

81 P. McCold & T. Wachtel, 'Restorative Justice Theory Validation', in: E.G.M. Weitekamp & H.J. Kerner (eds.), *Restorative Justice: Theoretical Foundations*, Devon, UK: Willan, 2002, p. 110–142, (p. 116).

once the funding period ended.[82] However, it has been influential in the establishment of a number of other programmes, including one in Auckland/New Zealand,[83] where referrals may be from court or from the community.[84] Today, conferencing in various forms is used apart from the USA,[85] worldwide, in Australia,[86] Canada,[87] New Zealand,[88] and European countries,[89] for resolving juvenile crime.

3.3.5. *Secure residential treatment programmes*[90]

This treatment programme is a residential measure for juvenile sex offenders, chronic high-risk juvenile offenders and juvenile offenders with acute substance abuse behaviours. The services are provided for male youth, ages 12 to 20 at its

82 E. McDonald & Y. Tinsley, *From "Real Rape" to Real Justice: Prosecuting Rape in New Zealand*, University of Wellington, Wellington/NZ: Victoria University Press, 2013, p. 406, footnote 89 (at: www.lawcom.govt.nz/content/extracts-elisabeth-mcdonald-and-yvette-tinsley-real-rape-real-justice-prosecuting-rape-new-zealand).

83 S. Jülich, 'Views of Justice among Survivors of Historical Child Sexual Abuse: Implications for Restorative Justice in New Zealand', 10 *Theoretical Criminology* 1 (2006), p. 125–138 (p. 125) (at: http://tcr.sagepub.com/content/10/1/125).

84 McDonald & Tinsley 2013, *op. cit.*, p. 406.

85 P. McCold & B. Wachtel, *Restorative Policing Experiment: The Bethlehem Pennsylvania Police Family Group Conferencing Project*, Pipersville, PA: Community Service Foundation, 1998 (at: www.iirp.edu/article_detail.php?article_id=NDYz); M.S. Umbreit, *The Handbook of Victim-Offender Mediation*, San Francisco: Jossey-Bass, 2001; Koss *et al.*, 2004, p. 1444–1445, *op. cit.*

86 K. Daly, 'Conferencing in Australia and New Zealand: Variations, Research Findings and Prospects', in: A. Morris & G. Maxwell (eds.), *Restorative Justice for Juveniles: Conferencing, Mediation and Circles*, Oxford, UK: Hart, 2002, p. 59–84; see also L. Sherman, H. Strang & D.J. Woods, *Recidivism Patterns in the Canberra Reintegrative Shaming Experiments*, Canberra: Australian National University, Centre for Restorative Justice, Research School of Social Sciences, November 2000 (at: www.aic.gov.au/criminal_justice_system/rjustice/rise/recidivism.html).

87 J. Bonta, J. Rooney & S. Wallace-Capretta, *Restorative justice: An evaluation of the restorative resolutions project*, Ottawa: Canada Solicitor General, 1998; N. Bala & J.V. Roberts, 'Canada's Juvenile Justice System: Promoting Community-Based Responses to Youth Crime', in: J. Junger-Tas & S. H. Decker (eds.), *International Handbook of Juvenile Justice*, New York, NY: Springer New York, 2008, p. 37–64 (at: http://dx.doi.org/10.1007/978–0-387–09478–6).

88 A. Morris & G. Maxwell (eds.), *Restorative Justice for Juveniles: Conferencing, Mediation and Circles*, Oxford, UK: Hart, 2002.

89 L. Walgrave, 'Community Service as a Cornerstone', in: G. Bazemore & L. Walgrave (eds.), *Restorative Juvenile Justice: Repairing Harm of Youth Crime*, Monsey, NY: Criminal Justice Press, 1999, p. 129–154; D. Miers, *An International Review of Restorative Justice*, B. Webb (ed.) (Crime Reduction Research Series Paper 10), London: Home Office, 2001 (at: www.restorativejustice.org.uk/resource/an_international_review_of_restorative_justice/#.UdxHoKyyyj0); R. Young & C. Hoyle, 'New Improved Police Led Restorative Justice? Action-Research and the Thames Valley Police Initiative', in: A. von Hirsch *et al.* (eds.), *Restorative Justice and Criminal Justice: Competing or Reconcilable Paradigms*, Oxford, UK and Portland, USA: Hart, 2003, p. 273–292.

90 Spectrum Human Services, Michigan (at: www.shswny.com/spectrum/AboutUs.aspx; www.spectrumhuman.org/SJJS/Programs.aspx).

two centres in Michigan/USA.[91] To earn a successful release, youth enrolled in the programmes must complete seven intensive cognitive behavioural treatment stages, "designed to change criminal thinking and delinquent behaviour". The scheme comprises family therapy, anger management and individualized treatment tasking. Juveniles are also taught social living skills and independent living skills. Normally, treatment lasts from 10–12 months; however, graduation from the programme is based on each individual's motivation and extent of previous delinquent involvement.[92]

4. CONCLUSIONS AND OPEN QUESTIONS

In the present article we examined community measures applied to persons or groups of persons been susceptible to follow antisocial behaviour, commit crimes or relapse into crime because of their individual and/or social circumstances.

During the last 10–15 years, the prediction and management of recidivism or commitment of crime among high risk groups has become increasingly important. The way in which 'risk' is defined, assessed and managed varies among research studies and agencies.[93]

Contemporary approaches to risk assessment and management focus on offender surveillance, parole, probation, individualised treatment, and outcome-orientated partnerships that integrate community measures (*e.g.* restore programmes, neighbourhood watch schemes), policing and judicial responses with health and welfare services (*e.g.* MST, community interventions, support and accountability circles, shelters for high-risk offenders in the community).[94]

Preliminary research suggests that interventions directly addressed to a person and taking into consideration individual risks and needs (*e.g.* MST, center for human development, secure residential treatment programmes) are more likely to be effective than interventions that adopt a standardised approach. The social bonds of the person are a significant determinant for dealing with his/her complex needs; further research is required into interventions that reduce risk.[95]

Specifically, this means that people who are concerned about the impact of arrest and other interventions upon their employment or social status, can react differently from those without such social connections and are thus more likely to escalate violence, or to repeatedly breach various orders (probation, PPOs

---

91 The Calumet and Lincoln Centers in Highland Park.

92 U.S. Department of Justice, Office of Juvenile Justice and Delinquency Prevention, *Balanced and Restorative Justice, Program Summary*, 8 June 1995, p. 1, 2 (at: www.ncjrs.gov/pdffiles/bal.pdf).

93 M. Salter, *Managing Recidivism Amongst High Risk Violent Men*, Issues Paper 23, Australian Domestic & Family Violence Clearinghouse, The University of New South Wales: Sydney, January 2012, p. 1, 7–18 (at: www.adfvc.unsw.edu.au/PDF%20files/IssuesPaper_23.pdf).

94 Salter, 2012, *op. cit.*, p. 11–18.

95 Salter, 2012, *op. cit.*, p. 14–16.

etc.).[96] However, social bonds can be catalytic to other antisocial behaviour, such as violent extremism, or hooliganism, as described above.

Kemshall and Wood restructure the previously mentioned, arguing that two approaches have been developed by governments in order to manage incalculable and high-consequence threats to life and security. "A 'community protection model' in which the appropriate containment and effective management of high-risk offenders is paramount ... and a 'public health approach' with an emphasis upon public awareness and educative campaigns to extend the remit of public protection to local communities and the general public".[97]

The community protection model exercises prevention by incapacitating dangerous persons (*e.g.* sex offender registration and public notification, electronic monitoring tracking, residency restrictions, various Public Protection Orders etc.), whereas the public health model attempts "to govern risky conditions, rather than categorically risky types of person" (*e.g.* neighbourhood watch schemes, Secure Residential Treatment Programmes etc.).[98]

Juveniles in risk contexts and risk contexts per se (*e.g.* peer pressure and group dynamics, sport milieu generating violent behaviour, drug scene) are an additional changeling and complex problem that deserves consideration. Moreover, attention should be paid to the intricate situation of dealing with the increasingly diverse forms and numbers of crime risk groups.

In May 2013 riots broke out in Sweden, initially in two suburbs of Stockholm (Husby and then Rinkeby) been predominantly populated by Muslim communities from Turkey, the Middle East and Somalia. Subsequently, the unrest spread to seven more of Stockholm's suburbs and four other cities, subsiding only after nine days. The unrest was triggered, as it is reported, by the fatal shooting by the police of an elderly man from Portugal wielding a knife and threatening to kill two police officers. Such situations put in question the 'public health' model and confirm that identifying not only which offenders are at high risk of causing serious physical harm in the future, but also which social circumstances can be developed into riskis a difficult task.[99]

---

96 For the significance of social bonds' and their effect on crime and delinquency, see the classic work of T. Hirschi, *Causes of Delinquency*, Berkeley: University of California Press, 1969.

97 H. Kemshall & J. Wood, 'Beyond public protection: An examination of community protection and public health approaches to high-risk offenders', 7 Criminology & Criminal Justice 3 (2007), p. 203–204; see also B. Hebenton & T. Seddon, 'From Dangerousness to Precaution. Managing Sexual and Violent Offenders in an Insecure and Uncertain Age', 49 *British Journal of Criminology* 3 (2009), p. 343 – 362 (p. 343).

98 P. O'Malley, 'The Uncertain Promise of Risk', 37 *Australian and New Zealand Journal of Criminology* 3 (2004), p. 323 – 343 (p. 328–329).

99 Sentencing Advisory Council, High-Risk Offenders: Post-Sentence Supervision and Detention, Discussion and Options, Paper Summary, Melbourne: Sentencing Advisory Council, 23 February 2007, p. 3, (at: https://sentencingcouncil.vic.gov.au/sites/sentencingcouncil.vic.gov.au/files/high_risk_offenders_post_sentence_supervision_and_detention_discussion_and_options_paper_summary.pdf).

Summing up, in any society there is a small group of offenders who pose a continued and serious danger of committing further serious offences. These people present a significant challenge for the justice system, a challenge that involves balancing the community's right to safety and the right of potential future victims to be protected from dangerous offenders on the one hand, against the rights of an offender who has already been punished for crimes committed on the other hand.[100]

100 Sentencing Advisory Council, 2007, *op. cit.*

LA GESTION DES DÉLINQUANTS À RISQUE ÉLEVÉ EN FRANCE

Francis CASORLA*

1. INTRODUCTION

La gestion des délinquants à risque élevé pose la question centrale de la récidive tant en droit pénal, qu'en procédure pénale et en droit pénitentiaire, car il est incontestable que certains types de délinquants présentent un risque élevé de récidive.[1]

Circonstance aggravante dans le Code pénal de 1810, la circonstance de récidive légale fut remplacée en 1885 par la relégation, peine d'enfermement perpétuel obligatoire, exécutée en Guyane, appliquée aux multirécidivistes. La loi du 17 juillet 1970 remplaça la relégation par la tutelle pénale, dont l'application par le juge était facultative et la durée maximum de 10 ans. La loi du 2 février 1981 supprima la tutelle pénale, et le nouveau Code pénal, entré en vigueur le 1er mars 1994, considère de nouveau la récidive comme une circonstance aggravante.

On se trouve ici dans la question classique de la prévention du risque. Mais la prévention de la récidive ne doit rien, ou fort peu, au hasard, à l'aléa, à la coïncidence, à l'imprévisibilité, de nombreuses études montrent des probabilités et même des constantes chez ces porteurs de risques que sont les délinquants récidivistes.

Il est étrange de constater que sur l'appréciation de la délinquance, pas de principe de précaution, mais des prises de risques des institutions judiciaires et pénitentiaires en laissant ou remettant en liberté des individus à risque élevé de passage à l'acte alors qu'avec la propagation du catastrophisme environnemental, les hommes, plongés dans une terrifiante culpabilité, sont invités à se vivre

* F. Casorla est Avocat général honoraire à la Cour de Cassation, et Chercheur au Centre de droit des affaires de la Faculté de Droit de Rennes.

1 Mon expérience d'ancien procureur et aussi d'ancien président de juridictions pénales m'a maintes fois permis d'entendre de certains délinquants, notamment d'agresseurs sexuels, de véritables demandes de les protéger de la récidive en les incarcérant, voire en les maintenant en détention, convaincus qu'ils récidiveraient dés leur sortie de prison. Ce qui ne manquait pas le plus souvent de se produire.

comme des criminels qui détruisent la planète en la pillant de ses ressources naturelles et en provoquant un réchauffement annonciateur des plus grandes catastrophes, d'où le célèbre principe de précaution.

La meilleure piste de réflexion se trouve dans un ouvrage capital[2], qui met en exergue dans la gestion des délinquants à risque élevé la théorie de la dissuasion qui tourne résolument le dos à la théorie thérapeutique du traitement médico-social, théorie de la dissuasion que l'auteur définit en une phrase «*plus la probabilité d'être arrêté, d'être condamné ou être emprisonné est forte dans un territoire donné, plus le taux de criminalité est bas*», tout en notant plus loin que «*plus les criminels sont punis sévèrement et fréquemment, plus ils récidivent*».[3]

C'est en effet toute la difficulté qui suppose une analyse approfondie de notre sujet. L'évaluation du risque de récidive se fait dans la réalité en trois étapes, lors de l'appréciation de la sanction, lors de la détention et enfin, et c'est la question la plus délicate, lors de la sortie de prison après l'exécution de la sanction.

2. LE RISQUE ÉLEVÉ DE RÉCIDIVE LORS DE L'APPRÉCIATION DE LA SANCTION

En droit français, la récidive s'entend comme l'état du délinquant qui, déjà condamné par un jugement définitif, commet une nouvelle infraction. De sorte que, au moment de l'arrestation du délinquant le procureur comme le juge d'instruction, comme le juge des libertés et de la détention à qui revient la décision finale, se poseront la question du risque élevé de récidive ou de réitération (lorsqu'il y a déjà eu une infraction mais pas de condamnation définitive antérieure) pour décider d'une mise en détention avant jugement. Et c'est à partir de ce moment que la détention sera en principe continue jusqu'à la plus ou moins complète exécution de la peine.

Comment analyser ce risque élevé de récidive? Bien entendu, et c'est l'indice le plus significatif, lorsqu'il y a déjà récidive, voire multirécidive. On constate hélas trop souvent plusieurs condamnations avec sursis et sursis avec mise à l'épreuve qui s'accumulent, avant qu'une décision ferme intervienne pour interrompre une carrière criminelle déjà bien installée. Il n'est pas rare que des policiers arrêtent dans la même journée deux fois les mêmes individus, le plus souvent des mineurs de 18 ans qui bénéficient de lois et de magistrats spécialisés plus cléments, relâchés par la justice quelques heures plus tôt.

---

2 Maurice Cusson, *Le contrôle social du crime,* Paris: PUF, 1983.

3 Chaque année, en France, 1,2 millions auteurs de crimes et de délits sont présentés à la justice, 1 sur 10 seulement, soit 120.000 sont condamnés à des peines de prison ferme, bien d'autres peines (sursis divers, remises à parents, amendes, rappels à la loi...) apparaissant comme purement symboliques notamment à l'égard de mineurs de 18 ans, de sorte qu'il est permis de se demander si ce n'est pas l'impunité plus que les courtes peines d'emprisonnement qui créent des délinquants à risque élevé.

D'autres indices interviennent: l'absence de domicile et de foyer, la toxicomanie y compris alcoolique, la nationalité étrangère souvent liée à l'absence de domicile défini, l'absence de travail et de ressources avouées, l'absence d'instruction et le défaut d'éducation, l'agressivité et la rébellion contre les policiers lors de l'arrestation, des antécédents psychiatriques sévères, la nature de l'infraction (l'incendie volontaire, l'agression sexuelle, le trafic de stupéfiants, ...) au point que l'on pourrait distinguer parmi les délinquants à risque élevé, les délinquants compulsifs et les «délinquants professionnels»[4], sans que la distinction entre ces deux catégories soit cependant bien claire, tant les uns comme les autres ont souvent des modes opératoires «personnels» qui constituent de précieuses signatures, notamment pour les policiers qui les recherchent.

Les délinquants compulsifs qui présentent souvent des caractères névrotiques, voire psychopathiques intéressent tout autant la médecine que le droit. Les délinquants professionnels, surtout quand ils règnent en bandes dans des territoires qu'ils considèrent avoir conquis, font de froides analyse coûts-bénéfices et pour eux, la réaction plus ou moins ferme des autorités, et notamment de la justice, est un élément d'appréciation non négligeable. De sorte que des analyses plus fines conduisent à observer différentes formes de récidives, différents types de récidivistes qui appellent donc des réponses diversifiées qui doivent être adaptées à des dangerosités spécifiques.

Des études françaises concordantes faites sur des échantillons de populations pénales montrent[5], bien qu'assez anciennes, que le récidivisme touche prés de la moitié des individus incarcérés, que l'importance de la récidive décroit avec l'âge et reste exceptionnelle au delà de 40 ans, que les condamnés à plus de trois condamnations récidivent à prés de 80 %, que les deux tiers des récidivistes commettent le même type d'infraction (récidive homogène) dans laquelle ils se sont spécialisés (ainsi sur 720 récidivistes, 450 ont commis une infraction identique), que dans un grand nombre de récidives hétérogènes et protéiformes, une aggravation progressive est notée (par exemple, vol, vol aggravé, vol avec violences, meurtre, le vol étant le plus souvent la première infraction, par exemple à hauteur de 96 % sur 705 cas de récidivistes).

La récidive n'est qu'exceptionnellement modifiée par les condamnations successives, elle en est même parfois aggravée ce qui permet de s'interroger sur l'effet dissuasif de certaines peines trop légères, car la prison crée des appartenances à des groupes asociaux, un phénomène analogue à celui des bandes. En revanche, le pourcentage de récidives est deux fois plus élevé parmi les détenus libérés en fin de peine que parmi les détenus placés en liberté conditionnelle.

---

[4] On lira avec intérêt à «la une» du journal *Le Parisien* du 22 avril 2013 le témoignage d'un cambrioleur se présentant comme un professionnel depuis 15 ans.

[5] Jean Marc Varaut, *La prison, pour quoi faire?*, Paris: La Table Ronde, 1972; *Rapport général de l'Administration pénitentiaire*, 1969.

Les évolutions récentes notent que les trajectoires délinquantes commencent dés l'adolescence, parfois dés l'enfance, que le vrai moteur de la délinquance n'est pas le besoin, mais l'envie qui crée des délinquants sur-actifs, prédateurs violents, dont l'activité criminelle abondante est hors de proportion avec leur faiblesse numérique, d'où l'importance des cartographies policières dans les villes qui repèrent activités délinquantes, modes opératoires et finalement délinquants sur-actifs forcément à risque élevé.[6]

L'Observatoire National de la Délinquance et des Réponses pénales dans un rapport récemment publié, note la part prépondérante des mineurs (53,4 %) dans les infractions commises par les délinquants sur-actifs (mises en causes pour 5 infractions ou plus en deux ans) ainsi que la part importante des étrangers, plus d'un tiers des mises en causes en globalité, mais majoritaire pour les vols et les cambriolages, les ciblages par nationalités indiquant une forte proportion de ressortissants des pays balkaniques essentiellement mineurs de 18 ans, puis des pays du Maghreb, puis des pays de l'Afrique sub-saharienne.[7]

3. LE RISQUE ÉLEVÉ DE RÉCIDIVE PENDANT LA DÉTENTION

Une circulaire du 19 mars 2008 émanant de la Direction de l'Administration Pénitentiaire est venue préciser et clarifier les missions et les conditions d'intervention des Services Pénitentiaires d'Insertion et de Probation (SPIP), dont la mission principale est devenue la prévention de la récidive avec un travail d'accompagnement autour du passage à l'acte. Le SPIP doit évaluer les risques puis construire un suivi *individualisé* et *progressif* dans le cadre du parcours d'exécution de peine en vue de responsabiliser le sujet et de prévenir la récidive.

Mais cela doit être mis en regard avec la réalité. Au 1er juin 2013, le nombre de personnes écrouées détenues est de 67 977, de personnes écrouées non hébergées de 12 181 ce qui met l'*ensemble des personnes écrouées à 80 158,* chiffres en constante augmentation[8] et chiffres à rapporter aux plus de quatre millions de

6 Xavier Raufer, *Les malfaiteurs sont-ils des victimes de la société?*, Publications de l'Institut pour la Justice, novembre 2010. Contra, le sociologue Antoine Chauvenet, 'Les longues peines: le «principe» de la peur', 6 *Champ Pénal* (2009). Dans la même veine du sociologisme, Laurent Mucchielli pour qui «la délinquance n'existe pas, la délinquance juvénile pas davantage» in L. Mucchielli, 'Une activité délinquante à défaut d'emploi', *Chroniques du Travail* 2 (2012).

7 Voir le site internet de *l'Observatoire*, également le journal *Le Figaro* du 28 juin 2013. Selon le *Washington Post* du 26 avril 2012, 60 à 70 % des détenus en France sont musulmans alors que les musulmans ne représenteraient que 10 % de la population. Voir aussi les travaux du Danois Nicolaï Sennels, auteur de *Among criminal muslims, A psychologist's experiences* with the Copenhagen Municipality.

8 68.569 détenus au 1er juillet 2013, chiffre jamais atteint, à comparer 47.837 détenus au 1er janvier 2001. Adde Laurent Obertone, *La France orange mécanique*, Paris: Ring, 2013. Adde Xavier Raufer, 'Enjeux Sécurité', *Revue Valeurs Actuelles*, 28 mars 2013.

procédures annuelles transmises aux parquets par les services de police judiciaire, ce qui fait de la France depuis plus de 20 ans, un pays au taux de délinquance l'un des plus élevés au monde.[9] Chiffres également à rapporter au nombre trop faible de places de prisons de *57.325*.

La France n'est pas seule dans cette situation de surpopulation carcérale. Selon un rapport du Conseil de l'Europe du 19 mars 2013. l'Azerbaïdjan, la Géorgie, la Lettonie, la Fédération de Russie et l'Ukraine dépassent, de plus du double, la moyenne des États membres du Conseil de l'Europe de 149 détenus pour 100.000 habitants, la situation étant tendue dans six pays, la Serbie avec 172 détenus, la France avec 108 détenus, la Turquie avec 115 détenus, la Grèce avec 123 détenus, Chypre avec 151 détenus et l'Italie avec 153 détenus pour 100 places, tandis que Andorre, la Bosnie-Herzégovine, le Danemark, la Finlande, l'Islande, le Liechtenstein, Monaco, les Pays-Bas, la Norvège, Saint-Marin, la Slovénie, la Suède et la Suisse affichent des taux d'emprisonnement correspondant à la moitié ou à moins de la moitié de la moyenne européenne. La plupart des pays d'Europe ont enregistré une tendance générale à l'augmentation de ces chiffres au cours des 10 dernières années, mais selon l'International Centre for Prison Studies (ICPS), en 2013, le taux d'incarcération pour 100.000 habitants est de 707 pour les États Unis, 475 pour la Russie, 294 pour l'Afrique du Sud et 98 pour la France (Source *Courrier International* n° 1211 du 16 janvier 2014).

Autre difficulté, alors même que la surpopulation carcérale «noie» les délinquants à risque élevé parmi les autres détenus, l'administration pénitentiaire privilégie l'évaluation de la dangerosité des détenus pour eux-mêmes (risque suicidaire), pour les personnels de surveillance et leurs codétenus (risque d'agression) ou pour l'institution (risque d'évasion) mais pas pour la société et les victimes potentielles (risque de récidive). L'occasion de la période de détention pour mesurer la dangerosité des condamnés et évaluer leur risque de récidive devrait constituer un impératif, d'autant qu'on sait que dans bien des cas le risque élevé de passage à l'acte demeure après l'exécution de la peine.

---

9 Chiffres également en augmentation dans un pays où plus de 13 000 policiers ont été blessés en service en 2012. Ainsi, *l'Observatoire* national de la délinquance et des réponses pénales note une augmentation de mai 2012 à mai 2013 selon les zones de 5 à 14 % pour les cambriolages (234 090 en 2012 soit plus de 10 000 qu'en 2011), de 3 à 5 % pour les vols avec violences, de 1,1 % à 28,6 % pour les agressions sexuelles. Journal *Le Figaro* 10 juin 2013. Un récent et très grave accident (ou attentat) ferroviaire près de Paris qui s'est produit dans l'un des nombreux «townships» qui entourent la capitale a vu les secours attaqués par des voyous qui détroussaient les cadavres dans les wagons disloqués, de sorte qu'il a fallu faire venir d'urgence la police de maintien de l'ordre pour protéger l'évacuation des blessés, Site Internet *Atlantico*, Alain Bauer et Xavier Lemoine, *Caillassage des secours à Bretigny sur Orge: y a-t-il une France sans morale?*, 14 juillet 2013.

4. LE RISQUE ÉLEVÉ DE RÉCIDIVE APRÈS L'EXÉCUTION DE LA PEINE

Devant la constatation généralement admise que 5 % des délinquants sont responsables de 50 % des infractions commises, et surtout à la suite de plusieurs assassinats et de viols barbares commis par des récidivistes et qui ont choqué l'opinion publique, la question de la mise à l'écart des récidivistes, et surtout des multirécidivistes violents s'est de nouveau posée. Plusieurs lois, intervenant à délais très rapprochés[10] vont tenter de neutraliser, d'exclure des individus considérés comme dangereux, certaines de ces mesures s'inscrivant très directement contre la faiblesse des sanctions prononcées par les juges contre les récidivistes.

La loi du 12 décembre 2005 relative au traitement de la récidive des infractions pénales réintroduit la notion de dangerosité abandonnée en 1981. Elle renforce la répression de la récidive et institue de nouvelles mesures de suivi des condamnés dangereux, élargit les catégories de délits assimilés en matière de récidive, prévoit l'incarcération obligatoire à l'audience des délinquants sexuels ou violents récidivistes, limite le nombre de sursis avec mise à l'épreuve dont les récidivistes pourront bénéficier, diminue la durée des réductions de peine applicables aux récidivistes, institue le placement sous surveillance électronique mobile pour les délinquants sexuels et violents, y compris à titre de mesure de sûreté dans le cadre d'une condamnation à un suivi socio-judiciaire[11], si la peine prononcée est d'au moins sept ans d'emprisonnement.

La durée de ce suivi est de deux ans, renouvelable une fois pour un délit et deux fois pour un crime. Ce placement peut également consister en une des obligations soit de la libération conditionnelle, soit d'une nouvelle modalité

---

10 Christine Lazerges, 'Le choix de la fuite en avant au nom de la dangerosité', *Revue de science criminelle et de droit pénal comparé* 1 (2012), p. 274; Contra et bien plus convaincant Jean Pradel, 'Que faire des criminels dangereux? Approche comparative' in: Michel Born, Fabienne Kéfer & André Lemaître, *Une criminologie de la tradition à l'innovation. En hommage à Georges Kellens,* Bruxelles: Larcier, 2006, p. 441-452. Adde Jean Pradel, *Droit Pénal Général,* Paris: Cujas, 2012.

11 Auparavant, une loi de 1998 a instauré pour lutter contre la récidive des infractions sexuelles une mesure de suivi médico-judiciaire, baptisée *suivi socio-judiciaire*, après exécution de la peine qui sera peu appliquée. Cette mesure emporte, pour le condamné, l'obligation de se soumettre, sous le contrôle du juge de l'application des peines et pendant une durée déterminée par la juridiction de jugement, à des mesures de surveillance et d'assistance destinées à prévenir la récidive. La durée du suivi socio-judiciaire ne peut excéder dix ans en cas de condamnation pour délit ou vingt ans en cas de condamnation pour crime. Toutefois, en matière correctionnelle, cette durée peut être portée à vingt ans par décision spécialement motivée de la juridiction de jugement; lorsqu'il s'agit d'un crime puni de trente ans de réclusion criminelle, cette durée est de trente ans; lorsqu'il s'agit d'un crime puni de la réclusion criminelle à perpétuité, la cour d'assises peut décider que le suivi socio-judiciaire s'appliquera sans limitation de durée, sous réserve de la possibilité pour le tribunal de l'application des peines de mettre fin à la mesure à l'issue d'un délai de trente ans... V. Dossier Eviter la récidive du délinquant sexuel, *AJ Pénal*, décembre 2012.

d'application des peines, la surveillance judiciaire. La mise en oeuvre de la mesure – mais non son prononcé – nécessite le consentement de la personne concernée et les mineurs en sont exclus.

La loi du 10 août 2007 renforçant la lutte contre la récidive des majeurs et des mineurs introduit des peines plancher pour les majeurs comme pour les mineurs au dessous desquelles les juges ne peuvent pas aller en principe lorsqu'il s'agit de juger des récidivistes.

La loi du 25 février 2008 relative à la rétention de sûreté et à la déclaration d'irresponsabilité pénale pour cause de trouble mental crée la rétention de sûreté, mesure permettant de retenir, à titre exceptionnel, dans un centre fermé, dénommé centre socio-médico-judiciaire, les personnes condamnées à une peine de réclusion criminelle d'une durée égale ou supérieure à quinze ans pour certains crimes et qui présentent à l'issue de leur peine, une probabilité très élevée de récidive et une particulière dangerosité résultant d'un trouble grave de leur personnalité.

Cette mesure ne peut être prononcée qu'à la suite d'une évaluation du détenu au moins un an avant la fin prévue de sa peine, évaluation dont le principe aura été expressément prévu par la décision de condamnation rendue par la cour d'assises. Cette évaluation est réalisée par la commission pluridisciplinaire des mesures de sûreté, créée par la loi du 12 décembre 2005 pour le placement sous surveillance électronique mobile, et composée d'un magistrat, d'un préfet, d'un psychiatre, d'un psychologue, d'un directeur des services pénitentiaires, d'un avocat et d'un représentant d'une association nationale d'aide aux victimes.

A cette fin, la commission demande le placement de la personne, pour une durée d'au moins six semaines, dans un service spécialisé chargé de l'observation des personnes détenues aux fins d'une évaluation pluridisciplinaire de dangerosité assortie d'une expertise médicale réalisée par deux experts. Si la commission conclut à la particulière dangerosité du condamné et au risque élevé de récidive, elle propose, par avis motivé, au procureur général son placement en rétention.

La décision de rétention de sûreté est prise par la juridiction régionale de la rétention de sûreté territorialement compétente, composée d'un président de chambre et de deux conseillers de la cour d'appel, après un débat contradictoire, et public si le condamné, assisté d'un avocat, le demande. Elle peut être contestée devant une juridiction nationale composée de conseillers à la Cour de cassation, dont la décision motivée peut faire l'objet d'un pourvoi en cassation. La décision de rétention est valable un an et peut être renouvelée selon les mêmes conditions de fond et de procédure.

La personne retenue est placée dans un centre socio-médico-judiciaire sous la double tutelle des ministères de la Justice et de la Santé et dispose de droits similaires à ceux des détenus en matière de visites, de correspondances, d'exercice du culte et de permissions de sortie sous escorte ou sous surveillance électronique mobile notamment.

Les personnes déjà condamnées à une peine de réclusion criminelle d'au moins quinze ans à la suite, soit de plusieurs condamnations pour les crimes d'assassinat ou de meurtre aggravé, de torture ou actes de barbaries aggravés, de viol aggravé, d'enlèvement ou de séquestration aggravé, soit d'une condamnation unique pour ces crimes commis sur des victimes différentes, peuvent être soumises au régime du placement sous surveillance de sûreté à l'issue de leur peine (placement sous bracelet électronique, injonction de soins, interdiction de se rendre dans certains lieux ou de rencontrer la victime). Si la personne viole ces obligations, elle peut être placée en centre de rétention de sûreté.

Le texte modifie, par ailleurs, la procédure qui s'applique lorsque l'auteur d'une infraction est atteint de troubles mentaux pouvant le rendre pénalement irresponsable. Le juge d'instruction en informe les parties et le procureur de la République qui peuvent alors demander la saisine de la chambre de l'instruction, qui devra statuer, à l'issue d'une audience publique et contradictoire, sur la question de l'applicabilité de l'irresponsabilité pénale.

La chambre de l'instruction peut, si elle estime qu'il existe des charges suffisantes contre la personne mise en examen, ordonner son renvoi devant la juridiction de jugement ou rendre un arrêt de déclaration d'irresponsabilité pénale pour cause de trouble mental par lequel elle déclare qu'il existe des charges suffisantes contre la personne poursuivie, prononce s'il y a lieu une ou plusieurs des mesures de sûreté à l'encontre de la personne (interdiction d'entrer en relation avec la victime de l'infraction ou certaines personnes spécialement désignées, de paraître dans tout lieu spécialement désigné, de détenir ou de porter une arme notamment), déclare la personne irresponsable pénalement en raison d'un trouble psychique ou neuropsychique ayant aboli son discernement ou le contrôle de ses actes au moment des faits, et si la partie civile le demande, renvoie l'affaire devant le tribunal correctionnel compétent pour qu'il se prononce sur la responsabilité civile de la personne et statue sur les demandes de dommages et intérêts.

Si un accusé ou un prévenu doit être déclaré irresponsable pénalement pour cause de trouble mental, la juridiction de jugement – cour d'assises ou tribunal correctionnel – rend également, non plus une décision de relaxe ou d'acquittement, mais une décision de déclaration d'irresponsabilité pénale pour cause de trouble mental.

Les décisions de déclaration d'irresponsabilité pénale pour cause de trouble mental sont inscrites au casier judiciaire. La loi prévoit, afin d'inciter les détenus qui ont besoin d'un traitement, que le refus de soins sera assimilé à une mauvaise conduite entrainant retrait des réductions de peine.

Les dispositions permettant le recours à un traitement utilisant des médicaments entraînant une diminution de la libido sont en outre, simplifiées puisqu'il n'est plus exigé que le traitement soit réalisé par un médecin agréé ni que ces médicaments figurent sur une liste fixée par arrêté. Enfin, en cas de risque pour la sécurité des personnes, les professionnels de santé intervenant au sein des établissements pénitentiaires ou des établissements de santé accueillant des personnes détenues ont l'obligation d'en informer le directeur dans les plus brefs délais.

La loi du 10 mars 2010 visant à amoindrir le risque de récidive criminelle complétant les dispositions issues de la loi du 25 février 2008 relative à la rétention de sûreté et à la déclaration d'irresponsabilité pénale pour cause de trouble mental prévoit que le placement en rétention de sûreté en centre socio-médico-judiciaire impliquera que l'intéressé ait, pendant sa détention, bénéficié d'une prise en charge médicale, sociale et psychologique adaptée au trouble de la personnalité dont il souffre.

Par ailleurs, elle affirme clairement que le placement en centre socio-médico-judiciaire doit demeurer l'ultime recours. Cette mesure doit intervenir lorsque le renforcement des mesures de surveillance de sûreté apparaît insuffisant pour prévenir la commission de nouvelles infractions graves. La mesure de surveillance de sûreté a été portée à deux ans.

Ce texte crée un répertoire des données à caractère personnel collectées dans le cadre des procédures judiciaires. Tenu par le service du casier judiciaire sous l'autorité du Garde des Sceaux et placé sous le contrôle d'un magistrat, il est destiné à faciliter et à fiabiliser la connaissance de la personnalité et l'évaluation de la dangerosité des personnes poursuivies ou condamnées pour l'une des infractions pour lesquelles le suivi socio-judiciaire est encouru. Il vise également à prévenir le renouvellement de ces infractions.

S'il existe un risque que le condamné puisse se trouver en présence de la victime ou de la partie civile et qu'au regard de la nature des faits ou de la personnalité de l'intéressé il apparaît qu'une telle rencontre paraît devoir être évitée, les juridictions de l'application des peines assortissent toute décision entraînant la cessation temporaire ou définitive de l'incarcération d'une interdiction d'entrer en relation avec la victime ou la partie civile et, le cas échéant, de paraître à proximité de son domicile et de son lieu de travail.

L'identité et l'adresse des personnes condamnées à une peine d'emprisonnement égale ou supérieure à trois ans sont communiquées par l'administration pénitentiaire aux services de police ou aux unités de gendarmerie du lieu de résidence des intéressés lorsque leur incarcération prend fin.

En cas de nouvelle inscription ou de modification d'adresse concernant une inscription ou lorsque la personne n'a pas apporté la justification de son adresse dans les délais requis, le gestionnaire du fichier des infractions sexuelles ou violentes et celui des personnes recherchées avise directement le ministère de l'Intérieur. Ce dernier transmet sans délai l'information aux services de police ou de gendarmerie compétents.

S'il apparaît que la personne ne se trouve plus à l'adresse indiquée, l'officier de police judiciaire en informe le procureur de la République qui la fait inscrire sans délai au fichier des personnes recherchées. Les services de police ou de gendarmerie peuvent procéder à toutes vérifications utiles et toutes réquisitions auprès des administrations publiques pour vérifier ou retrouver l'adresse de la personne.

Des lois du 14 mars 2011, 10 août 2011 et 29 février 2012 complèteront ces dispositifs en aggravant encore leur sévérité. Comme l'écrit le Rapporteur de la loi du 29 février 2012 :

« Alors qu'il se fondait jusqu'en 2002 de façon quasiment exclusive sur une logique de responsabilité pénale aboutissant au prononcé de peines, notre droit est passé à une logique prenant en compte non plus seulement la question de la responsabilité mais également la dangerosité, dont la reconnaissance est susceptible de donner lieu au prononcé de mesures de sûreté ».[12] Il écrit également : *Notion relativement neuve et complexe, la dangerosité comporte en réalité une double dimension : psychiatrique, d'une part, et criminologique, d'autre part. S'agissant de la dimension psychiatrique, Le rapport de la commission Santé – Justice, présidée par Jean-François Burgelin avait défini la dangerosité psychiatrique comme « un risque de passage à l'acte principalement lié à un trouble mental et notamment au mécanisme et à la thématique de l'activité délirante ». Quant à la dangerosité criminologique, qui fait l'objet dans la doctrine de plusieurs définitions, elle se caractérise par un critère principal : l'existence d'un risque de récidive ou de réitération d'une nouvelle infraction empreinte d'une certaine gravité. La commission Santé – Justice avait ainsi défini la dangerosité criminologique comme un « phénomène psychosocial caractérisé par les indices révélateurs de la grande probabilité de commettre une infraction contre les personnes ou les biens ».*

Devant cet impressionnant dispositif législatif qui mêle à la fois dissuasion et traitement auquel elle s'est toujours opposée, la récente majorité politique en France a entrepris de le modifier radicalement. Tout d'abord, le projet du précédent gouvernement de construire 25 000 places de prison supplémentaires a été « gelé » bien que le constat soit toujours fait d'un « stock » de 87 000 peines non exécutées, en partie faute de places dans les prisons. Ensuite, une « Conférence de consensus » a été réunie avec essentiellement des opposants à la récente évolution législative mise en œuvre de 2005 à 2012, pour préparer l'opinion à une importante involution dont les contours ne sont pas encore clairement annoncés sinon que les peines planchers seraient supprimées comme elles le sont déjà de facto dans les juridictions où les magistrats adhérents du Syndicat de la Magistrature qui soutient la nouvelle majorité politique, sont fortement implantés.[13] Ce projet, hors de toute réalité, prévoit également une

12 Jean Paul Garraud, Député, Assemblée Nationale, Rapport n° 4112. Constatant que la justice française refuse de penser la punition remplacée par l'idéologie de la victimité, le philosophe Emmanuel Jaffelin vient de publier un passionnant ouvrage *Apologie de la punition* chez l'éditeur PLON, qui fait une intéressante synthèse des punitions dans les sociétés premières et modernes.

13 Ainsi seulement 2 % des récidivistes se voient appliquer des peines planchers dans le département de la banlieue parisienne selon la revue *Droit et Liberté*, avril-juin 2013, p. 1 et 2.

nouvelle peine, variante du sursis avec mise à l'épreuve, qui s'appellera la probation et qui sera d'application très générale, y compris pour les récidivistes…

Mais la « Conférence de consensus » fait l'objet de l'intervention à notre Colloque de notre éminent Collègue Jean Pradel auteur, entre autres, d'une lumineuse chronique sur le sujet[14], mais qui, étrangement bien qu'un des tous premiers spécialistes du droit pénitentiaire français, n'a pas été invité à la mal nommée « Conférence de consensus ».

14 Jean Pradel, *Les recommandations de la conférence de consensus sur la prévention de la récidive. Les réponses d'un incrédule*, Recueil Dalloz, 21 mars 2013, p. 725; Martine Herzog-Evans, *Conférence de consensus: trop de droit, pas assez d'envergure institutionnelle et scientifique*, Recueil Dalloz, 21 mars 2013, p. 720; Contra, voir aussi dans le camp du consensus Christine Lazerges, 'Du consensus sur la prévention de la récidive', *Revue de science criminelle et de droit pénal comparé* 1 (2013), p. 191.

GESTION DES DÉLINQUANTS À RISQUE ÉLEVÉ DE RÉCIDIVE – LE CAS DU DROIT FRANÇAIS

Jean PRADEL*

1. INTRODUCTION

La récidive, surtout celle des délinquants dangereux, est l'un des problèmes majeur qui se pose aux pénalistes, qu'ils soient théoriciens, législateurs ou juges. Certains ont vu dans ce phénomène un échec du système pénal alors pourtant qu'il n'a jamais été question de l'éradication totale de la récidive. La tolérance zéro est un slogan, non une réalité pouvant être atteinte.

D'abord quels sont ces délinquants à risque élevé de récidive ? Ce sont pour l'essentiel des hommes, souvent jeunes (moins de 40 ans) qui ayant commis une infraction grave (viol, meurtre, vol aggravé ...) offrent, de par leur éducation et leur parcours personnel et professionnel une grande probabilité de recommencer dans la grande criminalité dans un certain délai.

Quelle est l'attitude du droit français à l'égard de ce phénomène ? Précisons d'emblée que notre analyse sera essentiellement d'ordre juridique, en portant sur la durée de la peine et ses modalités d'exécution.

1) A titre de *menace*, à titre *préventif*, la loi prévoit une aggravation de la peine – le doublement du maximum encouru – en matière délictuelle et en matière criminelle : dans le premier cas, l'aggravation pour récidive joue si le nouveau délit est commis dans les cinq ans (art. 132-10 C.P.P.), mais dans le second, hypothèse plus grave, aucun délai n'est fixé (art. 132-8 C.P.).[1] Toutefois, il faut bien reconnaitre que l'efficacité de cette menace pénale est subordonnée à certaines conditions : 1° Il faut que les candidats à un nouveau passage à l'acte sachent qu'ils ont légalement de forte chances d'être pris, ce qui pose le problème

---

* J. Pradel (1933) est Professeur émérite de l'Université de Poitiers, France. Après ses études à la Faculté de droit de Poitiers, il a été magistrat pendant dix ans. Il est notamment l'auteur d'un Droit pénal comparé (2008) et le co-auteur d'un Droit pénal européen (2009). Il est membre titulaire de l'Académie internationale de droit comparé.

1 En matière criminelle, le nombre de personnes condamnées en cas de récidive est de 5,6 %. En matière correctionnelle, il est de 10 %, pour l'année 2010, Les chiffres de la justice 2012, Ministère de la justice, p. 19.

de l'efficacité du système de justice criminelle ; 2° Il faut que les peines appliquées aux récidivistes soient plus lourdes que celles appliquées aux délinquants primaires[2] ; 3° Il faut que les candidats à la récidive connaissent judiciairement le degré d'aggravation qu'ils encourent, ce qui peut poser un problème de sévérité variant selon les ressorts géographiques puisque la politique répressive, ou plutôt les pratiques répressives, peuvent varier d'un ressort judiciaire à l'autre.

2) Si une sanction forte a été *effectivement prononcée* à l'égard d'un délinquant présentant un risque élevé de récidive, comme le droit français va-t-il réagir ? Telle est la question posée par les organisateurs de ce congrès. Concrètement, la sanction est en principe une peine privative de liberté à durée déterminée (jusqu'à 30 ans de privation de liberté) ou indéterminée (réclusion à perpétuité pour quelques crimes comme l'assassinat). Or il se trouve qu'il y a une grande différence entre la peine prononcée par la juridiction de jugement et la peine exécutée par le condamné, qu'il s'agisse de la durée d'exécution de la peine ou de ses modalités d'exécution à l'intérieur de cette durée. Et ces deux aspects de l'exécution sont entendus bien plus sévèrement à l'égard des criminels dangereux dont on redoute la récidive qu'à l'égard des délinquants primaires, surtout s'ils sont l'auteur d'un délit « ordinaire ». Subsiste ainsi en droit français (et pas seulement en droit français) la vieille distinction positiviste des criminels dangereux et des criminels non dangereux.[3]

2. UNE DURÉE D'EXÉCUTION PLUS LONGUE

En droit commun, c'est-à-dire pour les délinquants ordinaires ou présumés non dangereux, la durée de la peine est systématiquement réduite par rapport à celle qu'avait été fixée par la juridiction de jugement. De plus, à l'usage de certains criminels dangereux, est institué un allongement, la rétention de sûreté qui s'ajoute à la peine et s'exécute à sa suite.

2.1. UNE MOINDRE RÉDUCTION DE LA DURÉE DE LA PRIVATION DE LIBERTÉ

La *libération conditionnelle* qui permet la sortie de prison avant le terme fixé par la juridiction de jugement mais qui implique des mesures de suivi peut intervenir à mi peine pour les délinquants primaires, mais au deux tiers pour les

2 On n'ignore pas que souvent les juges répugnent à appliquer strictement les aggravations prévues par la loi.

3 Illustrée notamment par E. Ferri, Des criminels dangereux étant des criminels nés ?, et d'habitude, v. R. Gassin, S. Cimamonti & P. Bonfils, *Criminologie*, 7ème éd., Paris : Dalloz, 2011, n° 219.

récidivistes. En outre, le « temps d'épreuve » (ou temps d'attente de la mesure)[4] ne peut excéder en principe quinze ans, mais il est porté à vingt à l'égard des récidivistes.

En outre, l'octroi de la libération conditionnelle est soumis à de très strictes conditions pour certains grands malfaiteurs.[5]

La *réduction de peine* permet également une sortie anticipée, mais en principe sans mesures de suivi est elle aussi accordée moins libéralement aux individus présumés dangereux. Lorsque le condamné est en état de récidive, le crédit de réduction de peine est calculé à hauteur de deux mois la première année et d'un mois pour les années suivantes, contre trois mois et deux mois pour les primaires (art 721 C.P.P.). Certes une réduction supplémentaire pour les détenus manifestant des « efforts sérieux de réadaptation sociale » est prévue : cependant si la personne a été condamnée pour crime ou délit commis sur un mineur, meurtre, assassinat, torture, viol, la réduction ne peut excéder deux mois par an ou quatre jours par mois, contre trois mois et sept jours par an dans les autres cas (art. 721-1 C.P.P.). Enfin dans les cas particuliers où la personne a été condamnée à une peine au moins égale à sept ans, elle peut être astreinte à une surveillance judiciaire : le matière est traitée dans une section du Code de procédure pénale au titre révélateur : « Dispositions relatives à la surveillance judiciaire de personnes dangereuses condamnées pour crime ou délit » (art. 723-29 et s.). La loi qualifie cette surveillance de mesure de sûreté et elle est prise par le tribunal de l'application des peines (non par le seul juge de l'application des peines). L'application de cette mesure est précédée d'une expertise faisant « apparaitre la dangerosité du condamné » (art. 723-31). Le condamné se trouve alors soumis à un réseau d'obligations : ne pas fréquenter certaines personnes, ne pas exercer une activité impliquant un contact habituel avec des mineurs, réparer les dommages causés par l'infraction, voire se plier à une injonction de soins notamment.

2.2. UN ALLONGEMENT DE LA DURÉE DE LA PRIVATION DE LIBERTÉ

Une loi du 25 février 2008 a créé la rétention de sûreté à l'usage de condamnés particulièrement dangereux, même s'ils ne sont pas récidivistes. Selon

[4] Donc le temps devant être passé en prison avant octroi de la libération conditionnelle. Le temps d'épreuve doit être distingué de celui d'épreuve ou temps pendant lequel le condamné, élargi du fait de l'octroi de la libération conditionnelle, fera l'objet d'un suivi.

[5] Si la personne a été condamnée à la réclusion à perpétuité ou d'au moins 15 ans ; ou en cas de commission d'un viol aggravé, d'enlèvement et d'assassinat à au moins 10 ans, la libération conditionnelle ne peut être accordée qu'après avis de la commission disciplinaire des mesures de sûreté rendue suite à une évaluation pluridisciplinaire de dangerosité effectuée par deux spécialistes, art. 730-2 C.P.P.

l'article 706-53-13 al. 1 du Code de procédure pénale, « à titre exceptionnel, les personnes dont il est établi à l'issue d'un réexamen de leur situation intervenant à la fin de l'exécution de leur peine qu'elles présentent une particulière dangerosité caractérisée par une probabilité très élevée de récidive parce qu'elles souffrent d'un trouble grave de la personnalité, peuvent faire l'objet à l'issue de cette peine d'une rétention de sûreté... ». Cette sanction prend donc la suite de la peine privative de liberté, une fois celle-ci accomplie. Le condamné passe d'un établissement pénitentiaire à un centre socio-médico-judiciaire de sûreté. Il s'agit là encore d'une mesure de sûreté et par conséquent cette mesure ne peut être prise qu'à l'issue d'une expertise de dangerosité. Sa durée est indéterminée et la mesure fait l'objet d'un réexamen une fois par an. Les décisions sont prises par une juridiction particulière, la juridiction régionale de la rétention de sûreté.[6]

En pratique cette mesure supplémentaire est peu prononcée. La loi a été critiquée par certains qui y ont vu « une peine après la peine »[7], ce qui est inexact puisqu'il s'agit d'une mesure de sûreté comme l'a d'ailleurs reconnu le Conseil constitutionnel.[8] On peut estimer que la rétention de sûreté est nécessaire pour protéger la société des crimes éventuels de grands délinquants. Elle existe d'ailleurs dans de nombreux pays d'Europe et au Canada, sous des modalités certes un peu différentes. Le Royaume Uni par exemple a institué les *Indeterminate Sentences for the Public Protection* (IPP Sentences) à l'usage des individus violents et des prédateurs sexuels; la CEDH a validé le système à la condition que des efforts soient faits par l'administration pénitentiaire aux fins de réhabilitation du détenu.[9]

La nouvelle majorité présidentielle, en place depuis mai 2012 a promis la disparition de la rétention de sûreté, ce qu'a confirmé la conférence de consensus sur la prévention de la récidive organisée par Mme Taubira, garde des sceaux en octobre 2012 et ayant rendu son rapport en février 2013.[10] Mais pour l'heure on ne sait si la promesse sera suivie d'effets.

On le voit, le législateur est sévère à l'égard des délinquants présumés dangereux en se montrant chiche pour leur rendre la liberté avant terme. Mais il va au-delà en se montrant avare également pour leur octroyer ces fameux

---

6 J. Pradel, 'Une double révolution en droit pénal français avec la loi du 25 février 2008 sur les criminels dangereux', *Recueil Dalloz* 15 (2008), 1000 en 1002; P. Bonfils, Commentaire de la loi n° 2008-174 du 25 février 2008, *RSC* 2008, 392. Le système français s'inspire largement du système allemand de la détention de sûreté.

7 R. Badinter, ancien ministre de la justice.

8 Cons. const. décision n° 2008-502 DC du 25 février 2008. Comp. CEDH qui y voit une peine et donc ne pouvant s'appliquer rétroactivement (arrêts du 17 décembre 2009, *M. c. Allemagne*, Req. 19359/04, *D.* 2010, 737, note Pradel), mais qui en admet le principe (arrêt du 9 juin 2011, *Mork v. Germany*, Req. 31047/04 et *Schmitz v. Germany*, Req. 30493/04).

9 CEDH 18 septembre 2012, *James, Wells and Lee v. The United Kingdom*, Req. 25119/09, 57715/09 and 57877/09.

10 J. Pradel, 'Les recommandations de la conférence de consensus sur la prévention de la récidive. Les réponses d'un incrédule', *Recueil Dalloz* 11 (2013), p. 725-731.

bénéfices pénitentiaires comme la semi liberté et institutions voisines : ce sont ainsi les modalités d'exécution de la peine qui sont affectées.

3. DES MODALITÉS D'EXÉCUTION PLUS STRICTES

L'idée générale du législateur est de mesurer une aux détenus présumés dangereux. On en donnera deux exemples.

3.1. LA PÉRIODE DE SÛRETÉ

Une loi du 22 novembre 1978 a créé la période de sûreté conçue comme une partie de la peine pendant laquelle les techniques habituelles d'exécution (suspension et fractionnement de la peine, placement à l'extérieur, permission de sortie, semi-liberté) ne pourront pas s'appliquer (art. 132-23 et 221-3 al. 2 C.P. ; art. 720-4 al. 2 à 4 C.P.P.). C'est la juridiction de jugement qui décide d'appliquer au condamné la période de sûreté. Ce régime, très sévère suppose évidemment que l'intéressé fasse preuve de dangerosité, ce qui correspond aux cas où il a commis des faits graves, pas forcément en récidive.

Or, pour certains faits particulièrement graves, la juridiction de jugement est tenue de prononcer la période de sûreté : ainsi en est-il du crime contre l'humanité, du trafic de stupéfiants, des actes de terrorisme, des meurtres aggravés. Dans ce dernier cas et plus précisément en cas d'assassinat, où l'accusé encourt la réclusion à perpétuité, la Cour d'assises si elle prononce cette peine peut porter la durée de la période à trente ans, et même à perpétuité si la victime est mineure de moins de quinze ans ou si le crime a été commis avec tortures et/ou actes de barbarie (art. 221-3 al. 2 C.P.).[11] Ainsi l'assassinat d'un mineur est puni de la peine la plus lourde que connait le droit français : la privation de liberté à vie, sans la moindre fenêtre comme des périodes de semi-liberté. Ceci il est vrai n'est qu'un principe car une once d'individualisation s'est glissée dans la législation.[12] Est en effet prévu un relèvement. Il est vrai que ce relèvement est soumis à des conditions très strictes. Par exemple, si la Cour d'assises a prononcé la réclusion à perpétuité et une période de sûreté elle-même à perpétuité, le tribunal de l'application des peines ne peut la réduire où la supprimer que si l'incarcération a déjà duré trente ans ; et encore faut-il qu'une expertise effectuée par un collège de trois experts près la Cour de cassation ait conclu à la cessation de la dangerosité (art. 720-4 C.P.P.).

---

11 Normalement le temps de la période de sûreté ne peut dépasser 22 ans, art. 132-23 al. 2 C.P.

12 Sinon le Conseil constitutionnel aurait invalidé la mesure, 20 janvier 1994, n° 93-334 DC, JO 26 janvier ; D. 1995, Somm. 340, obs. T. Renoux, les principes posés par l'article 8 DDHC ne concernent pas seulement les peines prononcées, mais s'étendent au régime des mesures de sûreté qui les assortissent.

3.2. LA SURVEILLANCE ÉLECTRONIQUE MOBILE

La personne condamnée à une peine d'au moins sept ans d'emprisonnement pou certaines infractions graves peut être placée sous surveillance électronique pendant la période où elle bénéficie de libération conditionnelle. Il faut que la condamnation ait porté sur une infraction pour laquelle le suivi socio judiciaire est encouru (art. 731-1 al. 2 C.P.P.). Cette sanction – mi-peine, mi mesure de sûreté – est applicable à une foule d'infractions traduisant une certaine dangerosité et donc un risque de récidive comme le meurtre ou l'assassinat lié ou non à un viol ou à des tortures, les atteintes sexuelles, les dégradations ou destructions… (art. 131-36-1 et s. C.P.).

La décision de lier la libération conditionnelle à une surveillance électronique est prise par le tribunal de l'application des peines ou par le juge de l'application des peines selon que la durée de la peine est supérieure ou non à dix ans. Cette juridiction détermine la durée pendant laquelle le condamné sera effectivement placé sous surveillance électronique mobile; cette durée ne peut excéder deux ans, renouvelable une fois en matière délictuelle et deux fois en matière criminelle (art. 731-1 al. 2 *in fine* C.P.P).

4. REMARQUES FINALES

Le système français s'est beaucoup donné depuis une dizaine d'années. Les mots sécurité, surveillance et mesures de sûreté apparaissent. La privation de liberté est le recours qui apparait indispensable. On y a vu la manifestation d'une politique populiste. Il faut y voir au moins autant la conséquence législative de la montée de la criminalité dans ses formes les plus violentes. On a pu parler d'un renouveau de la sanction pénale.[13]

Ne croyons pas cependant que ce renouveau est à sens unique, inexorablement lié à une politique de répression. La criminalité étant parfois le produit d'individus présentant des anomalies psychiques ou des troubles graves de la personnalité, le législateur a inventé le suivi socio judiciaire qui tend à soigner plus qu'à punir. Finalement, on peut constater que la paix sociale s'obtient au prix d'une alchimie entre répression et soins *lato sensu*. Mais il apparait bien difficile de savoir où placer le curseur.

---

13 S. Jacopin, *Le renouveau de la sanction pénale. Evolution ou révolution?*, Actes du colloque organisé au sein de la Faculté de droit de Caen, les 2-3 avril 2009, Bruxelles: Bruyland, 2010.

LA GESTION DES DÉLINQUANTS À RISQUE ÉLEVÉ EN ITALIE

Franco Della Casa*

1. INTRODUCTION

La loi n° 354 du 26 juillet 1975 (par la suite, l. pénit.) a négligé la question de la gestion des délinquants à risque élevé. En effet, elle a prévu pour l'ensemble des condamnés un seul type de traitement pénitentiaire et, du point de vue des structures carcérales, n'a pas prévu la création d'établissements ou de quartiers de sécurité renforcée. Ce n'est qu'avec la référence aux mesures alternatives à la détention, qui, à ce moment-là, n'étaient qu'au nombre de deux, c'est à dire le sursis avec mise à l'épreuve et la semi-liberté, que l'on a interdit leur bénéfice aux condamnés pour vol, extorsion, séquestration de personnes.

Ce choix du législateur peut être expliqué sur la base de deux considérations: en premier lieu, il faut dire que la loi n° 354 de 1975 est l'expression d'une grande (peut être, excessive) confiance dans le traitement pénitentiaire et dans la possibilité qu'il s'en suit d'atteindre l'objectif de la réinsertion sociale des condamnés; en second lieu, il faut tenir compte du fait qu'au moment de son émanation, certaines formes spécifiques de criminalité qui auraient justifié une réglementation différente pour certaines catégories de détenus ne s'étaient pas encore manifestées.[1]

Malheureusement, justement dans la seconde moitié des années soixante-dix et donc peu de temps après l'entrée en vigueur de la loi pénitentiaire, s'est avérée une longue et sanglante série de délits de matrice terroriste. Pour le terrorisme

---

* Dr. F. Della Casa est Professeur de Procédure pénale et de Droit pénitentiaire à la Faculté de Droit, Université de Gênes. Il fait partie du comité scientifique de la revue «Rassegna penitenziaria e criminological», publiée par le Ministère de la Justice, et est membre de l'Association des spécialistes du procès pénal. Il a participé aux travaux de deux commissions nommées par le Ministère de la Justice, pour l'élaboration de projets de loi. Il est auteur de nombreuses publications dans le domaine de la procédure pénale et du droit pénitentiaire.

1 Il faut souligner que ce n'est qu'en 1982 que le Comité des Ministres du Conseil de l'Europe a consacré la Recommandation N° R (82) 17 au thème du «traitement des détenus dangereux», en faisant rentrer dans cette catégorie aussi bien ceux qui mettent à risque «la sécurité publique», que ceux en mesure de compromettre «l'ordre dans les établissements pénitentiaires et leur fonctionnement».

politique de ces années, la prison a été considérée comme une institution à combattre de front, comme l'ont démontré les blessures et assassinats de personnes qui à différents titres s'engageaient ou s'étaient engagées dans ce secteur spécifique. En même temps, la prison a été, à raison, considérée comme un lieu qui se prêtait à une action de prosélytisme, un terrain fertile où les organisations terroristes pouvaient divulguer leurs idées et recueillir de nouvelles adhésions.

Pour ne pas subir passivement cette offensive, le Ministre de la Justice et l'administration pénitentiaire ont eu recours à l'article 90 l. pénit., qui avait été formulé pour faire face à d'autres situations d'urgence transitoires (par ex. révolte ou tremblement de terre qui aurait endommagé une partie de la structure pénitentiaire). Cette disposition, abrogée par la suite par l'article 10, alinéa 1° de la l. n° 663 du 10 octobre 1986, permettait au Garde des Sceaux de « congeler » ces articles de la loi pénitentiaire – par exemple la réglementation sur les visites (article 18 l. pénit.) ou sur la constitution des représentations des détenus (article 31 l. pénit.) – qu'il n'était pas possible d'appliquer tant que durait la situation d'urgence.[2] Les accusés ainsi que les condamnés pour terrorisme furent donc concentrés dans un certain nombre d'établissements de sécurité renforcée, mis en place en urgence grâce au décret ministériel du 4 mai 1977, et, en même temps, le Ministre de la Justice disposa que, dans ces établissements, une série d'articles de la loi pénitentiaire ne devaient pas être appliqués.[3]

Sur le plan des résultats, cette manœuvre a été sans doute efficace, mais elle a soulevé de fortes interrogations sur les pouvoirs excessifs réservé à l'appareil administratif ainsi que sur l'inexistence de garanties adéquates aux détenus soumis à ce régime spécial de détention. D'une part, les conditions, la durée, les contenus du régime spécial restaient obscurs, et d'autre part, on avait pu constater que le détenu ne pouvait exercer aucun type de recours contre la décision qui le soumettait à un régime de détention beaucoup plus dur que le régime ordinaire: en effet, aussi bien le juge administratif que le juge de surveillance ont déclaré le défaut de juridiction. Toute cette affaire a fait comprendre combien il est important que la loi pénitentiaire réglemente dans le détail aussi – ou mieux, surtout – ces mesures qui compriment les droits des détenus. Une fois passées les années du terrorisme et abrogé, comme on l'a dit, l'article 90 l. pénit., le législateur italien a essayé de s'adapter à ce principe.

---

2 Le texte de l'art. 90 de la loi n° 354 du 26 juillet 1975 était le suivant: « Quand il existe de graves et exceptionnels motifs d'ordre et de sécurité, le Ministre de la justice a la faculté de suspendre, complètement ou en partie, dans un ou plusieurs établissements pénitentiaires, pour un temps limité, strictement nécessaire, l'application des règles de traitement et des bénéfices prévus par la loi présente qui pourraient être en désaccord avec les exigences d'ordre et de sécurité ».

3 Sur ce thème, v. Tullio Padovani, 'Ordine e sicurezza negli istituti penitenziari: un'evasione dalla legalità', dans: Vittorio Grevi (éd), *Diritti dei detenuti e trattamento penitenziario*, Bologna: Zanichelli, 1981, p. 285-308.

2. UNE VUE D'ENSEMBLE SUR LA GESTION DES DÉLINQUANTS À RISQUE ÉLEVÉ

Alors que la Recommandation n° R (82) 17 fait rentrer dans la définition de détenus dangereux aussi bien ceux qui constituent un danger pour la sécurité publique, que ceux qui constituent une menace pour l'ordre de l'établissement pénitentiaire, dans la loi pénitentiaire italienne, ces deux catégories sont considérées séparément. Dans le premier cas, on fait ressortir le concept de « dangerosité pénitentiaire », dans le second celui de « dangerosité sociale ». Et, en conformité avec cette distinction, les article 14-*bis*, 14-*ter* et 14-*quater* l. pénit., introduits par la l. n° 663 du 10 octobre 1986, réglementent le régime de surveillance spéciale, alors que l'article 41-*bis*, introduit par le décret-loi n° 306 du 8 juin 1992 (converti en la loi n° 356 du 7 août 1992), dicte les règles d'un régime d'incarcération différencié qui, en l'absence d'une dénomination « officielle » de la part du législateur, est communément appelé régime d'incarcération dure. En considération du fait qu'il s'agit de deux régimes spéciaux, créés pour répondre à des exigences différentes, la Cour de cassation a décidé qu'un détenu peut être soumis en même temps aussi bien à la surveillance spéciale réglementée par l'article 14-*bis* l. pénit., qu'au régime prévu par l'article 41-*bis* l. pénit.[4]

Dans les paragraphes suivants seront décrites les caractéristiques essentielles des régimes spéciaux auxquels nous avons fait référence. Avant de procéder à cette description, il peut cependant être opportun, afin de présenter un cadre complet des catégories auxquelles ne s'appliquent pas les règles qui valent pour la majeure partie des condamnés, de faire brièvement référence à la gestion des auteurs d'infractions sexuelles. A partir du décret-loi n° 11 du 23 février 2009 (converti en la loi n° 38 du 23 avril 2009), un condamné pour délit sexuel ne peut être autorisé à travailler à l'extérieur et il ne peut bénéficier ni de permissions de sortie (article 30-*ter* l. pénit.), ni de mesures alternatives à la détention si, indépendamment de l'entité de la peine infligée, il n'a pas été soumis, pendant au moins un an à partir du moment où le jugement de condamnation est devenu définitif, à une période d'observation de la personnalité.[5] En outre, suite à la loi n. 172 du 1° octobre 2012, avec laquelle nous nous sommes conformés aux directives découlant de la « Convention du Conseil de l'Europe sur la protection des enfants contre l'exploitation et les abus sexuels » (Convention de Lanzarote), si le délit sexuel a été commis sur un mineur, pour bénéficier d'une quelconque mesure

4 Cass., Ière section, 23 octobre 2008, Bagarella, dans *Rivista penale*, 2009, p. 1176.

5 V. Angela Della Bella, 'Accesso ai benefici penitenziari per gli autori di reati sessuali', dans : Stefano Corbetta, Angela Della Bella, Gian Luigi Gatta (éds), *Sistema penale e « sicurezza pubblica ». Le riforme del 2009*, Milano : Wolters Kluwer, 2009, p. 437-444. Sur la « Unité de traitement intensif pour délinquants sexuels » opérant auprès de la prison de Bollate (Milan), v. Paolo Giulini, 'Le problematiche dell'osservazione scientifica della personalità : l'operatore penitenziario tra aspettative deluse e nuove prassi trattamentali' (à l'adresse htpp:// astra. csm.it/incontri/relaz/15365.pdf; consulté le 15 juillet 2013).

extra-muros, le condamné est tenu de se soumettre à un traitement psychologique spécifique.[6] Il faut souligner que ce type de traitement n'est pas obligatoire, même s'il s'agit d'une *condicio sine qua non* pour pouvoir bénéficier d'une permission de sortie ou d'une mesure alternative à la détention. Cette dernière observation nous permet de préciser que, conformément aux dispositions de l'article 27, alinéa 3° Const. ainsi que de l'article 13, alinéa 5° l. pénit., dans l'ordre juridique italien, il n'est en aucun cas permis d'obliger un condamné à se soumettre à une quelconque forme de traitement.

3. LE RÉGIME DE SURVEILLANCE SPÉCIALE (ARTICLE 14-*BIS* L. PÉNIT.)

Comme nous l'avons déjà mentionné, le régime de surveillance spéciale a pour objectif de garantir l'ordre et la sécurité dans les établissements pénitentiaires et est appliqué dans les cas où, en raison de la gravité de l'infraction ou de la personnalité du détenu, les sanctions disciplinaires – même la plus sévère d'entre elles (l'isolement du détenu pendant quinze jours au plus)[7] – sont jugées inadaptées par défaut.[8] Par exemple, dans un cas assez récent, le tribunal de surveillance de Bologne, sollicité par un recours de l'intéressé, a estimé qu'étaient réunies les conditions pour soumettre au régime de surveillance particulière un détenu qui avait noté sur une feuille les roulements, avec leurs horaires, des différents surveillants.[9]

Ce régime peut être appliqué initialement pour une durée maximale de six mois (article 14-*bis*, alinéa 1° l. pénit.), mais peut être prorogé, même plusieurs fois, pour des périodes égales ou inférieures à trois mois chacune. L'application est fixée par décision motivée de l'administration pénitentiaire à l'encontre des accusés, des condamnés et des internés[10] qui : a) de par leur comportement compromettent la sécurité ou troublent l'ordre dans les établissements ; b) avec la

---

6 V. Anna Maria Capitta, 'Legge di ratifica della Convenzione di Lanzarote : le modifiche al codice di procedura penale e alla legge sull'ordinamento penitenziario' (à l'adresse : www.penalecontemporaneo.it, 5 novembre 2012 ; consulté le 15 juillet 2013).

7 V. l'art. 39, al. 1°, n. 5 l. pénit.

8 Laura Cesaris, 'Commento agli artt.14-*bis*, 14-*ter* e 14-*quater* l. pénit.', dans : Vittorio Grevi, Glauco Giostra, Franco Della Casa (éds), *Ordinamento penitenziario commentato*, 4ème ed., Padova : Cedam, 2011, p. 182-202.

9 Trib. sorveglianza Bologna, 27 séptembre 2011 (à l'adresse : www.penalecontemporaneo.it, 15 mars 2012 ; consulté le 15 juillet 2013). Voir aussi Ministère de la Justice, Département de l'administration pénitentiaire, décret 4 avril 2013 (inédit), avec lequel a été soumis au régime spécial, pour une période initiale de trois mois, un détenu de la maison d'arrêt de Pavia qui a été trouvé en possession d'un téléphone portable.

10 Sont appelées «internati» les personnes soumises à une mesure de sûreté (par exemple : maison de travail, colonie agricole, hôpital psychiatrique judiciaire). Les mesures de sûreté sont infligées en fonction de la dangerosité sociale d'une personne qui a été reconnue coupable d'un délit (art. 202, al. 1° c. pén.).

violence ou la menace entravent les activités des autres détenus ou internés ; c) dans la vie pénitentiaire, se prévalent de l'état de sujétion des autres détenus à leur égard (article 14-*bis*, alinéa 1° l. pénit.).[11]

En référence au contenu du régime de surveillance spéciale, l'article 14-*quater* l. pénit. se limite à préciser que les restrictions, en plus d'être strictement nécessaires pour le maintien de l'ordre et de la sécurité, ne peuvent graver sur une série de droits fondamentaux garantis par la Constitution (droit à la santé, droit de défense, droit d'exercer *sa* religion, etc.). Dans la mesure où le législateur ne le précise pas, on se demande si la soumission au régime de surveillance spéciale peut amener à l'isolement continu du détenu. On doit retenir exacte la réponse négative, dans la mesure où l'article 33 l. pénit., qui fournit une liste exhaustive des situations d'isolement continu, ne mentionne pas le régime de surveillance spéciale. Ceci dit, il faut par ailleurs considérer qu'il est suffisant de faire passer une très brève partie de la journée avec ne serait-ce qu'un seul détenu pour contourner l'obstacle de l'article 33 l. pénit.

En règle générale, le régime de surveillance spéciale n'entraîne pas le transfèrement du détenu ; cependant, si l'établissement se révèle inadapté, l'administration pénitentiaire peut décider son transfèrement dans un autre établissement approprié (article 14-*quater*, alinéa 5° l. pénit.).

Un recours devant le tribunal de surveillance peut être présenté par l'intéressé à l'encontre de la décision qui établit ou proroge le régime de surveillance spéciale. La procédure se déroule selon les dispositions de l'article 14-*ter* l. pénit. Le tribunal de surveillance peut nier que soient remplies les conditions pour l'instauration du régime de surveillance spéciale, ou peut se limiter à déclarer injustifiées certaines restrictions et n'accueillir que partiellement le recours, qui, de toute façon, n'a pas d'effet suspensif.

4. L' « INCARCÉRATION DURE » DÉCOULANT DE L'ARTICLE 41-*BIS*, ALINÉA 2° L. PÉNIT.

4.1. LA GENÈSE ET L'ÉVOLUTION DE L'ARTICLE 41-*BIS*, ALINÉA 2° L. PÉNIT.

L'article 41-*bis*, alinéa 2° l. pénit. a été introduit en 1992 à un moment de grande inquiétude face à la criminalité organisée : en effet, cette année-là, deux attentats

11 Alors qu'en ce qui concerne le soi-disant régime d'incarcération dure les données statistiques sont détaillées et faciles d'accès (v. *infra*, § 4.3), on ne peut en dire de même pour le régime spécial prévu à l'art. 14-*bis* l. pénit. Les chiffres reportés ci-après (période : 2007-2012), et qui ont été obtenus grâce à la gentillesse du Directeur de la séction « Detenuti e trattamento » de l'administration pénitentiaire, sont peu parlants car ils se réfèrent aux nouveaux régimes intervenus au cours d'une année « x », mais n'indiquent pas les prorogations des régimes précédemment instaurés. Ceci dit, les nouveaux décrets ont été : 115 en 2007 ; 176 en 2008 ; 158 en 2009 ; 149 en 2010 ; 170 en 2011 ; 129 en 2012.

sanglants qui coutèrent la vie aux magistrats Falcone et Borsellino ainsi qu'à leurs escortes furent commis par la mafia.

Comme le régime de surveillance spéciale, examiné dans le précédent paragraphe, le régime de détention prévu à l'article 41-*bis*, alinéa 2° l. pénit., implique de fortes restrictions pour les accusés, les condamnés ainsi que les internés qui y sont soumis. Par contre, il doit être distingué du régime de surveillance spéciale, car il a pour objectif d'empêcher que les détenus et les internés membres de la criminalité organisée, même incarcérés, gardent contact avec leur association criminelle et soient en mesure de mettre en danger la sécurité de la société.[12]

Cependant, tous les commentateurs ne partagent pas ce qui vient d'être affirmé. En effet, pour certains, l'objectif réel que l'on veut atteindre avec l'article 41-*bis*, alinéa 2° l. pénit. serait tout autre, c'est-à-dire la création d'un régime de détention particulièrement rigoureux, permettant d'amener les membres de la criminalité organisée à collaborer avec la justice.[13] A noter que si cette condition est remplie, les condamnés pour les délits de criminalité organisée non seulement évitent d'être soumis au régime spécial prévu à l'article 41-*bis*, alinéa 2° l. pénit., mais peuvent jouir des permissions de sortie et des mesures alternatives à la détention dont le bénéfice est admis par l'article 4-*bis* l. pénit. uniquement à condition que les condamnés appartenant à la criminalité organisée collaborent, précisément, avec la justice.

Au moment de son introduction, prévu par le décret-loi n° 306 du 8 juin 1992 (converti en la loi n° 356 du 7 août 1992)[14], l'article 41-*bis*, alinéa 2° l. pénit. était caractérisé par des analogies marquées avec l'article 90 de la loi n. 354 de 1975 (v. *supra*, § I). Le législateur n'avait précisé ni les contenus, ni la durée du régime d'incarcération dure et, surtout, n'avait pas prévu que l'intéressé puisse présenter un recours contre la décision du Ministre de la Justice.

L'article 41-*bis*, alinéa 2° l. pénit. est considéré sans aucun doute comme le produit d'une législation d'urgence et le législateur semble en avoir été lui-même conscient, car il en a circonscrite la durée dans le temps : initialement, jusqu'au 8 août 1995, délai maintes fois prorogé jusqu'au 31 décembre 2002. Cependant, la l. 23 décembre 2002, n. 279 a éliminé toute clause temporelle, par conséquent ce texte ne cessera d'être en vigueur que suite à une éventuelle abrogation.

---

12 V., entre autres, Sebastiano Ardita, *Il regime detentivo speciale 41-bis*, Milano : Giuffrè, 2007.

13 Giovanni Torrente, 'Il regime speciale dell'art. 41-*bis* ord.penit. tra funzioni manifeste e funzioni latenti della norma giuridica', V *Antigone* 1 (2010), p. 149 et suiv. ; Leonardo Filippi, 'La « novella » penitenziaria del 2002 : la proposta dell'Unione delle camere penali e una « controriforma » che urta con la Costituzione e con la Convenzione europea', *Cassazione penale* (2003) 1, p. 24 et suiv.

14 « Quand il existe de graves motifs d'ordre et de sécurité publique, même sur demande du Ministère de l'intérieur, le Ministre de la Justice a [...] la faculté de suspendre, complètement ou en partie, à l'égard des détenus pour un des délits indiqués par l'alinéa 1 de l'article 4-bis, l'application des règles de traitement et des bénéfices prévus par la loi présente qui pourraient être en désaccord avec les exigences d'ordre et de sécurité ».

Grâce aussi à l'apport fondamental de la Cour constitutionnelle, qui a indiqué des modifications jugées nécessaires pour harmoniser le régime d'incarcération dure avec la Constitution[15], le législateur est intervenu, dans un premier temps, avec la loi n° 11 du 7 janvier 1998 et, par la suite, avec la déjà citée loi n° 279 du 23 décembre 2002. Ces deux textes ont introduit des garanties en faveur du détenu placé en régime différencié : le premier a prévu la possibilité d'un recours devant le tribunal de surveillance contre la décision du Ministre de la Justice ; le second, en plus de définir en termes moins génériques les conditions, a spécifié les contenus, la durée de la période initiale (au moins un an et deux ans au plus) et des éventuelles prorogations (d'une durée d'un an chacune) ; en outre, du point de vue procédural, les garanties inhérentes aux voies de recours ont été renforcées, et il a été prévu par la loi le recours en cassation – de la part du ministère public, de l'intéressé et de son défenseur – contre l'ordonnance prononcée par le tribunal de surveillance.

En voulant compléter notre *excursus*, il faut préciser, qu'après la loi n° 279 de 2002, est intervenue la loi n° 94 du 15 juillet 2009, à laquelle il faut relier la réglementation en vigueur du régime d'incarcération dure. C'est pour cela qu'elle mérite une plus grande attention par rapport à celle réservée aux textes législatifs mentionnés jusqu'ici.

4.2. LA RÉGLEMENTATION ACTUELLE DU « RÉGIME D'INCARCÉRATION DURE »

Comme il ressort explicitement du débat parlementaire, les modifications au régime d'incarcération dure apportées par la loi n° 94 du 15 juillet 2009 ont eu pour objectif de rendre encore plus difficile aux détenus appartenant à la criminalité organisée la possibilité de garder un lien avec les associations criminelles dans lesquelles ils opéraient avant leur entrée en prison. Plus d'une voix s'était en effet levée pour soutenir que la barrière du placement en régime différencié n'était pas toujours impénétrable. Non seulement : les critiques s'étaient aussi tournées contre le travail des tribunaux de surveillance, lesquels, selon certains organismes de l'Etat (Procureur national « anti-mafia », administration pénitentiaire), annulaient avec une facilité excessive les décrets avec lesquels le Ministre de la Justice instaurait ou prorogeait le régime de détention spéciale prévu à l'article 41-*bis*, alinéa 2° l. pénit. Par conséquent, en synthèse, on peut affirmer que les deux caractéristiques principales de la réforme du régime spécial mise en œuvre par le législateur en 2009 ont été, d'une part, le

---

[15] V. Cour const. 28 juillet 1993, n° 349 ; Cour const. 18 octobre 1996, n° 351. Il faut rappeler, en particulier, Cour const. 5 décembre 1997, n° 376, où il est affirmé que le placement en régime différencié n'implique pas la suspension des activités d'observation et de traitement, même si il est inévitable que ces dernières soient concrètement diversifiées par rapport à celles garanties aux condamnés soumis au régime ordinaire de détention.

durcissement des conditions de détention réservées aux détenus soumis au régime différencié, et, d'autre part, la diminution des pouvoirs de contrôle attribués au tribunal de surveillance.[16]

Ceci dit, il est indispensable de mettre en évidence les aspects les plus importants de la réglementation actuelle[17] :

1. le régime dont nous nous occupons s'applique aux accusés, condamnés ou internés pour un des délits prévus au premier alinéa de l'article 4-*bis* l. pénit. (il s'agit de délits qui font présumer l'appartenance à la criminalité organisée ou à des associations terroristes) ou aussi pour un délit commun – on pense à un incendie volontaire d'un magasin – derrière lequel on peut envisager la présence de la criminalité organisée. Cette condition n'est pas suffisante, étant également nécessaire de démontrer concrètement l'existence de liens avec une association criminelle.
2. Le régime a une durée initiale de quatre ans, mais des prolongations sont admises – d'une durée de deux ans chacune – à moins qu'il ressorte que la capacité de maintenir des contacts avec la criminalité organisée ou terroriste n'a plus lieu d'être. L'établissement doit regrouper uniquement des détenus soumis au régime spécial et être de préférence situé sur une île. La surveillance est confiée à des services spécialisés de la police pénitentiaire.
3. Un point particulièrement important, est celui du contenu du régime examiné : a) en ce qui concerne les visites, elles sont admises – au nombre d'une par mois[18] – uniquement celles de la famille et des personnes vivant sous le même toit et doivent se dérouler dans des locaux équipés de manière à empêcher le passage d'objets. L'entretien, d'une durée maximum d'une heure, est écouté par des surveillants et est aussi enregistré, avec autorisation préalable de l'autorité judiciaire ; b) uniquement pour les détenus ne bénéficiant pas de visites, un entretien téléphonique par mois avec la famille et les personnes vivant sous le même toit est prévu : il est enregistré et dure dix minutes au maximum[19] ; c) en ce qui concerne les entretiens entre l'accusé et son avocat – entretiens qui, évidemment se déroulent hors de portée d'écoute d'un tiers – sont admis trois entretiens en vis à vis d'une heure maximum chacun ou trois entretiens téléphoniques hebdomadaires de

16 Carlo Fiorio, 'La stabilizzazione delle « carceri-fortezza » : modifiche in tema di ordinamento penitenziario' dans : Oliviero Mazza & Franco Viganò (éds), *Il 'pacchetto sicurezza' 2009*, Torino : Giappichelli, 2009, p. 402 et suiv.

17 Pour une description plus détaillée, v. Paola Corvi, *Trattamento penitenziario e criminalità organizzata*, Padova : Cedam, 2010, p. 148 et suiv.

18 Il faut signaler que sur la base de l'art. 37, al. 8° règl. appl. loi pénitentiaire, les condamnés soumis au régime ordinaire de détention bénéficient de six visites par mois.

19 Sur la base des dispositions de l'art. 39, al. 2° et 6° règl. appl. loi pénitentiaire il est permis aux condamnés soumis au régime ordinaire de détention de passer un appel par semaine d'une durée maximum de dix minutes.

la même durée[20]; d) la correspondance épistolaire est censurée, sauf celle avec les membres du Parlement et avec les organismes internationaux; e) il est admis de disposer de limitations – plus sévères que celles concernant les détenus soumis au régime ordinaire de détention – des sommes d'argent et d'objets qui peuvent être reçus de l'extérieur; f) le séjour en plein air, d'une durée maximum de deux heures par jour, est effectué par groupes de quatre personnes maximum; g) les mesures nécessaires sont adoptées pour empêcher les communications avec d'autres groupes de détenus, ainsi que pour empêcher l'échange d'objets et la cuisson d'aliments en cellule.

4. Il reste à examiner le rôle du tribunal de surveillance, auquel le détenu peut s'adresser par un recours aussi bien au moment de la mise en place, qu'au moment de la prorogation. Attendu que le recours n'a pas d'effet suspensif, on peut observer que les modifications les plus significatives sont au nombre de deux: avant tout, le seul tribunal compétent est le tribunal de surveillance de Rome (alors que précédemment la compétence était repartie entre les vingt-neuf tribunaux de surveillance, chacun desquels était légitimé à contrôler le décret du Ministre de la Justice lorsqu'il concernait un détenu situé dans un établissement sur lequel le tribunal exerçait sa juridiction).[21] Avec cette modification, on a poursuivi l'objectif d'éliminer la variété des orientations jurisprudentielles qui avaient caractérisé la période précédente. En second lieu, le tribunal de surveillance ne peut plus exercer son contrôle sur le fond du décret ministériel, afin d'annuler les restrictions non cohérentes avec les objectifs du régime différencié.[22]

---

20 A ce sujet, voir, cependant, récemment, Cour constitutionnelle, 17 juin 2013, n° 143, qui a déclaré l'illégitimité constitutionnelle de la dernière période de l'art. 41-*bis*, al. 2-*quater*, let. *b* l.pénit., retenue contradictoire avec le droit de défense garanti par l'art. 24, al. 2° Const. D'une part, les juges constitutionnels ont observé que, comme le détenu peut être impliqué dans plusieurs procédures (et avoir divers défenseurs), la limite des trois heures hebdomadaires peut avoir une incidence négative sur l'effectivité de la défense; d'autre part, ils ont souligné que, comme les entretiens ne sont ni écoutés, ni enregistrés, limiter leur durée ne sert pas à neutraliser la communication d'éventuelles directives que le détenu désire faire parvenir à son organisation criminelle.

21 On appliquait en effet le critère de compétence territoriale prévu par l'art. 677, al. 1° c.p.p.

22 Il est sans aucun doute, de toute façon, que si le détenu soumis au régime d'incarcération dure se plaint de la violation d'un de ses droits – faisons l'hypothèse que ne lui soient pas administrés les médicaments prescrits par le médecin qui l'a ausculté – il peut présenter un recours, comme tout autre détenu, au juge de surveillance. A ce sujet, il faut cependant signaler l'existence d'un problème important non résolu: il manque un instrument adapté pour garantir l'exécution forcée de la décision du juge de surveillance, avec la conséquence que si l'administration ne s'adapte pas, le succès du détenu est purement théorique. A ce sujet, v. récemment Carlo Renoldi, 'Poteri del giudice di sorveglianza e doveri dell'amministrazione penitenziaria', *Antigone* 2-3 (2011), p. 80-101. Le problème du refus de l'administration pénitentiaire n'est pas seulement italien: en référence à l'Allemagne, v. Johannes Feest, Wolfgang Lesting, 'Contempt of Court. Zur Wiederkehr des Themas der renitenten Strafvollzugsbehörden', dans Henning Ernst Müller, Günther M. Sander & Helena Válková (éds), *Festschrift für Ulrich Eisenberg zum 70. Geburtstag*, München: C.H. Beck, 2009, p. 675 et suiv.

Sur ce dernier point, on a par ailleurs soutenu que le redimensionnement du rôle du tribunal de surveillance est une pure et simple conséquence du fait qu'après la loi n° 94 de 2009, le Ministre n'a plus aucune marge de discrétion, car les limites provenant de sa décision sont entièrement prédéfinies par le législateur.[23] Sauf que cette explication n'est vraie qu'en partie : il suffit de penser au séjour en plein air, qui peut durer une ou deux heures et qui peut se dérouler par groupes de deux, trois ou quatre personnes (article 41-*bis*, *al* 2°-*quater*, let. *f*). Et surtout, on pense aux dispositions de l'article 41-*bis*, alinéa 2°-*quater*, let. *a*, où il est prévu que le décret du Ministre de la Justice implique l'adoption de « mesures de sécurité internes et externes élevées » non précisées. Concrètement, cela signifie que c'est l'administration pénitentiaire qui décide, par exemple, si la lumière de la cellule doit rester allumée durant la nuit et si le détenu doit aussi être soumis à vidéosurveillance lorsqu'il utilise les toilettes.[24]

S'il est vrai que ces modifications dernièrement mises en évidence sont les plus significatives, il est aussi vrai qu'avec la loi n° 94 de 2009 le législateur a également effectué des mises au point qui désavouent explicitement certaines orientations précédentes des tribunaux de surveillance. En particulier, il est établi que, si la condamnation concerne cumulativement une pluralité de délits, il est licite d'appliquer le régime d'incarcération dure « même lorsque la partie de la peine [...] relative aux délits cités à l'art 4-*bis* l.pénit. » (article 41-*bis*, alinéa 2°, dernière période) a été purgée. En outre, dans la mesure où les tribunaux de surveillance avaient fréquemment annulé les prorogations disposées envers des détenus soumis depuis longtemps au régime spécial, le législateur souligne que, en soi, le passage du temps ne peut permettre d'exclure l'absence de liens avec la criminalité organisée (article 41-*bis*, alinéa 2°-*bis* l.pénit.). Les tribunaux de surveillance doivent désormais tenir compte de ces directives, qui ont manifestement une incidence sur leurs pouvoirs d'annulation.

Il faut rappeler, enfin, que si un détenu est soumis au régime en objet, il ne lui est pas permis de participer personnellement aux audiences pénales qui le concernent. Le motif de cette interdiction est facilement compréhensible : on veut empêcher qu'une fois conduit au palais de justice, à travers des gestes ou des messages verbaux chiffrés, il communique avec les membres de l'association criminelle présents dans la salle d'audience. D'un autre point de vue, il faut cependant tenir compte de l'article 24, alinéa 2° Const. qui déclare « inviolable » le droit de défense. De ces deux exigences opposées est née une solution de compromis : selon les articles 45-*bis* et 146-*bis* des dispositions d'application, de coordination et des dispositions

23 Cour const., 28 mars 2010, n°190.

24 Il faut signaler un arrêt de la Cour de cassation, dans lequel il est affirmé qu'il est contraire à l'art. 8 CEDH et avec l'art. 27 Const. de disposer pour un détenu soumis au régime de l'art. 41-*bis* l. pénit. la vidéosurveillance continue (en particulier durant l'usage des toilettes), lorsque pour cette surveillance un contrôle visuel direct de celui-ci pourrait être suffisant : v. Cass., Vème section, 15 mars 2011, Lopiccolo, dans *Archivio penale*, 2011, fasc. n°2, p. 613, obs. Benedetta Bocchini.

transitoires du Code de procédure pénale, il ressort que cette catégorie particulière de détenus ne peut participer aux débats qu'à distance, grâce à une liaison audiovisuelle entre un poste prévu à cet effet dans la prison où ils sont détenus et la salle d'audience. La Cour constitutionnelle a exclu que la réglementation sur la participation à distance soit en opposition avec la loi fondamentale.[25]

4.3. APERÇU PLUS DÉTAILLÉ ...

Après avoir complété l'exposé du cadre règlementaire, il peut s'avérer utile de fournir quelques statistiques sur le régime spécial qui a été sommairement décrit : fin 2012, le nombre de détenus soumis à ce régime s'élevait à un total de 699. Pour obtenir les chiffres concernant les années comprises entre 1992 et 2011, voir le tableau ci-dessous[26] :

Année	Nouveaux décrets d'application émis par le Ministre au cours de l'année	Total des détenus article 41-*bis* en fin d'année
1992	510	498
1993	129	473
1994	94	445
1995	129	485
1996	59	476
1997	80	422
1998	115	461
1999	146	582
2000	30	564
2001	151	645
2002	106	659
2003	91	623
2004	49	604
2005	53	577
2006	70	526
2007	129	586
2008	90	587
2009	116	646
2010	91	680
2011	82	673

[25] V. Cour const. 14 juillet 1999, n. 342 ; v. aussi *Zagaria c. Italie*, CEDH, 2ème section, Arrêt du 27 novembre 2007, Req. n° 58295/00, paragr. 29, où la Cour affirme : « la participation de l'accusé aux débats par vidéoconférence n'est pas, en soi, contraire à la Convention ».

[26] Pour les chiffres reportés dans les deux tableaux, v. Ministero della giustizia. Relazione al Parlamento ai sensi dell'art. 5 della legge n° 279 del 2002. Periodo : 2009/2011, (à l'adresse : www.ristretti.it/commenti/2013/maggio/pdf5/circolare_41*bis*.pdf ; consulté le 15 juillet 2013).

Il peut être également intéressant de fournir le cadre des décrets ministériels annulés, ces dernières années, par les tribunaux de surveillance. Le tableau ci-dessous fait clairement ressortir aussi bien un nombre élevé d'annulations lors des trois années précédant l'entrée en vigueur de la loi n° 94 de 2009, qu'une inversion de tendance significative après l'entrée en vigueur de ladite loi.

Année	Décrets ministériels annulés par les Tribunaux de surveillance
2006	89
2007	66
2008	68
2009	37
2010	33
2011	27

Un dernier chiffre à notre disposition concerne le nombre de suicides des détenus soumis au régime de détention spéciale : depuis que ce régime a été mis en œuvre – dans la période comprise entre juin 1992 et mars 2013 – trente-neuf suicides se sont produits, ce qui représente un pourcentage trois fois et demi supérieur à celui enregistré au cours de la même période pour ce qui est des détenus soumis au régime ordinaire de détention.[27]

Dans la mesure où le chiffre relatif au nombre de suicides soulève des interrogations immédiates sur l'éventuel caractère inhumain de la détention mise en place selon les dispositions de l'article 41-*bis*, alinéa 2° l. pénit., il convient de préciser qu'à maintes reprises la Cour européenne a abordé la question et que, dans tous les cas examinés par ses soins, elle a exclu le contraste entre le régime d'incarcération dure et l'article 3 CEDH. Elle a toujours estimé que le régime spécial visé à l'article 41-*bis*, qui comporte un simple *isolement social relatif*, ne constitue pas, en soi, un traitement inhumain ou dégradant. En partant de la prémisse selon laquelle seul l'isolement sensoriel et social complet serait à même de détruire la personnalité d'un détenu[28], la Cour européenne n'a

27 Source : Osservatorio permanente sulle morti in carcere (à l'adresse : www.ristretti.it/commenti/2013/marzo/pdf6/comunicato_opera.pdf; consulté le 15 juillet 2013).

28 Pour cette argumentation qui remonte à quelques années, v. notamment, *Messina c. Italie*, CEDH, 2ème section, Arrêt du 8 juin 1999, Req. n° 25498/94, (paragr. 1 des considérations « en droit »), où il est dit que : « la Cour rappelle que l'isolement sensoriel complet associé à un isolement social total peut détruire la personnalité et constitue une forme de traitement inhumain qui ne saurait se justifier par les exigences de la sécurité ou toute autre raison ». Cependant il a été ajouté que : « la Cour observe d'emblée que le requérant n'a pas été soumis à un isolement sensoriel ni à un isolement social absolu. En revanche, il a été soumis à un *isolement social relatif*, découlant de l'interdiction de voir des détenus soumis à un régime de détention différent, de l'interdiction de recevoir des visites de personnes autres que les membres de sa famille et de l'interdiction de téléphoner ». A ce propos, v. Emanuele Nicosia, 'Il c.d. 41-bis è una forma di tortura o trattamento crudele, inumano o degradante?', 52 *Rivista italiana di diritto e procedura penale* 3 (2009), p. 1267; Carmelo Minnella, 'La

jamais modifié son orientation n'accordant aucune véritable importance à la durée du régime différencié : preuve en est qu'elle n'a même pas changé d'opinion quand lui a été soumis un cas où l'application de ce régime s'était prolongée durant plus de douze ans.[29]

Après avoir identifié le fil conducteur de la jurisprudence de la Cour européenne pour ce qui est de l'article 41-*bis* l. pénit., il convient de préciser que les conclusions des juges de Strasbourg seraient très probablement toutes autres si le régime spécial était appliqué à un détenu très âgé, ou ayant un mauvais état de santé[30] ou – même si, dans cette hypothèse le diagnostic est plus difficile – à un détenu mineur. Pour ce dernier cas, il convient de préciser qu'il n'existe en Italie aucune loi pénitentiaire réservée exclusivement aux personnes mineures. Par conséquent, l'article 79 l. pénit. continue de s'appliquer. Cet article établit que, tant que le législateur n'aura rien fait en ce sens, les dispositions contenues dans la loi pénitentiaire de 1975 continueront de s'appliquer aux détenus mineurs. Cela a pour conséquence que, en théorie, un détenu mineur pourrait être soumis au régime visé à l'article 41-*bis* l. pénit.[31]

5. LE CIRCUIT PÉNITENTIAIRE DE HAUTE SÉCURITÉ

A partir de 1993 (circulaire n°3359/5809 du 21 avril 1993) l'administration pénitentiaire, en reprenant les dispositions de l'article 14, alinéa 2° l. pénit.[32], a instauré trois circuits destinés, respectivement, aux membres de la criminalité organisée (circuit de haute sécurité, indiqué avec le sigle A.S.), aux toxicomanes ayant une faible dangerosité sociale (circuit de peines aménagées, indiqué avec le

giurisprudenza della Corte europea dei diritti dell'uomo sul regime carcerario *ex* art. 41-bis ord. penit. e la sua applicazione nell'ordinamento italiano', *Rassegna penitenziaria e criminologica* 3 (2004), p. 197 et suiv.

29 V. *Gallico c. Italie*, CEDH, 4ème section, Arrêt du 28 juin 2005, Req. n° 53723/00, paragr. 20.

30 En ce qui concerne la jurisprudence italienne, il convient de rappeler un cas où le régime visé à l'art. 41-*bis* l. pénit. avait été appliqué à un détenu psychotique qui, après examen médical, avait été déclaré être atteint du syndrome de Ganser; pour l'annulation de la mesure de prorogation du régime, v. Trib. sorveglianza L'Aquila, 14 juin 2005, n°1062, dans *Diritto & giustizia*, 2 juillet 2005 (à l'adresse: www.dirittoegiustizia.it; consulté le 14 juillet 2013), où justement il avait été observé que la maladie diagnostiquée faisait que le détenu n'était plus à même de maintenir des contacts avec une quelconque organisation criminelle.

31 Dans le même sens : v. Massimo Ruaro, 'I diritti dei detenuti e le misure alternative alla detenzione' dans : Maria Grazia Coppetta (éd), *L'esecuzione penitenziaria a carico del minorenne nelle carte internazionali e nell'ordinamento italiano*, Milano : Giuffrè, 2010, p. 98.

32 En se référant à une compétence réservée de manière exclusive à l'administration pénitentiaire, l'art. 14, al. 2° l. pénit. prévoit que : « l'affectation des condamnés et des internés à chaque établissement et le regroupement dans les sections de chaque établissement sont organisés avec un soin particulier en fonction de la possibilité d'appliquer un traitement rééducatif commun et à l'exigence d'éviter de nuisibles influences réciproques ».

sigle C.A.) et aux détenus ne rentrant dans aucune des deux précédentes catégories (circuit de moyenne sécurité, indiqué par le sigle S.M.).

Dans un tel contexte, notre attention se portera tout particulièrement sur le circuit de haute sécurité, dont l'existence est désormais légitimée également par l'article 32 règl. appl. de la loi pénitentiaire, approuvé par décret n° 230 du Président de la République de l'an 2000. A l'heure actuelle, le circuit de haute sécurité est unique[33], bien qu'il comprenne trois sous-circuits (indiqués avec les sigles A.S. 1 – A.S. 2 – A.S. 3), et est régi par la circulaire de l'administration pénitentiaire n°3619/6069 du 21 avril 2009.

Il n'est pas possible de fournir, ici, une indication détaillée des catégories de détenus affectés au circuit de haute sécurité. Par conséquent, nous nous limiterons à citer les catégories les plus significatives, c'est-à-dire les détenus précédemment soumis au régime visé à l'article 41-*bis*, alinéa 2° l. pénit., qui continue de produire ses effets également après sa cessation formelle, et les détenus emprisonnés pour des délits liés au terrorisme ou au renversement de l'ordre démocratique.

Dans sa circulaire de 2009, l'administration pénitentiaire tient à préciser que l'affectation d'un détenu au circuit de haute sécurité n'entraîne pas que ce dernier soit soumis à un régime spécial, étant donné que l'exécution de la peine reste encore et toujours régie par les dispositions dictées, de manière générale, par la loi pénitentiaire. Toujours selon l'administration pénitentiaire, l'affectation constitue la prémisse de l'individualisation du traitement pénitentiaire. C'est dans une telle optique que doivent être prises en considération les principales particularités du circuit de haute sécurité comme les meilleures garanties de sécurité offertes par la structure carcérale, ainsi que la présence de dispositifs électroniques en mesure de garantir un niveau élevé de surveillance.

Toutefois, si l'on tient compte de la réalité des choses, il est difficile de ne pas affirmer que l'affectation d'un détenu au circuit de haute sécurité implique des conditions de détention différentes de celles des détenus affectés au circuit de sécurité moyenne. Selon nous, le fait d'affirmer qu'il n'est pas possible, dans un tel cas, de parler techniquement d'un véritable régime différencié finit par n'être qu'une simple subtilité terminologique. L'exécution de la peine de détention est sans nul doute plus contraignante et l'administration pénitentiaire jouit d'un vaste pouvoir discrétionnaire, étant donné que les critères d'affectation au circuit pénitentiaire, ainsi que ses contenus effectifs ne sont pas régis par la loi, mais par les circulaires, ainsi que par les ordres de service du directeur de la prison et les dispositions contenues dans le règlement intérieur de l'établissement pénitentiaire.

Il reste à préciser que la décision par laquelle un détenu est affecté au circuit de haute sécurité est considérée comme non contrôlable par le tribunal de surveillance: en effet, la Cour de cassation a toujours considéré un tel acte

33 Par la circulaire du 9 juillet 1998, n° 3479/5929, la mise en œuvre du circuit de haute sécurité a été accompagné par la création d'un «circuit de haute vigilance» (sigle: E.I.V.), que la circulaire successive du 21 avril 2009, n° 3619/6069 a inclus dans le circuit de haute sécurité.

comme étant l'expression du pouvoir discrétionnaire de l'administration pénitentiaire qui reste libre d'organiser, comme bon lui semble, la vie à l'intérieur des établissements pénitentiaires.[34] Toutefois, à partir de l'arrêt n°26/1999 de la Cour constitutionnelle, qui a reconnu au magistrat de surveillance la faculté de se prononcer sur les recours déposés par les détenus dénonçant la violation de leurs droits par l'administration pénitentiaire, la Cour de cassation a mis à jour sa jurisprudence, en affirmant que la garantie reconnue par l'arrêt n°26 de 1999 vaut également pour le détenu soumis au régime de haute sécurité.[35] A titre d'illustration, il est possible de citer l'exemple des fouilles à nu réalisées selon des modalités ne respectant pas la dignité de la personne qui les subit. Compte tenu de cette forme de protection juridique, la Cour européenne a exclu que l'affectation du détenu au circuit de haute sécurité puisse contenir des éléments en contraste avec la CEDH[36], renversant ainsi l'orientation contraire qui avait abouti, quelques années auparavant, à une condamnation de l'Italie pour violation de l'article 6 § 1 CEDH.[37]

Malgré cela, de nombreuses perplexités subsistent. Ces dernières concernent, d'une part, la diversité, seulement partiellement justifiée, par rapport aux mesures qui encadrent le régime de surveillance spéciale (voir § 3 ci-dessus) et le régime visé à l'article 41-*bis* l. pénit. (voir § 4.1 ci-dessus). Le détenu peut déposer un recours auprès du tribunal de surveillance contre des mesures qui mettent en œuvre ou prolongent le régime auquel il est soumis. D'autre part, les perplexités sont de caractère plus général et doivent être rattachées à l'absence du mécanisme, mentionné précédemment, qui garantit l'exécution forcée des arrêts du magistrat de surveillance quand ces derniers sont favorables au réclamant (voir la note de bas de page n° 22). En définitive, pour le détenu affecté à un circuit de haute sécurité, la somme de ces deux éléments négatifs donne l'image d'un droit pénitentiaire qui en est pas encore suffisamment évolué.

6. CONCLUSION

Après avoir surmonté l'« état de nécessité » auquel il a été fait face en recourant à une application anomale de l'article 90 l. pénit. (v. *supra*, § 1), le législateur italien

---

34 Vont dans ce sens, Cass., I ère section, 6 novémbre 2008, Musumeci, dans *Cassazione penale*, 2009, p. 3980; Cass., I ère section, 9 juin 1994, Cella, *ibidem*, 1996, p. 307; Cass., I ère section, 21 octobre 1993, Della Zoppa, *ibidem*, 1994, p. 3110.

35 V. Cass., I ère section, 24 novémbre 2009, Lo Piccolo, dans *Rivista penale*, 2011, p. 94; Cass., 28 novémbre 2007, I ère section, Barreca, *ibidem*, 2008, p. 948; Cass., I ère section, 24 octobre 2007, Musumeci, *ibidem*, 2008, p. 1206; Cass., Ière section, 3 février 2004, Pazienza, dans *Cassazione penale*, 2005, p. 2351.

36 *Enea c. Italie*, CEDH, Grand Chambre, Arrêt du 17 séptembre 2009, Req. n° 33695/96, paragr. 118 et suiv.

37 *Musumeci c. Italie*, CEDH, 4ème section, Arrêt du 11 janvier 2005, Req. n° 33695/96, paragr.48 et suiv.

a affronté le problème de la gestion des détenus dangereux et a, en règle générale, opté pour le principe de limiter, le plus possible, les marges de manœuvre du pouvoir discrétionnaire de l'appareil administratif. Toutefois, un tel objectif n'a pas été atteint à cent pour cent. Par exemple, en ce qui concerne le régime de surveillance spéciale (v. *supra*, § 3), il aurait été préférable que le législateur indique plus précisément les limites d'un tel régime plutôt que d'en établir les restrictions non autorisées (article 14-*ter*, alinéa 4° l. pénit.). Pareillement, dans le secteur de l'incarcération dure, la loi de 2009 a redéfini les pouvoirs de contrôle du tribunal de surveillance en lui interdisant de censurer les différentes restrictions sous prétexte qu'elles sont désormais fixées directement par le législateur. Cela ne correspond pas entièrement à la réalité. En effet, comme nous l'avons précédemment dit (v. *supra*, § 4.2), le Ministre de la Justice et l'administration pénitentiaire conservent d'importantes marges de manœuvre en ce qui concerne leur pouvoir discrétionnaire.

Quoi qu'il en soit, la violation la plus importante du principe de légalité est représentée par les modalités de fonctionnement du circuit de haute sécurité. Contrairement à ce qui se produit dans d'autres systèmes judiciaires – notamment en France où la décision de l'administration pénitentiaire de prononcer le placement d'un détenu en régime d'incarcération différenciée est susceptible de faire l'objet d'un recours pour excès de pouvoir devant le juge administratif[38] – en Italie les tribunaux administratifs déclarent leur absence de compétence juridictionnelle à propos des décisions qui, comme celle examinée, affectent directement des positions juridiques subjectives rentrant dans la sphère de la liberté personnelle.[39] Si l'on tient compte de la jurisprudence de tels tribunaux, le juge de surveillance devrait donc intervenir. Or, cette autorité judiciaire, comme nous l'avons vu précédemment, ne peut s'opposer aux arrêtés de transfert d'un détenu d'un établissement pénitentiaire à un autre. Il peut toutefois intervenir si, durant la permanence d'un détenu à l'intérieur du circuit de haute sécurité, il constate la violation de ses droits. Mais il ne faut pas oublier qu'alors le dernier mot … revient toujours à l'administration pénitentiaire (v. *supra*, § 5).

---

38 Julien Boucher & Béatrice Bourgeois-Machureau, 'Le juge administratif et le détenu', *Actualité juridique. Droit administratif* 7 (2008), p. 128; Serge Slama, 'Régimes de détention différenciés: consécration d'un recours permettant d'ouvrir les « portes fermées »' (CE, 28 mars 2011, M. A.) (à l'adresse: combatsdroitshomme.blog.lemonde.fr; consulté le 15 juillet 2013).

39 V. Trib. admin. Emilia-Romagna (Parma), 16 novembre 1998, n.592, M.P. e altri c. Min. Giustizia, dans T. A. R, 1999, I, p. 201; Trib. admin. Puglia, 28 septembre 1994, Modeo c. Min. Giustizia, dans Foro amministrativo, 1995, p. 448; Trib. admin. Lazio, 13 septembre 1984, n. 771, Rivellini c. Min. Giustizia, dans Foro italiano., 1986, III, p. 87 et suiv.

SICHERUNGSVERWAHRUNG – A SUMMARY OF RECENT DEVELOPMENTS REGARDING PREVENTIVE DETENTION IN GERMANY

Johannes FEEST*

1. RENAISSANCE OF PREVENTIVE DETENTION

The German system of criminal sanctions is based on the distinction between punishments on the one hand and "Reform and Prevention Measures" *(Maßregeln der Besserung und Sicherung sec. 62 ff. Penal Code)* on the other hand. The former are to be applied on the basis of past criminal behavior and mens rea (Vorsatz). The latter are social defense measures designed to prevent future "dangerousness" of the offender to society. Such preventive measures include sentencing offenders to be kept in a mental hospital (usually served instead of a prison term), but also sentencing offenders to preventive detention (*Sicherungsverwahrung*) to be served after the completion of the prison term. In principle, these measures are of unlimited duration; the offenders are, however, to be released whenever they are considered not any more dangerous. All of these Reform and Prevention Measures were first introduced by Nazi Germany in 1933 and implemented in a big way. They were kept on after the Second World War in a version somewhat more compatible with the rule of law. The measure of preventive detention (*Sicherungsverwahrung*) was reduced to a mere 50 cases per year and was limited, when applied for the first time, to a duration of ten years.

---

* Dr. J. Feest (Berlin, 1939) is em. Professor for Criminal Law and Criminology, Law Department, Universität Bremen (1974–2006). He was Director of the International Institute for the Sociology of Law, Oñati, Spain (1995–1997), and President Research Committee on Sociology of Law (2000–2003). His research and publications are in the field of criminal justice, since 2006 mainly on prisons and prisoners' rights.

Since 1998, new Federal legislation extended preventive detention in several ways:

- it reduced, in 1998, the formal requirements for preventive detention (*Sicherungsverwahrung* = sec. 66 *Criminal Code*) especially for the group of violent and/or sex offenders
- it changed retroactively, in 1998, the situation for those detainees serving a preventive detention order: now the first preventive detention was no longer limited to ten years, but could last the whole life of the detainee.
- in 2002, it introduced the new sentencing option of "reserved preventive detention" *(vorbehaltene Sicherungsverwahrung)*
- [in 2004, the Federal Constitutional Court declared that retroactive changes in 1998 did not violate the prohibition of retroactive criminal laws, since preventive detention was not regarded a criminal penalty in German law].
- in 2004, the Federal legislature introduced the new measure of "retrospective preventive detention" *(nachträgliche Sicherungsverwahrung)*
- in 2008, it introduced preventive detention for the first time into German Juvenile Criminal Law (retrospective preventive detention).

The number of offenders sentenced to preventive detention has more than doubled by 2010; the number of detainees had risen to more than 500 (with the tendency to further increases).

This was the situation at the time of the IPPF conference in Stavern in 2008, when we reported on prison policies in Germany.[1] Since then, a lot has happened. In what follows, these recent developments will be briefly listed and commented upon.

2. CHALLENGE TO PREVENTIVE DETENTION BY THE EUROPEAN COURT OF HUMAN RIGHTS

The developments since 1998 became problematic through a series of decisions by the European Court of Human Rights. They concerned mainly two points:

- The retroactive elimination (in 1998) of the ten-year limit for first-time preventive detention was held to be in violation of Art. 5 §1a and Art. 7 §1 ECHR.[2]

1 Axel Boetticher & Johannes Feest, 'German criminal and prison policy', in: Peter Tak & Manon Jendly (eds), *Prison policy and prisoners' rights. The protection of prisoners' fundamental rights in international and domestic law*, Nijmegen: Wolf Legal Publishers, 2008, p. 361–390.

2 The first of a number of cases was ECtHR, Judgment of 17 December 2009, *M. v. Germany*, Appl. 19359/04.

- The introduction (in 2004) of "retrospective preventive detention" (*nachträgliche Sicherungsverwahrung*) was held in violation of Art. 5 §1 ECHR.[3]

In all of the cases, Germany had to pay – more or less symbolic – damages (between 20.000 and 30.000 € per person). There will probably be many more decisions from the Strasbourg Court, since in many similar cases the detainees are still fighting for their release.

3. REACTIONS IN GERMANY TO THE DECISIONS OF THE ECTHR

Reactions in Germany were characterized by surprise and, partly, by open resistance. Some high courts (*Oberlandesgerichte*) decided to release the prisoners, because they felt bound by the Strasbourg decisions. Other courts refused to do so, because they felt bound by the 2004 decision of the Federal Constitutional Court.

As a result, for the past three years, there has been a heated debate in the media and in legal circles about what to do with the released detainees, especially those which are still diagnosed as highly dangerous. Some of them are still under a 24-hour surveillance by the police; others find themselves under attack by "concerned citizens", who stage protests wherever ex-detainees try to live; still other released detainees have "voluntarily" agreed to remain, for the time being, in institutions (prisons or hospitals).

The federal legislature reacted by passing a law that came into effect on January 1, 2011. The law envisaged that detainees released on the basis of the Strasbourg decisions may be placed, by civil courts, into psychiatric custody if they are seen as dangerous because of a "psychic defect" (*psychische Störung*). This was supposed to be legitimized by Art. 5 §1 lit e of the ECHR, which makes it possible to deprive of their liberty "persons of unsound mind".

On May 4, 2011, the Federal Constitutional Court finally reacted to the Strasbourg decisions. It declared unconstitutional all legal provisions relating to security detention and demanded new comprehensive legislation in this respect. The older norms remain, however, applicable until the entry into force of new legislation, for which the court set 31 May 2013 as a deadline.[4] The Court based its decision not directly on the European Convention of Human Rights (and its

---

3 The first of these cases was ECtHR, Judgment of 24 November 2011, O.*H. v. Germany*, Appl. 4646/08. See also ECtHR, Judgment of 7 September 2012, *K. v. Germany*, Appl. 61827/09.

4 In the meantime, a retrospective or retroactive detention may only be continued in cases of a *high* risk of *heavy* cases of violent or sexual crimes, committed as a consequence of a *psychic defect* ("psychische Störung").

interpretation by the Strasbourg Court) but on its own interpretation of the German Basic Law. It stressed especially the need to establish a difference between preventive detention and the detention for serving a term of imprisonment (*Abstandsgebot*).

This decision has led to a flurry of legislation. The federal legislature has passed a law on the principles of the *Abstandsgebot* and the sixteen parliaments of the Länder-states have by now passed their respective laws governing the conditions in the facilities for preventive detention.

4. THE THEMES OF THE IPPF CONFERENCE: A FEW REMARKS FROM GERMANY

4.1. THE JUSTIFICATION FOR TAKING MEASURES TO PREDICT OFFENDING/REOFFENDING AND MANAGE RISK

Theoretically, the prediction (and management) of risks is relegated in Germany to the realm of the measures for reform and prevention, *i.e.* the second part of the dualistic system. There, the law requires that the possibility of serious future offences, *i.e.* the dangerousness of the offender for society is taken into account (sects. 63, 64, 66 Penal Code). If placement in a psychiatric institution, a drug clinic or a preventive detention facility is envisaged, expert witnesses are to be heard by the courts before a decision is made (sect. 246 a Code of Criminal Procedure). But the distinction between penalties and measures has become less clear over the years.

4.2. THE RELEVANCE OF THE RISK OF REOFFENDING IN DETERMINING THE TYPE AND LENGTH OF SENTENCES (*i.e.* PENAL SANCTIONS FOR REOFFENDING)

Theoretically, the risk of reoffending has no place in sentencing. The courts have to find the sentence on the basis of the offender's guilt. The offender's guilt is usually seen as criterion for the upper limit of the penalty. Within that frame, the courts are supposed to take into account "the consequences of the punishment for the future life of the offender in the society" (sect. 46 StGB), *i.e.* the rehabilitation potential of the offender. In practice, recidivism is a major factor in sentencing.

While the risk of reoffending does not enter explicitly at the sentencing stage, it has major and growing importance in the implementation of the sentence. The possibility of releasing prisoners before the end of their sentence (at half-time at the earliest) requires a risk based court decision. In some cases, the law makes the calling of expert witnesses mandatory, *e.g.* in the case of life sentences, psychiatric detention or preventive detention.

4.3. SPECIAL MEASURES AFTER THE EXPIRY OF A PENAL SENTENCE TO MANAGE RISK

So far, nothing of this kind exists. Security detention, as introduced in 1933 by the Nazi government, has to be fixed by a court of law in the context of penal sentencing, not afterwards. In recent years, however, some politicians (and parts of the media) have advocated such retrospective measures, in cases of "dangerous" persons. They succeeded in 2004, but their success was stopped by the ECtHR in 2009 (for a loophole, see however footnote 5). But this has not silenced the fans of such measures, who now advocate them under the terminology "therapeutic detention", in view of Art. 5 §1e ECHR. Since 1.1.2011, a law on therapeutic detention (*Therapieunterbringungsgesetz*) exists. But this law is limited to persons released on the basis of the recent decisions of the ECtHR. A number of justice ministers are pushing, unsuccessfully so far, for widening the scope of this statute.

4.4. CIVIL MEASURES TO MANAGE RISK WITHOUT CRIMINAL CONVICTION

In Germany, the management of risks, is, in general, seen as a police function. If persons are seen as a danger to themselves or to others because of a mental illness, they may be held by the police and presented at a psychiatric clinic. If the psychiatrists decide that compulsory placement in the clinic is called for, this needs to be authorized by a judge, within 48 hours. This decision will have to be reviewed every six weeks. This does not apply in cases where no mental illness has been diagnosed. For such cases, the police have developed elaborate programs of close control and supervision.

5. CONCLUSION

The fight over the institution of preventive detention in Germany is not over yet. On the one hand, this institution is still seen by most politicians as a necessary instrument to prevent sexual crimes and crimes of violence and it is regarded by the relevant courts as compatible with the European Convention on Human

Rights as well as with the German constitution. On the other hand, recent research shows that the prognostic instruments in use cannot predict individual cases, *i.e.* one has to imprison a lot of people unnecessarily to prevent one of them to commit a major crime. While some politicians still want to devise some form of retrospective preventive detention, there is a growing consensus among legal experts against such tendencies. But there is also a small number of scholars[5] and practitioners[6] that push for the abolition of the institution of Sicherungsverwahrung as such.

5 *E.g.* Lorenz Böllinger & Axel Dessecker, 'Kommentierung zu §66–66b StGB', in: U. Kindhäuser, U. Neumann & H. Paeffgen (eds.), *Strafgesetzbuch*, Baden-Baden: Nomos, 2013; Ralf Eschelbach, '§66', in: H. Matt & J. Renzikowski (eds.) *Strafgesetzbuch, Kommentar*, München: Vahlen, 2013.

6 *E.g.* Peter Asprion, *Gefährliche Freiheit? Das Ende der Sicherungsverwahrung*, Freiburg: Herder, 2012; Katholische Bundesarbeitsgemeinschaft Straffälligenhilfe u.a., *Gegen Menschenverwahrung. Ein Plädoyer zur Abschaffung der Sicherungsverwahrung*, Berlin, Stuttgart, Freiburg 2003 (joint manifesto of the Catholic and Protestant organisations in the field of offenders' aid).

DEALING WITH HIGH RISK OFFENDERS – GENERAL SYNTHESIS AND CONCLUSIONS

Johannes FEEST*

1. INTRODUCTION

It seems that in the history of the IPPC/IPPF, this topic has not been a central one. In preparing for the Wellington conference, I checked the records for earlier treatments of this topic. In the Proceedings of the IPPC congresses until 1951 only one major discussion of the topic can be found.[1] At the tenth congress of the (then) IPPC in Prague in 1930, the following question was raised:

> "In view of the more general adoption of security measures, which of these would be most suitable and how could they be classified in a rational way?"[2]

On the basis of nine written reports by members from Great Britain, Germany, Norway, Spain, Poland, Czechoslovakia, Austria, Yugoslavia and Italy and a prolonged discussion, the general reporter, Dr. Cornil (Belgium) was able to produce a formula which found unanimous support:

> "It is necessary to supplement the system of penalties by the adoption of security measures in order to assure social defense whenever the penalty imposed is inapplicable or insufficient. Measures of security are intended to rehabilitate the

* Dr. J. Feest is em. Professor for Criminal Law and Criminology, Law Department, Universität Bremen (for further information, see the previous chapter).

1 IPPF proceedings were published in a uniform format (and re-issued in that format by Kraus Reprint in 1979). When the IPPC was restructured and renamed IPPF, this uniformity was abandoned. Congress proceedings and other IPPF publications were published in different formats and with different publishing houses. Among the 43 publications listed by the Max Planck Institute in Freiburg, not one deals with the present topic.

2 J. Simon van der Aa, *Actes du Congrès Pénal et Pénitentiaire International de Prague, Procès-Verbaux des Seances*, Berne: Bureau de la Commission internationale pénale et pénitentiaire, 1931, vol. I b, p. 32. The proceedings were in French, the official language of the congresses. The translation follows the one offered by Negley K. Teeters, *Deliberations of the international penal and penitentiary congresses*, Philadelphia: Temple University Book Store, 1949, p. 168.

delinquent, to eliminate him, or to take away from him the opportunity of committing crime. They are applied by the courts".[3]

With respect to the deprivation of freedom in such cases, the IPPC congress foresaw the following categories of persons a potential objects of such security measures:

- insane and abnormal delinquents, who represent a social danger (with the objective of cure);
- alcoholics and drug addicts (with the objective of cure);
- mendicants and vagrants (with the objective of training them to earn a living);
- habitual delinquents (with the objective of eliminating or improving them).[4]

This list of suitable candidates for security measures involving deprivation of liberty strikes me as a very mixed and problematic one.[5] It does, however, confirm the notion, put forward by Warren Young during our colloquium, that the focus at that time tended to be the persistent or habitual offender rather than the dangerous, the high risk offender. According to Warren Young, it was only in the 1970ies that the latter "emerged as a major theme in policy-making" and has become "the catalyst for a great deal of legislative activity ever since".

But the quotation from this earlier congress also brings to mind an interesting formal change in the method of our organization. At least up until the Second Word War, the congresses were organized and proceeded by explicitly asking questions, discussing them and trying to find acceptable answers to them. I have started to wonder whether this might be still a model worth coming back to.

---

3 J. Simon van der AA, *Actes du Congrès Pénal et Pénitentiaire International de Prague, Procès-Verbaux des Seances*, Berne: Bureau de la Commission internationale pénale et pénitentiaire, 1931, vol. I a, p. 116–118. Again, I have adopted Teeters' translation, p. 168.

4 The discussion on security measures was supposed to be continued at the next IPPC conference in Berlin (1935). By then the Nazi regime had replaced the democratic government in Germany. Right at the beginning of their regime, the Nazis had introduced measures of security, including security internment (Sicherungsverwahrung) and put them to use in a big way. This could have led to a controversial discussion at the congress. But German scholars and practitioners dominated the congress and this seems to have intimidated some of the foreign participants. Not one critical word on Nazi criminal policy can be found in the Proceedings of the XIth International Penal and Penitentiary Congress held in Berlin August 1935, published in Bern 1937 (in English).

5 A lasting effect of this list can still be found in Art. 5(1)(e) of the European Convention of Human Rights. Only the habitual offenders are not specifically named in the ECHR, probably because they were seen by the framers of the Convention as covered by the penal law proper in Art. 5(1)(e).

And I have tried this out by rephrasing the four subtopics of our colloquium into questions. Here are the results:

- Can it be justified to base penal measures on the prediction of future behaviour? If so, under what conditions?
- What relevance has the risk of reoffending for determining type and length of custodial sentences in different countries? What do we know about the effectiveness of such innovations, *i.e.* do they reduce the incidence of major crimes?
- What special measures have been developed to manage the hypothetical risk of (ex-) offenders released from prison? How effective are they? Can they be justified under Human Rights criteria?
- What non-penal alternatives have been devised to manage the risk posed by high risk offender?

Interestingly enough, some fundamental questions have not explicitly been raised in the program of our colloquium. But they were likely to pop up anyway:

- What, if anything, is the factual difference between imprisonment as punishment and imprisonment as a measure of security?
- What is the relationship between security measures and rehabilitation? Should security measures always have a rehabilitation component? Shall there be institutions for "treating the untreatables"? Or can longstay institutions be justified that just provide a humane environment for those who refuse treatment or are seen as "untreatable"?
- Should the dual system or two-track system used in Switzerland, Germany and the Netherlands be seen as a progressive model to be adopted by others? Or should it rather be abandoned?

I will concentrate on the issues as raised in these questions.

2. THE PROCEEDINGS OF THE COLLOQUIUM

The conference was addressed by Chester Borrows, the Minister of Courts and Associate Minister of Justice of New Zealand. He indicated that he saw a "window of opportunity for criminal law reform in New Zealand, because the major parties agreed on the goals to distinguish between low, middle and high risk offenders, which requires to improve risk prediction. New Zealand is about to introduce Public Protection Orders as a civil, not criminal tool. He envisages 5–12 people to be eligible for such orders.

2.1. FIRST SESSION/THEME: THE JUSTIFICATION FOR TAKING MEASURES TO PREDICT OFFENDING/ REOFFENDING AND MANAGING RISK: A THEORETICAL PERSPECTIVE

Warren Young and Andrew Butler were the key-note speakers on this subject.

Warren Young (New Zealand) started from the point that assessment of risk underpins today almost all stages of criminal justice decision-making. He argued that we cannot avoid a risk-based approach, but need "to apply risk considerations in a fair and principled manner". In dismissing three fundamental objections (violation of the presumption of innocence; denial of individual free will; problem of "false positives"), he acknowledged that the "assessment of risk is often done on the basis of subjective judgements and lack of empirically validated foundation". He argued, however, that methods of risk prediction have improved "dramatically" in the last 20 years and that at least "some predictive tools have a high degree of accuracy". At the same time, he insisted that what he calls "risk shifting" be done in a "principled and consistent" manner".[6] In analogy to the presumption of innocence, he suggests a presumption of harmlessness, similar to the "presumption against threat" proposed recently by Lucia Zedner.[7] "Risk-shifting", according to Young, is justified only if a person has forfeited that right. Among the conditions of such a forfeiture are in his opinion the following indicators:

- past offending behaviour;
- robust and empirically validated tools, which the decision-makers are required to use;
- the risks have to be unacceptable (*i.e.* some notion of proportionality);
- the measures have to be clearly targeted at the risk (and be the least intrusive to reduce that risk).

Andrew Butler (New Zealand), focussed in his paper on preventive detention, leaving aside the many other preventive measures cropping up in national legislations and he stressed the central importance of what he called a "Human Rights perspective" in this regard. He started out by outlining human rights standards with respect to liberty, referring both to the International Covenant on Civil and Political Rights and to the European Convention of Human Rights. Criticising what he called a certain "roguishness of science", he called for a "culture of justification" and a "right level of scepticism". In contrast to a mere

6 This is based on reflections published in: Jean E. Floud and Warren Young, *Dangerousness and Criminal Justice*, London: Heinemann, 1981.

7 Lucia Zedner, *Security*, London, New York: Routledge, 2009, p. 171.

reliance on principles, he insisted on the specifics, the "granularity" of cases. Prediction of risk may be necessary, but the question is when and for what particular form of intervention.

Butler exemplified his arguments by discussing a number of cases from the UN Human Rights Committee, the European Court of Human Right and the Federal Constitutional Court of Germany. Taken together, these cases demonstrate that, as of today, human rights standards do not completely rule out preventive detention. They do, however, show a high level of concern and scepticism in respect to a number of issues, *e.g.*

- boundaries between imprisonment as punishment and as a prevention of dangerousness;
- questioning newly evolving practices from first principles;
- treating preventive detainees as people subject to change;
- keeping due proportionality between perceived danger and preventive measures;
- robustness of predictive instruments.

Andrew Butler feels that we find ourselves in a "moral panic", in a "war on fear". This asks for a preparedness to question prevention measures. In his opinion, exceptions need to be justified; mere extensions of the usual risk-assessment logic will not do. Furthermore, the presumption of innocence is in his view valid also in cases of preventive detention. This is the main point in which he signals disagreement with Warren Young: the presumption of innocence, in Butler's view, can serve to remind us of important moral values that are as relevant to predictive justice as they are to retributive justice. For him, the central question is a moral and political one: the justification for taking pre-emptive action based on possible future conduct. Human rights law requires that such assessments should never be made mainly on the basis of a person's membership in a group. As for the rest, Butler appreciates Young's insistence on a coherent theory of preventative justice and suggested ways of strengthening such an approach.

In the discussion

Warren Young replied that he still feels that the presumption of innocence is too narrow as a criterion with respect to preventative justice. Also from his point of view, preventive detention can only be justified in narrowly defined areas.

Andrew Butler received some support for his sceptical views. Warren Brookbanks (New Zealand) felt that risk assessment undermined the principles of criminal law. Others argued that security measures should be used only in cases involving lack of mental responsibility (Luis Miranda Pereira). Peter Tak

(Netherlands) argued that governments should not promise a completely safe world. They should rather apply the criminal justice system properly.

Lech Paprzycki (Poland) wondered what to do with "psychopaths". He informed the audience about new legislation in Poland in this regard.

Johannes Feest (Germany) briefly explained recent developments in Germany: media panics around violent sex crimes, hasty legislation extending the existing laws on preventive detention, a series of decisions by the European Court of Human Rights finding Germany in violation of Art. 5 §1 lit. a of the ECHR, resistance by politicians, media and courts against the release of detainees, new legislation trying to base the continuing detention on Art. 5 §1 lit.e ECHR ("persons of unsound mind").

2.2. SECOND SESSION/THEME: THE RELEVANCE OF THE RISK OF REOFFENDING IN DETERMINING THE TYPE AND LENGTH OF SENTENCES (*i.e.* PENAL SANCTIONS FOR OFFENDING)

Andre Vallotton and Peter Tak were the key-note speakers on this subject, while Lech Paprzycki and Bent Carlson offered prepared interventions.

André Vallotton (Switzerland) started out by deconstructing the concept "dangerousness", which he feels is not a scientific but a political notion. He backs this up by contrasting a "humanist anthropology" with a "warrior anthropology". As a starting point, he finds acceptable the following definition produced in 2010 by the Council of Europe: "an offender, who has caused very serious physical or psychological harm and who presents a high probability of re-offending causing similar (*i.e.* very serious) harm". He insists, however, that every delinquent act as well as each offender committing such an act requires by itself a thorough analysis. This leads him to a critical analysis of the assessment process in use. He points out that the certainty of committing a new crime predicted by instruments like OASyS or SARA do not go beyond 30 or 40 percent in extreme cases. The best method would, therefore, seem to be the combination of different methods of assessment, based on multidisciplinary approaches. "But even that can only produce a short-term prediction. There is no way to take into account the process of aging, of changing life situations, of the possibility that the delinquent becomes aware of his troubles or develops a desire to realize new existential objectives at a moment when one would last expect it". Therefore, Vallotton concludes, our distinctions between responsibility and irresponsibility are too clear, too "Cartesian". This, for him, becomes particularly obvious when actuarial evaluations are included into the sentencing guideline in the USA or

Canada. But it is also the case in the European systems following the model of social defense, practicing eliminatory measures of security detention. Vallotton finds some hope in the fact that the ECtHR (in his recent German cases) has started to break up the system of measures as practiced in Austria, Denmark, Italy, Liechtenstein, Saint Marino and Slovakia. Vallotton goes on to argue that it appears impossible to reconcile the two conflicting goals in one decision: "How can we retribute for the past and at the same time take into account the future".

He ends his paper by proposing five fine principles for further reflection, hoping that we might be able to "reconcile the irreconcilable".

Lech K. Paprzycki (Poland) offered some reflections on the risk of re-offending from the point of view of a judge. He considers it "an open question whether we can punish someone for possible misconduct in the future" and followed this up with a number of questions:

- is the public expectation sufficient enough for imposing longer sentences, when the state cannot accurately predict re-offending?
- should the legislature fix standards for the assessment of re-offending?
- do we need a special service for this assessment (or should the task remain with judges?)
- doesn't the expectation of accurate prediction bring us close to the science fiction presented in the movie "Minority Report"?

Peter Tak (the Netherlands) gave an overview over legislation based on the offender's dangerousness in Denmark, England, France, Germany, the Netherlands and Norway. For this purpose, he distinguished between the sentencing of mentally normal offenders and the sentencing of mentally ill offenders.

For *mentally sane offenders* considered "dangerous" basically two systems are in use:

Long prison sentences or secure preventive detention. In many countries life sentences traditionally serve this purpose. In most countries, however, a life sentence is not a real life sentence. Only in the Netherlands, the life sentence is a "whole life" sentence. Lifers in England, France and Germany can apply for parole, but in the parole decision, the assessment of the risk of reoffending plays a major role.

In 2003/2005 England introduced indeterminate sentences of imprisonment for "dangerous offenders" under the title of Imprisonment for Public Protection (IPP). In 2012 this system was abolished and replaced by making life imprisonment mandatory for a second serious offense. The new English legislation also includes the concept of "extended sentences" for sexual and violent crimes. This again implies a risk assessment by the court. Before 2008 this assessment was mainly based on previous convictions (presumption of dangerousness); now the assessment may take into consideration all available information on the nature and circumstances of the offence (including previous convictions).

Secure preventive detention for public security reasons is known in many countries such as Austria, Belgium, Denmark, France, Germany and Norway. In principle this is an indeterminate sanction, subject, however, to regular reviews and the possibility of release in case they are no longer seen as dangerous. In Germany and Norway preventive detention presupposes a prison sentence and it is to be served if at the end of the prison sentence the danger to society still exists. In Germany, this institution has survived scrutiny by the Federal Constitutional Court and by the European Human Rights Court. It has been embroiled in legal controversy only after attempts in the last fifteen years to extend its implementation retroactively and to create the possibility of a new measure of "retrospective preventive detention". Both were criticised by the ECHR as violating Art. 5 para 1 lit a and Art 7 of the ECHR respectively. Germany is presently undergoing a complete legislative overhaul, trying to distinguish between punishment and secure detention. Meanwhile, France has also introduced the institution of retrospective secure preventive detention. According to Peter Tak the decisions of the ECtHR in its German cases may affect similar institutions in Denmark, France, Norway and the Netherlands, since Art. 5 of the ECHR does not mention dangerousness.[8]

The situation is different for *mentally ill offender*, since they are covered by Art. 5 para 1 lit e of the ECHR ("persons of unsound mind").

In Denmark secure preventive detention is used only for mentally ill offenders.

In the Netherlands, the Entrustment order for mentally ill offenders is in existence since 1928. Rather than being sent to prison, mentally ill offenders are entrusted by the criminal courts to special psychiatric institutions. They can only be releases if they are considered not dangerous any more. The institution of entrustment has recently seen a major reform in the release policy in order to improve its security effects.

In Germany, mentally ill offenders are also entrusted by the criminal courts to psychiatric hospitals (since 1933). And their numbers have seen a sharp increase over the last twenty years. No reform is foreseen.

Peter Tak concluded by emphasizing that that there is no research showing a decline of major sexual or violent crime because of such measures. He feels that the public is misled and needs to be informed that there are other things at least

8 I think that this is most likely in the case of France and of Switzerland.

as dangerous as those so-called "dangerous" criminals. He doubts that it will ever be possible to reduce criminality and recidivism by way of imprisoning people.

In the discussion

Bent Carlson (Denmark) underscored that the Criminal Justice System is in general not able to prevent criminality. He thinks that the most interesting development is the separation of the criminal and civil systems to deal with risk. He argues for the avoidance of indeterminate sentences.

Piet Hein van Kempen (the Netherlands) points out that there might be negative consequences of the ECtHR's decisions on secure preventive detention with respect to life time prisoners. This particularly applies to jurisdictions where life imprisonment in most cases actually constitutes imprisonment for life, because in those jurisdictions judges in criminal trials might opt for a life sentence instead of applying entrustment orders.

2.3. THIRD SESSION/THEME: SPECIAL MEASURES AFTER THE EXPIRY OF A PENAL SENTENCE TO MANAGE RISK

Emilio Viano and Stephen Shute served as key note speakers, Nils Erik Lie made a prepared intervention.

Emilio Viano (USA) gave a broad overview over new trends and applications concerning "Supervision and Electronic Technology during Reentry". The most salient points concerned different forms of technology, *e.g.*

- ankle bracelets;
- location technologies (inclusion zones vs. exclusion zones);
- tracking devices (cell phones, GPS technology).

He reported that there are currently about 140.000 offenders supervised by such technologies; 49 states have made the tracking of sexual offenders obligatory for sex offenders. While electronic monitoring requires staff and space, it is still cheaper than prisons. Furthermore he informed us about the existence of standards for offender tracking developed by the National Institute of Justice.

In the discussion

The issue of Human Rights with respect to these powerful monitoring devices was raised. Emilio Viano's answer was that "we all have become accustomed to invasion of privacy". Furthermore, he felt that there was a trade-off between draconian penalties and using the new technology.

André Vallotton informed us that the Council of Europe will publish a paper on electronic monitoring later this year. The paper will emphasize the necessity to gain the consent of the person being tracked. According to him this means that this will be useless for high risk offenders.

Stephen Shute reported some results of his empirical research of satellite tracking. Key results were that about 25% of the monitored clients committed new offenses while being tracked. On the other hand 40% of those interviewed thought that the tracking helped them stay out of trouble.

Stephen Shute (United Kingdom), briefly reported in his keynote address on the overall developments in the British government's attempts to "break the cycle of reoffenders". The main contribution of the Labour government was the introduction of the Internment for Public Protection (IPP) in 2003. While this was meanwhile abolished, there still more than 6000 offenders imprisoned (serving the retribution part of their sentence), while only 500 have been released. The new coalition government has legislated a package that includes

- repeal of the IPP statute;
- a new two-strikes provision;
- a new "extended sentence";
- a new license period beyond the normal end of the sentence.

He then spent the major part of his address on the new Civil Preventive Orders that are can be imposed after the serving of a sentence. Historical antecedents were "anti-social behaviour orders" and the possibility to bind over offenders for public protection. Now the government has introduced four new types of orders:

- sexual offenses protection orders;
- foreign travel orders;
- risk of sexual harm orders (irrespective if conviction of any offense);
- violent offenders orders (for a specific list of offenses).

They all follow more or less a three-step procedure: risky behaviour, formal legal warning (by court), if ignored: conviction and punishment up to 5 years. It appears that most of these orders are breaches, detected and prosecutes.

Stephen Shute estimates that there are about 100 Sexual Prevention Orders per year. He presented three cases by way of illustration of the new Sexual Prevention Orders:

He thinks that the three-steps procedure is basically OK, but that predicting future offenses will be difficult (because of low base rate). He finished with four additional points:

- research shows that the reconviction rate after six years is 92%;
- concern that these orders may not be effective;
- he doubts the wisdom of using SPOs with people without a new offence;
- concern about the labelling effect of SOPOs.

Nils Eric Lie (Norway) states that practical assessments are not far from guesswork. He asks himself: which tools do we need to assess these problems as good as possible. Shall we really take dangerousness in consideration as aggravating circumstances. Or should we rather have as few freedom-restrictions as possible and take an ethical and Human Rights perspective?

2.4. FOURTH SESSION/THEME: CIVIL MEASURES TO MANAGE RISK WITHOUT CRIMINAL CONVICTION

The only keynote speaker here was Effi Lambopoulou (Greece), with a prepared intervention from Malcolm Luey (New Zealand).

Effi Lambropoulou (Greece) defined civil measures largely in terms of measures and resources of civil society. Consequently, she gave a broad, well documented, overview over a wide array of programs, mainly dealing with high-risk young offenders. As far as possible, she also indicated the results of the evaluations of such programs.

In a first section of her paper, the speaker concentrated on alternatives to formal court-processing and by implication on alternatives to custody. Examples were different sorts of community interventions on the one hand and the Multisystemic Therapy Approach on the other hand.

She then turned her attention to "support and restore schemes" with respect to such offender groups as hardcore drunk drivers, hooligans, religious and political extremists.

A separate group of programs referred to are local neighbourhood watch schemes about high risk offenders (USA and UK).

Another group of programs deal with the re-entry along with support of high-risk offenders into the community. Here Lambropoulou discussed Circles of Support and Accountability (Canada), and the different variations of restorative justice programs (Australia, Canada, Europe, New Zealand, USA), including the Reintegrative Shaming Experiments (in Australia).

Also with such civil programs there is, as the speaker pointed out, a need to balance the community's right to safety on the one hand and the rights of ex-offenders on the other.

She also mentioned the need to have another look at our definitions of "high risk groups". Should multinational companies involved in corruption, environmental pollution, stock exchange deceits and the like be included in such a definition? What civil measures would be appropriate to prevent such corporate crimes?

Malcolm Luey (New Zealand) identified, in his prepared intervention, four general groups of measures to address future offending risk:

1. Population targeted crime prevention measures – these are social initiatives aimed at large population groups with the general objective of safer communities or restoring community networks to prevent criminal activity from happening in those communities (*e.g.* community programmes to reduce football hooliganism, safer community environmental design, social welfare and health programmes aimed at economically disadvantaged families etc.).
2. Alternative Justice Systems (not involving courts) – alternative systems for dispute resolution for the community or family group to determine the how to address the offending and risk posed by the individual (*e.g.* Family Group Conferences, Restorative Justice, Diversion schemes, Police issued warnings etc.).
3. Civil Court Orders – civil orders imposed by courts based on assessments of individual risk, usually associated with on-going community treatment, monitoring and some restrictions of identified activities or associations (*e.g.* Compulsory Mental Health Treatment, Family Violence Orders, Child Abuse Prevention Orders etc.).
4. Criminal (Penal) Sanctions – On-going penal or community detention imposed as part of, or associated with, a requisite criminal conviction and based on determinations of the individual's continued risk of offending (*e.g.* Preventive Detention, Extended Supervision etc.).

Having set out the range of possible interventions used by governments to address the risk of future offending, Mr Luey discussed the challenge of ensuring that the correct intervention is used and proportionate to the appropriate type and level of risk posed by the individual or group. Getting this choice right was key to ensuring that any measure was consistent with individual human rights obligations. But disproportionate measures were often chosen by governments due to lack of resources, bureaucratic notions of efficiency, media driven public sentiment and reactive decisions to extreme cases.

3. A FEW BRIEF CONCLUSIONS

This was an extraordinarily stimulating colloquium. Fundamental questions as to the justifications and the efficacy of our dealing with the risks posed by the release of ex-offenders were discussed.

As to the questions raised at the beginning of this report, it was not always possible to find clear and consensual answers. But here is at least a short attempt, in the style of the IPPF congresses before 1945:

From a human rights point of view, penal measures based on the prediction of future behaviour should, if at all, only be permissible under narrow conditions. More work on a coherent theory of preventive justice is required.

Risk of re-offending is used in many countries and in different ways to determine type and length of custodial sentences. Because of inherent difficulties to evaluate the outcome of preventive detention, there exists only little empirical research on the question of how many major crimes are prevented by such measures.

Non-custodial measures to manage the hypothetical risk of ex-prisoners usually take the form of Public Protection Orders, with or without electronic supervision. The effectiveness as well as the conformity with basic human rights of such programs is in doubt.

Non-penal alternatives are mainly used for groups of offenders that are not considered "high risk". This implies important definitional and therefore political questions.

As to other questions mentioned in my introductory remarks and not explicitly envisaged by the organizers of this congress, I will limit myself to the following brief remarks:

Our different systems of dealing with these questions (one track, double track, post- track) appear as problematic and partly crumbling;

As Vallotton stated, it may be time to conceive "a new system of punishment, more pragmatic, more individualized, capable of integrating the demands of law and of public security".

The International Penal and Penitentiary Foundation: history and purpose

International efforts to harmonize criminal justice policy date back to the nineteenth century, when representatives of various European nations met periodically to exchange information and to consider common standards in the treatment of offenders. In 1872, cooperation took a step forward when an International Prison Commission (IPC) was set up to collect national prison statistics and make recommendations for prison reform in Europe. When the League of Nations was formed in 1919, it saw as part of its mandate the promotion of the rule of law in the international community. The IPC became affiliated with the League and continued to hold conferences, meeting in 1925, 1930 and 1935. In the latter year, the IPC became the International Penal and Penitentiary Commission (IPPC).[1] When the new United Nations was created in 1954, it incorporated crime prevention and standards of criminal justice into its policy-setting role. In December 1950, the IPPC was dissolved, to be replaced by the International Penal and Penitentiary Foundation. The IPPF is a foundation governed by the Swiss Civil Code and created on the 5th of July 1951. The Foundation shall have as its aim to promote studies in the field of the prevention of crime and the treatment of offenders, especially by scientific research, publications, teaching and international colloquiums.

See for further information:
http://internationalpenalandpenitentiaryfoundation.org

---

1 See: United Nations, *The United Nations and Crime Prevention*, New York: United Nations, 1991, p. 3–4.

La Fondation internationale pénale et pénitentiaire: histoire et objectif

Les efforts internationaux entrepris pour harmoniser la politique pénale et pénitentiaire remontent au 19e siècle, quand des représentants de plusieurs Etats européens ont commencé à se réunir périodiquement pour échanger de l'information et élaborer des standards communs dans le domaine du traitement des délinquants. En 1872, la coopération s'intensifia avec l'instauration de la Commission Pénitentiaire Internationale (CPI), chargée de réunir des statistiques nationales sur la prison et de formuler des recommandations pour la réforme des institutions carcérales en Europe. Instituée en 1919, la Société des Nations s'est vue confier le mandat de promouvoir des règles de droit en la matière auprès de la communauté internationale. La CPI devint affiliée à la Société des Nations et continua d'organiser des conférences et rencontres, en 1925, 1930 et 1935, avant de devenir la Commission Internationale Pénale et Pénitentiaire (CIPP).[1] Quand en 1954, à la suite de la Société des Nations, fut créée l'Organisation des Nations Unies, cette dernière maintint parmi ses objectifs principaux la promotion de la prévention du crime et de standards en matière de justice criminelle. En décembre 1950, la CIPP fut dissoute et remplacée par la Fondation internationale pénale et pénitentiaire. Instituée le 5 juillet 1951, la FIPP est une fondation, au sens du Code civil suisse. La Fondation a pour but d'encourager les études dans le domaine de la prévention du crime et du traitement des délinquants, notamment par la recherche scientifique, les publications, l'enseignement et par l'organisation de colloques internationaux.

Voir pour plus d'informations:
http://fondationinternationalepenaleetpenitentiaire.org

1 Traduction libre tirée de: United Nations, *The United Nations and Crime Prevention*, New York: United Nations, 1991, p. 3–4.

The IPPF series

The International Penal and Penitentiary Foundation (IPPF) has a long history and can trace its roots back to 1872. It shall have as its aim to promote studies in the field of the prevention of crime and the treatment of offenders, especially by scientific research, publications, teaching and international colloquiums. The IPPF's members are from around the world, are recognized experts in penal and penitentiary matters, and are either high judges, high officials of the prison system, or university professors. Recent publications of the IPPF regard, *e.g.*, *Prison policy and prisoners' rights*, *Minorities and cultural diversity in prison*, and the *Implementation of prison sentences and aspects of security*. The most recent publication discusses *Pre-trial detention*.

La collection de la FIPP

La Fondation internationale pénale et pénitentiaire (FIPP) est une institution vénérable dont les origines remontent à 1872. Elle vise à promouvoir les études dans le domaine de la prévention de la criminalité et le traitement des délinquants, plus particulièrement en menant des recherches scientifiques, en éditant des publications, des cours et par l'organisation de colloques internationaux. La FIPP compte des membres dans le monde entier, tous experts reconnus dans les matières pénale et pénitentiaire: hauts magistrats, hauts fonctionnaires du système pénitentiaire ou professeurs d'université. La FIPP a entre autres récemment publié *Politiques pénitentiaires et droits des détenus*, *Minorités et diversité culturelle en prison*, et *L'exécution des sanctions privatives de liberté et les impératifs de la sécurité*. La publication la plus récente discute *Détention avant jugement*.

www.ingramcontent.com/pod-product-compliance
Ingram Content Group UK Ltd.
Pitfield, Milton Keynes, MK11 3LW, UK
UKHW051846100926
8556IPUK00005B/487